Censorship Is a Drag

This book is number 16 in the Library Juice Press Series
on Gender and Sexuality in Information Studies,
Emily Drabinski, series editor.
_____

Censorship Is a Drag

LGBTQ Materials and Programming
Under Siege in Libraries

Jason D. Phillips and Jordan Ruud

rary Juice Press
mento, CA

Published in 2025 by Library Juice Press.

Litwin Books
PO Box 188784
Sacramento, CA 95818

http://litwinbooks.com/

This book is printed on acid-free paper.

Names: Phillips, Jason D. | Ruud, Jordan.
Title: Censorship is a drag : lgbtq materials and programming
under siege in academic libraries /
Jason D. Phillips and Jordan Ruud.
Description: Sacramento, CA : Library Juice Press, 2025. | Includes
bibliographic references and
index.
Identifiers: LCCN 2024941126 | ISBN 9781634001519 (paperback)
Subjects: LCSH: Academic libraries – Censorship. | Sexual minori-
ties – Library resources. |
Academic libraries – Activity programs. | Libraries and sexual
minorities. | Academic freedom.
Classification: LCC Z711.92.S49 C46 2025 | DDC 026.3059--dc23
LC record available at https://lccn.loc.gov/2024941126

Contents

Acknowledgments

The editors would both like to thank:

- Our crew and "brain trust"—Drs. Lindsy Lawrence, Nicki Stancil, and Laura Witherington—for moral support, thoughtful feedback, and cheerleading throughout this project. You are the very ideal of the kind of friend, colleague, and partner one needs to both survive and thrive in academia.

- Anne Liebst, our colleague, friend, and fellow soldier in the trenches during some tough, dark days.

- Our contributors, for your patience, grace, and exceptional work in this project together. We are so very proud of what you accomplished.

- Our series editor, Emily Drabinski, for taking a chance on the idea we presented to you back in March 2022 and for your faith and trust in us during this process while you were busy doing ALL the things.

- Vanessa Rayne and Bookish: An Indie Shop for Folks Who Read, for gorgeous photos and gracious hospitality

Jason would like to thank:

- My mother, Pam Phillips, for those trips to the library that nurtured a lifelong love of reading and learning.

- Dr. Karma Chavez, for encouraging a spark to grow into a flame.

- Drs. Howard Jones and George Williamson, for your many years of patient tutelage—any greatness in my writing and critical thinking can be attributed to them and any flaws are solely my doing.

- My Sister-Wives, for indulging me with coffee, good food, and lots of dark and/or inappropriate humor.

- Amanda Price, for still being along for the ride, and I'm the better for it.

- Jeremy Woody, who is living proof that your best friend can also be your soulmate. Thank you for being a friend.

- Jordan Ruud, whose friendship and years of collegiality have been one of the great gifts of my life.

- A.D., "You are the tenant of my heart. Sometimes behind on the rent, but impossible to evict." (From the 1998 film, *Playing by Heart*)

Jordan would like to thank:

- Finn, for not running out of the house in horror when I first mentioned this project, and for lovingly coaching me through many mini-meltdowns all the while.

- My parents, for teaching me to love reading.

- My teachers, especially Yael Abrahamsson, Bill Bradley, and James Watson, for their patience and mentorship.

- Jason Phillips, for years of great talks and Laura Dern memes, stress-inducing Gala planning, and heated discussions of what exactly emo is.

Foreword

Emily Drabinski

In July 2023, I listened in to an online meeting of the Montana State Library Commission as they discussed whether or not to cancel the state library's membership in the American Library Association because of ALA's Marxist, lesbian president: me. Tom Burnett, vice-chair of the commission, argued that "our oath of office and resulting duty to the Constitution forbids association with an organization led by a Marxist." People who spoke in favor of canceling the state library's membership said little about the struggle between capital and labor. None of this was about my political or philosophical views. Instead, speakers quoted Leviticus as evidence that I was condemned and argued that books with LGBTQ+ content were perverting our children. A smaller number spoke in favor of retaining the state library's membership in the organization. They pointed to the importance of continuing education and professional development opportunities as well as the need for "a seat at the table" in order to influence ALA's national agenda. Others argued that the ALA president is purely ceremonial, a figurehead who has little power or influence over the field. I was directed by ALA staff to keep quiet. There would be no comment from me. It would not be "strategic."

Strategy matters. Institutions matter. We make the best decisions we can with the evidence we have at the time. Since I had become a flashpoint for the right, it seemed strategic to many of us to keep me out of the public eye the moment that particular storm hit.

From the distance of many months, I am finding that my silence has proved costly. Silence breeds something that too many queer folks know too much about: shame. Staying silent in the face of these personal and public attacks installed a small, hard stone at the center of myself. I was afraid. I felt guilty. As my identity continued to be weaponized against public and school librarians across the country, that stone grew. This was my fault. The people and institutions I cared most about, library workers and libraries, were under threat because I said who I was in public. That shame grew, day after day, week after week, month after month. I have been out and proud, brash and bold, queer and Marxist, since 1995. What happened to push me back into the closet?

While I kept quiet, organized groups of censors got louder. My face appeared in extremist slide decks at library board meetings in Louisiana. In meetings, in person, on email, and over the phone, librarians were accused of being Marxists and groomers by people demanding to know their connections to the ALA. State libraries across the country canceled their memberships, often with direct reference to me. A state senator in Georgia introduced a bill that would prohibit spending any state funds for ALA products, programs, or services because of the radical agenda that supports the right for LGBTQ+ people to have their lives and experiences reflected in library collections. Montana's withdrawal was followed by multiple state libraries canceling their memberships. A woman screen-recorded my online talks, and then broadcasted them with her vile commentary to a vast right-wing network. Then she showed up in Chicago, where she secretly recorded me in a session talking about the importance of libraries for socialist organizing. I believe libraries should be at the forefront of every movement for social justice and equity, including the political movement of which I am a part.

Those who would eliminate access to materials and programs about LGBTQ+ life are never asked to be quiet. Their voices are celebrated and amplified by those who agree with them, whipped into the frenzies we're now accustomed to seeing at library and school board meetings, on the news, in front of our buildings and in our classrooms. The voices of those of us who know how important our stories are, how urgent our narratives, especially when so many are organized against us—those voices must be just as loud.

Censorship Is a Drag gives voice to the many of us who have been on the front lines of unprecedented attacks on libraries and librarians, books and their authors, and the young people we serve. Editors Jason D. Phillips and Jordan Ruud have gathered scholars and practitioners whose work in these pages contextualizes the ongoing assaults on the right to read, which we know are also assaults on the right to be who we are, as we are, where we are. They help us understand how we got here and where we are going, offering grounded analysis into the crisis facing queer people, queer books, and the people who love us. In amplifying personal narratives, Phillips and Ruud give the many of us who have been told to be quiet the microphone we deserve.

I penned this brief foreword in late February 2024, two-thirds of the way through my term as the first publicly open LGBTQ+ president of the American Library Association. Reflecting on the challenges of this year opened up some painful wounds, but also some beautiful reminders. I have met so many amazing librarians during my term, some of them represented in these pages, who understand quite clearly the impact of censorship on queer people like me and, perhaps, like you, the person reading this book. Read these chapters as I did, embracing the hope and deep belief that we have the power to shape our collective future, to win the world we want, one where all our stories can be told.

Emily Drabinski

Brooklyn, New York

February 2024

Part 1
Understanding the Challenges We Face

Introduction

Jason D. Phillips and Jordan Ruud

This collection is not about us (the editors), but we've brought our experiences to it anyway. And our experiences, in part, inspired this project in the first place, which has been a source of catharsis and a full-circle moment—"someday this pain will be useful to you."

During our professional lives, we've experienced queer battle fatigue and witnessed censorship of LGBTQ+ materials and public pushback to a drag story hour firsthand, and we've watched the political atmosphere in the United States rapidly devolving into disdain for—and even stochastic terrorism directed against—LGBTQ+ materials and programs and the professionals responsible for providing them.

Both of us are old enough to remember when the military policy of "Don't ask, don't tell" (1994-2011) was widely regarded as a measure in the direction of "increased tolerance." We're old enough to remember when Ellen DeGeneres came out as a lesbian and caused a media frenzy (1997), the death of Matthew Shepard (1998), and when years later, Barack Obama was elected on a platform of civil unions rather than gay marriage (2008). Then we remember seeing the May 2014 issue of *Time* magazine with "The Transgender Tipping Point" as its cover story, featuring Laverne Cox, showing up in our library. A little over a year later came the Supreme Court's *Obergefell* decision (2015) and love won.

Then, a year and a half later, social conservatism won the 2016 election, and we felt a sense of foreboding and fear. Would the gains achieved in recent years be overturned? Year by year, cultural developments followed that frightened the LGBTQ+ people around us—leading up to today's social environment, in which states are systematically oppressing trans people, interfering with curricula, and restricting speech.

These developments in the culture have been mirrored in libraries, and it was seeing this in the country as a whole, as well as close to home, that made us want to hear others' stories, find out how others resisted or fought back, and develop a toolkit of strategies to help others resist or fight back. To this point, we make the argument that libraries and librarians cannot be neutral as collections and services for underserved, threatened communities—both LGBTQ+ and people of color—are under assault.

We're writing about libraries here, but the theme of *resistance* carries beyond the strict professional context of library operations. It's been widely noted that, after decades of slow cultural evolution, the conservative incursion against LGBTQ+ rights came suddenly and with little warning. While we've seen encouraging signs that the oppressive measures of the past several years are facing real pushback and even exhaustion within the ranks (as one "Mom for Liberty" noted in early 2024, "I guess there wasn't as much willingness to do the work that's required to propel the movement forward"), there's no reason this can't happen again (Daly, 2024, para. 4). And there's no reason libraries shouldn't be prepared for that. This collection is meant in part as a document of this moment, but also as a toolkit for the future—for libraries unsure of exactly what's to come.

This collection draws on the stories and the strengths of our contributors. Many states or areas seem to be in a "race to the bottom," almost like a competition to see who can ban the most LGBTQ+ books or programs. It's no surprise that many of our contributors are living and working in these states, presenting voices and perspectives from the front lines of this conflict. We've included authors whose experiences represent the challenges of carrying out work in LGBTQ+ materials and programs and those who point to the fulfillment and joy of serving this community. True to this collection's "toolkit" goal, some of our chapters are practical accounts of the nuts and bolts of handling LGBTQ+ materials and programs, while others convey, personally, what it means to do this work. We hope that these stories and lessons can stand as encouragement in a time where—as our title puts it—these materials, these programs, and indeed, our libraries and their staff who support inclusion, *are* indeed under siege.

* * *

The following section offers some background information about this collection, the hows and whys involved in our thinking process and approach as we put the book together.

Given the relative dearth of scholarship specific to censorship of LGBTQ+ materials in academic libraries, the editors initially envisioned this as a text speaking to and for the academic library community. Our plans evolved as we received chapter proposals from public, school, and special libraries. We have tried to balance the representation of this audience so that everyone can take something away from the toolkits.

The voices in this collection include librarians from various career stages, from recent graduates to those eyeing retirement. Each author brings a clear vision and distinct voice, and we worked with them to ensure that all the chapters will be accessible to even lay readers, though you may want to brush up on your theory for a chapter or two. But it was important to us to not have a book filled with "academic speak" that's only accessible to a limited audience.

The editors also made every effort to represent the full spectrum of our community in the voices included in this book, in terms of sexualities, gender identities, and ethnic or racial identities. To this end, we are thankful to our colleagues who shared our initial call for chapter proposals to a wide variety of listservs and social media. We are also proud to include voices from Canada, Ireland, and the Philippines in our collection.

Both the editors were surprised by the response we received from our call for chapter proposals. We received many excellent proposals, some of which we were unable to include lest this book run the length of a Tolstoy novel. We also want to give a nod to the authors who did submit chapter drafts that ultimately were not included in this collection. Sometimes you end up at a different destination than you intended at the start of a writing project. We applaud their efforts, and they will undoubtedly find a home in a peer-reviewed journal or another collection. We would be remiss if we did not acknowledge their fine work—it was a very difficult decision to not include their chapters in this collection.

As we approached editing this book, we wanted to give authors the freedom to use community identifiers as they see fit. So, the reader may see "LGBTQ+," "LGBTQ2SIA+," or "2SLGBTQQIA+." We very much hope that this book speaks to and for the full spectrum of marginalized sexualities and gender identities.

There are some instances where authors decided against specifically citing a source, like a blog, tweet, or TikTok, for example. This decision was born from a desire not to give a platform to or amplify hate or untruths from known malicious actors. The editors fully support this thinking and decision and also received approval from our series editor. The editors did check the sources provided and can affirm the existence of items mentioned in the initial drafts but not cited in the final form.

In closing, progress can be incremental. And as we have witnessed, there can even be setbacks to progress. As you are reading this collection five, ten, fifteen years from now, consider the context of the times in which it was written. We may not get it 100% right, but we're trying, and our hearts are in the right place.

References

Daly, M. (2024, February 7). *Even Moms for Liberty are tired of Moms for Liberty*. The Daily Beast. https://www.thedailybeast.com/even-moms-for-liberty-are-tired-of-moms-for-liberty

Stochastic Terrorism
An Old Tactic Becomes a New Tool for Censorship[1]

Bryn Nelson

Introduction

On March 21, 2023, the Twitter account of the right-wing Libs of TikTok site denounced Northwest Junior High School in Coralville, Iowa, for making *This Book Is Gay* by Juno Dawson available to students. Chaya Raichik, who runs the highly influential social media account, had repeatedly attacked the bestselling LQBTQ+ guidebook for young adults as "pornographic" over its depiction of gay sexuality. "These are the books they're giving your kids to read in school," she wrote. The day before, an identical tweet calling out West High School in Sioux City, Iowa, had yielded a quick thank you note from the school district, which suggested that the book's contents could "compromise" student safety. The note assured Raichik, "It has been removed from our library" (Yamada, 2023; Siouxland News, 2023). Libs of TikTok claimed victory, responding on Twitter, "Big win for students of Iowa!"

Raichik's March 21 tweet, however, seems to have inspired a more extreme response in the form of multiple, coordinated bomb threats. On March 22, an emailed pipe bomb threat against the Hilton Central School District in suburban Rochester, New York, cited *This Book Is Gay*

---

1   Editorial note: This chapter is about the dangerous amplification of inflammatory rhetoric. As such, the author made the conscious decision to avoid direct links to certain statements made by public figures, primarily on social media. Where possible, however, footnotes and references to academic and journalistic sources have provided the necessary documentation and context for such rhetoric.

and mirrored parts of the Libs of TikTok tweet. The threat continued, "You are disgusting degenerates that belong on cross. We will ensure all of you degenerates are killed which is why we placed a bobm [sic] in those people's houses, they are responsible for the grooming of our children." In response, the Monroe County Sheriff's Office bomb squad mobilized and evacuated five schools, the district office, and the superintendent's home (Frelle, 2023; Wiggins, 2023b). Two days later, a second email repeated the bomb threat, while also warning of Molotov cocktails, though a subsequent bomb sweep again found nothing. Two more bomb threats followed; police said both were hoaxes, and the district superintendent suggested they were an attempt to create division in the community (Gandy, 2023).

On March 23 and 24, consecutive threats against Northwest Junior High in Coralville, the school specifically named in the March 21 Libs of TikTok tweet, also prompted evacuations and bomb sweeps. As with Hilton Central School District, police later deemed the threats against the Iowa school district "not credible." As in New York, the Iowa district temporarily pulled *This Book Is Gay* from library shelves for a reevaluation (Gandy, 2023; King, 2023).

The dramatic incidents fit a larger pattern. In April 2023, PEN America's *Banned in the USA* report described a sharp escalation of book bans and censorship efforts that have figured prominently in a broader campaign to exercise ideological control over primary and secondary education (Friedman, 2022; Meehan & Friedman, 2023). Although polls suggest that book bans are widely unpopular in the U.S., a vocal minority has exerted outsized political pressure with the help of sympathetic Republican politicians, rightwing groups such as Moms for Liberty, and other influencers such as Libs of TikTok. In 2022, they challenged more than 2,500 books in the nation's schools and libraries (American Library Association; Pengelly, 2023; Salvanto, 2023). "Overwhelmingly, book banners continue to target stories by and about people of color and LGBTQ+ individuals," the PEN America report asserts; combined, such books accounted for 30 percent and 26 percent, respectively, of all banned titles during the first half of the 2022-2023 school year (Meehan & Friedman, 2023, para. 7).

The banning of books about race, sexual orientation, and gender identity has not happened by chance. Instead, the bans track an escalation in verbal and physical threats and attacks against people of color and LGBTQ+ individuals amid a disturbing spike in inflammatory rhetoric aimed at them by conservative public figures (Equal Justice Initiative, 2021; Armed Conflict Location & Event Data Project, 2022; Martiny & Lawrence, 2023; Anti-Defamation League & GLAAD, 2023; Margolin & Grant, 2023; Lyngaas, 2023). Anti-LGBTQ+ tropes have also frequently overlapped with anti-Semitic and racist tropes, "creating a toxic brew of hateful conspiracy theories and beliefs" (ADL & GLAAD, 2023). Right-wing pundits, politicians, and influential figures have repeatedly used emotion-laden insults and derisive appropriations of words like "thug," "woke," "animal," "indoctrination," "groomer," "pedophile," "genital mutilation," "predator," and "pornography," to incite anger, disgust, and contempt (Monroe & Savillo, 2021; Avery & Yurcaba, 2021; Robinson, 2022; Kruesi & Phan, 2022; ADL & GLAAD, 2023).

"It's hard to get people to demonize human beings and lives and history," said Michael Harriot, author of *Black AF History: The Unwhitewashed Story of America*, in a 2022 interview with the Legal Defense Fund (Robinson, 2022, para. 31). "But it's easy to get them to demonize a word. And if you can use that word as a placeholder for those people, for caring about those people, then it's easy to demonize instead of saying, 'We're just gonna stop caring about people.'" Repeated demonization and dehumanization of people or groups of people, in turn, can inspire and encourage acts of violence against them (Hodson, Kteily & Hoffarth, 2014; Nelson, 2022).

Direct or indirect threats, in fact, have shaped book bans and the responses to them by instilling fear (Davies, 2023; Oliver, 2023). In particular, terrorist acts of violence and threatened violence are having the intended effect of intimidating librarians, teachers, and those who fund and govern them in order to ban books and literary events. Librarians and teachers have quit, been fired, or have been threatened with physical harm or criminal prosecution; libraries have been targeted by bomb and mass shooting threats; and books and lessons have been banned outright, heavily restricted, or self-censored by frightened employees (Harris & Alter, 2022a; King, 2023; Flora, 2023; Jayswal & Miller, 2023). In April 2023, the independent literary site Book Riot asked, "How long until a library worker is killed?" (Jensen, 2023).

Conservative thought leaders and organizations are radicalizing individuals—some of whom have committed acts of terrorism—in part by demonizing and dehumanizing LGBTQ and Black people, other vulnerable minorities, and teachers and librarians who are advancing intellectual freedom. Some extremists, in turn, are being supported by politicians and others in power who have repeated some of the same lies and distortions to justify censorship through policies and laws. Even if the vilification of individuals or groups doesn't precipitate violence, the fear that it *might* often suffices to achieve the same end goal: ensuring that students lose ready access to books targeted for political or ideological reasons. The chain of events—starting with denunciations by some participants and ending with dangerous criminal acts by others that intimidate or coerce civilian populations in order to force a social or political change—is based on an age-old practice that was named only recently: stochastic terrorism.

The Origins and Dimensions of Stochastic Terrorism

The broad outlines of the stochastic terrorism phenomenon have existed for centuries and supported a wide range of ideological, religious, and political ends (Amman & Meloy, 2021; Kleinfeld, 2021; Goldfarb Styrt, 2023). The formal term, however, was first used in 2002 and subsequently expanded to characterize unpredictable but targeted acts of violence inspired by demagoguery (Woo, 2002; G2geek, 2011; Keats, 2019).

In short, public speakers who repeatedly demonize other individuals or other groups of people in pursuit of political or ideological goals can inspire a supporter or a group of like-minded followers to act out violently toward the targets (Amman & Meloy, 2022; Snodgrass, 2022). The phenomenon has been likened to heating a pot of water: given sufficient fuel, a physical attack may be as predictable as the eventuality that the water will boil. "But the exact time and place of each incident will remain as random as the appearance of the first bubbles in the boiling pot" (G2geek, 2011).

As currently construed, stochastic terrorism requires three main elements: a pundit, politician, or other public speaker whose inflammatory words can influence others; one or more amplifying conduits such as a television or radio broadcast or social media channel to widely disseminate those words; and one or more receivers who internalize the messages of hostility and respond by committing acts of terrorism (Amman & Meloy, 2022). One key trait that distinguishes stochastic terrorism from incitement to violence, however, is that the threat from the former is veiled or implicit; "violence is never explicitly suggested and plausible deniability remains intact," meaning that the speaker can often avoid legal repercussions or direct blame for the random threats and acts of terrorism inspired by their words (Amman & Meloy,

2022). The initial hate speech or verbal attacks may be protected as free speech as long as they don't rise to the legal level of incitement, the latter of which can be a criminal offense.

Certain words, though, can invite a particularly aggressive response. Studies suggest that a combination of anger, contempt, and disgust is most effective at producing a feeling of hostility toward a perceived opponent or social outgroup (Matsumoto et al. 2016). Disgust, in fact, can contribute to systematic degradation and dehumanization that serves to justify violence toward a "sub-human" threat (Hodson et al. 2014; Nelson, 2022). Propagandists have used disgust to dehumanize Jewish people as "rats" or members of an "alien race" (United States Holocaust Memorial Museum); Black people as subhuman apes (Goff et al. 2008); Indigenous people as "savages" (Newcomb, 2012); immigrants as "animals" (Qiu, 2018); and LGBTQ people as sexual deviants and "predators" who prey upon children (Schlatter & Steinback, 2011). At a November 2023 rally, former U.S. President Donald Trump echoed Adolf Hitler in calling his political opponents "thugs" and "vermin" (Kurtzleben, 2023).

Influential figures and their allies have often reinforced the pejoratives with disinformation campaigns that deliberately spread misinformation about the targets. As a result, they have repeatedly emboldened some members of radicalized audiences to carry out horrific acts of terrorism. Historians, for instance, have tied stochastic terrorism fomented by racist politicians' inflammatory rhetoric to lynching attacks throughout the U.S., particularly in the late 19th and early 20th centuries (Equal Justice Initiative, 2017; Kleinfeld, 2021). In 1931, after the *Tulsa Tribune* printed false and inflammatory allegations about a Black man, a thwarted lynching by a white mob sparked the Tulsa Massacre that charred 35 blocks of the city's "Black Wall Street" and killed as many as 300 people (Balkansky, 2021).

Similar dehumanization and disinformation inspired a wave of violence against Jewish people in Germany in the lead-up to World War II. In May of 1933, students in 34 university towns across the country burned "un-German" books by the thousands—a chilling prelude to the increasingly violent acts openly encouraged and perpetrated by the Nazi party (Rittenberg, 2022). Other examples of stochastic terrorism incidents include the 2015 murder of nine African American church congregants in Charleston by a gunman who was radicalized by a white supremacist website (Hersher, 2017); the 2018 attack on the Tree of Life synagogue in Pittsburgh by a gunman who was heavily influenced by anti-Semitic rhetoric (Keller, 2018); the 2019 massacre of 20 people at an El Paso, Texas, Walmart by a gunman who feared a "Hispanic invasion" (Kayyem, 2019); and the attempted March 2023 firebombing of a church in Chesterland, Ohio, by a white nationalist who was upset over the church's plans to host a Drag Queen Story Hour (Sarnoff, 2023).

Whether groups or individuals feel compelled to act, multiple scholars agree that increasingly volatile and aggressive rhetoric by influential figures such as Donald Trump is becoming part of mainstream discourse and setting the stage for violence (Edwards & Rushin, 2018; Burchill, 2022). Before, during, and after Trump's presidency, analysts have repeatedly documented his clear encouragement of political violence, including his incendiary and mendacious speech about a "stolen election" that directly presaged the violent January 6, 2021 insurrection at the U.S. Capitol (Edwards & Rushin, 2018; Brice-Sadler, 2019; Grueskin, 2020; Cineas, 2021; Burchill, 2022; Select January 6th Committee, 2022; Basu, 2023).

How Surging Threats Support Censorship

Amid the current backdrop of false and inflammatory rhetoric, violent threats have targeted schools, libraries, churches, businesses, and other venues—along with scores of individuals (ADL & GLAAD, 2023). The first requirement for stochastic terrorism, that of public speakers vilifying individuals or groups, has been filled by far-right groups such as Moms for Liberty, a fast-growing political organization that has pledged to fight "woke indoctrination" and has spearheaded the most recent book banning movement in the U.S. (SPLC, n.d.). In Tennessee, the group's local chapter argued that books about Martin Luther King Jr. and fellow civil rights activist Ruby Bridges were "anti-American" and "anti-white" in an attempt to remove them from a second grade curriculum (Martiny & Lawrence, 2023). On Twitter, the group falsely claimed that "gender identity indoctrination" is one of the most dangerous threats facing U.S. children, and at a school board meeting in Wauwatosa County, Wisconsin, members of the local Moms for Liberty chapter accused other attendees of being "groomers"—another word for pedophiles (ADL, 2022; GLAAD, 2023). Other conservative groups and public figures have latched onto similar rhetoric in portraying objectionable books as "indoctrination" or "indecent and offensive" threats to children (Harris & Alter, 2022b).

Rightwing activist Christopher Rufo, who orchestrated the conservative backlash against critical race theory and used the controversy to target diversity, equity, and inclusion programs in schools, helped to abolish the gender studies program at the New College of Florida as a member of the school's board of trustees. Rufo has attacked the notion of "trans ideology" and smeared Drag Queen Story Hour as an attempt to "sexualize children" and normalize pedophilia, while he has encouraged his Twitter followers to use phrases like "ideological grooming" and "political predators" to harass teachers who "indoctrinate their students" (Meckler & Dawsey, 2021; Grasso, 2022; Nelson, 2022). Despite his prominent role in encouraging the use of inflammatory words and promoting censorship efforts in public institutions, Rufo has claimed that the concept of stochastic terrorism is itself a "lie" and a conspiratorial attempt by "the Left" to suppress speech. Likewise, he has sought to redefine the word "ban" to suggest that opposition to censorship in libraries and schools is an overreaction. "There are no 'book bans' in America," he wrote in one tweet.

Of the many rightwing instigators, however, Libs of TikTok has arguably inspired the most threats against librarians and other educators. On Twitter, Media Matters for America reported that the account run by Raichik had targeted more than 220 teachers, schools, and districts in 2022 alone, often over their efforts to promote inclusion and diversity (Lawton, 2022). Immediately thereafter, many were inundated with online harassment and threats. A subsequent investigation of threats against LGBTQ+ targets by *USA Today* "confirmed dozens of bomb threats, death threats and other harassment after Libs of TikTok's posts since February 2022" (Carless, 2023, para. 7).

The second requirement of stochastic terrorism—a means of publicizing and amplifying hate speech and hostility—has been met by media channels like Fox News and Infowars, and social media sites like Twitter, Telegram, Gab, 4chan, TikTok, Facebook, YouTube, and Instagram (Frenkel et al., 2018; Monroe & Savillo, 2021; Andrei, 2023). One study found that bots on Twitter helped to significantly amplify hate speech in online conversations about racism during the Covid-19 pandemic (Uyheng et al., 2022). The amplification of misinformation likewise surged in the immediate aftermath of the site's acquisition by billionaire Elon Musk (Brewster et al., 2022).

A separate report on media manipulation explains how far-right groups have developed "attention hacking" techniques via social media, memes, and bots to amplify extreme content (Marwick & Lewis, 2017). In his book *Weaponized Words*, American University researcher Kurt Braddock describes how online disinformation can radicalize people over time (Braddock, 2020, pp. 212-213). "Disaffected individuals who are steeped in Internet culture often come together in online forums and through social media platforms. There, they can find other individuals who share their frustrations within closed communicative systems. When disinformation is shared within these systems, it can reverberate within the ideological echo chamber, eventually becoming normalized among the individuals within it," he writes. Repeated demonization, with disinformation added as "proof," can solidify hostile attitudes and trigger violence.

As for the third requirement for stochastic terrorism, a diverse network of extremist groups and individuals have responded to the amplified rhetoric by appearing in force, sometimes armed, at Drag Queen Story Hour events (Martiny & Lawrence, 2023). In its 2023 report, the Institute for Strategic Dialogue identified multiple, often overlapping agitators at these events: far-right groups like the Proud Boys; anti-LGBTQ+ groups like Gays Against Groomers and Project 171; Neo-Nazi organizations like NSC-131, Blood Tribe, and the Aryan Freedom Network; Christian nationalist groups like FEC United, Warriors for Christ, the New Columbia Movement, and the American Society for the Defense of Tradition, Family and Property; and white supremacist groups like Active Clubs. In New York, a small but vocal anti-vaccine group called Guardians of Divinity had already organized nearly two dozen anti-drag events by mid-2023 (Martiny & Lawrence, 2023).

In some incidents, multiple groups drawn by media and social media posts have converged on the same location in a mass show of force. In March 2023, hundreds of far-right extremists—some of whom were armed, chanting "Sieg Heil!" and hurling racial and homophobic slurs—disrupted a Drag Queen Story Hour in a park near Akron, Ohio. One report identified members of the Proud Boys, Patriot Front, III Percenters, White Lives Matter of Ohio, Blood Tribe, and other extremist groups among the demonstrators (Wiggins, 2023a). After being repeatedly targeted with racial slurs by some of them, a Black reporter from the *Akron Beacon Journal* left for his own safety (Livingston, 2023). Police arrested two people after the demonstration turned violent, though no one was injured.

News stories and reports illustrate how the cycle of stochastic terrorism works: After an inflammatory tweet by Libs of TikTok about a Drag

Queen Story Hour at the San Lorenzo Library in California in 2022, a group of "extremely aggressive" Proud Boys stormed the room and shouted homophobic and transphobic threats, prompting police to investigate a possible hate crime (Bartlett, 2022). Such incidents, in turn, have inspired other threats and confrontations. One compilation tallied 203 separate incidents targeting drag events from June 2022 through May 2023 (100 of those were Drag Queen Story Hours), making the U.S. the worldwide epicenter of anti-drag activity (Martiny & Lawrence, 2023). In all, local Proud Boys chapters were implicated in 60 of those incidents across 20 states.

Thirteen events were canceled after the venues or organizers received violent threats; even then, the harassment continued for some, suggesting that acquiescence doesn't always forestall further harm. In September 2022, an Illinois library that canceled one drag event over mailed and online threats subsequently received a note threatening more disruptions, with a bullet included inside; the library then stopped hosting all drag events, underscoring how terroristic threats can lead to self-censorship (Martiny & Lawrence, 2023).

Some experts argue that a surge of incendiary speech and ideas once relegated to the fringes is inspiring violence by a growing legion of radicalized "lone actors" or "lone wolves" (Hamm & Spaaij, 2017). Others instead urge greater attention to a group phenomenon in which online channels of like-minded individuals foster a pack mentality supported by terrorist rhetoric (Kayyem, 2019). One 2023 review of anti-LGBTQ+ hate and extremism incidents found that roughly half were committed "wholly or substantially by associates of known extremist groups" (ADL & GLAAD, 2023, para. 4).

A Cascade of Downstream Consequences

After a violent incident or the threat of one, multiple downstream repercussions can bolster the end goal of censorship. A wave of threats and bullying has temporarily closed libraries and prompted some librarians to quit, while others have lost their jobs after opposing bans (Harris & Alter, 2022a; Woodcock, 2022; Grant, 2023). On March 28, 2023, the Indiana Suicide Prevention hotline fielded a call by someone claiming that they had entered the Lebanon Public Library armed with a rifle and two pistols, and that they intended to harm employees and bystanders. Law enforcement found no threat, but the incident closed the library for six days (Flora, 2023). Others have risked permanent closure after losing public funding, like the Patmos Library in Jamestown Township, Michigan. After complaints about four young adult books that included sexual orientation and gender identity themes, a successful defunding campaign featured inflammatory signs that read, "Stop sexualizing our children with cartoon porn" (Kransz, 2022; Smith, 2023).

Multiple legislative and legal efforts in U.S. states have adopted similar language in portraying objectionable books or Drag Queen Story Hour as "pornographic" and "age-inappropriate" and in trying to defund public libraries because of them (Melhado & Nguyen, 2023; Smith, 2023). After the passage of Florida's "Stop WOKE Act" and "Don't Say Gay" bill, as they were dubbed, teachers preemptively cleared or blocked off classroom bookcases for fear of felony prosecution if their books didn't pass muster with a "certified media specialist" (Siegel & Rubin, 2023; Walker, 2023). The specialist must ensure that every book is "free of pornography," that it is "appropriate for the age level and group," and that it doesn't contain "unsolicited theories that may lead to student indoctrination"—vague wording that has no legal meaning but mirrors the inflammatory rhetoric of ban advocates (American Civil Liberties Union, 2006). On Twitter, U.S. Rep. Clay Higgins (R-Louisiana), vilified public libraries as "liberal grooming centers" and called for dismantling them altogether—an oft-stated goal of far-right activists.

Although libraries may remove challenged books following a review, "controversial" books may be preemptively removed to avoid further strife or the threat of prosecution; notably, the bomb threats targeting schools in Iowa and New York over *This Book Is Gay* directly preceded the districts' decision to reevaluate it (Gandy, 2023; King, 2023).

Here too, stochastic terrorism has reinforced the dynamic by deterring individuals who oppose censorship from speaking out and fighting back for fear of violent reprisals. The revival of the "groomer" smear against LGBTQ+ people and their defenders as a stand-in for "pedophile" offers one case study (Lavietes, 2022). Amid the push to enact laws banning discussions of sexual or gender identity in schools, including Florida's "Don't Say Gay" law, the "groomer" label gained traction as a pejorative eliciting anger, contempt, and disgust. After pushback by the law's opponents, Republican Gov. Ron DeSantis's spokesperson, Christina Pushaw, responded on Twitter in March 2022, "The bill that liberals inaccurately call 'Don't Say Gay' would be more accurately described as an Anti-Grooming Bill" (Migdon, 2022).

In a follow-up tweet, she went even further: "If you're against the Anti-Grooming Bill, you are probably a groomer or at least you don't denounce the grooming of 4–8-year-old children." Both tweets were liked thousands of times and widely amplified on social media.

In a subsequent interview with *Florida Politics*, Pushaw doubled down by repeatedly conflating discussion of LGBTQ+ people in elementary schools with inappropriate sex education and "grooming" (Powers, 2022). Equality Florida responded, "Governor DeSantis' spokesperson said the quiet part out loud: that this bill is grounded in a belief that LGBTQ people, simply by existing, are a threat to children and must be erased" (Equality Florida, 2022, para. 3). By then, however, the "groomer" slur had begun expanding and metastasizing to become a catchall pejorative against LGBTQ+ people *and* their defenders. Conservative activists like Christopher Rufo, Chaya Raichik, and Moms for Liberty members have used it to justify the need for anti-drag and anti-trans policies and legislation, while conservative politicians like Clay Higgins have used it to call for the dismantling of public libraries. Through repetition, the insult of "groomer" and its implied permission to act upon an ongoing threat to children has inspired others toward violence. Proud Boys members have shouted it in libraries like the one in San Lorenzo, California, and anonymous terrorists have included it in bomb threats like the one sent to Hilton Central School District in upstate New York.

A Practical Toolkit for Fighting Stochastic Terrorism

Countering the multifaceted threat of stochastic terrorism as it relates to book bans and censorship first requires keeping in mind that at its core, the phenomenon uses words and emotions to establish distorted narratives that encourage violence or the threat of it toward an ideological or political end. As centers of learning and education that can help counter false narratives and the disinformation propping them up, libraries—and their books—are themselves frequent targets of extremists and oppressive regimes seeking to destroy a region's knowledge, memory, and cultural identity (Haq, 2015). Libraries, however, can also play an important role in disrupting the links that fuel radicalization and the cycle of violence and intimidation.

As with other public threats, some experts have argued that prevention is the best medicine and have proposed a public health-like approach in which a large-scale "information vaccination" program provides preemptive truths (Braddock, 2020). Lessons from Germany and

Norway also suggest that bottom-up grassroots efforts to counter violent extremism may lead to better outcomes than a top-down approach (Hardy, 2019). Their experience suggests that local institutions, including libraries and schools, could partner with nonprofit groups to reach and persuade at-risk individuals. As part of a more holistic approach that focuses on the "wider social, family and community contexts in which extremist ideas spread and people become radicalized," the European efforts have emphasized better choices, mentorship, and empowerment through dialogue rather than countering any specific ideology (Hardy, 2019, p. 275).

What might such a campaign look like in the U.S.? Unlike in many European countries, most hate speech is protected by the First Amendment and content moderation has been handled by media and social media companies themselves, leading to lax, erratic, and inconsistent policies and enforcement. A 2023 national survey by the Anti-Defamation League recorded a sharp rise in online hate and harassment for both adults and teenagers (ADL, 2023). For influential figures who repeatedly engage in dehumanizing and vilifying speech, limiting or taking away their virtual soapbox often requires a groundswell of pushback from the public, advertisers, or both.

Libraries, on the other hand, may be uniquely well positioned to help disrupt the links between amplifier and receiver by countering disseminated propaganda with something they do particularly well: tell stories. As one set of tools in the broader toolkit, counter-narratives have proven useful in combatting the messaging of a range of extremist groups, not only through traditional stories, but also through the visual power of videos and memes (Allchorn, 2022).

Braddock cautions, though, that stochastic terrorism poses a singular challenge "given that it requires counter-radicalization specialists to refute messages that are not overtly stated" (2020, p. 210). Because of the random and isolated distribution of stochastic terrorism-inspired actors, he suggests, a persuasion campaign that challenges implicit calls for violence could be disseminated via the Internet, mass media, or other means to increase the likelihood of reaching at-risk individuals (Braddock, 2020). Such a campaign requires not only overcoming the initial speaker's persuasiveness, but also the receiver's beliefs and attitudes about why a vilified group poses such a threat that it deserves to be targeted, whether the receiver would have control over a violent act, and whether that act might yield a positive outcome (Braddock, 2020).

For example, a counter-narrative against the "groomer" pejorative aimed at LGBTQ+ people might need to dispel pedophilia myths *and* persuade the receiver that a violent act would further someone else's agenda, harm innocent people who pose no threat to children, and ruin the receiver's future in the process. Braddock suggests that the preventive approach of "attitudinal inoculation," which uses storytelling, rhetoric, values, and emotion to fight misinformation and disinformation, may be useful here. "[A]n inoculation message could suggest that the would-be terrorist would not be acting on his own accord but would essentially be a puppet of the stochastic terrorist," he explains (2020, p. 229). Regretful and disillusioned January 6, 2021 participants who felt like they were misled into storming the U.S. Capitol at the behest of Trump and his supporters have provided another rich source of narratives that underscore stochastic terrorism's toll on its own conscripts (Blundo, 2022).

At a local level, storytelling might include visual displays, oral history projects, community partnerships that help counter physical threats and intimidations, and testimonies at school board and library board meetings. Libraries could use Black History Month and Pride Month to offer historical facts and stories that help humanize the minority groups, for example. On Twitter, the Auschwitz-Birkenau Memorial and Museum has used its platform to great effect by telling the stories of individuals imprisoned in the Polish concentration camp, offering an emotional and humanizing dose of reality that might reach some of those at risk of anti-Semitism and Holocaust denialism.[2] The storytelling could also highlight tales of support and affirmation from unlikely sources, such as conservative parents supporting a transgender child juxtaposed with the devastating consequences that inflammatory words and stochastic terrorism can have on families spanning the political spectrum (Rodríguez, 2023).

In the face of violent threats, the ALA has compiled a Resource Guide for Library Safety and Preparedness (ALA, 2023). Other groups have provided additional support. The nonprofit Parasol Patrol, for example, uses colorful umbrellas to shield children and young people from extremists aiming to disrupt Drag Queen Story Hours and other events featuring LGBTQ+ and BIPOC content (Parasol Patrol, 2023). In addition to providing a visual display of support, the volunteers'

---

2   https://twitter.com/AuschwitzMuseum

presence helps to disrupt the made-for-social-media recruitment videos of hateful messages and threats of violence that lead to the desired outcome of intimidation, acquiescence, and event cancellation. Similar counter-protests, with the active support of community members, have used oversized angel wings to effectively shield families and friends of LGBTQ+ people who have died from extremists picketing their funerals (Stelloh, 2016).

At school board and library board meetings, testimonials from librarians and patrons can also help counter hostile messaging. Stories of individual empowerment and community building that have emanated from local libraries can be contrasted with the significant harms that can come from injecting disinformation and dehumanization into local dialogue. From book burning in Nazi Germany to bomb threats in the U.S., shining a light on the tactics of ideological extremists and their ability to tear communities apart may help mobilize people against the mutually reinforcing dangers of inflammatory language, censorship, and violence that target specific groups of people.

At a higher level, storytelling could include educational and ad campaigns that portray libraries as critical resources and gathering spaces for diverse and vibrant communities, and that emphasize the importance of critical thinking to resist the pull of toxic influences. Braddock, for instance, suggests that "citizens should be trained to engage in critical thinking in a new media environment where extremist groups can produce content and watch it propagate within online social networks not based on its authority, but on its popularity" (Braddock, 2020, p. 216). Educational campaigns could help the public learn to spot disinformation and understand how instigators use inflammatory words, slurs, or misappropriated terms to target others.

In collaboration with other educational institutions and even app developers, libraries could present some counter-narratives as online experiences, where many users already spend much of their time. Some research suggests that "choose your own adventure" storylines or other options that allow individuals to customize how they receive content can give them a sense of autonomy, improve the content's perceived credibility, and enhance the persuasiveness of the information they encounter (Braddock, 2020).

In the hands of ideological and political extremists, stochastic terrorism can be a dangerous and potent weapon with the power to bolster censorship and destroy communities. But it is not insurmountable, and libraries can play a key part in exposing the threat, helping to de-fang it, and defending free speech and the deep value of public insti-tutions in the process.

References

Allchorn, W. (2022). *Moving beyond Islamist extremism: Assessing counter narra-tive responses to the global far right.* ibidem Press.

American Civil Liberties Union (2006, August 30). *What is censorship?* https://www.aclu.org/documents/what-censorship

American Library Association (n.d.-a). *Resource guide for library safety and pre-paredness.* https://www.ala.org/advocacy/resource-guide-library -safety-and-preparedness

American Library Association (n.d.-b). *Voters oppose book bans in libraries.* https://www.ala.org/advocacy/voters-oppose-book-bans-libraries

Amman, M., & Meloy, R. (2021). Stochastic terrorism: A linguistic and psychological analysis. *Perspectives on Terrorism. 14(5), 2-13.*

Amman, M., & Meloy, R. (2022). *Incitement to violence and stochastic terrorism: Legal, academic, and practical parameters for researchers and investiga-tors. Terrorism and Political Violence.* https://doi.org/10.1080/09546553. 2022.2143352

Andrei, M. (2023, May 6). *What stochastic terrorism is and why the US may see more of it.* ZME Science. https://www.zmescience.com/feature-post/ history-and-humanities/sociology/stochastic-terrorism-matters/

Anti-Defamation League (2022, September 16). *What is "grooming?" The truth be-hind the dangerous, bigoted lie targeting the LGBTQ+ community.* https:// www.adl.org/resources/blog/what-grooming-truth-behind-danger-ous-bigoted-lie-targeting-lgbtq-community

Anti-Defamation League (2023, June 27). *Online hate and harassment: The American experience 2023.* https://www.adl.org/resources/report/ online-hate-and-harassment-american-experience-2023

Anti-Defamation League & GLAAD (2023, June 22). *Year in review: Anti-LGBTQ+ hate & extremism incidents, 2022-2023.* https://www.adl.org/resources/report/ year-review-anti-lgbtq-hate-extremism-incidents-2022-2023

Armed Conflict Location & Event Data Project (2023, June 30). *UPDATE: Fact Sheet: Anti-LGBT+ Mobilization in the United States.* https://acleddata.com/2022/11/23/ update-fact-sheet-anti-lgbt-mobilization-in-the-united-states/

Avery, D., & Yurcaba, J. (2021, February 26). *Rand Paul criticized for trans 'gender mutilation' remarks in Rachel Levine hearing. NBCNews.com.*https://www. nbcnews.com/feature/nbc-out/rand-paul-criticized-trans-gender-mutila-tion-remarks-rachel-levine-hearing-n1259004

Balkansky, A. (2021, May 27). *Tulsa Race Massacre: Newspaper complicity and coverage. Headlines and Heroes: Library of Congress Blogs.* https://blogs.loc.gov/headlinesandheroes/2021/05/tulsa-race-massacre-newspaper-complicity-and-coverage/

Bartlett, A. (2022, June 12). *Hate crime investigation underway after alleged Proud Boys storm Drag Queen Story Hour at Bay Area library. SFGATE.* https://www.sfgate.com/bayarea/article/Proud-boys-storm-Bay-Area-Drag-Queen-story-hour-17236693.php

Basu, Z. (2023, October 4). *Trump's words turn violent as pressure on him builds. Axios.* www.axios.com/2023/10/04/trumps-words-turn-violent-pressure-builds

Blundo, J. (2022, November 6). Regrets, they've had a few: Joe Blundo examines Jan. 6 rioters' expressions of remorse. *The Columbus Dispatch.* https://www.dispatch.com/story/lifestyle/columns/2022/11/06/joe-blundo-compiles-a-list-of-jan-6-rioters-sentencing-day-apologies/69596470007/

Braddock, K. (2020). *Weaponized words: The strategic role of persuasion in violent radicalization and counter-radicalization. Cambridge University Press.*

Brewster, J., Wang, M., & Pavilonis, V. (2022, November 11). *Twitter misinformation superspreaders see huge spike in engagement post-acquisition by Elon Musk. NewsGuard.* https://www.newsguardtech.com/special-reports/twitter-misinformation-superspreaders-see-huge-spike-in-engagement-post-acquisition-by-elon-musk/

Brice-Sadler, M. (2019, April 16). He easily found hundreds of death threats against Rep. Ilhan Omar. He wants Twitter to stop them. *Washington Post.* https://www.washingtonpost.com/technology/2019/04/16/he-easily-found-hundreds-death-threats-against-rep-ilhan-omar-he-wants-twitter-stop-them/

Burchill, R. (2022, January 12). *Stochastic terrorism: Why this is a worrying trend and who bears responsibility to curb this phenomenon. European Eye on Radicalization.* https://eeradicalization.com/stochastic-terrorism-why-this-is-a-worrying-trend-and-who-bears-responsibility-to-curb-this-phenomenon/

Carless, W. (2023, November 2). When Libs of TikTok tweets, threats increasingly follow. *USA Today.* https://www.usatoday.com/story/news/investigations/2023/11/02/libs-of-tiktok-tweets-death-bomb-threats/71409213007/

Cineas, F. (2021, January 9). *Donald Trump is the accelerant. Vox.* https://www.vox.com/21506029/trump-violence-tweets-racist-hate-speech

Davies, D. (2023, June 22). *Facing book bans and restrictions on lessons, teachers are scared and self-censoring. NPR.* https://www.npr.org/2023/06/22/1183701813/facing-book-bans-and-restrictions-on-lessons-teachers-are-scared-and-self-censor

Edwards, G. S. & Rushin, S. (2018, January 14). *The effect of President Trump's election on hate crimes. SSRN.* https://doi.org/10.2139/ssrn.3102652

Equal Justice Initiative (2017). *Lynching in America: Confronting the legacy of racial terror (3rd ed.).* https://lynchinginamerica.eji.org/report/

Equal Justice Initiative (2021, September 9). *FBI reports hate crimes at highest level in 12 years.* https://eji.org/news/fbi-reports-hate-crimes-at-highest-level-in-12-years/

Equality Florida (2022, March 7). *Equality Florida condemns anti-LGBTQ remarks by DeSantis spokesperson.* https://www.eqfl.org/statement-equality-flori-da-condemns-anti-lgbtq-remarks-desantis-spokesperson

Flora, M. (2023, April 3). Threat closes Lebanon library for six days. *The Lebanon Reporter.* https://www.reporter.net/news/local_news/threat-closes-lebanon-library-for-six-days/article_21f58154-cf36-11ed-b640-1bcd7e-c2ac8d.html

Frelle, V. E. (2023, March 22). Bomb threat forces evacuation of all schools in Hilton school district. What we know now. *Rochester Democrat and Chronicle.* https://www.democratandchronicle.com/story/news/2023/03/22/hilton-school-district-evacuates-all-schools-following-bomb-threat-updates/70037183007/

Frenkel, S., Isaac, M., and Conger, K. (2018, October 29). On Instagram, 11,696 examples of how hate thrives on social media. *New York Times.* https://www.nytimes.com/2018/10/29/technology/hate-on-social-media.html

Friedman, J. (2022, February 23). *Goodbye Red Scare, hello Ed Scare. Inside Higher Ed.* https://www.insidehighered.com/views/2022/02/24/higher-ed-must-act-against-educational-gag-orders-opinion

G2geek (2011, January 10). *Stochastic terrorism: triggering the shooters. Daily Kos.* https://www.dailykos.com/stories/2011/1/10/934890/-

Gandy, G. (2023, March 30). *Hilton School District announces re-evaluation of 'This Book is Gay.' RochesterFirst.com.* https://www.rochesterfirst.com/news/education/hilton-school-district-announces-re-evaluation-of-this-book-is-gay/

GLAAD (2023, June 27). *Moms for Liberty.* https://glaad.org/gap/moms-liberty/

Goff, P. A., Eberhardt, J. L., Williams, M. J., & Jackson, M. C. (2008). Not yet human: Implicit knowledge, historical dehumanization, and contemporary consequences. *Journal of Personality and Social Psychology, 94(2), 292.* https://doi.org/10.1037/0022-3514.94.2.292

Grant, M. G. (2023, March 16). Conservatives are trying to ban books in your town. Librarians are fighting back. *The New Republic.* https://newrepublic.com/article/170920/conservative-book-bans-libraries-fighting-back

Grasso, S. (2022, April 15). *It was never about 'grooming.'* discourse blog. https://www.discourseblog.com/p/it-was-never-about-grooming

Grueskin, B. (2020, August 10). Stop calling racist rhetoric a 'dog whistle.' *Columbia Journalism Review.* https://www.cjr.org/criticism/racist-rheto-ric-dog-whistle.php

Hamm, M. S., & Spaaij, R. (2017). *The age of lone wolf terrorism. Columbia University Press.*

Haq, H. (2015). *ISIS burns Mosul library: Why terrorists target books. The Christian Science Monitor.* https://www.csmonitor.com/Books/chapter-and-verse/2015/0225/ISIS-burns-Mosul-library-Why-terrorists-target-books

Hardy, K. (2019). Countering right-wing extremism: Lessons from Germany and Norway. *Journal of Policing, Intelligence and Counter Terrorism. 14(3),* 262-279. https://doi.org/10.1080/18335330.2019.1662076

Harris, E. A., & Alter, A. (2022, June 6). With rising book bans, librarians have come under attack. *New York Times.* https://www.nytimes.com/2022/07/06/books/book-ban-librarians.html

Harris, E. A., & Alter, A. (2022, December 12). A fast-growing network of conservative groups is fueling a surge in book bans. *New York Times.* https://www.nytimes.com/2022/12/12/books/book-bans-libraries.html

Hersher, R. (2017, January 10). *What happened when Dylann Roof asked Google for information about race? NPR.* https://www.npr.org/sections/thetwo-way/2017/01/10/508363607/what-happened-when-dylann-roof-asked-google-for-information-about-race

Hodson, G., Kteily, N., & Hoffarth, M. (2014). Of filthy pigs and subhuman mongrels: Dehumanization, disgust, and intergroup prejudice. *TPM: Testing, Psychometrics, Methodology in Applied Psychology. 21(3),* 267-284. https://doi.org/10.4473/TPM21.3.3

Jayswal, P. & Miller, J. (2023, September 24). Bomb threat cancels drag story time at King's English Bookshop, store closes for day. *The Salt Lake Tribune.* https://www.sltrib.com/news/2023/09/24/bomb-threat-cancels-drag-story/

Jensen, K. (2023, April 7). *How long until a library worker is killed?: Book censorship news, April 7, 2023. Book Riot.* https://bookriot.com/how-long-until-a-library-worker-is-killed/

Kayyem, J. (2019, August 4). There are no lone wolves. *Washington Post.* https://www.washingtonpost.com/opinions/2019/08/04/there-are-no-lone-wolves/

Keats, J. (2019, January 21). *Jargon watch: The rising danger of stochastic terrorism.* Wired. https://www.wired.com/story/jargon-watch-rising-danger-stochastic-terrorism/

Keller, J. (2018, October 29). *To discuss the Pittsburgh synagogue shooting, we have to discuss Trump. Pacific Standard.* https://psmag.com/news/to-discuss-the-pittsburgh-synagogue-shooting-we-have-to-discuss-trump

King, G. (2023, March 29). Northwest Junior High bomb threats last week 'not credible.' *The Gazette.* https://www.thegazette.com/k/northwest-junior-high-bomb-threats-last-week-not-credible

Kleinfeld, R. (2021). The rise of political violence in the United States. *Journal of Democracy. 32(4),* 160-176. https://doi.org/10.1353/jod.2021.0059

Kransz, M. (2022, November 6). *Public library defunded over LGBTQ themes going back to voters. See the book challenges filed. MLive.* https://www.mlive.com/news/grand-rapids/2022/11/public-library-defunded-over-lgbtq-themes-going-back-to-voters-see-the-book-challenges-filed.html

Kruesi, K., & Phan, K. (2022, March 29). *'Grooming': The ubiquitous buzzword in LGBTQ school debate*. Associated Press. https://apnews.com/article/education-gender-identity-adf10ff5f169fae9c9af4d08a7b0c2bc

Kurtzleben, D. (2023, November 17). *Why Trump's authoritarian language about 'vermin' matters. NPR.* https://www.npr.org/2023/11/17/1213746885/trump-vermin-hitler-immigration-authoritarian-republican-primary

Lavietes, M. (2022, April 12). *'Groomer,' 'pro-pedophile': Old tropes find new life in anti-LGBT movement. NBCNews.com.* https://www.nbcnews.com/nbc-out/out-politics-and-policy/groomer-pedophile-old-tropes-find-new-life-anti-lgbtq-movement-rcna23931

Lawton, S. (2022, April 28). "Libs of TikTok" has used Twitter to target over 200 individual teachers, schools, and districts in 2022 for supporting LGBTQ students. Media Matters for America. https://www.mediamatters.org/twitter/libs-tiktok-has-used-twitter-target-over-200-individual-teachers-schools-and-districts-2022

Livingston, D. (2023, March 11). Two arrested after protesters and supporters clashed at Wadsworth drag queen story hour. *Akron Beach Journal.* https://www.beaconjournal.com/story/news/2023/03/11/dozens-demonstrate-at-drag-story-hour-for-children-at-wadsworth-park/69997506007/

Lyngaas, S. (2023, May 24). *US remain in 'heightened threat environment' with recent racist and ethnically motivated attacks, DHS says. CNN.* https://www.cnn.com/2023/05/24/politics/dhs-threat-bulletin/index.html

Margolin, J., & Grant, T. (2023, May 15). *Threats against the LGBTQIA+ community intensifying: Department of Homeland Security. ABCNews.com.* https://abcnews.go.com/US/threats-lgbtqia-community-intensifying-department-homeland-security/story?id=99338137

Martiny, C., & Lawrence, S. (2023, June 22). *A year of hate: Anti-drag mobilization efforts targeting LGBTQ+ people in the United States. Institute for Strategic Dialogue.* https://www.isdglobal.org/isd-publications/a-year-of-hate-anti-drag-mobilization-efforts-targeting-lgbtq-people-in-the-us/

Marwick, A. E., & Lewis, R. (2017, May 15). *Media manipulation and disinformation online. Data & Society Research Institute.* https://datasociety.net/library/media-manipulation-and-disinfo-online/

Matsumoto, D., Hwang, H. C., & Frank, M. G (2016). The effects of incidental anger, contempt, and disgust on hostile language and implicit behaviors. *Journal of Applied Social Psychology. 46, 437-452.* https://doi.org/10.1111/jasp.12374

Meckler, L. & Dawsey, J. (2021, June 21). Republicans, spurred by an unlikely figure, see political promise in targeting critical race theory. *Washington Post.* https://www.washingtonpost.com/education/2021/06/19/critical-race-theory-rufo-republicans/

Meehan, K. & Friedman, J. (2023, April 20). *Banned in the USA: State laws supercharge book suppression in schools. PEN America.* https://pen.org/report/banned-in-the-usa-state-laws-supercharge-book-suppression-in-schools/

Melhado, W. & Nguyen (2023, March 6). Texas lawmakers pursued dozens of bills affecting LGBTQ people this year. Here's what passed and what failed. *The Texas Tribune.* https://www.texastribune.org/2023/03/06/texas-legislature-lgbtq-bills/

Migdon, B. (2022, March 7). *Gov. DeSantis spokesperson says 'Don't Say Gay' opponents are 'groomers.' The Hill.* https://thehill.com/changing-america/respect/equality/597215-gov-desantis-spokesperson-says-dont-say-gay-opponents-are/

Monroe, T., & Savillo, R. (2021, May 26). *Fox news has attacked Black Lives Matter over 400 times in a 6-month period. Media Matters for America.* https://www.mediamatters.org/black-lives-matter/fox-news-has-attacked-black-lives-matter-over-400-times-6-month-period

Nelson, B. (2022, November 5). How stochastic terrorism uses disgust to incite violence. *Scientific American.* https://www.scientificamerican.com/article/how-stochastic-terrorism-uses-disgust-to-incite-violence/

Newcomb, S. (2012, June 20). On historical narratives and dehumanization. Indian Country Today. https://ictnews.org/archive/on-historical-narratives-and-dehumanization

Oliver, D. (2023, February 22). What happens to our culture when books are banned: 'A chilling effect.' *USA Today.* https://www.usatoday.com/story/life/health-wellness/2023/02/22/book-bans-what-happens-culture/11262643002/

Parasol Patrol (n.d.). https://parasolpatrol.org/

Pengelly, M. (2023, May 6). Moms for Liberty, meet John Birch: the roots of US right-wing book bans. *The Guardian.* https://www.theguardian.com/books/2023/may/06/moms-for-liberty-john-birch-society-far-right-book-bans

Powers, S. (2022, March 7). *Gov. DeSantis spokesperson labels sex ed bill opponents 'groomers.' Florida Politics.* https://floridapolitics.com/archives/504879-gov-desantis-spokesperson-labels-sex-ed-bills-opponents-groomers/

Qiu, L. (2018, May 18). The context behind Trump's "animals" comment. *New York Times.* https://www.nytimes.com/2018/05/18/us/politics/fact-check-trump-animals-immigration-ms13-sanctuary-cities.html

Rittenberg, J. (2022, April 6). *The history of Nazi book burning. Book Riot.* https://bookriot.com/nazi-book-burning/

Robinson, I. (2022, August 26). *How woke went from "black" to "bad." Legal Defense Fund.* https://www.naacpldf.org/woke-black-bad/

Rodríguez, J. (2023, July 24). She was a GOP congresswoman. Her son is a transgender activist. *Washington Post.* https://www.washingtonpost.com/lifestyle/2023/07/24/republicans-and-transgender-issues/

Salvanto, A. (2023, May 8). *CBS News poll analysis: How do people view book bans, trans rights issues as GOP presidential primary fight ramps up? CBSNews. com.* https://www.cbsnews.com/news/cbs-news-poll-views-book-bans-trans-rights-issues-gop-presidential-primary/

Sarnoff, M. (2023, April 25). *'White Lives Matter' protestor who allegedly tried to firebomb a church over drag event hit with hate crime charge. Law & Crime.* https://lawandcrime.com/high-profile/white-lives-matter-protestor-who-allegedly-tried-to-firebomb-a-church-over-drag-event-hit-with-hate-crime-charge/

Schlatter, E., & Steinback, R. (2011, February 27). *10 Anti-gay myths debunked. Southern Poverty Law Center.* https://www.splcenter.org/fighting-hate/intelligence-report/2011/10-anti-gay-myths-debunked

Select January 6th Committee (2022, December 22). Final Report and Supporting Materials Collection. https://www.govinfo.gov/collection/january-6th-committee-final-report?path=/GPO/January%206th%20Committee%20Final%20Report%20and%20Supporting%20Materials%20Collection

Siegel, E. & Rubin, E. (2023, June 3). *Same fears, new tactics: How efforts to ban 'bad books' reached a record high in 2022. WBAY.com.* https://www.wbay.com/2023/06/03/same-fears-new-tactics-how-efforts-ban-bad-books-reached-record-high-2022/

Siouxland News (2023, March 20). *Book removed from West High School library after right-wing Twitter account protest.* https://siouxlandnews.com/news/local/book-removed-from-west-high-school-library-after-right-wing-twitter-account-protest

Smith, T. (2023, May 4). *Missouri escalates battle over books with rule threatening state funds for libraries. NPR.* https://news.stlpublicradio.org/government-politics-issues/2023-05-04/library-funding-becomes-the-nuclear-option-as-the-battle-over-books-escalates

Snodgrass, E. (2022, November 8). Stochastic terrorism appears to be on the rise globally. Extremism experts explain how this form of violence has gone mainstream. *Business Insider.* https://www.businessinsider.com/stochastic-terrorism-meaning-definition-form-of-extremist-political-violence-2022-11

Southern Poverty Law Center (n.d.). *Moms for Liberty.* https://www.splcenter.org/fighting-hate/extremist-files/group/moms-liberty

Stelloh, T. (2016, June 19). *Angels quietly block Westboro protesters at Orlando funeral.* NBCNews.com. https://www.nbcnews.com/storyline/orlando-nightclub-massacre/angels-quietly-block-westboro-protesters-orlando-funeral-n595311

Styrt, P. G. (2023, January 3). *Stochastic terrorism, January 6, and medieval monarchy.* The Sundial. https://medium.com/the-sundial-acmrs/stochastic-terrorism-january-6-and-medieval-monarchy-dd8b19055e04

United States Holocaust Memorial Museum (n.d.). *Defining the enemy. Holocaust Encyclopedia.* https://encyclopedia.ushmm.org/content/en/article/defining-the-enemy

Uyheng, J., Bellutta, D., & Carley, K. M. (2022). Bots amplify and redirect hate speech in online discourse about racism during the COVID-19 pandemic. *Social Media + Society, 8(3), 20563051221104749.* https://doi.org/10.1177/20563051221104749

Walker, S. (2023, January 23). Manatee County teachers close class libraries, fearing prosecution under new Florida law. *The Palm Beach Post*. https://www.palmbeachpost.com/story/news/education/2023/01/23/fearing-prosecution-manatee-county-teachers-cover-up-classroom-books/69832276007/

Wiggins, C. (2023, March 13). *Neo-Nazis chanting 'Sieg Heil' target drag queen story event*. Advocate. https://www.advocate.com/news/ohio-nazi-drag-story-hour

Wiggins, C. (2023, March 22). *5 N.Y. schools evacuated after bomb threats over LGBTQ+ books*. Advocate. https://www.advocate.com/news/groomer-bomb-threat-new-york

Woo, G. (2002). Quantitative terrorism risk assessment. *Journal of Risk Finance*. *4(1)*, 7-14. https://doi.org/10.1108/eb022949

Woodcock, C. (2022, September 27). *Libraries across the US are receiving violent threats*. Motherboard. https://www.vice.com/en/article/v7vyvb/libraries-across-the-us-are-receiving-violent-threats

Yamada, C. (2023, March 21). Sioux City Community School District removes book after being featured on Libs of TikTok Twitter account. *Sioux City Journal*. https://siouxcityjournal.com/news/local/education/sioux-city-community-ty-school-district-removes-book-after-being-featured-on-libs-of-tiktok-twitter/article_163cfd8a-c293-58ad-8a2d-8c60597d63dc.html

Beyond the Library Walls
This Censorship is Not About the Books

Maureen Babb

Introduction

Recent years have seen a persistent and highly organized effort to censor LGBTQ materials[1] in libraries (Friedman & Johnson, 2022; Natanson, 2023). These efforts have been most pronounced in the United States but are certainly not limited to that country; many of the same techniques for book banning have bled across the border into Canada (Manitoba Library Association, 2023). Attempts to ban books are nothing new, but the frequency and vitriol of these latest attempts are noteworthy and have startled librarians and the general public with their fervor. Current book-banning attempts target multiple libraries and many books at once. Queer materials are framed as explicitly pornographic and therefore inappropriate (especially for children), regardless of the actual content of the works. Librarians themselves have been targeted in these book banning efforts as well, framed and harassed as being pedophilic groomers (Friedman & Johnson, 2022; Smith, 2023). In some cases, librarians have had the police called on them for sharing "pornography" (actually young adult novels) with children (Legum, 2023). In others, librarians have faced death threats for their role in opposing book bans, with attackers framing them as "pedos." (Smith, 2023).

Some libraries have capitulated to these censorship demands, either by choice or through coercion from their governing bodies (Bloom,

---

1   LGBTQ materials are not the only materials that have been targeted; notably materials about racial minorities have also been targeted

2023; Friedman & Johnson, 2022; Kienlen, 2023). Other libraries have responded to censorship attempts with the traditional library stand-bys of freedom of expression and neutrality. Libraries frequently use claims of neutrality to assert a sense of apolitical detachment from the world at large. But it is critical that librarians understand these recent book-banning attempts in their full context and recognize them for what they are; an explicitly political attempt to silence certain groups of people, and moreover, a small part of a much larger plan to invoke large-scale political change.

Additionally, the targeting of queer works must be understood in the broader context of queer history in the Western world. While in recent years there has been a flourishing of queer literature, coinciding with increased acceptance of queer individuals, it is essential for librarians to recognize that this is a relatively new development. Rather than the exception, widespread censorship of queer materials has been the norm for much of recent history (Brownworth, 1994; Cossman, 2013; Jaeger et al., 2023). Likewise, suppression or even outright criminalization of queer identities has also been the norm. Indeed, such suppression still occurs, with social media algorithms that flag any LGBTQ content as mature, hiding it from view or discoverability (Monea, 2022). Criminalization of queer lives occurs still as well; in many countries, homosexuality is illegal even today (Human Dignity Trust, 2023; Kelleher, 2022). But even in countries that have been more tolerant to queer individuals, we see attempted or enacted laws designed to hamper queer existence. In particular, transgender individuals are targeted with laws affecting everything from their access to medical care, to their ability to participate in sports, to their ability to use public washrooms (Trans Legislation Tracker, 2023). As librarians seek to respond to requests to censor materials, this state of affairs should be kept in mind, for these targeted requests cannot be removed from the context of this history, nor can they be divorced from current efforts to legislate against queer individuals. Nor can this be viewed as an aberration; vitriolic organized censorship attempts in response to the increased acceptance and visibility of queer lives have occurred before and must be fervently countered.

The History of Queer Censorship

With regard to materials with LGBTQ content, censorship has been the norm more than not. The history of queer media is one of censorship;

queer publications were seized by police under obscenity laws, prevented from crossing borders into other countries, and generally prevented from being accessed (Cossman, 2013). While censorship in the strictest sense refers to censorship by a government organization, censorship as discussed in this chapter will refer to a wider form of censorship that includes censorship from other organizations, including libraries themselves, as well as any other organizations that have a role in information dissemination, censorship by classification, and self-censorship. All of these forms of censorship have played, and indeed continue to play, a role in how queer content exists in the world. Famous examples include the Hays Code, ironically created to prevent the introduction of formal government censorship in the United States during the McCarthy era, which kept queer content out of movies by disallowing the inclusion of "sexual perversion" in movies (Mennel, 2012). The Comics Code of America did the same for comics, and similar structures existed for television shows and publishing (Grunzke, 2021). Many of these codes were in place until the 1980s and have lasting legacies in the presentation of queer content even today.

Libraries too played their role in censorship. The modern idea of libraries as beacons of neutrality, that house content that will appeal to all, is an idea that did not develop until World War II, in direct response to the harsh censorship of the Nazi regime (Popowich, 2019). Historically, libraries were seen as a means by which to better society and to provide access to a certain quality of reading material that promoted a hegemonic worldview that aligned with the dominant white, straight, male, and wealthy perspective.

In more recent times, libraries have contributed to censorship by classification, often while denying their own culpability by making claims to neutrality. Until the 1970s and the work of the *Task Force on Gay Liberation of the American Library Association*, queer content in libraries catalogued using Library of Congress classification was listed under the subject heading "sexual perversion." Despite a change in subject headings, the legacy of this can still be seen today, as queer books are still catalogued next to sex crimes in the Library of Congress classification. This is because while the subject headings had changed, the physical placement within the collection still reflects the original positioning of queer content as a form of sexual deviancy or criminality (Adler, 2013, 2015; Berman & Gross, 2017). The concept of "perversion" being used interchangeably with queer content is something we still see echoes of today, both in inflammatory right-wing rhetoric, and in more subtle ways, such as corporate algorithms in search engines and discoverability functions, marking all queer content as adult in nature and/or making such content more difficult to find on their websites or platforms. YouTube is a prime example of this and is known to have discriminatory practices and algorithms that suppress queer content that is not deemed sufficiently palatable (Rodriguez, 2023). Likewise, the linking of queer content and activities with sex crimes has been a standby of anti-queer rhetoric; the accusation of "pedophile" and "corruption of the innocent" was used frequently against gay men in the past, and those arguing against gay marriage frequently argued that it would open the doors for pedophilic relationships (Adler, 2015). Today, similar accusations are leveled at transgender individuals, and increasingly at individuals providing access to queer resources, such as librarians (Bombaro, 2023).

It should not be lost in this discussion that the censorship of queer materials is not, and never has been, exclusively about the materials. Rather, it is about queer people: queer materials are censored as a side effect of attitudes towards, and attacks on, queer people. This is perhaps most clearly epitomized in the now-defunct American military policy of "Don't Ask, Don't Tell," which barred LGBTQ people from serving, and thus functionally placed limitations on speech by preventing members of the military from acknowledging their LGBTQ status. The existence of such individuals in the military was accepted only if their queerness was kept out of sight. It is also worth noting that when this policy was implemented, it was considered a step forwards, as prior to it, suspected LGBTQ status could be used to dismiss members, and this limited such possible dismissals to those with explicit LGBTQ status (Goldbach & Castro, 2016). In the previous example, one could focus on the censorship of speech if one desired, but of course, the larger problem is what the censorship represents: control over the lives and livelihoods of LGBTQ individuals. So, too, is this the case with the censorship of queer materials.

Censorship of queer materials is tied up with a desire to control the lives of LGBTQ individuals. This may manifest as a desire to keep queer individuals out of sight, to keep them from "corrupting" others, to prevent knowledge of queer lives from becoming widespread and normalized, to wanting queer individuals to feel as though their existence is shameful and wrong, to, at the most extreme edges, wanting queer individuals to cease to exist. Today, queer rights have reached extents that have not been seen before; since 2001, many countries have legalized same-sex marriage, and protections exist to prevent discrimination based on gender or sexuality in many places. Queer representation is increasingly common in mainstream media, and its depiction no longer comes with archaic rules that require queer lives to only be shown in a negative light. The recent attempts at censorship of queer material represent a pushback against this increasing acceptance of queer people, a desire to return to a previous (or perceived previous) status quo from conservative quarters. We are seeing a desire to effectively push queer people *back* into the closet.

Such pushbacks against increasing acceptance of queer lives have been seen before. The Weimar Republic in Germany saw a greater acceptance of queer individuals than had previously been the case and was noteworthy within Europe at the time for it (Marhoefer, 2015). Though queer individuals were generally expected to keep their queerness out of public view, they could be accepted as long as their queerness was kept private. Queer spaces were generally tolerated in an underground context, societies of gay and lesbian people were formed, serious attempts were made to decriminalize homosexuality, and Magnus Hirschfeld's *Institute for the Science of Sexuality* (*Institut für Sexualwissenschaft*) was opened. But with the Nazi rise to power in 1933, that progress was destroyed (Anonymous, 2013b; Marhoefer, 2015). Homosexuality had long been a target (one of many) of the far right in Germany and was explicitly singled out as undesirable by Nazi doctrine. The famous book burning conducted by the Nazis on May 10, 1933, included the works and research housed at Hirschfeld's *Institute*, after a violent and most likely deadly raid on the building on the 6th, alongside books from other locations, such as public libraries and universities (Marhoefer, 2015). Under Nazi rule, gay men were persecuted, with many ultimately killed or imprisoned in concentration camps (Anonymous, 2013a; Heger, 1980; Plant, 1986). Here we see an extreme example of how censorship of queer materials is not about the books, but rather, about a desire to see an end to queer existence.

While the comparison between modern censorship attempts and Nazi censorship in the form of book burnings may at first seem hyperbolic, it must be noted that anti-trans hostility in the United States was identified as being genocidal in nature in a statement made by the Lemkin Institute for Genocide Prevention in late 2022 (Lemkin Institute for Genocide Prevention, 2022). Transgender individuals in particular have been the target of the American far right; hundreds of anti-trans bills have been proposed in the United States since 2021; as of the writing of this chapter, 83 of those bills have passed (Trans Legislation Tracker, 2023). The bills target transgender individuals' ability to use public washrooms or changerooms, to access gender-affirming care, to perform in public in drag[2] or to refer to transgender individuals by their correct pronouns, among other things (Trans Legislation Tracker, 2023). The ultimate goal of such bills is to remove transgender people from existing in public spaces.

Other bills have targeted the wider queer community, notably the "Don't Say Gay" bill in Florida, which prevents educators from teaching on sexual orientation (Associated Press, 2022). Similar bills have started finding their ways into other Western countries such as Canada (Hunter, 2023). These bills present queer individuals as being explicitly obscene or unsuitable for public spaces or unsafe around children. This framing is reflected in the calls for the banning of queer books, which frequently describe even the mildest queer content as pornographic and unsuitable for children.

The Bigger Picture

As with previous attempts to censor queer content, recent attempts to ban queer materials should be acknowledged as part of a larger movement. In the current case, the attempt at censorship is part of an organized, rather than an organic, pushback against a society increasingly accepting of those not historically in power, including, but certainly not limited to, queer people.

The organized nature of recent censorship attempts cannot be denied; the *American Library Association* (ALA) has reported alarming increases in its tracked book banning attempts, with 1,269[3] attempts in 2022 alone (American Library Association, 2023a). This number is likely to significantly underestimate the true number of proposed book bans, as only those reported to the ALA are tracked. The *Washington Post* has reported that the majority of attempted bans originated from only 11 zealous individuals, who filed similar or identical multi-item complaints at libraries across the United States (Natanson, 2023). Likewise,

---

2   It is worth noting here that so-called drag bans are themselves a way to target transgender individuals, as they could be perceived as "dressing in drag" at all times by bad faith actors.

3   Not all of these attempted bans target queer content specifically, but a significant number do. As noted earlier, though queer censorship is the focus of this chapter, it is not the only content being targeted.

many attempts at censorship have been facilitated by organizations such as Moms for Liberty, a Florida-based group (Harris & Alter, 2022). Without attention to a broader context, recent censorship attempts could be viewed as the actions of a handful of malcontents, able to make noise, but with little power. However, when viewed in context, it is clear that these censorship attempts represent a single wing of a much greater attack force targeting many fronts. The anti-trans bills discussed earlier represent another front, and there are yet others targeting other marginalized groups not discussed here as they are out of the scope of this chapter.

It is also worth noting that these organized efforts from small-but-vocal groups do inspire more local individuals to confront their libraries with censorship requests as well. Framing these requests as a way to protect children allows for a much more palatable excuse to ban books than simply finding them distasteful. Additionally, these organized groups provide guidance to those wishing to send their own book removal requests to libraries; a prime example of this is the Moms for Liberty affiliated *BookLook* "Book Reports" for parents, which note "concerns" about specific books, and highlight individual passages and pages that can be pointed to in boilerplate book removal requests (BookLook, 2023). Similar sites with an array of different books can likewise be found, several of which use the rating system and techniques used by *BookLook*; another example is *Rated Books* which provides information on many more books (RatedBooks, 2023). In short, it is simple to find the details necessary to file a book removal request, meaning that not only will attacks on books come from a small number of people external to most library jurisdictions, but the systems have been put in place by the organized right to make it simple for discontented locals within a jurisdiction to file takedown requests as well. This organization and the simplicity of the process no doubt contribute to the volume of book banning requests in recent years.

Moms for Liberty is a member of the Advisory Board of *Project 2025*, an initiative of the Heritage Foundation, an $86 million conservative think tank (Heritage Foundation, 2023). In July 2023, *Project 2025* released its *Mandate for Leadership,* a 920-page framework—functionally, a wish list—for a Republican leader to follow, should they win the 2024 American election (Project 2025, 2023). The *Mandate* is clear in its desire to push back against queer rights. For instance, it notes that the hypothetical 2024 Republican president should "rescind regulations prohibiting discrimination on the basis of sexual orientation, gender identity, transgender status, and sex characteristics" (Project 2025, 2023, p. 584). The *Mandate* also refers to the normalization of transgender individuals as "toxic" and equates queer content with pornography (which it claims should be outlawed) and the "sexualization of children," in a move that reflects the manner in which queer content has been censored previously (Project 2025, 2023, pp. 1-5). It also outlines plans to expand censorship attempts to target research funders such as the National Institutes of Health, and regulate what research can be produced, specifically calling attention to transgender individuals in the process:

> The incestuous relationship between the NIH, CDC, and vaccine makers—with all of the conflict of interest it entails—cannot be allowed to continue, and the revolving door between them must be locked. As Severino writes, "Funding for scientific research should not be controlled by a small group of highly paid and unaccountable insiders at the NIH, many of whom stay in power for decades. The NIH monopoly on directing research should be broken." What's more, NIH has long "been at the forefront in pushing junk gender science." The next HHS secretary should immediately put an end to the department's foray into woke transgender activism. (Project 2025, 2023, p. 284)

Anti-transgender activists denigrate the research that supports gender-affirming care, despite a medical establishment that overwhelmingly supports it; the above quote indicates a desire to censor and shape research so that it might not interfere with bills targeting access to gender-affirming healthcare. With Moms for Liberty as a member organization of *Project 2025*, we can see clearly that the censorship attempts are only a step in a much larger plan, one that targets queer rights and lives, though even this does not encompass the extent of the larger plan.

Necessity of Context

This context, both historical and political, is essential for librarians to keep in mind as they confront attempts at censorship in their libraries. This rash of targeted, organized, attempted book banning that frequently frames librarians and other educators as indoctrinators, pedophiles, and groomers cannot be treated like run-of-the-mill attempts to remove books from library collections, for the simple reason that these efforts represent a much broader scope than one-off book removal requests. These censorship attempts are not raised in good faith, but as part of a grand plan to remove queerness from the public eye and queer people from public society.

Addressing book banning requests is a time-consuming process. When libraries are inundated with book banning requests by organized groups, that time commitment is multiplied. Policies for addressing these book challenges may require reading or assessing each individual book, removing the book from circulation until the book has been assessed, or otherwise demanding significant parcels of staff time be devoted to the request. For challenges targeting multiple books, the time required to assess them all, and the fact that libraries may remove the books from their shelves while the assessment is ongoing, means that those challenges may effectively remove queer books from circulation, even if it is only for a short time (Sterbenz, 2023). In the current situation, library workers often also face harassment for refusing to bow to censorship demands. This harassment ranges from the leveling of terms like "pedophile" and "groomer" at librarians, to explicit death threats, to hate groups appearing at library board meetings to intimidate librarians and others (Smith, 2023; Sterbenz, 2023). The stress of the situation has caused some library workers to quit, and it is unfortunately likely more will follow (Smith, 2023).

Viewing these censorship attempts in the broader context allows for better assessment with how they should be dealt with. Situating these attempted book bans as part of a targeting of queer, particularly transgender, individuals should indicate to librarians that these challenges run counter not only to intellectual freedom, but also to the professional commitment to social justice. The ALA code of ethics states both:

> We uphold the principles of intellectual freedom and resist all efforts to censor library resources

and

> We affirm the inherent dignity and rights of every person. We work to recognize and dismantle systemic and individual biases; to confront inequity and oppression; to enhance diversity and inclusion; and to advance racial and social justice in our libraries, communities, profession, and associations through awareness, advocacy, education, collaboration, services, and allocation of resources and spaces. (American Library Association, 2021, paras. 9-16)

These censorship attempts should be confronted not only on the grounds of protecting intellectual freedom and resisting censorship, but also, perhaps especially, on the grounds that they represent a serious affront to social justice.

Social justice has not always fit comfortably into librarianship. Indeed, it is a concept that is often framed as running counter to neutrality. Neutrality itself is often framed as being essential to librarianship and intellectual freedom in particular, but as a recent ALA working group pointed out, it is not something that is well-defined in librarianship, and is not positioned centrally in ALA documentation (American Library Association, 2022). The place of neutrality has long been debated in the profession, with many highlighting that true neutrality is impossible, and that attempting to follow a framework of neutrality privileges those already in power (American Library Association, 2022; Lewis, 2008). Neutrality, however, is not essential to intellectual freedom, and the ALA Working Group on Intellectual Freedom and Social Justice has recently proposed alternative frameworks to neutrality, including radical empathy, trauma-informed response, and cultural humility (American Library Association, 2022). This is to say that social justice can be centered in the profession, and doing so is not an affront to the values of the profession, as neutrality, a historically fraught paradigm that is ultimately mythical in its ability to be applied practically, is not the only lens through which one can approach librarianship and intellectual freedom.

Recent situations in libraries have seen neutrality pitted directly against social justice, most especially in controversies involving the booking of library spaces to anti-transgender speakers, sometimes even in the face of library policies that allow for the discretionary cancellation of events (Popowich, 2021). In these situations, neutrality historically wins out in nearly all cases, often resulting in an unsafe environment for queer individuals. The argument goes that if queer people are to be protected, then we must allow those who wish to deny or erase their existence to voice that in library spaces. However, as others have pointed out, neutrality benefits the status quo, and does not benefit minority groups, such as queer, and particularly transgender people. Accepting neutrality as a framework for enforcing intellectual freedom implies a starting point of equality within society that does not exist, and therefore neutrality unfairly benefits those already in power.

These power dynamics are of particular interest in the current situation, where well-funded, organized groups are directly attacking queer (particularly transgender) rights in the political and social spheres. Attacks on books and libraries are a single wing of a much larger front, epitomized by offenses such as *Project 2025*. The current response in libraries to these attacks prioritizes neutrality, which misses the broader picture. Social justice should be of equal or increased importance in librarian responses to the current book challenges, because what is at stake is more than merely whether or not queer books exist in libraries, but whether queer people are permitted to exist in public spaces. Neutrality as a framework has librarians confront these book challenges on a symptom level, when what librarians should confront is the reason that the challenges are being issued to begin with, that is, a desire to roll back queer rights and queer visibility. Addressing this only at the book challenge level will be akin to playing a game of whack-a-mole and will be largely futile. As such, bad faith attempts to censor books, particularly those that come with a larger goal of silencing queer voices, should be dismissed without needing to waste hours of librarians' time responding. Spending time on these challenges takes away from the true work of librarianship: ensuring access to information for all. Ignoring the broader context of the book challenges ignores their targeted nature; not only are queer individuals being targeted, but so too is the role of libraries, librarians, and any who would seek the free flow of information of all sorts within a society. By contrast, viewing the book challenges in their proper context, as the wing of a broader attack against both queer individuals and those in a society who allow information about queer lives to be accessible, demonstrates the need to approach from a social justice perspective.

The organized nature of these recent censorship attempts merits organized response, and libraries and librarians should be a part of that response, both to protect queer lives and to protect the profession. The ALA has already created a *Fight Censorship*[4] page with resources, including legal resources, for those facing censorship challenges (American Library Association, 2023b). As these censorship attempts increasingly reach beyond the borders of the United States, library organizations in other countries should consider developing similar toolkits, with resources suited to their particular country's laws, and

---

4   https://www.ala.org/advocacy/fight-censorship

potentially build legal defense funds to help library workers who face harassment. Ultimately the goal of library organizations should be to see that no librarian faces these censorship challenges on their own. Suggested responses to these calls for censorship and to the harassment of librarians have included responding to threats with legal action, and changing or streamlining book challenge policies (Sterbenz, 2023). These attempts are to be lauded and should be continued, but efforts should also be made at a grander and more political scale.

While politics have long been considered anathema to libraries working from a neutrality framework, the current context highlights how libraries are themselves political. Library boards are often controlled politically, and in some cases, boards have been deliberately stacked with individuals hostile to libraries as places of freely available information. In response, librarians should foster attempts to populate boards with those friendly to the information-accessibility mission of libraries. Political awareness of the issue should be raised as well; while endorsing specific candidates in elections would likely be unacceptable, ensuring that the voting public considers these issues when casting their ballots is something that librarians could do, through advertising or leafleting campaigns, organized within the larger community. These campaigns should be organized through library organizations, as a direct response to a current crisis in the profession; organizing it in this fashion allows the response to be greater than any single librarian or library and solidifies the effort as worthy of professional attention and organized response.

The professional credentials of librarians should also be more clearly vocalized to the public, who often do not recognize the degree of specialized education required of librarians; highlighting this educational background and vocalizing our expertise in this area may help articulate why just anyone should not be making content decisions for libraries.

Conclusion

It is clear that the recent attempts at censorship of queer materials have implications far beyond the library walls. Current censorship attempts are part of an attack against transgender individuals that has been identified as genocidal in nature. Despite the severity of this, even the attacks on transgender and other queer individuals represents only a small part of a larger plan. The organized nature of this pushback against queer acceptance is unusual, but not unprecedented. Nor is censorship unusual in the history of queer material.

This context *must* be kept in mind when responding to these censorship attempts. Examining the history of the censorship of queer materials shows both the long-lasting effects of successful censorship and the way that such censorship is often tied to broader political agendas that can have dire consequences for queer individuals. If librarians ignore the context—by imagining these censorship attempts as the vendettas of a few organized malcontents, for example—they miss that this is part of a broader agenda that seeks censorship not just of library materials, but of education and research on a much larger scale. If librarians view this censorship as something that can be dealt with effectively by responding to it on the microscale of individual book bans at individual libraries, they will be unable to counter it as the organized attempt that it is. Librarians should forge alliances within and across libraries, and with those in other professions, to counter these censorship attempts and to pre-empt additional and more hidden censorship attempts, such as those that could occur if organized anti-queer activists target research funders.

The librarian's commitment to social justice is an essential tool in combating the recent wave of attempted censorship, as the goals of the bodies organizing the censorship attempts run directly counter to social justice. Because this censorship is a means to an end (one of many being employed) that seeks to remove queer, particularly transgender, individuals from public existence, the social justice lens allows librarians to view this censorship in its proper context, rather than as a hodgepodge of individual book banning attempts. As removal of queer lives from the public eye is the goal, librarians should be particularly cautious when responding to censorship attempts that they do not acquiesce to the demands of censors by quietly removing contested books from public view, even if they remain in the collection, for example. In this moment, it is not merely queer books at risk, but queer rights and queer lives. Moreover, these organized efforts threaten libraries as freely available sources of information more generally—a direct attack on the purpose of our profession. The goal of the current censorship movement is to roll back the progress that queer people have experienced in recent years, and to curtail the free flow of information about queer lives: librarians must resist this completely.

References

Adler, M. A. (2013). The ALA task force on gay liberation: Effecting change in naming and classification of GLBTQ subjects. *Advances in Classification Research Online, 23*(1), 1-4. https://doi.org/10.7152/acro.v23i1.14226

Adler, M. A. (2015). "Let's not homosexualize the library stacks": Liberating gays in the library catalog. *Journal of the History of Sexuality, 24*(3), 478-507. https://doi.org/10.7560/JHS24306

American Library Association. (2021). *Professional Ethics.* https://www.ala.org/tools/ethics

American Library Association. (2022). *Final Report of the Working Group on Intellectual Freedom and Social Justice.* https://www.ala.org/aboutala/sites/ala.org.aboutala/files/content/governance/ExecutiveBoard/20222023Docs/ebd%2010.0%20IF_SJ%20Final%20Report%207.12.2022.pdf

American Library Association. (2023a, March 22). *American Library Association reports record number of demands to censor library books and materials in 2022* http://www.ala.org/news/press-releases/2023/03/record-book-bans-2022

American Library Association. (2023b). *Fight censorship.* https://www.ala.org/advocacy/fight-censorship

Anonymous. (2013a). 1935 Revision to Paragraph 175 of the Penal Code. In A. G. Rabinbach & S. L. Gilman (Eds.), *The Third Reich sourcebook* (pp. 374-375). University of California Press.

Anonymous. (2013b). How Magnus Hirschfeld's Institute for Sexual Science Was Demolished and Destroyed (1933). In A. G. Rabinbach & S. L. Gilman (Eds.), *The Third Reich sourcebook* (pp. 367-369). University of California Press.

Associated Press. (2022). 'Don't Say Gay' bill becomes law in Florida, banning sexual orientation instruction from K-3. https://www.cbc.ca/news/world/florida-don-t-say-gay-bill-desantis-1.6400087

Berman, S., & Gross, T. (2017). Expand, humanize, simplify: An interview with Sandy Berman. *Cataloging & Classification Quarterly, 55*(6), 347-360. https://doi.org/10.1080/01639374.2017.1327468

Bloom, M. (2023, September 22). *Former Weld County librarian wins settlement after district fired her for promoting LGBTQ, anti-racism programs.* CPR News. https://www.cpr.org/2023/09/22/weld-county-fired-librarian-settlement-high-plains-library-district/

Bombaro, C. (2023). The future of libraries did not happen–But don't let history repeat itself. *The Reference Librarian*, 1-5. https://doi.org/10.1080/02763887.2023.2244934

BookLook. (2023). *Book Reports.* https://www.booklook.info/public-book-reports

Brownworth, V. A. (1994). Gagging ourselves. *Lambda Book Report, 4*(6), 11-12.

Cossman, B. (2013). Censor, resist, repeat: a history of censorship of gay and lesbian sexual representation in Canada. *Duke Journal of Gender Law & Policy,
21*(1), 45-66.

Friedman, J., & Johnson, N. F. (2022). *Banned in the USA: The growing
movement to censor books in schools.* https://pen.org/report/
banned-usa-growing-movement-to-censor-books-in-schools/

Goldbach, J. T., & Castro, C. A. (2016). Lesbian, gay, bisexual, and transgender
(LGBT) service members: Life after Don't Ask, Don't Tell. *Current Psychiatry
Reports, 18*(6), 1-7. https://doi.org/10.1007/s11920-016-0695-0

Grunzke, A. (2021, 2021/12/01). Graphic seduction: Anti-homosexual censorship of
comics in the postwar era. *The Journal of American Culture, 44*(4), 300-317.
https://doi.org/10.1111/jacc.13295

Harris, E. A., & Alter, A. (2022, December 12). A fast-growing network of conservative groups Is fueling a surge in book bans. *The New York Times.* https://
www.nytimes.com/2022/12/12/books/book-bans-libraries.html

Heger, H. (1980). *The men with the pink triangle.* Alyson Publications.

Heritage Foundation. (2023). Advisory Board. Retrieved September 8, 2023, from
https://www.project2025.org/about/advisory-board/

Human Dignity Trust. (2023). *Map of Countries that Criminalise LGBT People.*
Retrieved August 12, 2023, from https://www.humandignitytrust.org/
lgbt-the-law/map-of-criminalisation/

Hunter, A. (2023). *Civil liberties association calls Sask. government school naming and pronoun policy discriminatory.* CBC. https://www.cbc.ca/news/
canada/saskatchewan/education-naming-policy-1.6946657

Jaeger, P. T., Jennings-Roche, A., Taylor, N. G., Gorham, U., Hodge, O. & Kettnich, K.
(2023.) The urge to censor: Raw power, social control, and the criminalization of librarianship. *The Political Librarian, 6*(1), 1-20. https://journals.
library.wustl.edu/pollib/article/id/8711/

Kelleher, P. (2022, December 10). *Here's all the places where it's illegal to be LGBTQ+ – and yes, it's all colonialism's fault.*
PinkNews. https://www.thepinknews.com/2022/12/10/
countries-lgbtq-illegal-criminalisation-britain-colonialism/

Kienlen, A. (2023, October 9). *Saline County library director fired.* KARK. https://
www.kark.com/news/local-news/saline-county-library-director-fired/

Legum, J. (2023, November 6). *Moms for Liberty members call the cops on
Florida librarians.* Popular Information. https://popular.info/p/
moms-for-liberty-members-call-the

Lemkin Institute for Genocide Prevention. (2022). *Statement on the genocidal
nature of the gender critical movement's ideology and practice.* https://
www.lemkininstitute.com/statements-new-page/statement-on-the-geno-
cidal-nature-of-the-gender-critical-movement%E2%80%99s-ideolo-
gy-and-practice

Lewis, A. M. (Ed.) (2008). *Questioning library neutrality: Essays from Progressive Librarian*. Library Juice Press.

Manitoba Library Association. (2023). *Letter of concern to the Canadian Anti-Hate Network following calls for censorship across a number of Manitoba public and school libraries in the past several months*. https://mla.mb.ca/wp-content/uploads/2023/09/Letter-of-concern-to-info@anti-hate.ca_.pdf

Marhoefer, L. (2015). *Sex and the Weimar Republic: German homosexual emancipation and the rise of the Nazis*. University of Toronto Press.

Mennel, B. (2012). *Queer cinema: Schoolgirls, vampires, and gay cowboys*. Wallflower Press.

Monea, A. (2022). *The digital closet: How the internet became straight*. The MIT Press. https://doi.org/10.7551/mitpress/12551.001.0001

Natanson, H. (2023, May 23). Objection to sexual, LGBTQ content propels spike in book challenges. *The Washington Post*. https://www.washingtonpost.com/education/2023/05/23/lgbtq-book-ban-challengers/

Plant, R. (1986). *The pink triangle: The Nazi war against homosexuals*. Henry Holt.

Popowich, S. (2019). *Confronting the democratic discourse of librarianship: A Marxist approach*. Library Juice Press.

Popowich, S. (2021). Canadian librarianship and the politics of recognition. *Partnership, 16*(1), 1-23. https://doi.org/10.21083/partnership.v16i1.6126

Project 2025. (2023). *Mandate for Leadership: The Conservative Promise*. https://static.project2025.org/2025_MandateForLeadership_FULL.pdf

RatedBooks. (2023). *Rated books*. https://www.ratedbooks.org/

Rodriguez, J. A. (2023). LGBTQ incorporated: YouTube and the management of diversity. *Journal of Homosexuality, 70*(9), 1807-1828. https://doi.org/10.1080/00918369.2022.2042664

Smith, T. (2023, August 11). *The plot thickens: The battle over books comes at a cost*. NPR. https://www.npr.org/2023/08/11/1192034923/the-plot-thickens-the-battle-over-books-comes-at-a-cost

Sterbenz, C. (2023, September 1). How we fight back: Library workers and advocates are turning to new policies, lawsuits, and legislation to stem the tide of book bans. *American Libraries*. https://americanlibrariesmagazine.org/2023/09/01/how-we-fight-back/

Trans Legislation Tracker. (2023). *2023 anti-trans bills tracker*. Retrieved September 7 from https://translegislation.com/

The Biopolitics of Moral Panic and Canadian Libraries

Donna Langille

Introduction

In recent years, Canadian libraries and the people who work for them have suffered an increase in violence for offering programs that support the 2SLGBTQIA+[1] community (Montpetit, 2022). Conservative and religious groups are targeting libraries under the guise of protecting vulnerable children from those they perceive as "deviants," and are accusing libraries of "grooming" young children (Doctorow, 2022). This has been evidenced by public protests of Drag Storytime events such as the ones in 2022 and 2023 in Kelowna, British Columbia at the Okanagan Regional Library discussed later in this chapter and the attempted banning of 2SLGBTQIA+ books within Canada such as Maia Kobabe's *Gender Queer: A Memoir*.

Public libraries in Canada are responsible for providing free access to information and resources to their communities, as well as inclusive spaces. This chapter understands that some of these libraries in Canada have become targets of what can be understood as moral panic, a concept framed by theories of Michel Foucault related to biopower and disciplinary power. While scholars such as Gayle Rubin and Janice M. Irvine have written about moral panic and sexuality, there is an evident gap in the scholarship regarding the connection between moral panic, biopolitics, and disciplinary power.

---

1 Two Spirit, Lesbian, Gay, Bisexual, Trans, Queer (or Questioning), Intersex, Asexual. "The '+' is for all the new and growing ways we become aware of sexual orientations and gender diversity" (University of British Columbia Equity and Inclusion Office, n.d.).

The work of French philosopher Michel Foucault (1926-1984) focuses on the ways in which power relations are embedded in social practices and institutions. Disciplinary power, as conceptualized by Foucault, refers to the strategies used to regulate and control individuals into conforming to societal norms. Norms are shared expectations and rules that guide and regulate the behavior of individuals within a particular society and include both gender and sexual norms. Biopower is concerned with the control and regulation of populations. One example of a technique of biopower is the policies that regulate biological aspects of life such as reproductive rights and family structures.

Libraries are affected and shaped by the political landscape. Chris Bourg writes "libraries also contribute to certain kinds of inequalities because of the way in which we exercise influence over the diversity (or lack thereof) of information we make available to our communities and the methods by which we provide access to that information" (Bourg, 2015, para. 11). In this way, libraries potentially disrupt disciplinary power—or the methods enacted by the State with which individuals are encouraged to conform to societal norms—by providing free and accessible services, including access to information about gender and sexuality. Emily Drabinski, a self-identified Marxist lesbian and President of the American Library Association (ALA), alludes to the non-disciplinary nature of libraries in a recent interview[2] with WNYC Studios, a public radio station in New York City. In this interview, she claimed that libraries are "non-coercive learning spaces... [the library] isn't something that the state needs to be involved in" (2022).

Through a critical and close reading of how conservative and religious groups are weaponizing moral panics to threaten Canadian libraries and stop Drag Storytime events and 2SLGBTQIA+ collections, I argue that the moral panic about libraries "grooming young children" is a technique of disciplinary power that operates to reinforce sexual norms such as heteronormativity and the gender binary. Libraries become targets of moral panic because they are spaces where people can potentially resist those norms, and learn and think about gender and sexuality outside of state mandates.

---

2   https://www.wnycstudios.org/podcasts/otm/segments/libraries-under-attack-on-the-media

Foucault and Biopower

In *The History of Sexuality* (1976), Foucault defines biopower as "a power to foster life or disallow it to the point of death" (p. 138). In other words, biopower is the power that States exercise over populations through the management, regulation, and surveillance of the population. Biopower includes but is distinguished from what Foucault calls the "anatamo-politics of the human body," which describes the techniques used to establish and conform individuals to societal norms, including, but not limited, to sexual norms such as the gender binary (Foucault, 2012, p. 139). These concepts are helpful for thinking about the power dynamics embedded within society.

Norms, which are produced and reinforced through institutional apparatuses like medicine, law, and schools, act to divide the population into groups based on what is normal or not normal so that these groups can be more efficiently optimized and regulated by the State. Writing about trans politics in 2015, and in conversation with Foucault, Dean Spade defines disciplinary power as "how racism, transphobia, sexism, ableism, and homophobia operate through norms that produce ideas about types of people and proper ways to be" (p. 52). These systems enforce the marginalization and oppression of groups of people based on normative standards.

Foucault argues that sex is not just about feelings—it is a tool that societies use to control and organize people. It is not just about individuals; it is a way to shape and manage entire populations by setting norms and organizing people into different groups based on those norms. In regard to sexuality, medical experts have historically played a significant role in labeling certain types of sexual behavior as either normal or abnormal. This has influenced the way people think about sexual characteristics and what is considered typical or not. The pathology of sex is also closely tied to and informed by racist, colonial, and patriarchal ideologies which reinforces Spade's argument that racism, transphobia, sexism, ableism, and homophobia operate together to produce norms. These systems of oppression cannot necessarily be analyzed in isolation (Bauer, 2009; Chauncey, 1993; Gibson, 2022; Somerville, 2000). In many Western and Eurocentric contexts, sexual norms reinforce the concept of cisheteronormativity, the assumption that everyone should identify with the gender assigned to them at birth and that we should be attracted to the opposite gender. According to Foucault's theories of biopower, behaviors that challenge norms, such as identifying as 2SLGBQIA+, are perceived to be a threat to the overall well-being of the population, and therefore are labeled as deviant and dangerous through policies and laws.

Moral Panic

Moral panics arise when "a condition, episode, person or group of persons emerges to become defined as a threat to societal values and interests" (Cohen, 1972, p. 1). Moral panics make people feel scared about something they see as a threat to how society is supposed to be (Rubin, 2006; Cohen, 1972; Irvine, 2008). I argue that moral panics produce disciplinary power by reinforcing discourses that define what bodies are normal/abnormal, safe/dangerous, natural/unnatural, etc. The intended outcome of moral panics is to expand State power and increase technologies of regulation such as security, policing, surveillance, and censorship that target marginalized and vulnerable bodies and populations (Irvine, 2008, p. 2). Janice M. Irvine (2008) writes, "moral panics legitimize enhanced state power through fostering the illusion of a singular public mobilized in support of traditional values" (p. 3).

There are many examples of moral panics that were fueled by the media throughout the 20th century. These examples include the AIDS epidemic, the War on Drugs, and Satanic panic in the 1980s, as well as critical race theory in schools today. A commonality among many of these examples is that these incidents revolve around conservative and religious groups perceiving that these events are a danger to children. Gayle Rubin, writing about sexual panics in 1984, argued that "the current wave of erotic terror has reached deepest into those areas bordered in some way, if only symbolically, by the sexuality of the young" (p. 153). The rhetoric of "protecting children," which is so often the catalyst for moral panics, resonates with the arguments that Foucault makes in *The History of Sexuality* about the biopolitical State's preoccupation with safeguarding society and ensuring the vitality of the species.

The preoccupation with children's well-being is a red herring, a rhetorical device that is perpetuated through the moral panic discourse. Conservative and religious groups often use the well-being of children to elicit a heightened emotional response and mobilize the wider community to take action. This can lead to more restrictive policies or regulations such as book banning, cancellation of events, and sometimes violence. Most importantly, this red herring distracts from the underlying threat, and main argument, that libraries are spaces where people can potentially resist disciplinary power and access information about gender and sexuality outside of state mandates.

Disciplinary power is often enforced through State institutions such as government, schools, and prisons. For example, schools often establish expectations for behavior, dress codes, and academic performance. When students violate these rules, disciplinary actions such as detention, suspension, or other consequences may be imposed. Libraries, however, are unique institutions because in multiple ways they both perpetuate and disrupt disciplinary power. First, I will draw on the literature in library and information studies to discuss the ways that libraries perpetuate disciplinary power, then I will offer suggestions for how libraries are resisting or challenging State-mandated strategies of disciplinary power.

nina de jesus (2014) discusses how libraries are colonial institutions that were "created to make citizens better" and therefore are complicit in "perpetuating settler states." Settler states are countries that have obtained their territorial presence through colonization or violent occupation. Libraries classify and categorize information using systems that are rooted in colonial and racist ideologies. The Library of Congress, a classification system that is used by academic libraries across North America, still uses the subject heading "Indians of North America," although a project plan is underway to change this (Library of Congress, 2022, p. 67; Frank, 2022, p. 1). Until very recently the Library of Congress Subject Headings also included the subject heading "illegal aliens." They only changed the new headings to "noncitizens" and "illegal immigration" in November 2021 (ALA News).

Emily Drabinski (2013) argues that the disciplinary classification and organization of information on sexuality is rooted in hegemonic ideologies. Hegemonic ideologies are the belief systems, values, or cultural norms that are widely accepted and internalized within a society. Heteronormativity is an example of a hegemonic ideology. Melissa Adler (2017) extends this argument by providing a detailed historical analysis of the ways that the pathology of sex is mirrored by classification and cataloging practices by the Library of Congress. Despite the evidence that libraries are political institutions, libraries continue to be mythologized as neutral spaces or spaces that offer support and services without promoting any political stance. Many have argued that library neutrality only serves the colonial state and further oppresses marginalized and vulnerable groups such as Indigenous, Black, People of Colour, and 2SLGBTQIA+ (Ferretti, 2019; Cooke et al, 2022). For example, treating homophobic and transphobic views as valid can reinforce existing power structures and dominant ideologies such as heteronormativity and the gender binary.

Libraries

Libraries are political spaces, but they also serve to potentially disrupt disciplinary power by claiming to value equitable access to information and providing free and accessible services to everyone in the community. Libraries are voluntary spaces, which means that most people can access them without any need to show identification. The ability to do so is particularly helpful for those who live on the margins, including people experiencing homelessness. Libraries also offer free access to washrooms, free access to the Internet, and in some cases access to social workers and even COVID vaccines. Libraries offer places for children to do their homework or access free literacy programs. They can offer warming or cooling centers in harsh climates. Most importantly, people can enter a library without the expectation that they need to spend money. Cory Doctorow writes "libraries are the last place in America where you are valued for your personhood, rather than the contents of your wallet. At the library, you are a patron, not a customer" (2022). Through their commitment to information accessibility and intellectual exploration, libraries inherently undermine disciplinary power and promote a more inclusive and informed society. Libraries can empower individuals to seek information beyond what is readily available through institutions, such as schools, that may seek to limit access to certain information.

Libraries also provide access to inclusive programs and collections that represent and include 2SLGBTQIA+ perspectives which may otherwise be marginalized in mainstream discourse such as popular television shows, books, and news stories. In the contemporary moment, the two most obvious examples of this representation within libraries are Drag Storytime and books that challenge normativity, such as 2SLGBTQIA+ books, but also books on critical race theory. These examples are the primary targets of a larger Canadian moral panic, spread by conservative and religious groups, that libraries—and library workers—are "grooming" children (Dreher, 2022).

The language of "grooming" is meant to evoke the presence of sexual abuse and "conjure public disgust" (Irvine, 2008, p. 10). This rhetorical strategy is a political tactic that produces disciplinary power over queer and trans bodies by suggesting that people who identify in these ways are dangerous to children and may cause them harm. "Grooming" also wrongly suggests that children who are exposed to this threat may become 2SLGBTQIA+ themselves. The two examples that I draw upon to illustrate this moral panic are the Drag Storytime events that took place at the downtown Kelowna branch of the Okanagan Regional Library from 2019 to 2023 in Kelowna, British Columbia, and the latest increase in 2SLGBTQIA+ book challenges in libraries across Canada. These examples illustrate a current moral panic that libraries are harming young children by exposing young children to "inappropriate" sexual content and "dangerous" 2SLGTBQIA+ individuals.

Drag Storytime

The downtown Kelowna branch of the Okanagan Regional Library (ORL) hosted its first Drag Queen Storytime (later referred to as Drag Storytime) on Saturday, September 14, 2019 (MacNaull, 2019; Moore, 2019). Drag Storytimes in libraries are inclusive and educational programs where drag performers, often in colorful and gender-bending costumes, read books to children and families in a fun and engaging way. These events aim to promote literacy, diversity, and acceptance by providing children with an opportunity to explore themes of self-identity, gender expression, and the value of individuality through storytelling. Drag Storytimes do not include nudity, profanity, or public displays of sexual behavior.

Roger Chabot and Davin Helkenberg (2022) recently published a paper on the discourse surrounding Drag Storytime at the ORL. In their paper, they examine 406 publicly available letters written by community members expressing either their support or their opposition to the event. Their preliminary findings demonstrate that the basis of the arguments in opposition to Drag Storytime reflect a fear that these events pose a threat to children and an assumption that children are not capable or mature enough to handle content about sexuality and gender. Chabot and Helkenberg wrote that "challengers were most fearful about the program influencing the identity of their/ others' children or causing psychological harm." They feared it would "promote gender questioning" or "manipulate" them. One community member wrote, "this library program is part of that agenda, to hijack the identity of our children."

Secondly, many challengers wrote that the library should be "neutral." This viewpoint was supported by the ORL CEO Don Nettleton.[3] In a memo to the library board on September 9, 2019, he wrote that the Drag Storytime event "deviated from [the library's] main purpose of early literacy encouragement in a safe and neutral environment that everyone in the community will find acceptable" (Nettleton, 2019, p. 33). He later added that the storytime event was not age-appropriate and that proceeding with the event will "reposition [the library] away from being an accepted, middle of the road, non-controversial neutral and safe environment for children's programming" (p. 33). The Drag Storytime event continued as planned and Don Nettleton was asked by the Okanagan Regional Library board of directors to attend diversity and inclusion training as well as issue an apology to the library staff for showing a lack of trust in their judgement (Moore, 2019).

In 2023, after pandemic restrictions had been lifted, the library introduced Drag Storytime back in its programming. This decision was met with both animosity and support from the Kelowna community, resulting in a large protest gathered outside the library on the day of the event. The ratio of supporters to protesters was staggeringly overwhelming, but the narrative that the library is somehow endangering children persists (King & Femia, 2023). This pattern echoes across the country with similar protests appearing in cities such as Winnipeg (Shebahkeget, 2023), Woodstock (Bhargava, 2023), Taber (Bay, 2023), Calgary (McGinn, 2023), etc. These events and subsequent protests all share the same characteristics of moral panic operating as biopolitical interventions in libraries. Each cited news article presents the same argument from protesters that Drag Storytimes are endangering children. This discourse perpetuates cisheteronormativity and furthers the ideology that nonnormative expressions of gender and sexuality are deviant and therefore not only inappropriate for children but outright dangerous.

Drag Storytimes support 2SLGBTQIA+ spectrum children by offering representations of diversity and inclusion "and supports healthy child development" (Barriage et al., 2021). Drag Storytime should be seen as a positive and enriching experience for children, helping them to develop values such as empathy and acceptance, while also empowering them to embrace their own identities and those of others. It is exactly this reason—the acceptance and understanding of non-normative

---

3   Don Nettleton has since retired from the Okanagan Regional Library.

identities—that underlines the fear produced by this moral panic. The library becomes a target because people within the community believe that the library is supposed to be a neutral space free from controversial activities. These fears about Drag Storytime suggest a deeper concern about the library as space and what libraries represent within a biopolitical state.

Book Challenges

The increase in challenges to books held in public libraries reveals anxieties toward children being given the opportunity to learn, read, and access information about non-normative sexualities and gender expressions outside of State mandates. In 2022, the American Library Association (ALA) published a report called *The State of Libraries*.[4] In this report, the ALA addresses the rise of book bans across North America challenging books and materials that "address racism, gender, politics, and sexual identity" (Hlywak). The ALA's Office for Intellectual Freedom reported that the number of book challenges has doubled since 2020 (729 challenges to 1597 books). The most banned book of 2021 was *Gender Queer*, a graphic novel memoir by Maia Kobabe. The graphic novel is a coming-of-age story about a person figuring out their gender identity. The book has been described in the media by conservative and religious politicians and groups as "pornographic" because of its depictions of non-normative gender identities (Alter, 2022). The discursive strategy to label 2SLGBTQIA+ books as pornographic, like the way libraries are described as "grooming" young children, acts as a tool of moral panic to cultivate fear and anger.

Also, like the moral panic discourse around drag storytime, the moral panic discourse around this book (and all queer books in libraries and schools) suggests that gender identities that do not adhere to the binary of male/female are abnormal, wrong, and dangerous for children. In Canada, one example of this occurred in 2023 when *Global News* reported that the Royal Canadian Mounted Police (RCMP) received complaints from a member of Action4Canada about an elementary school in Chilliwack containing materials with pornographic content (Little, 2023). Action4Canada is an anti-2SLGBTQIA+ and anti-Sexual

---

4   https://www.ala.org/news/state-americas-libraries-report-2022

Orientation and Gender Identity (SOGI)[5] Inclusive Education organiza-tion that advocates against the education of non-normative genders and sexualities in schools. The RCMP found that the books in question did not fall under this definition. As highlighted by this example, mor-al panics are not based on a real threat of causing significant harm to children and they often misinterpret or misrepresent the content.

Book bans are also rarely successful and sometimes even counter-productive to their initial cause. For example, book bans can produce more discourse about a book through media representation (as is the case with *Gender Queer*) and inadvertently increase interest in and curiosity about the material leading to more young readers seeking out the book. Secondly, book bans often fail to achieve their intended goals, as determined readers can still access banned books through alternative means, such as other libraries, bookstores, or the Internet. Despite their lack of success, book bans continue to increase in Canada which suggests that the books are not solely the problem. 2SLGBTQIA+ books in libraries are important because they can offer support, guid-ance, and representation for young 2SLGTBQIA+ people. Seeing one-self reflected in stories can help validate our identities and experienc-es. On a societal scale, 2SLGBTQIA+ books can reduce misinformation and misconceptions and lead to wider acceptance and understanding of non-normative sexualities and genders. For these reasons, I argue that moral panic toward 2SLGBTQIA+ books in libraries indicates a fear of libraries as spaces that potentially disrupt disciplinary power by providing access to information about gender and sexuality to society.

Conclusion

Biopolitical states, like Canada, exercise governance and control pow-er over the population through biological aspects of life such as our health and our bodies. Moral panics about libraries operate as bio-political interventions because they arise when there is a perceived threat to societal norms and a disruption to disciplinary power. The moral panic aims to "correct" this threat through increased regulation, surveillance, security, and censorship. My first case study of Drag Sto-rytime in Canadian libraries demonstrates that the moral panic that

---

5   Sexual Orientation and Gender Identity (SOGI) (https://www2.gov.bc.ca/gov/content/erase/sogi) is an inclusive education program in British Columbia, Canada designed to support 2SL-GTBQIA+ youth.

libraries are "grooming" young children is a technique of disciplinary power that operates to reinforce sexual norms and perpetuate the myth that libraries are neutral spaces. Book bans in Canada also underline how moral panics target libraries because they are spaces that offer access to information about non-normative sexualities and genders thereby circumventing State control. The two case studies highlighted in this chapter, Drag Storytime and the increase in 2SLGBTQIA+ book challenges, indicate that libraries are targets of moral panic because they are spaces where people can potentially resist disciplinary power within a biopolitical State.

References

Adler, M. (2017). *Cruising the Library: Perversities in the Organization of Knowledge.* Fordham University Press.

Alter, A. (2022, May 1). *How a debut graphic memoir became the most banned book in the country.* The New York Times. https://www.nytimes.com/2022/05/01/books/maia-kobabe-gender-queer-book-ban.html

American Library Association. (2022, April 1). *State of America's Libraries Report 2022.* https://www.ala.org/news/state-americas-libraries-report-2022

ALA News. (2021, November 12). *ALA welcomes removal of offensive 'Illegal aliens' subject headings.* https://www.ala.org/news/member-news/2021/11/ala-welcomes-removal-offensive-illegal-aliens-subject-headings

Bhargava, I. (2023, March 16). *Supporters outnumber protesters at drag queen storytime in Woodstock, Ont.* CBC. https://www.cbc.ca/news/canada/london/supporters-outnumber-protesters-at-drag-queen-storytime-in-woodstock-ont-1.6781291

Bauer, H. (2009). Theorizing female inversion: Sexology, discipline, and gender at the Fin de Siècle. *Journal of the History of Sexuality, 18*(1), 84–102. https://doi.org/10.1353/sex.0.0040

Barriage, S., Kitzie, V., Floegel, D., & Oltmann, S. M. (2021). Drag queen storytimes: Public library staff perceptions and experiences. *Children and Libraries, 19*(2), 14-22.

Bay, T. (2023, June 2). *Protest expected at Taber drag story time event.* Global News. https://globalnews.ca/news/9742722/protest-taber-drag-queen-story/

Bourg, C. (2015, January 28). Never neutral: Libraries, technology, and inclusion. Feral Librarian (blog). https://chrisbourg.wordpress.com/2015/01/28/never-neutral-libraries-technology-and-inclusion/

Chabot, R., & Helkenberg, D. (2022, August 6). The discourse of drag queen story time challengers and supporters: A case study from the Okanagan Regional Library. *Proceedings of the Annual Conference of CAIS / Actes Du Congrès Annuel de l'ACSI.* https://doi.org/10.29173/cais1253

Chauncey, G. (1993). From sexual inversion to homosexuality: Medicine and the changing conceptualization of female deviance. In N.F. Cott & K.G. Saur (Eds.), *Sexuality and Sexual Behavior* (pp. 324–56). De Gruyter. https://doi.org/10.1515/9783110976342.324

Cohen, S. (1972). *Folk Devils and Moral Panics.* Routledge.

Cooke, N. A., Chancellor, R., Shorish, Y., Dahlen, S. P., & Gibson, A. (2022, June 10). Once more for those in the back: Libraries are not neutral. *Publishers Weekly.* https://www.publishersweekly.com/pw/by-topic/industry-news/libraries/article/89576-once-more-for-those-in-the-back-libraries-are-not-neutral.html

de jesus, n. (2014). *Locating the library in institutional oppression.* In the Library with the Lead Pipe. https://www.inthelibrarywiththeleadpipe.org/2014/locating-the-library-in-institutional-oppression/

Doctorow, C. (2022, November 13). *They want to kill libraries.* Medium. https://doctorow.medium.com/they-want-to-kill-libraries-ec045c06097e

Dreher, R. (2022, August 1). *ALA guide to grooming young readers.* The American Conservative. https://www.theamericanconservative.com/ala-guide-to-grooming-young-readers/

Ferretti, J. A. (2019, August 20). *Neutrality is hostility: The impact of (false) neutrality in academic librarianship.* Medium. https://citythatreads.medium.com/neutrality-is-hostility-the-impact-of-false-neutrality-in-academic-librarianship-c0755879fb09

Foucault, M. (2012). *The history of sexuality: An introduction* (Robert Hurley, Trans.). Vintage Books. (Original work published 1976)

Frank, P. (2022, June 3). *CaMMS Subject Analysis Committee Report from the Library of Congress Liaison.* https://connect.ala.org/core/discussion/sac-2022-annual-meeting-lc-ptcp-report

Gibson, M. (1996). Clitoral corruption: Body metaphors and American doctors' constructions of female homosexuality, 1870-1900. In V.A. Rosario (Ed.), *Science and Homosexualities*, (pp. 108-131). Routledge.

Hlywak, S. (2022, April). Editor's note. *State of America's Libraries 2022.* American Library Association.

Irvine, J. M. (2008). Transient feelings: Sex panics and the politics of emotions. *GLQ: A Journal of Lesbian and Gay Studies, 14*(1), 1–40.

Italie, H. (2022, September 16). *Book ban efforts surging in 2022, library association says.* AP News. https://apnews.com/article/libraries-american-library-association-book-banning-af7c9f312266b572c3dc189b1d109de4

King, J., & Femia, V. (2023, January 28). *Drag Queen Story Time sparks protest outside Kelowna, B.C. library.* Global News. https://globalnews.ca/news/9444184/drag-queen-story-time-protest-kelowna-library/

Library of Congress. (2022, June 10). *LCSH I*. https://www.loc.gov/aba/publica-
tions/FreeLCSH/I.pdf

Little, S. (2023, February 23). *No, books in Chilliwack school libraries aren't
child pornography, RCMP says*. Global News. https://globalnews.ca/
news/9505240/chilliwack-school-books-not-child-pornography/

MacNaull, S. (2019, December 23). *Year in review: Drag queen story time a story in
itself this year*. Daily Courier. https://www.kelownadailycourier.ca/life/ar-
ticle_1fb99c14-260f-11ea-865a-177b55f95111.html

McGinn, D. (2023, March 11). *Anti-gay activists target children's libraries and
drag queen story hours*. The Globe and Mail. https://www.theglobeand-
mail.com/canada/article-anti-gay-activists-target-childrens-librar-
ies-and-drag-queen-story/

Montpetit, J. (2022, June 27). *Libraries in Canada hit by wave of hate, threats, as
right-wing groups protest all-age drag events*. CBC. https://www.cbc.ca/
news/investigates/libraries-threats-all-age-drag-1.6501247

Moore, W. (2019, November 20). *Controversial drag queen storytime will remain at libraries*. Kelowna News.
https://www.castanet.net/news/Kelowna/270900/
Controversial-Drag-Queen-Storytime-will-remain-at-libraries

Nettleton, D. (2019, September 18). Children's programming policy discussion. Notice of Meeting. Okanagan Regional Library. https://www.orl.
bc.ca/docs/default-source/library_board/meeting_agendas/bod-ag-
d_18sep19.pdf

Rubin, G. (2006). Thinking sex: Notes for a radical theory of the politics of sexuality. In R. Parker & P. Aggleton (Eds.), *Culture, Society and Sexuality: A
Reader*. Routledge.

Shebahkeget, O. (2023, August 15). *Despite protest, drag queen storytime event a
source of pride, Headingley librarian says*. CBC. https://www.cbc.ca/news/
canada/manitoba/drag-queen-story-time-headingley-library-1.6936496

Somerville, Siobhan B. (2000). *Queering the color line: Race and the invention of
homosexuality in American culture*. Duke University Press. https://doi.
org/10.1215/9780822378761-002

Spade, D. (2015). *Normal life: Administrative violence, critical trans politics, and the limits of law*. Duke University Press. https://doi.
org/10.1215/9780822374794-004

University of British Columbia Equity and Inclusion Office. (n.d.). *Equity
and inclusion glossary of terms*. https://equity.ubc.ca/resources/
equity-inclusion-glossary-of-terms/

Building and Defending LGBTQ+ Collections

Jason D. Phillips and Jordan Ruud

A good library, whether public or academic, will develop its collections to speak to and for every segment of the community it serves. To this end, libraries should have a collection development policy that speaks to the needs of their communities, the formats they will and will not collect, collection priorities, and ways to handle challenges. Further, these should be "living documents" that are periodically updated to keep up with current or expected trends.

Some in our profession take it for granted that every library has a collection development policy, or that it's readily available, or that it has been updated within the last five years or so. This, unfortunately, is not always the case. For example, both the authors worked at an academic library whose collection development policy was a single typed page, drafted in the 1970s, that resided in a forgotten folder in the library director's file cabinet. It was only ever referenced in passing, no one actually knew or remembered what it said, and it was not publicly available or accessible. And when faced with an internal challenge, it was not available or useful in responding to the challenge, either in terms of creating a defense for the item challenged or a set of procedures to adjudicate the challenge. (For more about this situation, see the later chapter "Enemies Within the Gates: Contending with Internal Censorship Challenges.")

In the case of academic libraries, a collection development policy creates a plan for what subject areas you will collect in based on the research, curricular, and, yes, extracurricular needs of the community you serve. Some of our academic colleagues might quibble with the need for an academic library to develop a leisure reading collection, but that too has a purpose in feeding the minds and spirits of our patrons. And to this point, and especially for public libraries, a collection development policy is a promise and a commitment that the library's collection will have something for everyone, especially to previously neglected and underserved communities, like LGBTQ+ people and people of color. In many instances, the availability of LGBTQ+ materials may be the only positive representations to which a closeted child, teen, or adult may have access.

Speaking within the context of this text and the challenges we face, a collection development policy also serves another important purpose: a strong collection development policy can be one bulwark against challenges. And "strong" means multiple things in this situation:

- "Strong" means relevant to the needs of your community. Collection development is often a delicate push-pull between providing exactly the kinds of materials users have indicated they want to see, building out a collection that is full in the relevant areas and maybe only has the essentials in less relevant areas, and predicting trends in usage. No library can respond with absolute precision to the needs of every user, and this is why policy must be written in broad strokes to be flexible enough to address all these needs as well as the matter of intellectual freedom—it is also a compelling reason for your policy to be revisited every two to three years.

- "Strong" means both a document and a mindset that is flexible and proactively responsive to potential threats, and this is precisely where the matter of policy written to be responsive to the community comes into play. Does your policy, whether explicitly stated or not, keep the makeup of your library's community in mind, including and specifically the aforementioned historically underserved communities? If you're in an academic library, are you addressing the needs of the campus' disparate groups? If you're in a public library, are you taking account of all the populations you serve?

- A challenge procedure is crucial to truly strengthen your policy. Think carefully, in crafting your procedure, about the outcome of a challenge process. Do you want these decisions made by non-librarians in positions of authority over you, for example, a provost's office or city council? By an independent body tasked with reviewing materials? You may well have the ability to control the mechanisms through which your collection potentially faces censorship, steering the process for your own part rather than having decisions made for you.

Once equipped with a strong collection development policy, your library will be in a position to collect materials susceptible to challenges and be in a better place to defend your collections from potential challengers. One important source you might consider consulting is the *Intellectual Freedom Manual* from ALA's Office of Intellectual Freedom, which has guidance on how to respond to challenges to both collections and programs.

Historically, collection practices have not favored collecting books and other materials written by or for underserved communities. In recent years, more scholarship and discussion has been devoted to this oversight and ways to rectify this deficiency through retrospective collection development and updating collection development policies. If your collections are going in this direction at all, prepare yourself for challenges—because they are a very real possibility. In libraries we take it for granted that a diverse collection is a virtue and a professional obligation, that a collection should represent and reflect the community it serves, with something for everyone. Given the matters at hand presented in the chapters of this book, obviously not everyone agrees.

Retrospective collection development, or the purchase of essential books and other materials from years past, is an important activity when responding to historical collection practices that disadvantaged communities like the LGBTQ+ population. While we do not want to delve too deeply into the specifics of how to build a truly diverse/DEI-oriented collection, as that's beyond this chapter's scope, we will offer this suggestion: you might consider looking at various awards from the American Library Association, like the Stonewall Book Awards or Rainbow Book List, or to other organizations like the Lambda Literary Awards. You also have a good opportunity to undertake outreach to underserved communities to solicit titles they would like to see and request.

In addition to grounding the basis for your collection decisions in a strong collection development policy, consider explicitly what it means to represent the community in one's collection. As we'll discuss later, "community standards" can often serve as a catch-all for the notion that a library should not represent minority interests. But the community a library serves is the community in its entirety, and in all but the most extreme cases of demographic homogeneity, a library truly reflective of its community will wind up housing materials that touch directly on minority interests—including those of LGBTQ+ people.

Considering one's allies may be a logical step for cultivating buy-in for a policy. Take the time to educate your allies and supporters about what a collection development policy is, what it means for a library and its collection, and why it is important in the defense of censorship challenges. If you're in an academic setting, consider reaching out to your faculty senate for an endorsement of the policy. If you're in a public setting, ensure that your leadership and board are fully aware of your policy and that they stand by it.

In addition to addressing the parameters of a collection under development, a policy may also address the specifics of ordering materials and the way that materials wind up hitting the shelf. An example from our own experience might speak effectively to the necessity of this. We attempted to support a diverse collection that would serve our diverse community. Jason started this project shortly after his arrival in 2013. The library director had conveyed to Jason (and Jordan) his dissatisfaction with the state of the library collection, namely, that it reflected a community college's needs and not the needs of a four-year university. Many of the titles in the collection were older, in poor shape, acquired through local donations, or more appropriate for a public library. Inspired by these discussions, Jason suggested a retrospective collection development project. Each year, he would focus on one underrepresented community and purchase approximately $2,000 of titles specific to this community. When the project was completed, he had managed to increase the allocation to $5,000 and had purchased titles for the Hispanic, African American, Asian American, Native American, and LGBTQ+ communities, which all reflected the demographics of the university's population. Or so he thought.

It was only later that Jason discovered many of the award-winning LGBTQ+ titles had not been ordered after all. At the time, the library primarily used Amazon to order books for the collection with the librarians submitting their book orders to one individual who coordinated the orders. We took it on faith that these titles were being ordered, but this created a situation where an individual, either on their own authority or at the behest of the library director, was able to exert their influence over the ordering process by not ordering requested titles, possibly due to their "controversial" nature. The library later moved to using GOBI by EBSCO as its book vendor, which allows librarians to track the status of their orders in a more transparent fashion than available under the previous arrangement. We highlight this situation as a potential pitfall and challenge you may face as you undertake collection development in areas some (wrongfully) consider to be "controversial."

It can be a great benefit for libraries to keep a careful ear out for developments in the communities they serve. This helps in guiding actions with regard to collections and programming. To give an example from one of the authors' locales, the recent legislative atmosphere in Arkansas has been one of intense pressure placed on libraries (public libraries in particular). There have been two examples in 2023 of library directors leaving their positions under controversial circumstances after challenges lodged against their libraries' materials, one in Crawford County and one in Salinas County.[1] Under statewide conditions like these—in addition to state legislation that has been widely discussed as placing librarians under the threat of jailing for providing materials "harmful to minors"—reluctance to put one's library or one's employment at risk would be absolutely understandable. We'll discuss these conditions of threats to librarians further in a later chapter, "At What Cost? The Personal Stakes of Intellectual Freedom." For the meantime, it suffices to say that in situations where one deems oneself personally at risk for controversial collecting/programming decisions, collection development policy can serve as one bulwark against controversy—but perhaps not always enough of one.

This said, with respect to having an informed sense of events and perspectives on the ground in one's library's vicinity, part of building a groundwork against challenges is keeping the public informed about what the library is doing and why. Libraries sometimes appear to find themselves in a defensive crouch against wild accusations of peddling filth to minors. Their relative lack of preparation in such situations is completely understandable—the accusation is not only outrageous on the face of things, but also unprecedented (consider some past censorship efforts, where materials *were* challenged as inappropriate, but the challenges didn't necessarily rise to the level of systematized personal attacks against library professionals. Yes, we're thinking here of Moms for Liberty).

---

1   In one of these cases, the director's resignation took place under a severance agreement. The other was an outright dismissal, and an Arkansas Times interview with the fired director is very much worth reading: https://arktimes.com/arkansas-blog/2023/11/02/she-regrets-nothing-a-qa-with-fired-saline-county-librarian-patty-hector

Outreach goes hand in hand with collection development: if you're collecting potentially controversial materials, you're doing this not for the pure sake of controversy—no one wants to invite that for its own sake—but, as with other collections, because you think they'll find an audience, because you believe they hold a place in your collection. The same goes for an event in the vein of a drag storytime: libraries aren't provocateurs doing this to spark outrage, but because there are concrete good reasons to do so.

By their nature, libraries as organizations tend to be optimistic and focused on progress. Strong policy, though, may require some clear-eyed perception that borders on pessimism. Libraries know themselves to be well-intentioned, focused on serving their communities in the best way possible. But casting the library's services and materials through a possible challenger's eyes can strengthen a preemptive response. Imagine the mechanisms through which an attack on your library might unfold—the people behind it, the authorities to whom they might appeal. Think about the likely trajectory of challenges, and plan policy and procedure accordingly.

References

Garnar, M. & Magi, T. (Eds.) (2021). *Intellectual freedom manual* (10th ed.). ALA Editions.

Part 2
Stories from the Front Lines

Many Fronts
Ketchikan Public Library and the Culture Wars

Patricia Tully

The Ketchikan Public Library has been in the thick of the culture wars since 2021. In that time the Library has received challenges to its displays, programs, funding, books, and policies. In this chapter I will briefly introduce our community and the library, describe recent challenges, and end by listing common elements of these challenges, the mistakes we made in addressing them, and the lessons we learned in the process.

Ketchikan, Alaska is a community of 13,700 residents on Revillagigedo Island in southern southeast Alaska. The island makes up the bulk of the Ketchikan Gateway Borough. Within the borough are the City of Ketchikan and the City of Saxman—both cities and the borough itself have their own governments.

Ketchikan's library was founded in 1901, and since 2013 it has been in a beautiful building on a hill above the city. The Ketchikan Public Library is a department of the City of Ketchikan, but it serves all residents of the island. Both the City of Ketchikan and the Ketchikan Gateway Borough contribute to its funding.

When the COVID-19 pandemic hit in early 2020, the library provided curbside service, take-home craft and tasting bags, and programming via Facebook, YouTube, and Ketchikan's local community radio station. Aside from a few objections to masking, most patrons were happy with the library and the books, programs, and other services we were able to provide. By the fall of 2021, the library was once again consistently open to the public and creating displays of important community events and milestones.

LGBTQIA+ Displays

One September 2021 display featured a new periodical called *Loud and Queer*, published by the Ketchikan Queer Collective, featuring essays, fiction, and artwork by LGBTQIA+ residents of southern Southeast Alaska. The library displayed it as a new local publication, on one of a number of display shelves along the main library aisle extending the length of the building. Around the same time, the Banned Book Week display in the children's library included the picture book, *Jacob's New Dress*, by Sarah and Ian Hoffman.

In early October 2021, several people posted vehement objections to the displays on a local private Facebook page. We learned about this from a library patron who sent screenshots of the posts to me as library director. After a few days, the posts were taken down. Library staff received many expressions of support from patrons, criticizing the posts and thanking them for the library's commitment to serving the entire community.

The next week a man came to visit me, representing a group that was upset about the displays. He sought a compromise—the library would retain books on gender roles and LGBTQIA+ issues in the collection, but not display them in the children's library. I explained that the library is obligated to treat all groups in the community equally, and we could not have different rules for one group because another group disapproved of them. The man regretted that we would not compromise on this matter and put on my desk the draft of a proposition to partially defund the library—specifically, to revoke the borough's nonareawide power to tax borough residents for library services. This power had been voted by borough residents outside the City of Ketchikan in 1985, as part of an agreement to extend full library privileges to all borough residents within and outside the city. (In Alaska, a nonareawide power is one that impacts residents who live in a borough but outside the city or cities within the borough. The proposition would be voted on by people living in the borough but outside the City of Ketchikan, since the nonareawide tax is levied on only these residents.) Borough funding accounts for about 40% of the library's budget, corresponding to the percentage of Ketchikan Gateway Borough residents who live outside the cities of Ketchikan and Saxman.

I responded that I would be happy to work with the group to develop services and programs they could support, and the man left saying that he would pass on my offer.

Drag Queen Storytime

In early 2022, Head of Children's Services Amie Toepfer and her staff planned a robust schedule of in-person summer programs. After two years of virtual programming, they were thrilled to be able to return to a more normal summer season.

At the suggestion of a parent, the library's June 2022 program schedule included a Drag Queen Storytime to celebrate Pride Month. A lifelong Ketchikan resident and respected high school teacher, who performs locally as the drag queen Luna, agreed to read to the children with Amie Toepfer.

Other Pride Month activities included a Rainbow Reading Challenge for all ages and a take-home Rainbow Family Maker Bag. These activities correspond to those the library regularly conducts to celebrate Indigenous Heritage Month, Filipino American History Month, African American History Month, Asian American and Pacific Islander Heritage Month, and Women's History Month. These Pride Month activities were separate from the library's many children's and teen Summer @ Your Library programs.

After releasing its June event calendar on May 26, the library received emails, letters, phone calls, and visits from people objecting to the Pride Month activities, and particularly to Drag Queen Storytime. Many of the objections were to the idea of legitimizing different forms of gender expression. The concern was that at best this would be confusing for small children, and at worst, it would sexualize children and groom them for sexual abuse.

People spoke at Ketchikan City Council and Borough Assembly meetings, beginning with the June 2 council meeting, speaking for or against the library's Pride Month activities. The Library Advisory Board held a public hearing on the matter on June 9. Public comment, pro and con, lasted an hour and a half, and in the end the board voted to recommend that the library's Pride Month events go forward. The Ketchikan City Council took up the matter at their June 16 meeting—the evening before the storytime was to take place. After much debate the council voted in favor of holding the Drag Queen Storytime.

Throughout all of this, Luna and Amie remained steadfast and determined to go forward with the storytime. As a staff, we prepared by reviewing our active shooter training and developing a plan to handle the expected overflow crowd. Each library staff person had an assigned task and location during the program, and substitute staff came in to help as well.

On the day of the Drag Queen Storytime, there were some protestors, but many more came to attend the program and show their support for Luna and the library. People with large umbrellas stood near the front entrance to shield attendees from protesters if necessary. Four police officers stood at the entrance as well. The local newspaper and community radio station were on hand to cover the event. A large number of families showed up to attend the storytime, and Amie and Luna ended up doing three back-to-back programs, to the delight of all those who attended.

Since then, people have requested a second Drag Queen Storytime. Others have said that after the 2022 controversy, the library would be ill advised—"stupid" was the word they used—to do another. In the spring of 2023, after much public comment, the city directed the library not to hold a second Drag Queen Storytime. This was disappointing, but a local resident and her daughter organized a Drag Queen Storytime with Luna at the local civic center, and it was very successful.

Bible Storytime Requests

In the late summer and fall of 2022 the library received several requests to sponsor a Bible storytime. The City Attorney advised the library not to sponsor a program with a particular religious point of view. However, the library could offer one of its meeting spaces for such a program, since these are available to all non-profit groups for public meetings. I passed this information along to those who requested the Bible storytime, with additional information about reserving a library meeting room. There was no response and no follow-up request to use a meeting room for this purpose.

Defunding Effort

In July 2022 the man who visited me months earlier about the banned book display asked the Ketchikan Gateway Borough Assembly to consider placing on the October 2022 municipal ballot a library defunding measure. The measure died for lack of a second. The man and a group of like-minded residents then went door-to-door with a petition and gathered enough signatures to place the measure on the borough ballot as Proposition 2. If the measure passed, it would revoke the borough's nonareawide power to tax borough residents for library services, limiting library services for borough residents who live outside the City of Ketchikan. The subsequent 40% reduction in the library's budget would have been devastating.

An independent group of library supporters, including the Friends of the Library, came together as Stand With Ketchikan Library, and raised almost $10,000 for the campaign to defeat Proposition 2. The group created and distributed signs and postcards, began a social media campaign, and organized two rallies north and south of the city. After some borough residents expressed concern about losing library privileges if the proposition passed, those in favor of Proposition 2 assured borough residents that regardless of the vote, the borough would find a way to provide their portion of library funding.

At the October 4, 2022 election, the voters defeated Proposition 2 by a narrow margin. Of the 38.5% of eligible borough residents who voted on the proposition, 818 or 43% voted for the proposition, and 1,066 or 57% voted against it. The library retained its full funding from the borough, and full services to all borough residents.

Proposed Change in Library Governance

In September 2022, a group floated a proposal to transfer governance of the library from the city to the borough. One reason for the proposal is that some in the borough feel they are taxed twice for the library—once through sales tax in city businesses, and again through the Borough Library Tax. Another reason for the proposal is that those who reside outside the city do not have a say in electing the body that ultimately governs the library—the Ketchikan City Council. The Library Advisory Board, established by city ordinance, does include a representative of the Borough Assembly and a resident of the borough outside the city, as well as several at-large members who can come from anywhere in the borough. However, there continues to be a feeling among some borough residents that their voices are not heard, and that if the library was a borough department, they would be.

If the library was transferred to the borough, it is not clear whether this would lead to changes in library policies or practices.

Book Challenges

In January 2023, for the first time in 14 years, the library received several formal requests to remove a book from the collection—or move it from the teen to the adult collection. The first book challenged was *Let's Talk About It* by Erika Moen and Matthew Nolan. The book is a teen's guide to sex and relationships in graphic novel form. There are illustrations depicting sex organs and sexual acts, as well as chapters on kinks, consent, respect for one's partner, and how to recognize when a relationship becomes abusive.

The library received ten initial challenges to the book. One person indicated that they had read it; the others had seen an online video that highlighted the most controversial pages.

The library followed its Request for Reconsideration policy in responding to these challenges. Head of Children's Services Amie Toepfer, who selected the book, responded to the initial challenges. Two of the ten complainants then appealed the decision to retain the book to me as library director—I responded with my decision to keep the book in the teen section. One of the two remaining complainants asked the Library Advisory Board to conduct a public hearing on the matter. The board did so and recommended that the library retain the book in the teen section. After subsequent complaints to the City Council, the council voted initially to retain the book in the teen section, then reversed itself at its next meeting, a last-minute amendment to the motion expressing the claim that the book is "pervasively vulgar" as a reason to move it to the adult section. The book is now in the adult section.

In September 2023, the library received another reconsideration request to move the book *Flamer*, by Mike Curato, from the teen to adult collection, claiming that the book encourages teens to consider suicide. This request is currently making its way through the reconsideration process.

Collection Development Policy Review

The library's collection development policy has been in place, with subsequent revisions, since 1984. At its July 2023 meeting, the Library Advisory Board began a review of the policy. One board member cited as a possible model recent proposed changes in the collection development policy of the Hamilton East Library in Noblesville, Indiana, which details the sexual content, profanity, and violence that their board considered inappropriate in children's and teen books. The Advisory Board's review and subsequent recommendations will in turn be reviewed by the Ketchikan City Council.

Common Accusations

The disparate challenges our library is facing have many elements in common. Here are a few of them:

Creating division

Accusation: The library and its staff have been accused of dividing the community by holding controversial programs and selecting books and other content on sensitive issues. As a community gathering space, they say, a public library should have nothing that makes anyone feel unwelcome. They believe that a public library should be a safe place, a haven—and that it is no longer safe.

Response: A public library is a safe place in that it is a place to explore new ideas, new discoveries, new points of view, and new modes of personal and artistic expression. It is a place to do these things even if they are controversial or unpopular—actually, especially if they are so. A public library is not, however, a place to be safe *from* new ideas and different perspectives. The library should not protect people from unwelcome opinions, modes of personal expression, or different points of view.

Being discriminatory

Accusation: The library has been accused of discriminating against those with a Christian point of view. By acquiring materials with alternative viewpoints on sex and gender roles and conducting programs that celebrate groups like the LGBTQIA+ community, the library demonstrates disrespect for Christian beliefs and values.

Response: A public library provides materials, programs, and services to meet the needs and interests of a diverse community. This includes fiction and nonfiction materials with a Christian point of view. Other points of view are represented in library collections and programming, and some find these viewpoints offensive. No one is compelled to read a book, view a DVD, or attend a program that they find objectionable. For the same reason, no one has the right to restrict the rights of others to choose the materials and programs that are best for themselves and their children.

Being unwilling to compromise

Accusation: The library has been accused of being unwilling to compromise on the display of LGBTQIA+ materials or the selection of teen and children's books on sexuality and other sensitive subjects. Why, they say, can't the library meet them halfway and not display or make accessible materials they find offensive?

Response   A public library's ability to compromise is limited to measures that will not infringe on the rights of others to find and check out materials that meet their needs and interests. Restricting or denying access to materials based on their content is prioritizing one set of values over others. The library cannot compromise other people's rights to free expression and unrestricted access to books for themselves and their minor children, even if another group believes these to be harmful.

Wasting the City Council's time

Accusation: Because the library does not compromise with individuals who complain about the viewpoints expressed in its programs and collections, they often take their concerns to city and borough governments. This is a waste of the Borough Assembly and City Council's time, when both bodies have much more pressing issues to deal with. If the library would compromise to begin with, it would not be necessary to bother the council or assembly with these matters.

Response   A public library is constrained by its mission from making compromises that restrict the rights of one group because of the beliefs of another. Any citizen has the right to appeal the decision of their public library to its governing body and receive a hearing by that body.

Common Difficulties in Responding to Challenges

Anonymous criticism

Although many people have voiced their concerns publicly, others have done so by sending anonymous notes or complaining to local officials on the condition that they remain anonymous. This makes it difficult to pinpoint and address rumors. For example, one official passed on a rumor that some children were brought to the Drag Queen Storytime without their parents' knowledge or consent. Without being able to contact the person making this claim, there is no way to determine whether this is true. In another instance, a staff member received an envelope at their home address, with no return address and no indication of who sent it, claiming that LGBTQIA+ groups are seeking to sexualize and groom children.

Unaccompanied children

Some people are afraid that unaccompanied children or adolescents will see displays of LGBTQIA+ materials, wander into a program, or check out a book that has content that will influence and damage them or of which their parents will disapprove. The library does not allow very young children into the building unaccompanied, but we do allow older children and teens to be in the library by themselves. We urge parents to accompany their children to the library if they have concerns about the children seeing certain content. Some feel that this would stigmatize their child and would instead like the library to make controversial material and programs less accessible.

Self-censorship

With all the unrest and upset over the past few years, we are having to guard against the tendency to self-censor, to decide not to acquire *that* book or conduct *that* program for fear that we will cause further upset in the community. We need to remind ourselves that our mission is to serve the entire community by providing a wide range of perspectives and points of view, particularly on controversial topics.

Social media

Our library has a very active social media presence. During the 2022 Drag Queen Storytime controversy, much of the debate took place on Facebook. Library staff initially began reacting with a "thumbs up" to comments defending the library's action—not as themselves on their personal Facebook accounts, but as the library. One critic of the library's programs was upset that the library was approving comments that they felt were critical of them and threatened legal action. We quickly undid the reactions, but the damage was done. In response, we discontinued a generic Facebook account for library staff, reviewed, as a staff, the city's Social Media Policy, and required that staff only post to the library's Facebook page at work. During a similar Facebook debate over the library's 2023 Banned Book Week posts, we largely ignored the flurry of comments, and eventually the furor died down.

Staff differences

When these challenges began, all of us as a staff were dismayed at hearing so much criticism and tended to vent amongst ourselves when in the workroom. What we did not initially realize was that not everyone on our staff was in favor of Drag Queen Storytime or other library activities that resulted in challenges, and the venting made some staff members feel unable to voice their concerns.

I had always considered myself a collaborative leader who respected and valued all library staff equally, but I had not considered that the staff might have greatly differing points of view on these issues. When I realized this, we talked as a staff about airing and respecting our internal differences about these issues.

Inadequate policies and practices

Some of our policies and practices are not as complete as they should be. For example, our Request for Reconsideration policy is many years old and did not explicitly include a mechanism for complainants who were unsatisfied with the Advisory Board's public hearing and recommendation. Since we had not had a challenge since 2009, we did not realize the inadequacy of the policy until we needed to use it. Similarly, the Library Advisory Board's meeting practices had been informal before the challenges began in 2022. The library and Library Advisory

Board will be working on amending policies and practices once the controversies have died down.

Communicating our mission

Our library is far better at advertising *what* we do—the programs, services, and collections we provide—than we are at expressing *why* we do it. We have the library's mission on our website, but we rarely talk about it. As a result, people in the community have disparate ideas about what a library is and should be.

We need to communicate better the mission and role of the public library in the community, consistently and often. Our mission is to respect, value, and serve the community—all of the community, and every group in it.

We are fortunate in having energetic, articulate, and dedicated local advocates, particularly our Friends of the Ketchikan Public Library. They have been indefatigable in their defense of the library and its mission. It is very important to have advocates throughout the community who understand and value the library.

Conclusion

In the introduction to the Ketchikan Public Library's collection development policy, there is the statement, "The Ketchikan Public Library subscribes to and supports the American Library Association's Library Bill of Rights and the American Library Association Freedom to Read statement." Recent challenges have included questions about our adherence to these statements, asserting that they advocate a set of values that are not universally held by our community. In developing a response to these questions, I found an interesting letter written by President Dwight D. Eisenhower in response to the original Freedom to Read Statement issued by ALA in 1953.

President Eisenhower wrote to the President of the American Library Association in a letter dated June 24, 1953, at the height of McCarthyism and the hearings of the House Un-American Activities Committee. Here are the last two paragraphs of President Eisenhower's letter:

> "But we know that freedom cannot be served by the devices of the tyrant. As it is an ancient truth that freedom cannot be legislated into existence, so it is no less obvious that freedom cannot be

censored into existence. And any who act as if freedom's defenses are to be found in suppression and suspicion and fear confess a doctrine that is alien to America.

The libraries of America are and must ever remain the homes of free, inquiring minds. To them, our citizens—of all ages and races, of all creeds and political persuasions—must ever be able to turn with clear confidence that there they can freely seek the whole truth, unwarped by fashion and uncompromised by expediency. For in such whole and healthy knowledge alone are to be found and understood those majestic truths of man's nature and destiny that prove, to each succeeding generation, the validity of freedom. Sincerely, DWIGHT D. EISENHOWER"[1]

The Ketchikan Public Library and libraries around the country will continue to face challenges in the foreseeable future. We will respond to them respectfully but with determination, defending the rights of everyone in our communities to freely access the books and other materials they want and need, and to celebrate their authentic selves. The more libraries communicate, with our communities and with each other, to explain this mission and role, the better position we will be in to continue to serve our communities for many years to come.

---

1   "Letter on Intellectual Freedom to the President of the American Library Association," Dwight D. Eisenhower to Dr. R. B. Downs, June 24, 1953. https://www.presidency.ucsb.edu/documents/letter-intellectual-freedom-the-president-the-american-library-association

Pride and Prejudice and Sunshine
Drag Story Events in a Floridian Academic Library

Maria Atilano

Introduction

The University of North Florida (UNF) is located in Jacksonville, Florida, and had an estimated FTE of 17,000 students as of Fall 2022. UNF's Thomas G. Carpenter Library is one of the busiest buildings on campus, with approximately 16,000 entries per week in 2018/2019 and 18,000 entries per week in 2022/23. The Carpenter Library hosts a variety of informational and fun events throughout the academic year, some of them in conjunction with other campus departments and organizations. Our outreach librarians and staff have worked diligently over the years to create a welcoming, personable environment that students look forward to visiting. We often encourage the UNF community to refer to their library as "Tommy G's" and to participate in our events not as students or staff, but as friends.

In partnership with UNF's LGBT Resource Center, and under the guidance of the official Drag Story Hour organization, the Carpenter Library hosted two successful drag story events in June and October 2019. This chapter will detail the many steps and precautions that we took to research, propose, plan, and promote these two events, as well as suggestions for other academic libraries that may wish to follow in our footsteps.

History

The Carpenter Library hosted and participated in more than 140 outreach events and tours during the 2017/2018 academic year, many of which were geared towards students. Examples of these initiatives included orientation tours and resource tables, an annual Halloween event, Blind Date with a Book, and numerous stress-relieving finals week activities. At the time, our outreach team included a librarian dedicated to student outreach, another dedicated to faculty outreach, support staff for all of outreach, and an administrative staff member who worked specifically with outreach to community members. Many of the student-focused events were in collaboration with other campus departments, organizations, and clubs, including Campus Life and Admissions.

In October 2018, the UNF LGBT Resource Center (LGBTRC) posted a Facebook post featuring an article from NBC News about "public libraries creat[ing] LGBTQ-affirming spaces" with drag story events (Truong, 2018). In its post, the LGBT Resource Center asked its followers: "Raise your hand if you would attend a drag queen book reading at Thomas G. Carpenter Library?!" tagging the library's Facebook account. The response was overwhelmingly positive, with 87 likes, 14 comments, and 10 shares expressing excitement about such an event at the Carpenter Library. Comments from students and staff included "YES PLEASE," "Gotta have this," and raised hand emojis.

As a result of these enthusiastic reactions, LGBT Resource Center staff reached out to the Carpenter Library in November asking about the possibility of a partnered event. Since our outreach team also runs the library's social media accounts, we had seen the Facebook post and were excited about the opportunity to partner on a new and trendy event. The library's director of public services responded positively to an email in late November from LGBT Resource Center staff and asked for more information to move forward. As a result, the associate dean asked the outreach librarians—who were under the public services umbrella—to create a proposal for the event, detailing how it would benefit the library and its constituents, especially current students. The rationale for such a report was to cover all bases in case there were questions or even possibly pushback from university administration or community members. Having seen the rise in popularity of drag story events, but also an increase in public concerns, we outreach librarians and library administration understood and agreed to the need to protect ourselves and our community with a well-researched event proposal.

Research

To receive approval from library and university administration to move forward, we needed to establish, via research, a precedent for hosting drag story events in academic libraries. We began searching for other academic libraries who had successfully hosted similar events. As student outreach librarian, I was put in charge of the event proposal and began research in January 2019.

The first step was a series of Google searches on drag story events that had made a splash on news media. I quickly found Drag Story Hour (DSH), which was created in 2015 to provide guidance for drag story library events. According to its official website, DSH is a national 501(c) (3) non-profit organization with a "global network" of local chapters that are independently managed. Their mission statement reads: "Drag Story Hour celebrates reading through the glamorous art of drag. Our chapter network creates diverse, accessible, and culturally-inclusive family programming where kids can express their authentic selves and become bright lights of change in their communities" (DSH, n.d.). We reached out to the organization when planning our first event. Because we were in uncharted waters, we thought it pertinent to provide an official source for why these events were popular and should be supported.

During my research, I also came across a helpful toolkit from the American Library Association (ALA) titled "Libraries Respond: Drag Queen Story Hour." The webpage states: "Many libraries across the country have been hosting or participating in Drag Queen Story Hours. A few have experienced pushback from some members of their community. To support libraries facing challenges we have established this collection of resources. We will continue to add to it and welcome your contributions" (Libraries Respond, n.d., para. 1). Resources on this webpage, including relevant ALA Library Bill of Rights interpretations, provided context for why libraries would plan and host drag story events. While most of these resources were created for and by public librarians, we found it helpful in writing our event proposal, especially while making a correlation between the ALA examples and our academic library's mission statement.

Seeking examples from other academic libraries, I reached out on Facebook to the ACRL Library Marketing and Outreach (LMaO) Discussion Group asking: "There has been plenty in the news and in library-land... about hosting such an event in a PUBLIC library, but does anyone know of any ACADEMIC libraries taking part? Any thoughts or ideas or experiences making this work on the college level? Do tell! ☺" The post received 15 likes and 26 comments. Several comments were supportive of such an initiative and offered advice or asked to be kept informed of any progress. One librarian at Webster University, who had hosted their own drag story event at their academic library the previous year to great success, offered to chat privately to discuss details and answer my questions.

These comments and interactions encouraged my colleagues and me and proved we were on the right path to hosting an exciting and successful event for our students.

Prospectus

In March 2019, I submitted a prospectus document on behalf of the Carpenter Library and LGBT Resource Center to co-host a drag story event in the library during the upcoming Summer semester. UNF's Summer semester is split into three sections that are referred to as Summer A, B and C. Summer B takes place during June and July and sees the highest enrollment during the Summer, with a high percentage of new freshmen choosing to begin classes during Summer B rather than during the Fall semester. The University's Campus Life department also hosts a Summer B Kickoff week with many events around campus. Since Pride Month is commemorated in June each year, the Carpenter Library and LGBT Resource Center agreed that Summer B would be the perfect time to host an inaugural drag story event.

The prospectus document included details about the proposed event at UNF as well as research regarding other academic libraries hosting similar events, and included the following:

- Our event goal: "To support and foster UNF campus diversity; to promote LGBTQ books from the library's collection; to promote the library as a Safe Space and as a resource for gender and sexuality research; to facilitate a discussion of LGBTQ identities in conjunction with literature."

- Description: "Drag Queen Story Hour events have taken place all over the world at numerous libraries, schools, bookstores, and other community spaces.… Our DQSH event will feature a local drag performer reading from one or two LGBTQ titles from the library's collection."

- Timeline: "The library proposes to host one event during Summer B as a pilot project in order to gauge student interest. If the event is successful, the library may host a larger-scale event in Fall"

- Examples of other drag story events: Stanford University's one-day conference, Equity in Education, on February 2, 2019 (modeled a Drag Story event to attendees), Webster University Library's events (earliest one was in 2017), and University of South Alabama's event on January 12, 2019. The prospectus included links to news articles about and photographs of Webster and South Alabama's events.

As requested by library administration, it was important that the prospectus address the event's intended target audience as being "UNF students and the campus community at large." While the University of North Florida is a public institution, and the Carpenter Library is open to Northeast Florida community members, the Carpenter Library and LGBT Resource Center agreed not to publicize the event to members of the public, so as to mitigate risk and pushback. In addition, the prospectus detailed promotion to be mostly internal, using UNF's official channels of communication such as the UNF Calendar of Events and Osprey Update, a weekly e-newsletter. The prospectus also noted that the Carpenter Library and LGBT Resource Center would publicize via social media, fliers, and during other events on campus.

Library administration also requested that our prospectus include UNF teaching faculty involvement. This suggestion was made to help make the event academic in nature, and not just for entertainment. The prospectus noted that after the drag performer's presentation, "a short, faculty-led discussion will take place where the performer discusses how literature influenced their identities." We knew that we would invite a UNF faculty member whose research included sexuality, DEI, and/or LGBT subjects, and we already had a few in mind who had previously collaborated with both the Carpenter Library and the LGBT Resource Center. The event would be scheduled for one hour, with 30 minutes for the performance and a 30-minute Q & A session.

Security and Safety Concerns

An important part of the proposal was to include security and safety concerns, not only for the library to mitigate risk but for the protection of our performer and attendees. The Carpenter Library and LGBT Resource Center agreed that a semi-private and secure location within the library was preferred to protect everyone involved. At the time, event spaces in the library were largely open and inviting, allowing anyone to see what was happening and join the festivities. The chosen location was the library's special Collections reading room, which is located on the first floor and has two large doors leading into the open study area. This study area had been used previously for speaker events.

As a precaution, we asked the University Police Department (UPD) to provide security before, during, and after the event. At the time, the library had a STOP Station at the first floor Information Desk, where a UPD officer would sit and complete paperwork at a desktop computer between shifts. This STOP Station was located directly across the hallway from special collections, providing a perfect view of the event entrance.

In addition to the private event location and the assistance from UPD, the Carpenter Library and LGBT Resource Center created a fact sheet of community questions and concerns to be shared as needed before and during the event. This FAQ (see Appendix 1) was created by LGBT Resource Center staff using a template available from the Drag Story Hour website and included the following information:

- What is DSH?
- Who is this program for?
- Why is this program necessary?
- What is a drag queen?
- Why is it important to talk about gender expression and gender fluidity?
- What if I have questions about gender and don't know how to answer them?
- Should I call the drag queen "she" or "he" or "they" or something else?

This FAQ was shared amongst Carpenter Library and LGBT Resource Center staff who volunteered to help during the event. Multiple copies were also printed out ahead of both events.

Once completed, the prospectus was then shared with library administration, which then consisted of the director of public services and the interim dean. Comments and suggested edits were made before the final draft was submitted to the provost. In March 2019, the first drag story event at the University of North Florida was approved to take place in June.

Performer Selection

As the trusted and knowledgeable partner on campus, it was important that the LGBT Resource Center oversee the drag story event's programming, which included contacting and securing the performer(s) and faculty presenter. LGBT Resource Center staff not only had local community connections and established partnerships with LGBTQ+ performers, but they had hosted other drag events on campus. While these events sometimes created minor scrutiny in the community, they were supported and encouraged by university leadership; at the time, the LGBT Resource Center was fully staffed and funded. As a department under Student Affairs, the LGBT Resource Center also had a budget in which to pay the performer for their time. The Carpenter Library did not contribute to the budget but provided support in other ways, including writing the prospectus, providing the event space, helping with promotion, and scheduling staff time to help before, during, and after the event.

A local drag performer, writer, and musician was invited to be the featured performer for UNF's inaugural drag story event on Tuesday, June 25, from 12 to 1 p.m. They had previously performed at other UNF events, including the "Laugh OUT Comedy Show" in November 2017 at the student union. Representatives from the Carpenter Library and LGBT Resource Center, as well as the invited faculty member and the performer met beforehand to discuss event logistics to make sure we were on the same page.

Promotion and Marketing

The Carpenter Library and LGBT Resource Center split the responsibility for promoting and marketing the event to the UNF community. A student assistant in our research and outreach unit created a flier for the event which would be shared via social media and around campus. This flier showcased the event's performer and listed the Carpenter Library, LGBT Resource Center, and the official Drag Story Hour organization as partners for the event. In addition, the Carpenter Library reached out to DSH to have the event listed on their website. The event was also promoted in official university communications, including the Calendar of Events and the Osprey Update email, which went out to UNF students, faculty, and staff.

Local Controversy and Challenges

Unbeknownst to event organizers at UNF, a controversy was brewing in Northeast Florida. The same performer was also scheduled to present at another Pride event for the Jacksonville Public Library, which was hosting a Storybook Pride Prom event around the same time as UNF's drag story event. We were aware of the Storybook Pride Prom event, since we were sharing a local performer, but we did not know the details of the other event. Teenagers were the intended audience for the Pride Prom and a branch of the public library would host it.

This event was promoted online via social media and received serious backlash from both local and out-of-state conservative media and influencers. One of the Jacksonville Public Library's social media posts prior to the Pride Prom event received 274 comments, many of them negative. Several comments included, "This is child abuse," "Its [*sic*] down right disgusting and tasteless," and "It is disgraceful what you are doing specially using tax payers [*sic*] money!!!" Although supporters of the event rallied to support the public library, because of this backlash, the Jacksonville Public Library canceled the Pride Prom due to safety and security concerns. The cancellation was announced one day before UNF's drag story event. Although we at UNF were aware of Jacksonville Public Library's event backlash and cancellation, we did not consider canceling our drag story event. If anything, I personally felt a responsibility to continue our event as planned. UNF did not officially comment on or respond to the public library backlash.

In the meantime, in the weeks leading up to UNF's event, negative comments were posted to both the Carpenter Library's and LGBT Resource Center's social media accounts regarding our drag story event. Example comments included: "Stop hosting child-sex indoctrination sessions," "Pure pedopily [*sic*]. Repent," and "Sickening... perversing [*sic*] kids." While we outreach team members did not interact with these negative comments, we forwarded them to library administration and our event partners, so they were aware of the response. UNF students and other supporters took it upon themselves to respond to the comments, supporting the event and our performer, much to our relief.

The negative publicity surrounding both the Jacksonville Public Library event itself and its cancellation put an unintended focus on UNF's event. Even though these were two separate events with different intended audiences, word spread online via social media that UNF's event was a rescheduled Pride Prom event. UNF decision-makers, including LGBT Resource Center leadership and library administration, maintained that while UNF's drag story event was still intended to reach a campus audience (i.e. adults) and not minors, the Carpenter Library was open to the public; therefore, if non-UNF community members with or without children decided to attend the event, for good or bad, they would not be barred.

To further protect our attendees, it was decided that no attendance sheet would be required during the June event, but the LGBT Resource Center would provide an informational table with handouts, swag, and an optional sign-up sheet to join the LGBT Resource Center's mailing list.

Summer B Kickoff/Pride Month Event

UNF's first drag story hour event took place on Tuesday, June 25 from 12 to 1 p.m., during the first week of Summer B classes. That week, the Carpenter Library also installed an interactive Pride display in the first-floor lobby, near special collections where the event would take place. The display featured LGBTQ-related books from the library's collection as well as a whiteboard with the prompt: "What does Pride mean to you?" Colorful sticky pads were provided for guests and attendees to contribute to the activity. Positive messages included the following sentiments: "Celebrating love without fear," "I am proud of my trans brother," "Bi and Proud," and "Love for yourself and everybody else! 0% shame!" By the day of the event, the whiteboard held dozens of uplifting sticky notes.

The event was one hour in length, with 30 minutes allocated for the performance and 30 minutes for the Q&A. Although the prospectus stated that the performer would read from select library materials, the performer requested that they read from books that they had personally written, and which were illustrated by their partner. The LGBT Resource Center and Carpenter Library happily agreed to this request; we thought it would not only make the event more unique and personal, but it would also align with our aim to have the performer discuss "how literature influenced their identities." We did request that stories be rated G for all audiences, so minor edits had to be made before the event; for example, one story was renamed to "Trans People Don't Owe You a Gosh Darn Thing." Several stories included audience participation and one story titled "Mind Ya Business Monster" featured a raucous puppet show, to the delight of all attendees. Slides from the books were projected onto a screen behind the performer, who both stood and sat throughout the performance, depending on the story.

Approximately 65 people attended the event, including a mixture of UNF students, staff, faculty, and community members, as well as half a dozen children. Having planned for roughly 50 attendees due to the capacity of the special collections reading room, many attendees resorted to standing during the duration of the event. The Q & A was so involved, including numerous questions about Jacksonville Public Library's canceled Pride Prom, that our event ended up going over time. Although the event officially went from 12 to 1 p.m., the last attendees didn't leave until nearly an hour after it was scheduled to end.

Due to controversy regarding the canceled Jacksonville Public Library event and the online threat of protesters being present, UPD provided two police officers for the event. While no protesters caused a scene, at least one conservative blogger did attend the event and livestreamed it to his followers. UPD was made aware of his presence. In addition, university and local news media were present during the event. The education reporter for Jacksonville's *Florida Times-Union* attended and published an article titled "Drag Queen Story Hour prevails at UNF" which positively lauded UNF's effort (Bloch, 2019).

Fall/Coming Out Week Event

Due to the success and positive press of the June event, the LGBT Resource Center and Carpenter Library quickly proposed hosting a similar event during the Fall semester during October's Coming Out Week celebration on campus. Our previous performer was invited back and another UNF faculty member was invited to participate in the Q & A session. Anticipating a similar-sized audience, the event was moved to the library's second floor, where an area that was regularly used as an event space could be blocked off and secured. We again worked with the UPD who provided security officers for the event. This was especially important because we received word that a local group planned to protest outside the Carpenter Library during the event.

Our Fall event took place on Tuesday, October 8, from noon to 1 p.m. The performer read three children's books from the library's collection, including a personal favorite of theirs: *Julien is a Mermaid* by Jessica Love. Their performance ended with a command performance of "Mind Ya Business Monster" from our summer event, complete with puppets and audience participation. The faculty member who facilitated the Q & A happened to be a friend of our performer, which made for an interesting and intimate discussion. Questions revolved around the performer's personal experiences with gender identity, current politics, and advice they may give to struggling students.

This second event proved to be less controversial than the first one but had even more attendees with approximately 85 people present. Unlike the first event, no children were present. This was likely due to the lack of publicity following a local controversy, which had been the case in June. UNF affiliates (students, faculty, and staff) made up most of the attendees for the October event. Thanks to professors in the College of Education and Human Resources, one of whom brought their entire Introduction to Diversity in Education class to the event, most attendees were undergraduate students. Unfortunately, we learned during the event that at least one protester was loitering outside of the library. Therefore, after the event, one UPD officer quietly escorted the performer and faculty member out the back exit of the library building for their security.

Praise and Prejudice

The University of North Florida, the Carpenter Library, and the LGBT Resource Center all received praise and positive publicity for hosting these drag story events in June and October 2019. Unfortunately, the COVID-19 pandemic dampened plans for future drag story events at the Carpenter Library in 2020 and 2021. During this time, many outreach librarians (both academic and public) struggled to either convert already existing events and programs to online formats or create whole new remote activities to reach their audiences. As student outreach librarian, I personally grappled with this task, and found some success but also a few failures. In 2020, I had several discussions with LGBT Resource Center staff where we considered hosting a drag story event via Zoom, but despite interest on both sides, it never came to fruition. Time and resources were spent elsewhere, especially on bolstering UNF's "Stronger Together" campaign highlighting mental health and campus safety initiatives.

Not only did these events at UNF open the door to other possible partnerships between the Carpenter Library and the LGBT Resource Center, but it also encouraged other academic libraries and librarians to plan their own similar events. In June 2020, I partnered with two other academic librarians and one public library employee to co-present an online session titled "Supporting Diversity in Campus Communities with Drag Queen Story Hour" for ACRL Together Wherever Virtual Event, with over 100 attendees (ACRL, 2020). One of my co-presenters was the librarian from Webster with whom I connected via Facebook while researching our event proposal.

The political climate in the State of Florida further chilled UNF's ability to successfully host another drag story event. In 2022, legislation restricting DEI classes and programs at Florida's State University System was proposed, causing confusion and concern across UNF. SB 266, also known as the "Stop WOKE" bill, banned Florida's public universities from spending funds on programs related to diversity, equity, and inclusion (Lu, 2023).[1] In May 2023, this legislation was signed into law along with SB 1438, Florida's anti-drag show bill, which contains vague language that may be used to attack public drag shows and performances.[2] These bills, uncertainties, and veiled threats were disheartening for me personally as an outreach librarian, but devastating to university faculty and staff whose jobs revolve around DEI. Several staff members in the LGBT Resource Center, including my main contact for programming and events, sadly left the university in early 2023, further stymieing my hopes for a third drag story event at UNF.

Conclusion and Suggestions

Drag story events are popular with all ages, not just with children. These events provide an opportunity for college students to discuss and reflect on themes relating to inclusion, belonging, pride, and more. To make this event work in an academic library setting where the audience is intended to be college students, here is a suggested plan of action:

---

1   https://www.flsenate.gov/Session/Bill/2023/266

2   https://www.flsenate.gov/Session/Bill/2023/1438

- Nurture Relationships: Successful library outreach isn't a one-way street. If you want to plan a drag story event, your library should partner with other entities across campus, especially offices and departments whose job is to support diverse student experiences. If your campus does not have an LGBT Resource Center or similar department, look for other possible relationships on campus that can provide similar support and knowledge.

- Secure Buy-In: Support from library and university administration is crucial, especially at the earliest planning stages. Ask your administrators what concerns or ideas they have and be sure to address them in your proposal. Had it not been for a suggestion to involve faculty members in our drag story events, we would not have had two enlightening and entertaining Q & A sessions.

- Research, Research, Research: Find precedent where you can. As already noted, official resources are available from both ALA and DSH, but there are also unofficial resources and experiences to be gleaned from both public and academic libraries, other librarians who have hosted similar events, and more. Network and reach out to other librarians who have already done the work, ask questions, and build upon their successes.

- Plan For the Worst: Because these events are not without their risks, use your university resources to protect your attendees as best you can. Create an FAQ in case you receive difficult questions, do not feed the trolls, and rely on your university police department to handle event security.

With the proper research and prospectus work, as well as a trustworthy network of campus supporters, a successful drag story event is attainable, even under the threat of prejudice.

References

ACRL. (2020). *ACRL Together Wherever Virtual Event*. Retrieved October 19, 2023, from www.ala.org/acrl/conferences/atw

Bloch, E. (2019, June 25). *Drag Queen Story Hour prevails at UNF*. Florida Times-Union. www.jacksonville.com/story/news/education/2019/06/25/drag-queen-story-hour-prevails-at-unf/4799493007/

Drag Story Hour. (n.d.). *What is Drag Story Hour?* www.dragstoryhour.org/about

Libraries respond: Drag Queen Story Hour. (n.d.). American Library Association. www.ala.org/advocacy/libraries-respond-drag-queen-story-hour

Lu, A. (2023, October 12). *Here's what Florida's proposed anti-DEI regulations would ban.* Chronicle of Higher Education. www.chronicle.com/article/heres-what-floridas-proposed-anti-dei-regulations-would-ban

Truong, K. (2018, October 16). *From Brooklyn to Wichita, public libraries create LGBTQ-affirming spaces.* NBC News. www.nbcnews.com/feature/nbc-out/brooklyn-wichita-public-libraries-create-lgbtq-affirming-spaces-n920446

Appendix 1

Drag Story Hour (DSH) at UNF – FAQ

What is DSH?

Drag Story Hour events have taken place all over the world at libraries, schools, bookstores, and other community spaces. An official national Drag Story Hour organization supports local chapters, librarians, and volunteers across the United States. While Jacksonville doesn't have a chapter, there is a Florida chapter in Tampa.

The DSQH at UNF event features a local drag performer who will read from one or two LGBTQ titles selected from her personal library. Attendees may also peruse the books and resources in Thomas G. Carpenter Library's collection. After the Story Hour, a short, faculty-led discussion will take place where participants will discuss how literature influences identity and promotes diversity through a social and academic lens.

The event promotes conversations about identity, culture, and gender in a fun, academic environment that connects the campus community and promotes utilization of library and student success services.

Who is this program for?

Drag Story Hour at UNF is geared towards college students and the UNF community. It takes place during UNF Summer B Kick-Off to welcome students to campus in a welcoming setting.

Why is this program necessary?

Programs like DSH are a vital part of making the world a safe and affirming place for *all* people. The program helps promote empathy, diversity appreciation, and understanding across human difference.

Additionally, with the rise of RuPaul's Drag Race and the recent MET Gala's Camp Theme, the late 2000s have been drag's big pop culture moment! This event helps to bring people together around an exploration of identity, pop culture, history, and community to understand the meaning and history of drag shows, performance, and gender.

What is a drag queen?

Drag is an artistic form of self-expression and showing the world different parts of who you are. Drag queens often express their feminine sides or different aspects of gender and personality through dressing up, putting on performances, marching in parades, and volunteering in their communities. There are drag queens, drag kings, drag princes, and drag princesses—anyone can be any of the above!

Why is it important to talk about gender expression and gender fluidity?

Many people express gender in different ways. DSH provides an opportunity for people to embrace gender diversity in themselves and in others. Additionally, events like these help to curb bullying of LGBTQ kids and adults who may be perceived as different.

What if I have questions about gender and don't know how to answer them?

Adults don't always have all the answers, but we can ask questions and learn together. A great place to start is Sez Me, a free LGBTQ web series appropriate for the whole family. We also recommend looking at resources from organizations like Gender Spectrum,[3] GLSEN,[4] and PFLAG, as well as local LGBTQ groups like JASMYN[5] and UNF's LGBTQ Center.[6]

Should I call the drag queen "she" or "he" or "they" or something else?

You can ask them! It's always OK to ask someone what gender pronoun they use. Examples of pronouns are she, he, and they. Some people have the same pronoun all the time. Some people have different gender pronouns at different times, like when they're in drag or not in drag.

---

3 https://www.genderspectrum.org/

4 https://www.glsen.org/

5 https://pflag.org/

6 https://www.unf.edu/lgbtqcenter/

Stop WOKE Gave Me Pause

David Benjamin

Introduction

> *This is a culture war to create an enemy that we can put all our fears onto...[The LGBTQ+ community is] easy to point at to distract people from looking at the real problems and that is eroding the educational opportunities of our students.*

Helene Gold (Greenfield, 2023)

This statement from Helene Gold, former associate dean of academic engagement at the New College of Florida, on the current culture wars reflects the contentious debate surrounding anti-woke and anti-DEI legislation in education in Florida. In today's complex sociopolitical landscape, Gold's words highlight the divisive nature of the discourse around these issues. This new legislation has caused many in education to panic because of the vagueness of these new laws regarding what is and what is not allowed in the classroom and its potential impact on the work of educators, administrators, and librarians. This chapter discusses how the uncertainty of new anti-woke legislation and rhetoric affected collection development and exhibit planning in an academic library's special collection department, from the viewpoint of a seasoned librarian caught in the middle of this culture war.

Stop WOKE and Politicization of Education

Merriam-Webster defines woke as "aware of and actively attentive to important societal facts and issues (especially issues of racial and social justice)" (Merriam-Webster, n.d.). Dictionary.com defines woke as "having or marked by an active awareness of systemic injustices and prejudices, especially those involving the treatment of ethnic, racial, or sexual minorities" (Dictionary.com, n.d.). In a 2023 interview on NPR, Dr. Elaine Richardson, professor of literacy studies at The Ohio State University, discussed the history of the term woke, tracing its meaning to the "experiences of Black people of knowing that you have to be conscious of the politics of race, class, gender, systemic racism, ways that society is stratified and not equal" (Montanaro, 2023). The term woke is not new; it appeared in writings and protest songs by Black authors and songwriters in the early and mid-20th century. In 1923, Jamaican philosopher Marcus Garvey included the phrase "wake up" in his writings, calling for Blacks to become more socially and politically conscious. Moreover, in 1938, singer and songwriter Huddie Ledbetter, better known as Lead Belly, included "stay woke" in the spoken afterword for his song "Scottsboro Boys" about nine Black teenagers accused of raping a white woman in Arkansas in 1931 (Romano, 2020). The resurgence of the use of woke occurred in 2008 when artist Erykah Badu used "I stay woke" throughout her 2008 song "Master Teacher" (Montanaro, 2023).

However, when pushed to define woke, there is little agreement on the meaning of woke from those sounding the alarm about "wokeness." When asked to define woke in a recent court case, lawyers representing Florida's governor responded, "the belief there are systemic injustices in American society and the need to address them" (Williams, 2022). While this meaning is not far from the definitions of woke above, the lawyers said that the Governor "doesn't believe that there are systemic injustices in the United States" (Williams, 2022). In the Governor's acceptance speech for his second term, he said, "We reject this woke ideology. We seek normalcy, not philosophical lunacy. We will not allow reality, facts, and truth to become optional.... We will never surrender to the woke mob. Florida is where woke goes to die" (Dixon & Fineout, 2023). However, there was no definition or clarification on what he was rejecting. When asked to define woke in a 2023 interview, conservative author Bethany Mandel struggled for 30-plus seconds, saying, "So, I mean, woke is, sort of, the idea that, um," and then, after a long and awkward silence, continued, "this is going to be one of those moments that goes viral" (Wiggins, 2023). While unable to uniformly define woke, conservative partisan rhetoric continued to push an anti-woke agenda.

The Florida Legislature passed two laws regulating the content of instruction, discussion, and training in public schools and workplaces in their 2022 Legislative Session. The Individual Freedom Act,[1] commonly known as the Stop WOKE Act (WOKE stands for Wrongs to Our Kids and Employees), regulates the content of instruction and training in schools and workplaces. Designed to combat "woke indoctrination," the bill prohibits instruction that might cause someone to "feel guilt, anguish or any form of psychological distress" due to their race, color, sex, or national origin (Mudde, 2023). Initially, this legislation targeted teaching critical race theory in K-12 education (Florida Governor's Staff, 2021). The second law, the Parental Rights in Education Act,[2] commonly referred to as the Don't Say Gay law, restricts instruction or discussion about sexual orientation and gender identity in public schools. The law initially only applied to kindergarten through third-grade students. However, in April 2023, the Florida Board of Education voted to expand the law to include fourth- through twelfth-grades (Pendharkar, 2023).

During this time, all public educational institutions throughout Florida came under the microscope as politicians sounded the alarm about "woke ideologies" invading the classroom with radical teachers and programs indoctrinating and grooming students. In October 2021, the University of Florida administration barred faculty members from testifying in a lawsuit challenging a new state law limiting the use of drop boxes or voting by mail in Florida (Klas, 2021). The Governor claimed that public college and university professors have no right to freedom of speech (Diep, 2022). Part of what many on the right call "America's culture war," they believe liberals are pushing a woke agenda on public education.

And the rhetoric did not stop with "wokeness." Local school and public library boards grappled with calls to ban LGBTQ+ books (Mazzei et al., 2023). Drag performers were accused of sexualizing children (del Barco, 2022). Walt Disney World was in the Florida Governor's crosshairs because of opposition to the Stop WOKE Act (Guynn, 2022).[3] The

---

1 Fla. Stat.§ 760.10(8)(a) (2022): http://www.leg.state.fl.us/statutes/index.cfm?App_mode=Display_Statute&URL=0700-0799/0760/Sections/0760.10.html

2 Parental Rights in Education, CS/CS/HB 1557, https://www.flsenate.gov/Committees/billsummaries/2022/html/2825

3 Although initially silent after Florida Governor Ron DeSantis signed the Parental Rights in Education Act (commonly known as the Don't Say Gay law) in 2022, Disney's then-chief executive eventually criticized the bill. The governor and republican legislators seized on Disney's response, using it to portray the company as pushing a woke agenda. Ultimately, the Florida Legislature rescinded Disney's special tax status, which had been in place since 1967, that essentially allowed the company to operate as its own governmental district. The legislature then put into place a new board to oversee the district. Both sides have gone to court over this issue. As of November 2023, the courts have not weighed in on the case.

Florida Department of Education banned high school students from taking some Advanced Placement history and psychology courses because they "indoctrinate students to 'a political agenda'" (Kim, 2023). State colleges and universities are required to report money, time, and staff involved in DEI programs and provide information about transgender health care sought or received by students and provided by colleges' or universities' health centers (Associated Press, 2023). The word "groomer" seemed to become a new catchphrase for anyone daring to stand against censorship, bigotry, and hate.

Then, in January 2023, Governor Ron DeSantis proposed legislation banning university gender studies and diversity programs (Bernstein, 2023). This legislation states that courses taught at public universities "may not suppress or distort significant historical events or include a curriculum that teaches identity politics." There were calls for abolishing gender studies programs and realigning the "core curriculum to the values of liberty and the Western tradition" (Bernstein, 2023).

Collecting LGBTQ+ Materials

In spring 2021, the LGBTQ History Museum of Central Florida selected the University of Central Florida (UCF) Libraries' Special Collections & University Archives department to house the Museum's archival holdings. The Museum, a grassroots effort run by volunteers, had acquired multiple archival collections documenting the stories of the LGBTQ+ community in Central Florida. Most of the material collected by the Museum is from individuals and mainly consists of correspondence, photographs, publications, ephemeral material, and memorabilia. The collections cover diverse topics, including community involvement, HIV/AIDS awareness, LGBTQ+ activism, local gay-owned businesses, local politics, local organizations such as the Orlando Gay Chorus and the Center[4], and national organizations such as PFLAG and GLAAD. Several collections include materials about UCF's Gay, Lesbian, Bisexual Student Union, a group/club that served the university's LGBTQ+ community when there was no official university support organization. With many of the founding members of the LGBTQ History Museum's

---

4   The Center, now known as the Center Orlando, is a nonprofit organization offering various programs and services for the LGBTQ+ community. According to the Center's webpage (https://thecenterorlando.org), "the mission of the LGBT+ Center Orlando is to promote and empower the LGBT community and its allies through advocacy, education, information, and support."

Board identifying as LGBTQ, the Museum had access to unique collections documenting the LGBTQ+ community of Central Florida. However, the Museum lacked appropriate archival storage spaces and staff to process and make the collections available for research. They realized they needed to partner with an archival organization to continue their mission of documenting the LGBTQ+ community.

Special Collections & University Archives (SCUA) houses the UCF Libraries' most unique and rarest items from the 13th century to the present day. The department's diverse collections cover a broad range of topics. The collections are particularly strong in book arts and typography, botany, Floridiana, the space program, and travel and tourism, as well as the history of the University of Central Florida. These collections allow the UCF community to understand history better and have a deeper connection to campus. From incorporating primary resource materials into class curriculum to providing students with internships and hands-on experiences not available anywhere else on campus, department staff work with faculty and students to offer unique learning opportunities. Although SCUA was not actively collecting LGBTQ+ history, I saw this as a chance to document an underrepresented community. Also, several collections included materials documenting efforts to establish staff and student LGBTQ groups at UCF, which is essential in telling the university's history. In addition to acquiring the Museum's existing archival collections, SCUA staff would work with the Museum Board to collect additional materials documenting Central Florida's queer community.

Staff began processing collections in late 2021 and early 2022—just as the governor and legislature started their "War on Woke." By early spring 2022, I was worried about potential issues around collecting LGBTQ materials and what effects new legislation would have on this collection. I had pushed to acquire the LGBTQ History Museum of Central Florida's collections. We were one of several institutions the Museum considered when looking to place their archival holdings. When speaking with Museum Board members, I discussed the advantages of giving the collection to the university as a permanent repository. Our current and future students could use the materials for research. Women and gender studies department faculty could integrate collections into class assignments. We had institutional support and funds to preserve existing collections and continue collecting. The materials would be at an institution that prides itself on diversity and inclusion initiatives. This was a win-win for everyone involved.

However, my win-win was quickly feeling like a potentially liable and losing situation. By spring 2023, I began doubting my decision to accept this material. Had I made the wrong decision in acquiring this material? Would the university continue to support efforts to collect LGBTQ+ archival collections? Would the library suffer because of a collecting decision I made? Florida's political environment began impacting my archivist and librarian work and decision-making. No one objected to my decision to take the Museum's archival collections. Library administration supported my decision. And yet, that decision was weighing heavily on me. Self-censorship was affecting how I did my job.

Creation of a Second-wave Feminist Exhibit

In 2019, the UCF Libraries opened a new exhibition gallery space, part of an expansion and renovation of UCF's main campus library. This new space, adjacent to the library's new reading room, was initially planned to showcase Special Collections & University Archives (SCUA) resources and increase the visibility of its holdings and exhibit program. As head of SCUA, I saw the gallery as much more. I envisioned the gallery as an extension of the classroom where our department worked directly with students to curate exhibits that would augment classroom learning outcomes using primary source materials.

Fast forward to late summer 2021 when a UCF women's and gender studies faculty member approached me about partnering on a service-learning project[5] with students in her First and Second Wave Feminism class. SCUA staff previously partnered with this faculty member on a service-learning digitization project. We wanted something different for this class. I suggested a student-curated exhibition.

Students would select materials from the department's manuscript holdings illustrating themes explored in their coursework during their fall 2021 class. Department staff chose several collections for the students to work with for this project. These included the *Judith and*

---

5   UCF defines service-learning as, "a teaching method that uses community involvement to apply theories or skills being taught in a course. Service-Learning furthers the learning objectives of the academic course, addresses community needs, and requires students to reflect on their activity in order to gain an appreciation for the relationship between civics and academics." "Service-Learning Course Designation." Experiential Learning Division of Student Success and Well-Being, University of Central Florida, https://academicsuccess.ucf.edu/explearning/faculty/course-approval-form/. Accessed 3 Aug. 2023.

Warren Kaplan Collection, Women's and Gender Studies,[6] the *Beatrice B. Ettinger Papers,*[7] the *Democratic Women's Club of Florida, Inc. Collection,*[8] and the *Lynda Van Scoyoc Women's Feminist Papers Collection.*[9] Materials and subjects in these collections touch on themes associated with feminism, including sexuality, family, reproductive rights, civil rights, the workplace, and inequality between the sexes. These collections contain manuscript and published materials, photographs, and ephemeral items, providing a cross-section of materials students could select for the project. The students would choose items for the exhibit during their fall 2021 class. In 2022, department staff would pull the student materials for the exhibit based on the students' work, write captions and exhibit labels, pull together student writings about second-wave feminism for the exhibition's description, and choose additional materials needed to supplement the student selections. We planned to install the exhibit in our gallery in January 2023, with a closing date of April 2023.

After some discussion, the faculty member and I refined the focus to second-wave feminism. This project was a win-win for everyone. The faculty member loved this idea, as it fit within the course's goals and met the university's criteria for service-learning projects. I was excited at the prospect of mounting a student-curated exhibit in the gallery and that students would be working with our manuscript and archival collections.

For the project, students selected items that illustrated themes discussed in class: "Feminist Consciousness Raising," "The Personal is Political," "Having It All Feminism," "Radical Feminism," "Second Shift," "Sisterhood," and "The Lavender Menace." To illustrate "Feminist Consciousness Raising," students selected pamphlets about women's

---

6   Judith and Warren Kaplan Collection, Women's and Gender Studies, Special Collections & University Archives, University of Central Florida, https://ucf-flvc.primo.exlibrisgroup.com/permalink/01FALSC_UCF/5okunq/alma990363614720306596.

7   Beatrice B. Ettinger Papers, Special Collections & University Archives, University of Central Florida, https://ucf-flvc.primo.exlibrisgroup.com/permalink/01FALSC_UCF/5okunq/alma990287404010306596.

8   Democratic Women's Club of Florida, Inc. Collection, Special Collections & University Archives, University of Central Florida, https://ucf-flvc.primo.exlibrisgroup.com/permalink/01FALSC_UCF/5okunq/alma990294188810306596.

9   Lynda Van Scoyoc Women's Feminist Papers Collection, Special Collections & University Archives, University of Central Florida, https://ucf-flvc.primo.exlibrisgroup.com/permalink/01FALSC_UCF/5okunq/alma990287409770306596.

health topics such as breast cancer awareness and reproductive health. Several students chose political buttons for "The Personal is Political," including an ERA (Equal Rights Amendment) button and an "I'm Pro-Choice, and I Vote" button. For "Having It All Feminism," one student selected an information packet and registration form from the Beatrice B. Ettinger Papers for a "Leadership Skills for Women Seminar" to empower women in the workplace. Another student chose a pamphlet titled *Women at Work Today and Tomorrow* for the same topic.

To illustrate "Radical Feminism," one student chose a button with the slogan, "Women's Place is in the House and Senate, too!" Several students used photographs of women working in the home and caring for children to illustrate "Second Shift." Finally, students pulled materials with slogans such as "Women Power" or NOW (National Organization for Women) buttons to represent the idea of "Sisterhood." However, none of the students selected materials they felt illustrated the Lavender Menace. After choosing the items, students wrote about each item's relevance to one of these themes and personally reflected on their meaning. I was thrilled with the students' work and excited about the exhibit.

During the 2022-2023 academic year, a graduate student from UCF's department of history interned in the department. Part of her internship was helping me curate this exhibition. She pulled the student-selected materials together, and we decided which items to include in the exhibit. She also identified materials to supplement the students' selections, ensuring women of color and the LGTQ+ community roles in second-wave feminism were represented. She found several publications documenting the impact of Black women in America; photographs, ephemera, and memorabilia from the *African American Legacy: The Carol Mundy Collection*; manuscript material from the *Judith and Warren Kaplan Collection, Women's and Gender Studies*; and photographs and newspaper clippings from the *Central Florida International Black Women's Congress Collection*. For the Lavender Menace, she found several lesbian publications in the LGBTQ History Museum of Central Florida materials, plus artists' books and zines from the department's *Book Arts & Typology Collection*. We were excited about the exhibit titled "Second-Wave Feminism in the Archives."

However, while we were planning the exhibit on second-wave feminism, the Florida governor and legislature were passing legislation eliminating gender studies programs and banning teaching of the very subjects covered by this exhibit. The 2022 Florida Legislative Session saw the legislature pass the Individual Freedom Act (Stop WOKE Act) and the Parental Rights in Education Act (Don't Say Gay). Then in January 2023, Governor DeSantis proposed legislation targeting gender studies and DEI programs. Between the local and state news coverage of the legislative session and Governor DeSantis' touting his "anti-woke" agenda as he toyed with a presidential run, it was hard to miss what was happening in Florida politics. The more I read and heard, the more concerned I became about the exhibition's subject matter.

My career in archives spans 30-plus years. I cut my teeth as an archivist at the University of Kansas, working with one of the country's most significant assemblages of US left- and right-wing political literature.[10] The collection documented white nationalism, Holocaust deniers, and eco-terrorism. I curated exhibits and worked with students and scholars using this material. Politicians and the public did not scrutinize higher education like they are currently. No one accused us of pushing a liberal agenda. I never worried that someone would object to or come after our work or people involved in an exhibit because of the subject matter. However, in January 2023, I was worried.

For the first time in my career, I let outside forces influence my thinking. I put the exhibit on hold and left the gallery dark. No one suggested I rethink this exhibit. I discussed my concerns with senior library administrators. They were sympathetic to my concerns but fully supported my decision; no one pressured me one way or the other. This was all me. I needed time to think about what was next. I needed time to revise the exhibition's focus to avoid perceived unwanted and unwarranted public or political scrutiny. I was worried about potential repercussions because the topic was second-wave feminism, a subject being eliminated from higher educational institutions in Florida because it "teaches identity politics" (Factora, 2023). I wanted to showcase the work of these students. I wanted to showcase our collections. I wanted to realize the goal of student-curated exhibits in the exhibition gallery. Again, self-censorship was affecting my decisions at work, decisions I had been making my entire career.

I do not believe my concerns were unwarranted. Across the state and the nation, teachers and librarians were being called out, harassed,

---

10 Wilcox Collection, Kansas Collection Regional History Library, KU, https://spencer.lib.ku.edu/collections/wilcox-collection

and fired for pushing a liberal agenda. Helene Gold, an associate dean at the New College of Florida's library, was fired without notice and cause. Gold was an outspoken member of the LGBTQ+ community and a champion of diversity, equity, and inclusion in higher education. Florida school districts threatened "librarians with third-degree felonies" if they allowed students to access books on race, sex, and gender (Woodcock, 2023). Public librarians throughout the country have faced harassment and firing by local governing boards for allowing LGBTQ books in children's and teen sections, even when the books are deemed age-appropriate (Gallardo, 2023).

Given all that was going on in Florida and the nation, I was concerned about the students whose work we featured in the exhibition. Initially, we planned to include the students' essays about their chosen items. While we would only identify them by their first name, it could be easy for someone to find them using class rosters. The students wrote some beautiful and moving reactions for this project. Excluding the student comments defeated the spirit of the exhibit. They chose the items for specific reasons. It was essential to include those reasons.

I worried how this would impact the history graduate student, my co-curator for the exhibit. Her work selecting materials to augment those from the class brought depth and additional voices to the exhibition. Much of her work was selecting materials representing women of color and the queer community to augment the exhibit content. She is just beginning her time in academia. I did not want this exhibit to derail her future.

I was concerned about the unwanted attention the exhibit might bring to the UCF Libraries. Higher education has been under a microscope for several years in Florida. Universities are quietly rewriting DEI policies, removing language that might conflict with ever-changing laws. Declining enrollments since the 2020 pandemic have seen budgets for staff and acquisitions on the line. I panicked that this exhibit could hurt the library financially.

I feared an exhibit on second-wave feminism would draw unwarranted attention to the department.

I feared that financial retaliation could occur.

I feared politicians and overly zealous community members would question why we had this material in our collection.

I feared university officials would feel under pressure to look at our collection, and I feared deaccession of so-called woke materials.

Curiously, I never feared for myself. I never worried about losing my job. I never worried someone would come after me. I was not concerned about my career. Frankly, I don't know why I wasn't worried for myself.

So, the gallery sat dark while I determined what was next.

Where We Go From Here

Continuing to Process and Collect LGBTQ+ Materials

When I began working in archives, archivists discussed the importance of being inclusive in collecting. Colleagues and mentors instilled in me the importance of telling the stories of underrepresented communities— people of color, LGBTQ+, women, etc. I believe archival collecting for too long had focused on documenting the lives of white, cisgendered men. In the early 1990s, while working in the Kansas Collection Regional History Library at the University of Kansas, the department began collecting the stories of Black Kansans. We were one of the first institutions in the Midwest to create a position specifically to collect materials on and about the Black community. The department head realized the need to acquire and preserve these materials before they were lost forever. Her thinking heavily influenced how I view archives to this day.

Even while I was uncertain how the political environment might affect our work, we continued working on the LGBTQ History Museum of Central Florida archival collections. Staff processed the materials, created finding aids, and published them on our collections guides page.[11] Despite worrying about what might happen with the exhibit and collecting new materials, I was not concerned that processing the LGBTQ collections would be a problem.

Looking back, I am unsure why I was not worried, considering how much I agonized about and questioned my decision to accept the collection. It could be because documenting marginalized communities is ingrained in my thinking about archives. It may be because processing and cataloging archives is where I feel most comfortable and secure in my profession. Perhaps it is because I suddenly grew

---

11   Special Collections & University Archives Collection Guides page, https://scua.library.ucf.edu

a backbone. However, most likely, it was because of something a co-worker said during a collection development meeting. Someone asked what impact the new Florida legislation would have on collecting. The response was—nothing. Nothing is going to change. She emphatically stated, "We are collecting history." These four words sounded so amazing to me. It was empowering. We are collecting history. This is why archivists do what we do. This is why I became an archivist.

Rethinking the Exhibition

Postponing the exhibit gave me time to think about what was next. Do I cancel the show? Do I shelve it until the effects of the "War on Woke" hysteria died down? When I had shared my concerns with library administrators, I had secretly hoped they would give me an official out and cancel the exhibit. This would have been the easy out for me. I did not want to cancel this exhibit curated by students. Working with students, getting students to think critically about history, and sharing our collections with students is the whole point of what I do. Canceling the exhibit was off the table.

As new legislation banning diversity, equity, and inclusive initiatives and departments went into effect, I asked friends in those areas what they were doing. While some were leaving the state and others looking for jobs outside higher education, those staying and working through this time talked about rethinking how we present the topics. Still believing what they do is essential, they quietly renamed programs and initiatives, avoiding the words diversity and inclusion.

This got me thinking. How could I still present the student work around second-wave feminism and avoid potential backlash? What if I rebranded the exhibit as part of a broader topic around women and history titled "Women Making History?" Could I take the materials selected by the students, add the materials chosen by our graduate intern, and augment this with additional materials documenting women who worked to make or change history? We could still use the student write-ups but not include their names. Statements about the exhibit could discuss partnering with faculty and students without mentioning the class name or topic.

Am I thrilled with this solution? No. It feels like a copout—like I chose the easiest solution. And I will always wonder if I overreacted.

Does it eliminate my fears? Not completely. One outcome of all the legislation, all the name-calling, and all the grandstanding is the creation of an atmosphere of fear. Perhaps this is the intended outcome.

Can I live with it? Yes, I can. It's a compromise. A compromise that I see more and more as state employees, educators, and librarians grapple with the impact of overreaching legislation. This may be the new reality at educational institutions in Florida. Keeping a low profile while strategically choosing when and how to counteract the atmosphere of fear. It avoids raising undue scrutiny and unwanted attention while pushing forward our ideas, even if done quietly.

And it doesn't silence us.

Conclusion

The past few years have been exhausting. We were finally returning to normalcy after the COVID-19 pandemic when educational institutions and libraries were scrutinized as our collective work was put under a cultural and political lens. Often viewed as intimidation, new laws and legislation seem to be less about substance and more about bullying, aiming "to empower a vocal and censorship-minded minority...and intimidate educators with threats of punishment" (Friedman et al., 2023; Gonzalez, 2023).

It makes doing my job, a job I love, difficult. I am proud of my library degree. Librarians, archivists, and anyone in the information profession are crucial to ensuring our shared history lives on. I am most proud that we collect and preserve all types of narratives—the good, the bad, and the ugly. As a librarian and archivist, I collect stories without judgment. However, the current climate makes this more and more challenging. It often feels like a personal attack. As Mary Grahame Hunter said in a recent article in *American Libraries*, "If you're a member of a marginalized group that's being targeted on top of also being a library worker...it can be just absolutely crushing" (Sterbenz, 2023, pp. 28-33). It has been crushing. But I cannot let this defeat me. I will not let this defeat me.

After the 2023 spring semester ended, I reevaluated my decision to postpone the exhibit. I contemplated how to continue collecting LGBTQ+ materials, given the current politics in Florida. Here are my takeaways from this experience:

First and foremost, trust your instincts if they tell you to be cautious.

Your concerns are valid. When confronted with difficult situations or choices, your gut reactions are an internal compass that helps guide your decision-making process. However, you must strike a balance between intuition and reason. You do not want to overreact. Gather all relevant information and weigh the pros and cons, assessing the situation and understanding your instincts. Part of me will always wonder if I overreacted by postponing the exhibition, but I trusted my instincts and delaying the exhibit proved to be the sound decision despite my uncertainty.

Step back and give yourself some breathing room and time to think.

Take your time with a decision, especially if the decision feels very personal. You need time to think through all the implications and possible outcomes. Allowing yourself some breathing room is crucial to effective decision-making. Take a step back and give yourself the time and space to think through the situation and concerns. Do not allow outside pressures to force you into making hasty decisions. Giving yourself this space enables you to process the information more thoroughly. Consider the consequences, weigh the alternatives, and then compare these to your values and priorities.

Moreover, giving yourself breathing room is an act of self-compassion. Postponing the exhibit and pausing collecting gave me the time to ensure I was comfortable with my decisions. Ultimately, if I am uncomfortable with my choices, I cannot confidently stand behind the decision.

Talk with others in similar situations.

Seek advice from colleagues and friends who have gone through similar situations. Discussing your thoughts and concerns gives you a fresh perspective and new insights. These conversations and feedback will inevitably lead to better decisions and outcomes. You can explore different angles of the decision, uncover things you might not have thought of, and identify solutions you might have missed when deciding in a vacuum. Moreover, talking with others provides much-needed emotional support and reassurance. It allows you to express your doubts, fears, and uncertainties in a safe environment.

Assess the pros and cons of moving forward.

Work through the pros and cons of a decision and identify the potential advantages and pitfalls. This enables you to clarify what you stand to gain or lose. However, excessive focus on the cons can lead to negativity and pessimism, potentially hindering your decision-making process. Also, you may unconsciously bias your decision one way or the other based on your emotions. Striking a balance can be difficult but results in a more informed and practical decision.

Rebrand the message.

Take a cue from my colleagues working in diversity, equity, and inclusion as they navigated the politicization of their jobs and responsibilities. They rebranded what they do. Whereas an exhibition titled "Second Wave Feminism in Special Collections & University Archives" seemed problematic, arguing about an exhibit titled "Women Making History" is more complex. It has the same content, just a different presentation. Tweak the wording and not the meaning when politicians and extremists have politicized and vilified words. Rebranding your message is a powerful tool to combat these efforts.

Sometimes, it is okay to postpone—even indefinitely.

Postponing something can be a means of avoiding hasty, impulsive choices that may lead to regret. By rushing headlong into something, especially where emotions on both sides are running high, you may need more depth of consideration to fully grasp the consequences and implications. Permitting yourself to delay a decision can result in more deliberate decision-making. It gives you time to gather additional information, seek advice, or wait for the right circumstances to align. There are times and situations when it is okay, or even prudent, to postpone something indefinitely. This is particularly true with emotionally charged decisions. They may require more time, reflection, or information to make an informed and thoughtful decision.

I am hopeful that current and future legal challenges to these new laws impacting education and marginalized people may see several of them overturned, and we can get back to collecting and sharing history. I will never know what would have happened had we installed an exhibition with feminism in the title or the reaction to an exhibit curated by students in a women's and gender studies class. No one has said to stop collecting the stories of LGBTQ+ people. Nevertheless, the anticipation of a struggle around censorship caused me to pause the work I was doing—work I have been doing for 30+ years. Perhaps this is the intended effect of legislation vilifying marginalized people. Maybe those crafting these laws want our stories forgotten. Stop WOKE may have given me pause—but, in the end, it will not silence me.

Exhibit Update

We continued working on the "Women Making History" exhibit through the summer of 2023 with a new install date of January 2025. However, on November 9, 2023, the Florida Board of Governors met to discuss the implications of Senate Bill 266, signed by the Governor on May 9, 2023. This bill "prohibits a university or university direct-support organization from expending any state or federal funds, regardless of the source, to promote, support, or maintain any programs or campus activities that…advocate for diversity, equity, and inclusion, or promote or engage in political or social activism" (Florida Board of Governors, 2023). UCF's legal counsel is looking into the impact of the new regulation; specifically, how it defines "political or social activism." Could an exhibit about women in history be considered some type of activism or political statement? That question has been asked. We await the answer.

References

Associated Press. (2023, January 19). *DeSantis seeks transgender university students' health care information*. Retrieved June 2023, from nbcnews.com: https://www.nbcnews.com/nbc-out/out-politics-and-policy/de-santis-seeks-transgender-university-students-health-care-information-rcna66495

Bernstein, S. (2023, February 24). *Florida bill would ban gender studies majors, diversity programs at universities*. Reuters. https://www.reuters.com/world/us/florida-bill-would-ban-gender-studies-majors-diversity-programs-universities-2023-02-25/

del Barco, M. (2022, June 16). *Some lawmakers hope to crack down on drag shows watched by children*. NPR. https://www.npr.org/2022/06/16/1105544325/drag-shows-children

Dictionary.com. (n.d.). Woke. In *Dictionary.com*. https://www.dictionary.com/browse/woke

Diep, F. (2022, September 22). *It's not clear whether public-college professors have First Amendment rights when they're teaching.* The Chronicle of Higher Education. https://www.chronicle.com/article/its-not-clear-whether-public-college-professors-have-first-amendment-rights-when-theyre-teaching

Dixon, M., & Fineout, G. (2023, January 1). *'Where woke goes to die': DeSantis, with eye toward 2023, launches second term.* Politico. https://www.politico.com/news/2023/01/03/desantis-2024-second-term-00076160

Factora, J. (2023, May 16). *Ron DeSantis just banned DEI programs at public colleges in Florida.* them. https://www.them.us/story/ron-de-santis-florida-dei-colleges-ban

Florida Board of Governors. (2023, November 9). *Notice of Proposed Amended Regulation* (9.016 Prohibited Expenditures) https://www.flbog.edu/wp-content/uploads/2023/11/Proposed_AmendedRegulationForm-9-016-1.pdf

Florida Governor's Staff. (2021, December 11). *Governor DeSantis announces legislative proposal to stop W.O.K.E activism and critical race theory in schools and corporations.* FLgov.com. https://www.flgov.com/2021/12/15/governor-desantis-announces-legislative-proposal-to-stop-w-o-k-e-activism-and-critical-race-theory-in-schools-and-corporations/

Friedman, J., LaFrance, S., & Meehan, K. (2023, August 23). *Educational intimidation.* PEN America. https://pen.org/report/educational-intimidation/

Gallardo, J. (2023, July 31). *Library director fired after refusing to resign.* Gillette News Record. https://www.gillettenewsrecord.com/news/local/article_748da054-d543-595c-896c-4d020be9570d.html

Gonzalez, X. (2023, May 15). *The librarians are not okay.* The Atlantic. https://www.theatlantic.com/ideas/archive/2023/03/book-bans-censorship-librarian-challenges/673398/

Greenfield, N. M. (2023, May 6). *Professors are victims as DeSantis' culture war hots up.* University World News. https://www.universityworldnews.com/post.php?story=20230506085146565

Guynn, J. (2022, April 22). *Why is DeSantis fighting Disney? It's a warning to 'woke' big business to stay out of culture wars.* USA Today. https://www.usatoday.com/story/money/2022/04/22/disney-desantis-florida-woke-capital/7415134001/

Kim, J. (2023, January 22). *Florida says AP class teaches critical race theory. Here's what's really in the course.* NPR. https://www.npr.org/2023/01/22/1150259944/florida-rejects-ap-class-african-american-studies

Klas, M. E., Mower, L, & Cohen, H. (2021, October 30). *University of Florida prohibits professors from testifying in voting rights suit.* Tampa Bay Times. https://www.tampabay.com/news/florida-politics/2021/10/30/university-of-florida-prohibits-professors-from-testifying/

Mazzei, P., Harris, E. A., & Alter, A. (2023, April 22). *Florida at Center of Debate as School Book Bans Surge Nationally.* The New York Times. https://www.nytimes.com/2023/04/22/books/book-ban-florida.html

Merriam-Webster. (n.d.). Woke. In *Merriam-Webster.com dictionary*. Retrieved September 2023, from: https://www.merriam-webster.com/dictionary/woke

Montanaro, D. (2023, July 19). *What does the word 'woke' really mean, and where does it come from?* NPR. https://www.npr.org/2023/07/19/1188543449/what-does-the-word-woke-really-mean-and-where-does-it-come-from

Mudde, C. (2023, February 6). *What is behind Ron DeSantis's Stop-Woke Act?* The Guardian Online. https://www.theguardian.com/commentisfree/2023/feb/06/what-is-behind-ron-desantis-stop-woke-act

Pendharkar, E. (2023, April 19). *Florida just expanded the 'Don't Say Gay' law. Here's what you need to know.* EducationWeek. https://www.edweek.org/policy-politics/florida-just-expanded-the-dont-say-gay-law-heres-what-you-need-to-know/2023/04

Romano, A. (2020, October 9). *A history of "wokeness" Stay woke: how a Black activist watchword got co-opted in the culture war.* Retrieved October 2023, from Vox.com: https://www.vox.com/culture/21437879/stay-woke-wokeness-history-origin-evolution-controversy

Sterbenz, C. (2023, September/October). How we fight back. *American Libraries*, pp. 28-33.

Wiggins, C. (2023, March 16). *Anti-Woke Book's Author Humiliated, Can't Define 'Woke' in Interview.* The Advocate. https://www.advocate.com/media/conservative-author-cant-woke

Williams, J. T. (2022, November). *One of the biggest critics of "woke" was forced to define what the word actually means–Here's what was said.* okayplayer. https://www.okayplayer.com/news/ron-desantis-woke-defintion.html

Woodcock, C. (2023, June 25). *College librarians in Florida are hoping for the best, but preparing for the worst.* Slate. https://slate.com/human-interest/2023/06/libraries-florida-dei-crt-college.html

Enemies Within the Gates
Contending with Internal Censorship Challenges

Jason D. Phillips

Introduction

Censorship challenges in academic libraries are not the norm, much less internal challenges. Perhaps this is because of the nature of academic libraries, given their mission to collect widely in order to serve the teaching, learning, and research needs of their respective communities. Or perhaps it's that the primary users of academic libraries are adults. In recent times, these challenges seem to be the province of school and public libraries. Yet censorship of LGBTQ+ materials *can* and *does* happen in academic libraries, in perhaps a less public or spectacular fashion than as seen recently with school and public libraries.

The literature on censorship in *academic* libraries seems largely (but not entirely) dedicated to discussions about censorship during the collection development process. There is ample scholarship describing the debates over acquiring materials potentially labeled as "controversial," especially LGBTQ+ books. For example, Tsang described this as a form of internal censorship where selectors opt to not purchase materials (nonselection) because they believe the material is "irrelevant, immoral or controversial" (1990, p. 168). More recently, Cooke describes not selecting books for fears of retaliation, age-appropriateness (or other reasons) as "soft censorship" (2023, para. 7).

Censorship may also take the form of quietly removing books from a library's collection by side-stepping any challenge processes a library has in place. Tsang noted "almost as endemic as nonacquisition" of

LGBTQ+ books is library workers borrowing books and not returning them, removing them from the shelf and not reshelving them, or even theft (1990, p. 169). Cooke also includes the quiet removal of books for their racial, sexual, or homosexual themes in her definition of "soft censorship" (2023, para. 7).

Academic libraries, despite their scope and mission, are not immune to censorship challenges. In this chapter, I document instances of internal censorship challenges to LGBTQ+ materials from library staff, librarians, and a former library director, conceivably motivated by moral objections to the content of the material or fears of public reaction or retaliation. These actions are "in direct opposition to the library profession's core values, the ALA's Freedom to Read Statement, and the ALA's Library Bill of Rights and are wholly detrimental to library collections and offerings" (Cooke, 2023, para. 10). Hindsight is 20-20, and I, after much reflection following these events, try to provide guidance on how to avoid or navigate these situations through a robust collection development policy, outreach to faculty, and internal conversations to head off potential internal censorship challenges.

Background Information

This chapter discusses my experiences at a smaller, regional public university located in the South. The university transitioned from a community college to a four-year, bachelor's granting institution in the early 2000s when it joined a state university system. Later, in the mid-2010s, it started master's degree programs. The geographic isolation of the university lends itself to largely employing staff from the area with little to no experience at other institutions. Many of the faculty who move to the area for employment tend to stay. So, by 2013, many of the university's employees—both faculty and staff—pre-dated the transition to university status, an important distinction because, in many respects, they continued to act and think like the university was still a community college.

The library was no exception. Most of its staff had worked there for decades. The collection and policies continued to reflect its former status as a community college. This created a static environment fostering the "we've always done it this way" mentality, where proposed changes to bring the library up to current standards of practice were treated with suspicion and met with fierce resistance.

Prior to 2016, the library did not actively engage in campus activities, with two notable exceptions: freshman orientation sessions and a biennial event where patrons would tour the first floor of the library, collecting stamps as they learned about the different services and collections from each stop. Our primary function was to provide reference services, order books, and teach library instruction sessions, and very little else in the way of outreach or engagement.

Why Should Academic Libraries Collect Diverse Materials?

In addition to supporting the teaching, learning, and research needs of your campus, an academic library should strive to build a collection that speaks to the diversity of the human experience and the population it serves. This is true with any leisure materials—books, newspapers, magazines, etc.—collected by the library. I would go a step further to say this is particularly incumbent upon academic libraries located in geographically remote areas where cultural opportunities, such as community building, events, or feeling a sense of place for the LGBTQ+ community, are limited or non-existent. The academic library almost serves as an oasis for those experiencing a sense of cultural isolation.

This sense of cultural or communal isolation is particularly keen for the LGBTQ+ community in this region. There are only one or two public establishments (bars) to serve as a gathering spot for LGBTQ+ people as well as a local nonprofit equality center that previously provided occasional activities such as Pride events and support group meetings. The college campus includes an LGBTQ+ student organization whose active status has varied over the years, but which at the time of the events under discussion (fall 2018) had a small membership and was in the process of restarting after it fell into abeyance. While I never personally experienced or witnessed overt acts of hostility toward members of the community or myself, the region's culturally conservative and religious values discourage many from leading open lives outside of the closet; you see many individuals come out publicly later in life.

Setting the Scene

Events in 2016 and beyond would prove consequential for the library in terms of increased campus outreach and engagement activities as well as the acquisition of diversity, equity, and inclusion (DEI) materials. While another newer librarian and I had attempted to introduce changes to the status quo, the tipping point was the hiring of a new access services librarian. Early in this person's tenure, at a weekly staff meeting, they proposed that the library host a Banned Books Week event and display, an idea greeted with general acceptance. Following the meeting, I searched the catalog for banned book titles against the lists provided by ALA. Finding that the library had few of the titles on the list, I used my retrospective collection development funds to purchase as many of these banned book titles as were then available. These titles would feature prominently in the library's Banned Books Week display and a corresponding event where librarians, faculty, and students read aloud passages from banned titles.

Part of our efforts to create diversity in the library's holdings was the addition of a regional periodical, the Gayly, serving the LGBTQ+ community. This periodical includes coverage of events and other activities in the region, which another librarian and I thought would be of interest to the campus LGBTQ+ population. Through connections with the local equality center, I was able to establish the library as a distribution point for free copies of the Gayly, with one copy added to the library's periodicals section. The free community copies reside on a table at the library's entrance with other free local periodicals, and all the copies are taken by the time the next month's issue is delivered.

Efforts to bring the library up to current standards of practice received a boost with the retirement of four longtime employees starting in December 2016-May 2019 and the arrival of new, fresh perspectives. The new library director increased the allocation for retrospective collection development, and for the first time, we had an opportunity to collect LGBTQ+ titles in earnest. Some of the titles purchased had direct relevance to the state or region, including works of fiction. The development of the DVD and graphic novels collections would also soon follow, which also included LGBTQ+ and other DEI-centric titles. The student success librarian and I, building on the campus outreach and engagement efforts started by the aforementioned access services librarian (who left in early 2018), drastically increased the library's activities and events with partnerships with campus units or registered student organizations. New activities included monthly displays of books aligning with various heritage months or special topics and hosting a drag storytime in December 2018. Fallout from the furor over the drag storytime chilled future LGBTQ+-oriented events (see chapter "At What Cost? The Personal Stakes of Intellectual Freedom"), though the library continued to collect LGBTQ+ materials and continued book displays for Pride month.

Internal Censorship Challenges to LGBTQ+ Materials

This progress, namely in terms of building up our collections, also proved to be a source of internal challenges. These challenges emerged from long-time librarians and library staff, and in one instance, a new library school graduate working in a staff position. Though long-time employees were resistant to changes, these challenges seemed, from my perspective, to be primarily motivated by fear of the potential public response, homophobia and transphobia, and self-censorship.

Another librarian and I also faced an uncomfortable situation in which the library director showed active hostility toward the acquisition of LGBTQ+ materials. The director approved the retrospective collection development of books for other underrepresented communities (African Americans, Asian Americans, Hispanic Americans, and Native Americans), but the director also feared the public response to LGBTQ+ books or materials in the collection. I submitted an order for Stonewall Book Award titles that was quietly denied behind the scenes, a situation I would not discover until later. (See chapter "Building and Defending LGBTQ+ Collections.")

First Example: LGBTQ+ Periodical

The director appeared to feel some surprise and consternation on discovering the aforementioned regional LGBTQ+ periodical. Like many of the processes and policies at the library, there was no formal or documented policy or process for adding free periodicals to the collection. Previously, I, as a then-new employee, sought permission to add a locally produced regional economic outlook newsletter to the library's collection. The library director approved the request in a dismissive fashion, skeptical that any patrons would want to use the periodical. Accustomed to this informal manner of handling free publications, neither myself nor another librarian formally raised the addition of the periodical to the director or in a staff meeting. Instead, as part of our normal work activities, we worked with library staff to create the space in the periodicals section, add it to the library's catalog, and include it in the list of periodicals to receive and process. Upon discovery, the director went to our respective offices and sharply interrogated us about the library serving as a distribution point and the addition of the title to the collection. No action was taken, but the author and the other librarian shared an uneasy feeling from the experience.

Second Example: Internal Book Challenge

Following on the heels of this incident, we faced an internal censorship challenge that would prove to be a more consequential and long-lasting debate. The latest edition of *The Joy of Gay Sex* by Charles Silverstein and Felice Picano—a classic in its area, but one (given its subject matter) with some explicit text and graphic illustrations, was purchased as part of our aforementioned acquisition of banned book titles. A library staff member, objecting to the explicit content and graphic illustrations, brought this item to a library staff meeting and demanded a justification for adding it to the collection. (Incidentally, Alex Comfort's heterosexual counterpart *The Joy of Sex* was part of the library's collection, and to the best of my knowledge, the staff member never raised any objection to the presence of that item.) Three librarians spoke up in defense of the book, arguing that it was purchased as part of the banned books project and that it has cultural significance and importance to the LGBTQ+ community. Those on both sides of the discussion sought faculty input. Then, one morning in October 2016, the director walked into my office and, in response to this situation, said, "A good librarian does not jeopardize his library or the institution that is the source of his paycheck." This felt like a veiled threat, which I then reported to the director's supervisor. The director retired in December 2016, leaving the situation unresolved.

When a new library director began employment in March 2017, I once again raised the issue of adding *The Joy of Gay Sex*—still in the building, still not cataloged—to the collection. The director supported this and sent it back to the technical services department for processing. At the following staff meeting, the aforementioned staff member renewed objections to the content and its addition to the collection. A librarian and another staff member suggested keeping the title behind the circulation desk. This caused concern from some of the other librarians: a closed-stacks or restricted access collection creates an additional barrier between patrons and the book, one where patrons may be reluctant to request the title, especially if the request might "out" someone who is still in the closet (Tsang, 1990, p. 167). The meeting ended with no resolution or action taken, and it remained that way for several months.

They say a dying mule kicks hardest. Before retiring, the staff member took the previous objections, and the book itself, to a university administrator. I do not know who made the final decision, but the book was removed from the library's collection. I would only learn of its final disposition several months later.

Third Example: Hiding Books

The next example involves internal censorship bordering on targeted microaggressions from the aforementioned staff member. One of this employee's responsibilities was processing new books to add to the collection and then place them on the new books bookcases. The library has three bookcases located within the entry atrium that prominently displays books new to the library. These bookcases also include book stands to highlight notable titles. On numerous occasions, librarians would select an LGBTQ+ title of particular importance, such as being relevant to the region or written by a local author, to display. The staff member would remove the LGBTQ+ books from the book stands and replace them with different titles; ironically, two of the victims were *Boy Erased* and *Out in the Country: Youth, Media, and Queer Visibility in Rural America*. On other occasions, it became clear that the new LGBTQ+ books were being placed directly in the stacks after processing rather than going on display.

Fourth Example: Creating Separate Collections

The final example involved the new library school graduate working as a staff member and a case of self-censorship within the collection. Like this person's predecessor, the new employee was in charge of physically processing new acquisitions for the library's collection. The library started a graphic novel collection at the request of faculty who teach using graphic novels or whose courses are explicitly about graphic novels as a form of art or literature. When processing new graphic novels, this staff member made the decision to catalog ostensibly "adult" graphic novels in a section separate from the main graphic novels collection—the rationale being concern that these "adult" graphic novels would be shelved side-by-side with young adult titles and that minors might wind up exposed to adult material. This was later brought up as an aside during a staff meeting, and steps were taken to quickly remedy the situation and reintegrate the targeted titles into the main graphic novel collection.

Discussion: Lessons Learned

This was years ago. Circumstances have drastically changed since the events under discussion took place, and the library in question is now in a situation where its professionals enjoy great latitude and support from administration in collection decisions. The library's atmosphere has drastically shifted. But these examples were all potentially preventable. Learning from these experiences, I have the following suggestions to offer:

Collection Development Policy

What these situations have in common, aside from all having taken place at the hands of the library's own staff, was that they could very well have been forestalled by a solid collection development policy. Unfortunately, as previously noted in the chapter "Building and Defending LGBTQ+ Collections," the library's collection development policy dated from an earlier time and consisted of a single, typed page. It was not publicly available and resided in a locked drawer in the director's office. My co-editor and I have already discussed in that chapter the necessity for a library to have such a policy to guard against external challenges. This is also a way to head internal challenges off at the pass.

A library's collection development policy needs to be a living document that is periodically reviewed and updated to reflect changes in the library's policies, collections, or germane matters. This policy should also explicitly address censorship, offer a specific mechanism for challenging items in the collection, and define the collection's scope. It should be publicly available and discussed with new employees, both internal to the library and with administrators in the library's reporting line.

When was the last time your library's collection development policy was updated? You cannot foresee every possible situation and document accordingly, but having some fundamentals in place, as described above, may spare you from the difficulties we experienced.

Faculty Outreach

The internal censorship challenge to *The Joy of Gay Sex* ultimately found no satisfactory resolution. In this situation, the librarians were left standing on their own seemingly against those who, evidently, did not want to see this item in the collection. The sub rosa nature of the situation, where the staff member escalated the challenge to an administrator's attention and the book's final status was determined behind closed doors by parties unknown, caught us unawares and we were unable to mount a response. Had we known in advance, then what other level of appeal could there be in a situation like this?

Outreach preceding the actual incident of censorship could have helped. We did not have a proper collection development/challenge policy in place, but we could have alerted interested faculty to the fact that there was a censorship incident unfolding, and perhaps they'd have intervened on our behalf. Everyone in the community a library serves—particularly an academic library—needs to be aware of the library's services, and, by extension, of how services and collections stand to suffer in the event of censorship.

In properly cultivating the grounds for external appeal or support, a library needs to communicate its worth to all of its stakeholders. In an academic library, this is what liaison work and outreach are meant to accomplish. One clear goal of outreach of this nature is to get interested parties using the library: to get faculty to recognize the value that library personnel and collections offer. Outreach in this vein, though, can also build stones in the metaphorical wall against administrative decisions interfering with collections. This can lead to letters of support or even more action in favor of intellectual freedom.

During the internal debate regarding *The Joy of Gay Sex*, the library director, seeking other perspectives on the matter, brought the book to a psychology faculty member. The faculty member evaluated the book and wrote a statement noting that "I would defend the right for the book to be available." Academic librarians can leverage the expertise of the faculty to give specific and pointed evidence for the value a title may possess for their teaching or research. Given that academic libraries exist to support the teaching, learning, and research of a university, these statements can provide ironclad proof of the necessity for including a challenged title in the library's collection.

Another recommendation is to appeal to other interested parties who can raise their voices on a library's behalf. In our specific situation, we could have brought the title to the attention of the Faculty Senate's Library Committee or the Faculty Senate itself. Other possibilities may exist if your university has a chapter of the American Association of University Professors (AAUP) or other union-like organizations that can address or protest such violations of academic and intellectual freedom.

Language and Attitude Matter

Libraries are often delicately poised between their popular imagination image as treasured storehouses of knowledge and what library workers themselves know to be their libraries' forward-thinking practices. In hitting on the right standpoint for developing potentially controversial collections and carrying out potentially controversial programming, libraries need to work with a degree of finesse that can be productively informed by keen awareness of the community and its potential attitudes.

When a library advocates for itself, language and attitude matter. One frequently hears the confrontational statement that "a good library has something in it to offend everyone," but another standpoint for this perspective is the idea that "this library is positively representing its community in these particular ways." Representation need not be a matter of "offense," but simply of ensuring that those who have not previously found their identities reflected in the library are now doing so. Treating the full representation of minority identities and controversial ideas as a matter of "offense" aggressively counterposes them to the majority, rather than accepting them as legitimate parts of the spectrum of identities and the ideological spectrum. The existence and representation of minorities is not offensive to anyone except bigots.

Libraries, though no longer as quiet as they once were, still have a hard time raising their voices when it comes to advocating for themselves and for the collections and programs they manage. There are certain categories of challenged material that, to be frank, are significantly easier to defend than others. Popular classics simply have more cultural cache. The likes of *To Kill a Mockingbird* and *1984* may still see challenges, and while these challenges are as egregious as ever, an appeal to the public on behalf of these materials doesn't carry the same potential for discomfort as an appeal on behalf of the more explicit *Gender Queer: A Memoir* or, indeed, *The Joy of Gay Sex*. But we owe it to the public we serve to advocate for the value of all these materials with the same passion—to lean, at times, into the uncomfortable.

Internal Conversations

Librarians with good intentions can disagree about whether certain materials belong in a collection. To give one example, a copy of *Mein Kampf* came back heavily damaged and the question rose whether it ought to be replaced. A replacement for the library's edition would have taken extra effort to acquire, since the publisher appeared to have taken it out of circulation, and an older translation is freely available online from Project Gutenberg. One librarian said yes, replace it, the other said no. This is an example of sincere good-faith disagreement.

Disagreement in bad faith, though, assumes that one particular perspective is inherently correct and that there is no room for debate. Again, this is where the final arbiter, the well-articulated and solidly grounded collection development policy, can benefit a library. No policy can address every possible situation in the level of detail it merits, and the final court of appeal in any library must ultimately be the librarians' professional judgment, but backed with a policy that is mindful of the community the library serves, such disputes may wind up resolved without acrimony.

In the case of *The Joy of Gay Sex*, consider an alternate path along which the situation could have unfolded. A staff member was left uncomfortable on seeing its graphic imagery and text. The staff member reacted by challenging this item's inclusion. Would the outcome have been different if there was additional communication between librarians and staff—for example, a statement that read "we are developing a collection of frequently challenged books, and you might see some discomfort-inducing titles rolling in as new acquisitions?" There was a potential learning opportunity for the new library graduate who attempted to create a separate graphic novel collection, namely that juvenilia collections are there as teaching materials for an adult audience—the primary consumer is not intended to be children or young adults.

Listen to concerns; sometimes people just want to feel heard. Then take the opportunity to chat about the collection development policy, the mission of academic libraries, and the need to collect materials that represent the full spectrum of the institution's community. The staff member may still resist adding it to the collection and they can then avail themselves of the challenge procedures, but there is also a chance the situation could be amicably resolved. Or at least documented if needed in the future.

Responding to Microaggressions

Censorship can take on other forms aside from direct challenges. In the third example, I mentioned that the staff member was placing new LGBTQ-related materials directly in the stacks rather than on the new books shelves after processing them and removing LGBTQ titles from book stands if selected for display by a librarian. This amounted to the microaggressive exclusion of a particular aspect of identity from a crucial area for library discovery. The location of the new books shelves is in a high-traffic area of the library where patrons will pause, look, and check-out titles; our circulation counts attest to the correlation between visibility and use.

Keep microaggressions in mind in your library. Be aware that censorship, beyond the matter of collections, can also be a matter of targeting specific identities. Are challengers seeking to censor the subject matter of the book itself or are they also trying to censor any representation of specific identities or communities? These situations require that you have a clear policy and set of procedures, like for new books shelves, so it is not the sole discretion of an individual to include or leave out titles as they choose. Be sure to document instances observed in case this is needed later for disciplinary action.

Conclusion

Public and school libraries have been the recent focus of censorship challenges, but academic libraries should also remain vigilant. Keep your collection development policies up to date. Have conversations with your staff about what you collect and why you collect it. But in the face of challenges, seek out your allies: the faculty. Be proactive in communicating the value of a diverse collection. And remember, your academic library's collection may be the only place an LGBTQ+ person can see themselves positively reflected, an oasis in a culturally conservative desert.

References

Cooke, N. A. (2023). The calls are coming from inside the library! *Against the Grain, 35*(5), 32-34. https://issuu.com/against-the-grain/docs/nov_2023_v35-5/s/38488318

Tsang, D. (1990). Censorship of lesbian and gay materials by library workers. In *Gay and Lesbian Library Service*. Cal Gough and Ellen Greenblatt (Eds.). (pp. 166-170) McFarland and Co.

Part 3
"Research Says…":
LGBTQ+ Collections
and Services
Analysis

Collecting "Good Gay Books"
Gay Bibliographies and the American Library Association's Task Force on Gay Liberation

Lisa N. Johnston

> *High school libraries, community libraries, and the smaller college and university libraries as a matter of policy refuse to purchase 'good gay books'...*
>
> Louis Crew and Rictor Norton, "The Homophobic Imagination: An Editorial," 1974, p. 280

For the past several years, library staffers and readers have had to focus on keeping LGBTQ books in libraries, particularly in school and public libraries. How did librarians and their readers locate and acquire the "good gay books" Crew and Norton describe? In this chapter, I consider the challenges faced by academic librarians and the students and faculty they serve to locate materials and justify their purchase for academic library collections. I discuss the essential role the Gay Liberation Movement, library advocates, publishing, and particularly the American Library Association's (ALA) Task Force on Gay Liberation had on developing library collections in LGBTQ studies from its founding in 1970 to 1990. I refer to the resources as gay and lesbian for historical context.

A Young Lesbian Searches a Card Catalog Circa 1949

The gay rights and library advocate Barbara Gittings describes her experience seeking information in an academic library as a first-year student at Northwestern University. In her 1978 chapter "Combatting the Lies in the Libraries," Gittings defines her phrase "the lies in the libraries" on the basis of her experience as a first-year student at Northwestern University in 1949 (Gittings, 1978, p. 107). Gittings recounts a story familiar to countless LGBTQ+ students in which she visited the university library to find herself as a lesbian woman. Upon searching the card catalog, she found, instead, works that were "cruelly clinical (there's nothing about love) and always bad (being this way seems grim and hopeless)" (Gittings, 1978, p. 107). In mid-century library catalogs as prescribed by the Library of Congress, the controlled vocabulary on the subject of "homosexuality" included the terms "sexual deviance" and "perversion." To the young Barbara Gittings, this was the discovery of what she described as "the lie."

Gittings spent her time searching for fiction in Evanston-area libraries and, as discussed in her chapter, read Donald Webster Cory's 1951 book, *The Homosexual in America: A Subjective Approach*, which included two lengthy bibliographies. Introducing his "Check List of Novels and Dramas" in his volume, Cory notes that he believes the 22-page list is the most comprehensive to date (1951, p. 296). Gittings describes meeting Cory and joining the gay rights movement. Donald Webster Cory, a.k.a. Edward Sagarin, was a sociologist, writer, and activist whose 1951 work *The Homosexual in America*, was the first non-fiction account of gay culture authored by an out gay person. Because of this work, he was known as the "father of the homophile movement" (Johnson, 2019, p. 79). Another work she likely consulted in her research on herself was academic librarian Jeanette H. Foster's essential *Sex Variant Women in Literature: A Historical and Quantitative Survey* self-published with Vantage Press in 1956. It is doubtful the lists in these two publications would have escaped the attention of a determined Barbara Gittings.

Prior to the work of ALA's Task Force on Gay Liberation, readers found books more readily as consumers. Gay- and lesbian-focused newsletters, newspapers, and magazines produced by early organizations reliably included book reviews and bibliographies. Readers with the means to buy books could order new publications from the privacy of their own homes. The Mattachine Society's publication *ONE* included advertisements for mail-order books, membership plans for book services, reviews, and notably advertisements for the Cory Book Service (CBS), founded in 1952 by sociologist Donald Webster Cory, just one year after the publication of *The Homosexual in America* (Johnson, 2019, p. 67). In *Buying Gay*, historian David K. Johnson describes the CBS as the first business established exclusively to sell books to *gay readers* (2019). Other services would follow. San Francisco-based *Dorian Book Quarterly*, a catalog and review source directed at librarians, collectors, and their customers, stated itself as "Defending YOUR Freedom to Read" in its April-June 1963 issue (Dorian Book Quarterly, 1963, p. 32).

Barbara Gittings began her career as an activist and bibliographer in 1958 when she founded the East Coast chapter of the lesbian rights organization, Daughters of Bilitis. Its national publication, *The Ladder*, established itself as an essential resource from its first issue published in October 1956. Book lists and reviews were featured in every issue. Annotated bibliographies were compiled by the Research Committee and books listed were available through the Daughter of Bilitis Book Service. Barbara Gittings became *The Ladder's* editor in 1963 and served until 1966. The magazine was renamed *The Ladder: A Lesbian Review*. Barbara Gittings had the experience of collaborating closely with the bibliographer/reviewer of the monthly "Lesbiana" book review section, Gene Damon (Damon was a pseudonym used by Barbara Grier, founder of Naiad Press) (Gallo, 2010). In 1971, Gittings would bring her new expertise to ALA's Task Force on Gay Liberation.

Typed and Photocopied: The Task Force on Gay Liberation's First Bibliographies

The American Library Association's Task Force on Gay Liberation was founded in 1970 by librarian Israel Fishman who at first sought to establish a way for gay library staffers to meet one another at conferences. He explains, "My most basic motivation in forming the Task Force was that I was lonely, and I wanted to meet other gay people— what could be more natural?" (Fishman, 1998, p. 108). One of Fishman's founding goals was for librarians to use their training to improve materials holdings on the topic of homosexuality in American libraries (Gittings, 1998, p. 81).

In 1971, Gittings, then a journalist reporting on the American Library Association's conference, learned the Task Force members were working on a bibliography of non-fiction titles. The organization's volunteers compiled their first list of the "most positive" resources or "good gay books" (Gittings, 1998, p. 83). The first bibliography lists 20 books, 12 pamphlets, and six citations for articles in periodicals. The titles included easy-to-acquire, best-selling works on human sexuality by Dr. Alfred C. Kinsey, 1948's *Sexual Behavior in the Human Male* and 1953's

Sexual Behavior in the Human Female. The volunteers compiling the first *Gay Bibliography* wanted to include books that were both familiar, hence the Kinsey bestsellers, and titles that might be new to collection development librarians. These titles by Kinsey appear in both editions of the 1971 *Gay Bibliography* as well as the 1974 revision (ALA Task Force on Gay Liberation, 1971-76, 1980). Pamphlets listed include publications on law and psychology, as well as four titles published by the Council on Religion and the Homosexual. All publications include addresses for ordering. The six articles recommended also include themes of law and religion that would lead them to be more likely considered by collections specialists in public and academic libraries.

This first bibliography was not titled *Gay Bibliography* as editions that followed would be, but "Brief List of Materials on Homosexuality." It was distributed to attendees of the January 1971 meeting of the American Library Association in Detroit. The last line on the verso lists the professional address of Israel Fishman, then a librarian at Upsala College. Readers were encouraged to write to the Task Force with their comments and suggestions for the next edition which promised to be annotated and to include more titles. The first bibliography was composed on a typewriter and printed on both sides of one sheet of off-white paper. The publication appeared as simply a bibliography that might be included in an academic publication submitted for review. There were no logos representing the Task Force, ALA, or the gay liberation movement on the document. Its lack of graphic design was due to a small budget, a small group of volunteers undoubtedly with limited time on their hands, and perhaps, was also to convey a sort of anonymity so ALA attendees, particularly closeted library workers, would be comfortable picking up a copy for themselves and sharing it with their collections specialists and library users.

The bibliography's second edition, distributed in June 1971, was a more polished leaflet: three pages printed on eye-catching, orange paper with the header reading *A Gay Bibliography* in bold lettering, subtitled: "A Brief List of Materials on Homosexuality" (ALA Task Force on Gay Liberation, 1971). It featured a GAY IS GOOD logo on the front page. As promised, the bibliography was revised and expanded to 48 items again including books, pamphlets, articles, and a new feature, periodicals published specifically for lesbian and gay readers. *A Gay Bibliography* was again passed by hand to librarians in attendance. The bibliography's description clearly states its intent "to draw attention to some worthwhile materials that have received little publicity, as well as to emphasize items that tend to move away from standard negative views about homosexuality" (Task Force, 1971, p. 3).

On the last page, it is noted that the Task Force was compiling an updated annotated bibliography of yet more titles. Interested parties were to contact Barbara Gittings via her post office box in Philadelphia. Three thousand copies of the 1971 revised edition were "aggressively leafletted" to ALA members (Gittings, 1998, p. 83). In her announcement of the revision published in the January 1972 issue of *American Libraries*. Gittings explains that one of the motivations for the Gay Liberation Task Force's decision to compile and distribute its own bibliographies was the volunteers' concern about the lack of listed materials on "women homosexuals" included in the bibliography distributed by the Homosexual Information Center, as well as the need for a listing of more positive publications (Gittings, 1972. p. 21).

A GAY BIBLIOGRAPHY

A Brief List of Materials on Homosexuality
Prepared by: TASK FORCE ON GAY LIBERATION [Text]
Social Responsibilities Round Table, American Library Association

Revised June 1971

This list is intended to draw attention to some worthwhile materials that have received little publicity, as well as to emphasize items that tend to move away from standard negative views about homosexuality.

GAY IS GOOD

Figure 1 (Task Force on Gay Liberation, 1971). Used with permission from the American Library Association.

The Publishing Industry Listened and the Bibliographies Grew

In her 1998 essay "Gays in Library Land: The Gay and Lesbian Task Force of the American Library Association: The First Sixteen Years," included in the essential anthology, *Daring to Find Our Names: The Search for Lesbigay Library History* edited by James V. Carmichael, Jr., Gittings remarks that the publishing industry had transformed after 1969's Stonewall Uprising. Prior to 1969, a majority of publications on LGBTQ+ themes were written by straight writers pathologizing and "dissect[ing] us," and by 1971 a new vanguard of LGBTQ+ authors were signing with prominent publishers (Gittings, 1998, p. 84). This change coincided with the Task Force's goal to change library collections, and hence the *Gay Bibliographies* compiled and distributed in June 1972 were more challenging to compile. "Now the first title on the list was no longer Atkinson's *Sexual Morality* but Abbott and Love's *Sappho Was a Right on Woman*" (ALA Task Force on Gay Liberation, 1971-76, 1980). By 1974, the 4th edition of the bibliography began including audio visual resources, but with the caveat: "We recommend that non-gay audiences who use these audio-visual materials do so only with knowledgeable gay persons present to answer questions" (ALA Task Force on Gay Liberation, 1971-76, 1980, p. 16). It had a print run of 30,000 copies distributed on request to librarians and members of the reading public. The 1980 edition increased to 16 pages, and there was a small fee attached to cover printing expenses. Pricing was as follows; 1 or 2 copies—$1 each, 3 to 9 copies—85¢ each, and 10 or more copies—70¢. The front page of the 1980 edition reminds the reader of the efforts of the members of the Task Force: "This bibliography was prepared by gay people who donated their time and efforts and skills." The statement is followed by an explanation of the costs involved as well as a copyright notice, and ends with a plea, "Help us to keep on helping you, by getting additional copies of our bibliography from us, not from copiers!" (ALA Task Force on Gay Liberation, 1971-76, 1980, p. 27).

Between the years 1971 and 1980, the Task Force had produced and distributed six general gay bibliographies and had begun to compile lists of materials on specific topics or for specific audiences. One of their most significant of the shorter bibliographies was the 1976 project *Gay Books in Format for the Blind and Physically Handicapped*, compiled using both the 1975 and 1976 supplements to the *Gay Bibliographies* and resources listed in the Library of Congress Division for the Blind and Physically Handicapped. Other specialized lists compiled in the 1970s included resources for teachers, counselors, religious studies scholars, and a core list for public libraries. The practice of compiling specialized lists continues today. All of the bibliographies and other publications have been digitized and are available through the American Library Association Archives maintained by the University of Illinois.[1]

Though the focus of this chapter is on the bibliographies, the Task Force's Gay Book Award, established in 1971, remains one of the premier

---

1   https://digital.library.illinois.edu/collections/2beaea30-4b0d-0136-4f6d-0050569601ca-5

honors for queer-themed literature (American Library Association, 2009, p. 21). In 1975, the winner included a bibliography. The award winner—one of the most significant works in the new field of gay studies—*Homosexuality: Lesbians and Gay Men in Society, History, and Literature*, published by Arno Press in 1975, collects 56 reprints of documents in English, French, and German dating from the late 19th century to the early 1970s. *A Gay Bibliography: Eight Bibliographies on Lesbian and Male Homosexuality* was one of the volumes. These annotated bibliographies were printed between 1958 and 1966 and included work by Gene Damon and popular science fiction and fantasy author Marion Zimmer Bradley. Jonathan N. Katz is an American historian specializing in gender and sexuality. His intent with this collection and compilation of bibliographies was to provide scholars with the basic materials needed to plan and establish courses (Gittings, 1978). Gittings quotes Katz on gay studies: "The development of gay studies is not a matter of academic interest only. Our rediscovery of our forgotten history, and our new knowledge of ourselves, will provide us with the spiritual nourishment we need for living, loving, and surviving in a genocidal society—for militant struggle against what Christopher Isherwood has aptly called 'the heterosexual dictatorship'" (Gittings, 1978, p. 113). Katz's Arno Press collection of reprints published in their original languages gave academic libraries a ready-made beginning to collecting for queer studies.

Gay Librarians Collecting for the New Gay Studies

Though abundant, curated scholarly and popular-press bibliographies were available to academic librarians by the mid-1970s, homophobic library workers remained an obstacle to overcome. Task Force founder Israel Fishman was employed as a circulation and reference librarian at Upsala College from 1970 to 1974. He describes the college library's technical services librarian refusing to process LGBTQ+ materials he brought to her. If he ordered in this subject area, acquisitions would languish uncatalogued. Due to an unsupportive environment, hostile coworkers, and as he explains, his own lack of maturity, this would be his final library position (Fishman, 1998, p. 110).

My chapter is prefaced by a quotation from an editorial by two scholars of literature. A special edition of the journal, *College English*, was published in November 1974. Titled "The Homosexual Imagination," this issue featured "The Homophobic Imagination: An Editorial" by guest editors Louis Crew and Rictor Norton. Crew and Norton analyze the effects that homophobia has on the study of literature and the literary imagination itself and consider the role of censorship beyond interpretation of literary works and biographies of authors. They list the contributors to the "excommunication" of homosexual literary history, including academic publishing and library services (Crew & Norton, p. 277). The regulation of gay and lesbian library materials to "cherry cabinets" (Crew & Norton, p. 280) or caged stacks in academic libraries can be blamed on the librarians' perception that any writing on homosexuality falls into the category of pornography. The act of shelving these books in a locked area, or in some cases not cataloging them, effectively disappears the works and the authors. The collection policies are rightfully called into question. Have all types of libraries had policies that do not allow the purchase of what Crew and Norton name "good gay books?" These "good gay books" are not unlike the titles included in the *Gay Bibliography* series, in that they present a more positive or at least balanced view of homosexuality that Crew and Norton request of academic libraries.

This edited issue of *College English* closes with a "Checklist of Resources." Crew and Norton, along with their literature colleague, Louis Crompton, curated this bibliography, thoughtfully combining scholarly works with popular magazines, newspapers, and directories for the gay and lesbian community. The authors rightfully address the lack of access to gay and lesbian newspapers and popular magazines as an erasure of culture by the libraries that refuse to subscribe to even a few titles, no matter how inexpensive they may be, thus depriving future as well as current scholars of primary research (Crew & Norton, 1974, p. 280). Incidentally, the ALA Task Force on Gay Liberation's bibliography series, described as "invaluable," and a 1974 bibliographic essay by John J. Crowden featured in *Choice* was included in that resource list (Checklist of Resources, 1974, p. 401).

Published since 1964, *Choice* is a book review journal produced by the Association for College and Research Libraries (ACRL). *Choice* is considered an essential resource for collection specialists in academic libraries and gives more support to librarians in justifying purchases for their collections. The bibliographic essay "The Love that Dares Now Speak its Name: Homosexuality" by John J. Crowden, a sociology professor at Berea College, includes discussion of books and journals, and even newsletters specific to organizations both local and national. Crowden writes a short disclaimer, explaining the need for librarians to review items "with an eye to 'community standards.'" There could be nudity, a "free use of the English language, and titillating ads and personals" (Crowden, 1974, p. 210). Would these works be regulated to the "cherry cabinets" Crew and Norton decry? Unlike the Gay Task Force's distributed bibliographies that clearly state their focus will be on works that are positive and supportive of gay and lesbian people, Crowder specifically includes four works that "do not argue for the life style [*sic*] of the homosexual" (Crowden, 1974, p. 210). For example, William Aaron's book, *Straight: A Heterosexual Talks About His Homosexual Past* (published in 1972 by Doubleday) instead considers conversion therapy to be an option (Crowden, 1974, p. 222). It is likely he is considering a collection development policy's best practice, both then and today, presenting different sides of an issue.

Interspersed with advertisements for microfiche readers were ads for three works in the area of gay and lesbian studies, the most significant being *The Journal of Homosexuality*—"The first serious journal on homosexuality from the professional community"—published by Haworth Press beginning in 1974 (Crowden, 1974, p. 219). Crowden includes information about the journal in his essay, noting the publication will be for "professionals in the fields of psychology, clinical social work, psychiatry, school counseling, education, criminology, sociology, and anthropology" (Crowden, 1974, p. 210). Though the journal will be "sympathetic" editorially, it will not adopt what it describes as an "advocacy position" (Crowden, 1974, p. 210). *The Journal of Homosexuality* is currently published by Routledge and as of this writing has just completed volume 70. The resources listed by Crowden and the Arno Press series together were an ideal cornerstone of a gay and lesbian studies collection for a liberal arts college library in the mid-1970s.

Librarians and Their Readers Lobby for Good Gay Books

While the availability of the *Gay Bibliographies*, Crowden's 1974 *Choice* article, and the Task Force's Gay Book Award list provided ready-made collection development tools for academic libraries, the question of how readers could lobby the library for their purchase and access remained. In 1979, the Gay Task Force produced the publication *Censored, Ignored, Overlooked, Too Expensive? How to Get Gay Materials into Libraries: A Guide to Library Selection Policies for the Non-Librarian*. The bright yellow cover was designed to get the attention of conference attendees who might be passing through the ALA exhibits area

(Sherbo, 1979, cover). This publication directly addresses censorship in collection development. The Task Force members have made the lists, and now it would be up to the library users to lobby the collection specialists in their libraries. The first section begins with anecdotal evidence of the lack of, and "cherry cabinet" location of, materials in an academic library: "At a New England liberal arts college, the library had only twelve books on homosexuality that the college's gay group considered positive. All twelve titles were kept behind the circulation desk and had to be asked for" (Miller, 1979, p. 1). The authors provide a detailed, jargon-free primer on the issues of collecting these materials, then they encourage library users to take matters into their own hands using the *Gay Bibliography* series as well as lists in other publications. The authors recommend consulting a variety of popular review resources such as *The New York Times*. The publication explains the importance of book reviews in journals librarians consult—*Choice* is specifically cited—that can be particularly influential (Miller, 1979, p. 3). Those library users seeking our LGBTQ+ information can become collection evaluators who get these books added to libraries in direct opposition to users who challenge the inclusion of these resources. In academic libraries, the authors explain, policies may dictate that materials support the curriculum. If an institution does not offer or plan to offer a "gay studies" course, readers should frame their arguments for the inclusion of a title to consider the interdisciplinarity of the field. Residential colleges could also argue that libraries need to provide LGBTQ materials in support of their students.

By the 1980s there were abundant lists of library materials and contact information for librarians seeking advice regarding collections to support gay and lesbian studies and student organizations. Included in the pioneering 1990 anthology *Gay and Lesbian Library Service* edited by librarians Cal Gough and Ellen Greenblatt, are articles on collection development that remain relevant. In her chapter "Collecting Gay and Lesbian Materials in an Academic Library," Suzy Taraba describes collecting due to increased academic interest in gay and lesbian studies, addressing not only the need for the library's support of the institution's curriculum, but the extracurricular needs of students in particular (1990, p. 27). In her chapter, she includes a sample proposal for her university library's collection development body and library administration. Taraba lists the meetings she conducted with stakeholders on her campus as examples for other collection development librarians to follow as part of a proposal. She emphasizes the importance of the new collection to the institution's curriculum. The proposal also outlines the steps taken to survey the current holdings and an outline of budget and action items (Taraba, 1990, p. 34).

Taraba's research remains relevant today, particularly considering the changes in laws that govern some state education systems that imperil academic freedom. The recent laws can be vague enough to make academic collections librarians pause and consider their state-funded budgets. Will every purchase be scrutinized? Librarians in 2023 can modify existing collections policies by looking back on Taraba's sample proposal from 1990. Taraba's chapter can easily be adapted for the challenging times for higher education in states like Florida and Texas.

Daniel Tsang's chapter in the same anthology, "Censorship of Lesbian and Gay Materials by Library Workers," concerns self-censorship by either closeted or out LGBTQ library workers (1990, p. 166). The scenarios and experiences he describes reflect the experience of Israel Fishman in the early 1970s. Though Tsang's chapter was written 33 years ago, it is relevant today, particularly when the concept of self-censorship is considered. A collections specialist, out of concern for their materials budget being tracked for purchases that might be on the topic of sexuality, may simply stop collecting those materials out of fear of censorship by their library staff colleagues, their need to stay closeted, the threat of losing funding, or offending a library user who could then challenge titles, even in an academic setting (Tsang, 1990, p. 170).

Conclusion

In order to face challenges in higher education in states such as Florida, Texas, and Tennessee, it is helpful to look to the past experiences of those colleagues who worked to bring the collections into existence. These colleagues' actions provide both a reflection of how far we have come as academic librarians and a toolkit of sorts. The currently named ALA Rainbow Round Table has a rich history of combining stealth with visibility that, unfortunately, might still be of use today. One can also refer to the work of Suzy Taraba, who lists the steps to take in academic libraries. It was the early bibliographies found in scholarly works from the 1950s, the early periodicals, and most significantly it was the efforts of librarians and readers who aimed to change what Barbara Gittings aptly named the "lie in the library." The "good gay books" listed and analyzed by Norton and Crew, and the "worthwhile materials" listed by the Task Force on Gay Liberation, moved these resources from the closed stacks and cabinets to inclusion as essential parts of academic library collections. Now in the 21st century, it is the mission of librarians and the readers to keep them there. As academic librarians, we should look to the past as we plan for the future.

Recommended Resources

- American Association of School Librarians (AASL). *LGBTQ+ Materials in School Libraries*. AASL, 2018. https://standards.aasl.org/project/lgbtq/

  - Produced by a team of ALA Emerging Leaders, this valuable resource provides information on book challenges and patron privacy, as well as a list of materials. Its theme is ultimately to defend intellectual freedom, and that applies to all libraries. Materials can be adapted for an academic audience.

- The American Association of University Professors (AAUP). https://www.aaup.org/about-aaup

  - Established in 1915, the AAUP remains at the forefront of the protection of intellectual freedom in higher education. From the classroom faculty to the library, their extensive resources have been essential. Whether or not you have faculty status, your institution might have a chapter with members you can consult to locate helpful resources. Their spring 2023 issue of *Academe, Academic Libraries and Academic Librarians* (vol. 109, no.1) includes articles about censorship.

- Martin Garnar and Trina J. Magi, editors. *Intellectual Freedom Manual*. Tenth edition. ALA Editions, 2021. https://www.alastore.ala.org/content/intellectual-freedom-manual-tenth-edition

  - In its tenth edition, this resource is essential for academic libraries, particularly considering the current political climate. It contains all of ALA's statements, resources for book challenges, use of space, etc.

- Rainbow Round Table of the American Library Association. *Open to All: Serving the LGBTQIA+ Community in Your Library*. ALA, 2022. https://www.ala.org/rt/sites/ala.org.rt/files/content/RRT/rrt-open-to-all-toolkit-2022.pdf

- Though written for public and school librarians, this resource can easily be adapted to academic libraries, particularly those at residential liberal arts colleges where a library can have two roles, serving as a place of research and study and as a public library for the academic community.

• Rainbow Round Table of the American Library Association. *Professional Tools*. ALA, 2022. https://www.ala.org/rt/rrt/tools

  - The oldest professional organization for LGBTQIA+ professionals provides an updated list of links to resources from award books to those famed bibliographies. This vibrant community includes all types of library professionals, students, and retirees.

• Sydney Jordan and Tomaro Taylor, *LGBTQ+ Studies Business and Implementation Plan*. University of South Florida, 2022. https://lib.usf.edu/special-collections/wp-content/uploads/sites/13/2022/07/LGBTQ-Studies-Designed-Plan-FINAL-07192022-1.pdf

  - Jordan and Taylor are special collections librarians at the University of South Florida. Their plan can be adapted into a toolkit for LBGTQ+ collections in general, particularly when justifying the impact of a particular collection with an emphasis on subjects a state might find controversial is a necessity.

References

American Library Association. 2009) *Stonewall Book Awards list*. Rainbow Round Table. http://www.ala.org/rt/rrt/award/stonewall/honored

Checklist of Resources. (1974). *College English, 36*(3), 401–404. http://www.jstor.org/stable/374860

Cory, D. W. (1951). *The homosexual in America: A subjective approach*. Greenberg.

Crew, L. & Norton, R. (1974). The homophobic imagination: An editorial. *College English, 36*(3), 272–290. https://doi.org/10.2307/374839

Crowden, J. J. (1974). The love that dare now speak its name: homosexuality. *Choice, 11*(4), 209-227.

"Dorian Book Quarterly." *Dorian Book Quarterly*, April-June 1963, p. 32. *Archives of Sexuality and Gender*.

Fishman, I. D. (1998). Reclaiming a founding. In J. V. Carmichael, Jr. (Ed.) *Daring to Find Our Names: The Search for Lesbigay Library History* (pp. 107-113). Greenwood Press.

Foster, J. H. (1956). *Sex variant women in literature: a historical and quantitative survey.* Vantage Press.

Gallo, M. (2010). *Introduction. The Ladder: A Lesbian Review, 1956-1972: An Interpretation and Document Archive.* https://documents.alexanderstreet.com/d/1003268047

Gittings, B. (1972). Revised gay bibliography. *American Libraries, 3*(1), 21–21. http://www.jstor.org/stable/25618737

Gittings, B. (1978). Combatting the lies in the libraries. In Crew, L. (Ed.), *The Gay Academic* (pp. 107-120). ECT Publications.

Gittings, B, (1998). Gays in library land: the Gay and Lesbian Task Force of the American Library Association: The first sixteen years. In Carmichael, J. V., Jr. (Ed.), *Daring to Find Our Names: The Search for Lesbigay Library History* (pp. 66-80). Greenwood Press.

Gough, C. & Greenblatt, E. (Eds.). (1990). *Gay and lesbian library service.* McFarland.

Johnson, D. K. (2019). Selling gay books: Donald Webster Cory's "business with a conscience." In *Buying Gay: How Physique Entrepreneurs Sparked a Movement* (pp. 53–80). Columbia University Press.

Miller, S.R. (1979). *Censored, ignored, overlooked, too expensive? How to get gay materials into libraries: A guide to library selection policies for the non-librarian.* American Library Association Archives Rainbow Round Table Issuances and Publicity Digital Surrogates (Box 1). American Library Association Archives, Normal, IL. https://digital.library.illinois.edu/items/c1789d80-4bca-0136-4f2e-0050569601ca-1

Sherbo, D. (1979). *Censored, ignored, overlooked, too expensive? How to get gay materials into libraries: A guide to library selection policies for the non-librarian.* Front cover design. [electronic]. American Library Association Archives Rainbow Round Table Issuances and Publicity Digital Surrogates (Box 1). American Library Association Archives, Normal, IL. https://digital.library.illinois.edu/items/c1789d80-4bca-0136-4f2e-0050569601ca-1

Taraba, S. (1990) Collecting gay and lesbian materials in an academic library. In Gough, C. & Greenblatt, E. (Eds.), *Gay and Lesbian Library Service* (p. 25-37). McFarland and Co.

Task Force on Gay Liberation. (June 1971). *A Gay Bibliography (1971-1976) (1980).*

American Library Association Archives Rainbow Round Table Issuances and Publicity Digital Surrogates (Box 1). American Library Association Archives, Normal, IL. https://digital.library.illinois.edu/items/c1803130-4bca-0136-4f2e-0050569601ca-5

Tsang, D. (1990). Censorship of lesbian and gay materials by library workers. In Gough, C. & Greenblatt, E. (Eds.), *Gay and Lesbian Library Service* (pp. 166-170). McFarland and Co.

LGBTQ+ Censorship in the Gov Info Sphere

Kaitlyn Moody

Introduction

Government documents might not be the first type of resource thought of when discussing the censorship of LGBTQ+ materials, but such issues still exist in the sphere of these special collections. As will be discussed, there have been various attempts throughout history to censor the creation and distribution of queer material by the federal government. In the present climate especially, there are a growing number of concerns surrounding the treatment of specific depository materials and whether state attempts at censorship will affect the mission of the Federal Depository Library Program. From the type and amount of LGBTQ+ resources published by government agencies, to the treatment of those resources by government officials, federal depositories face a variety of roadblocks when it comes to serving their LGBTQ+ patron populations today.

Background on the FDLP

The Federal Depository Library Program (FDLP) was first established by Congress in 1895 and is currently overseen by the Government Publishing Office (GPO). Today, there are over 1,100 designated federal depository libraries (FDLs), located in all 50 states. The founding tenet of this program was, and still is, to "make Government publications available for the free use of the general public" (44 U.S.C. § 1911).[1] Consequently, government document collections include anything published by or for the federal government.

---

[1]   https://www.govinfo.gov/app/details/USCODE-2021-title44/USCODE-2021-title44-chap19-sec1911

To become an FDL, libraries must receive a special designation. This designation can come from one of two places: Congress or the GPO. The most common type of designation is a congressional designation, in which a state representative may designate a library within their congressional district should a vacancy exist. The other type of designation is a by-law designation, in which the GPO director may designate a library with special circumstances, such as land-grant colleges or law schools. FDLs can, mostly, be housed in any kind of repository, be it a college, university, public library, etc. Additionally, while special exceptions exist, there are two main types of federal depositories: regionals and selectives. The primary difference between the two is that regionals must collect every publication published by the federal government and selectives only collect based on the needs of their patronage.

The role a government documents department plays in a library's overall collection development policy varies from institution to institution. For example, here at the University of South Alabama, our government documents department works collaboratively with the university libraries' collection management as a whole but is allowed flexibility in its overall selection of materials. This decision primarily stems from the fact that our patronage extends further than the university's student population to also include everyone within Alabama's 1st Congressional District. That being said, each FDL collects based on its individual item selection profile. The item selection profile is how a depository selects which publications they want distributed to their library. Depositories are provided a List of Classes, which consists of various item numbers that correspond to specific groups of materials from specific government agencies or sub-agencies.[2] For example, when the item number "0786-A-23" is selected, a library has chosen to receive all reference guides published by the Library of Congress. There are thousands of item numbers available through the List of Classes, making the creation and maintenance of an FDL's item selection profile incredibly time consuming. While certain materials are mandatory for depository collections, most selections are based solely on a library's very specific needs and wants.

Since depository documents received through the program are technically government property, a federal depository ultimately wishing to weed or deaccess materials from its collection must follow a very

---

2   https://www.fdlp.gov/instruction/list-of-classes

detailed set of procedures. While these procedures may vary between types of depositories, three general rules are always followed. The primary rule revolves around the five-year holding period. Once an item is officially processed as part of a depository's collection, an FDL must keep that item in its collection for at least five years. There are then two main exceptions to this rule. The first is when an item is superseded. If a new edition or a revised copy of something is released, libraries are allowed to switch older copies with these newer versions. The second exception is when libraries wish to substitute formats. For example, if there is a legitimate electronic version of a title, libraries are allowed to switch their paper copy for that digital copy. While there are other possible exceptions to this five-year rule, these are the most common.

History of Government Censorship

While the FDLP's mission is to ensure open access to government information, the federal government still has a history of widespread censorship, especially in regard to LGBTQ+ material. Perhaps one of the biggest examples of this was the Library of Congress's lesser-known Delta Collection. While it is generally unknown when or why this collection first started, it is posited to have begun sometime within the 1880s and was not made public until 1964. In *Cruising the Library: Perversities in the Organization of Knowledge*, Melissa Adler (2017) delves into the known history of this collection in more detail, though it should be noted that written knowledge of the collection is sparse. In short, however, the Delta Collection was a restricted section of materials collected and sequestered by the Library of Congress because of their "obscene" nature.

While this primarily included things like erotica or pornography, "obscenity" at the time also included anything the government thought of as perverse. Consequently, materials dealing with homosexuality were shut away in an attempt to "protect citizens" and "serve as a repository of sample materials for consultation by federal agencies" (Adler, 2017, p. 63). According to Adler, the collection itself was "far from cohesive" (p. 64), as beyond housing generally explicit material, it also contained items seized by the Postal Service and Customs Bureau as evidence for crimes handled by the Morals Division of law enforcement agencies (p. 68). Additionally, according to Meg Metcalf, other Delta Collection material included various queer periodicals such as

Turnabout magazine and even a number of rare books such as *Venus Castina* (Metcalf, 2021).

Government attempts at censorship are not relegated to the past, however. Since the creation of the Internet, there has been a major shift in how information is both published and distributed. In 1993, the GPO Access Act provided the Government Publishing Office "a means of enhancing electronic public access to a wide range of Federal electronic information" (44 U.S.C. § 4101).[3] Since then, the focus on digital formats has only grown. For example, the number of paper titles offered by GPO in FY 1995 totaled 17,466. Contrastingly, the number of paper titles offered in FY 2020 totaled to only 2,688 (Task Force on a Digital FDLP, p. 63). Paper has slowly become the less popular format, and while this shift certainly has its benefits, it also has some major drawbacks.

While the GPO works tirelessly to capture and catalog as much of the government's digital footprint as it can, things are still liable to slip through the cracks. In the past, documents published and distributed by the GPO were provided by each government agency. However, agencies would not, and still do not, send the GPO every single publication. This often causes issues with lost documents, or what FDLs call "unreported publications." Essentially, an "unreported publication" is identified as any federal publication, within the scope of the FDLP, that cannot be found in CGP (Catalog of U.S. Government Publications) or was not distributed by the Government Publishing Office. This presents a fairly serious problem, especially in the digital age when agencies are less likely to report on their online content. To combat this problem of unreported publications, the GPO began web harvesting agency websites in 2013, but even this strategy is liable to miss relevant resources.

In addition to these general pitfalls, changes in administration can also lead to the temporary loss, and sometimes total erasure, of certain material. For example, immediately after the inauguration of Donald Trump in 2017, LGBTQ+ content was removed from the White House, Department of Labor, and State Department websites. Documents from this batch deletion included former Secretary of State John Kerry's apology for the 1950s/60s "Lavender Scare," information on Pride Month observances, and much more. While some of these materials *were* immediately archived, this systematic removal of LGBTQ+ content

---

3   https://www.govinfo.gov/content/pkg/STATUTE-107/pdf/STATUTE-107-Pg112.pdf

from government websites still proved that certain material is made especially vulnerable when provided in digital-only format.

Censorship Issues Today

The preceding discussion ultimately leads to the most recent influx of censorship attempts from local and state legislatures. FDLs are not immune to these efforts just because they collect material by and for the federal government. In April of 2023, the Depository Library Council penned a letter to the GPO asking for guidance on how to handle any potential conflict in adhering to state legislation while keeping with the legal requirements of the FDLP, as it is a real possibility that these newly enacted laws might label specific depository resources as "harmful, obscene, inappropriate, or explicit" (Pritchard, 2023). The GPO was quick to respond but ultimately unable to provide any blanket guidance, asking libraries to keep vigilant and to notify the agency when or if specific issues arise (Halpern, 2023). While there have been no demands for the removal of specific depository materials at present, there are still plenty of resources to monitor. For example, the Department of Education has various guidance documents on how to support transgender youth in schools. With the current climate surrounding trans youth in particular, these types of resources might be made especially vulnerable.

Consequently, while it is not yet clear to what extent depository libraries will be affected by these censorship attacks, it is still essential to step up and ensure that the LGBTQ+ materials in government document collections receive the same amount of care as the ones in a library's general collection. To get started, it would be of use to discuss what sort of LGBTQ+ resources are actually available from the federal government and then look at the possible promotional issues that arise when dealing with a disparity in print material.

The Catalog of U.S. Government Publications

The first and most basic resource to reference when searching for LGBTQ+ government documents is the Catalog of U.S. Government Publications (CGP).[4] CGP is the official search tool for all titles listed

---

4   https://catalog.gpo.gov

in the National Bibliography of U.S. Government Publications, which is a GPO-published bibliography composed of all the cataloged publications from all three branches of the federal government. As mentioned previously, government documents are more than just print resources. Electronic resources are on the rise, and since depository libraries only receive materials specified on their own item selection profiles, certain titles can often still slip past a library's purview. With CGP, libraries are able to create blanket searches for resources that might not be available through their own catalogs.

While this tool might be a good starting point, it does present some key disadvantages. Primarily, there seems to be a general lack of cataloged LGBTQ+ resources. To showcase this, a brief bibliometric analysis was completed with data compiled from a batch of rough keyword searches. Seven individual searches were completed with the following keyword terms: LGBT, LGBTQ, queer, gay, lesbian, bisexual, and transgender. No other limiters were used in these searches, as the aim was to gather everything relevant to each keyword term. Each results list was then collated and further narrowed. This meant the deduplication of records with entries for both paper and electronic formats, and the removal of other questionable titles such as resources that simply populated because the author's last name was "Gay." In total, there were only 162 unique titles (see Figure 1).

Search Term(s)	Preliminary Results	Individual Titles
LGBTQ	26	20
LGBT	16	13
Queer	20	14
Gay	241	118
Lesbian	55	41
Bisexual	56	46
Transgender	95	73
COLLATED RESULTS		162

Figure 1 CGP Search Results

While there were certainly LGBTQ+ resources undetected during this batch search due to the selected keyword scheme, such as individual landmark Supreme Court opinions, these results still provide a fairly good look at what CGP has to offer. Of those titles, some had both print and electronic records, while others had only one or the other. In total, there were 130 electronic records and 76 records for paper/fiche. This surplus in digital material is both a positive and a possible setback, which will be further discussed in later parts of this chapter.

Additionally, the types of LGBTQ+ resources present in these results show a fairly inadequate collection of historical queer perspectives and stories. For example, the two most recurrent types of resources were congressional material (50) and other policy or data-driven resources like documents from the Department of Health & Human Services (33). While these are certainly fundamental government resources, the LGBTQ+ community is more than just numbers and legislative issues. Key agencies and departments that typically publish relevant historical material include the National Park Service, Smithsonian Institution, and the Library of Congress, but queer voices do not seem present in the catalog itself.

There could be a number of reasons for this, but the primary seems to be that historical LGBTQ+ content has not been actively documented until recently. The National Park Service (2016) states:

> Traditionally, history as a formal discipline and a cornerstone for national heritage represented little or nothing of LGBTQ lives.... LGBTQ people similarly saw scant reflection of their own past in museums, public monuments, local historical societies, and the popular history distributed by mainstream media, let alone at officially recognized historic places (p. 04-2).

On May 30, 2014, the National Park Service announced the creation of the LGBT Heritage Initiative, a plan that aimed to identify and document places, people, and events connected to the queer community's story in America. However, while this initiative has ultimately led to the creation of more historical material, that material is still largely undiscoverable through CGP. Whether this be an oversight issue on the part of web harvesting efforts or a "reporting" issue on the part of individual agencies, it is hard to say. In any case, it becomes even more important to consider a variety of other search methods to broaden the pool of relevant LGBTQ+ resources.

Department & Agency Websites

CGP is not the only resource available when searching for LGBTQ+ resources. The purview of government documents should not be limited to cataloged publications only. Any and all information produced by and for the federal government should be considered when looking to promote specific resources in a depository's collection. This includes material found in both department and agency websites. As mentioned previously, agencies are often responsible for reporting which publications they wish to have distributed through the GPO. As a result, not every agency publication or resource is sent GPO's way, making these resources undiscoverable through CGP. Therefore, *USA.gov* is another wonderful search tool to utilize.[5] As the official web portal of the U.S. government, it is incredibly comprehensive and links to nearly all federal and state websites. A broad search on *USA.gov*, then, provides another good starting point for finding relevant LGBTQ+ material.

There are a couple drawbacks to this method, however; namely, it can be difficult to narrow searches through the portal's general search bar, often making the number of results overwhelming. Consequently, it can sometimes be more fruitful to search agency websites more directly. There are numerous departments and agencies that provide LGBTQ+-focused material, ranging from emerging census data on *Census.gov* to real-time updates on current queer legislation through *Congress.gov*. But where CGP seems to be lacking in historical perspectives, a plethora of wonderful resources can be found when exploring the websites of the three previously mentioned entities: the National Park Service, the Smithsonian Institution, and the Library of Congress.

The National Park Service

The official mission of the National Park Service (NPS) is to preserve and protect both the natural and cultural resources of the United States. Consequently, the NPS's reach far exceeds the parks themselves to also cover prominent American heritage monuments. In regard to the LGBTQ+ community, this includes places like Stonewall and people like Marsha P. Johnson. The National Park Service's website includes various profiles leading to some wonderful resources on prominent queer figures and landmarks.[6]

---

5   https://www.usa.gov/

6   https://www.nps.gov

One such example is the *Finding Our Place: LGBTQ Heritage in the United States* article series.[7] The NPS states, "Historical references to LGBTQ contributions to American heritage are rare…In recent years, scholars have focused on uncovering the history of LGBTQ communities and expanding our understanding of American history" (Crippen, 2018). In this particular series, NPS contributors profile various people and places from queer history, including things like The Names Project and areas such as the Castro District.

The Smithsonian Institution

Founded by James Smithson, the Smithsonian Institution was first bequeathed to Congress in 1836 and has steadily grown in mission and scope ever since. With 21 museums, a National Zoo, and nine research facilities, it has become an epicenter for education and knowledge throughout the United States. It is no surprise, then, that the Smithsonian has a wonderful collection of artifacts from LGBTQ+ history in America, many of which can be viewed through the Smithsonian's official website. On the Smithsonian's page for "LGBTQ History," patrons and libraries alike can access past exhibitions, digitized collection pieces, and even queer-focused posts from an official blog.[8]

For example, "Illegal to Be You: Gay History Beyond Stonewall" was an exhibition at the National Museum of American History that ran from June 2019 to July 2021.[9] It aimed to showcase the diversity within gay American history and included a collection of pieces spanning throughout the 50 years since the Stonewall uprisings. On the exhibition's official webpage, photographs of individual items can be found, including a collection of buttons from the first Christopher Street march, matchbook covers from popular gay bars in the early 90s, and so much more. Similarly, on the *O Say Can You See?* blog, relevant posts include topics such as the origin of the rainbow as a symbol of pride, the rise of drag ball culture in the 1920s, and even a look at the inclusion of the LGBTQ+ community in 90s skateboarding culture.[10]

---

7   https://www.nps.gov/articles/series.htm?id=0B81BB73-1DD8-B71B-0B676B91F1D446A7

8   https://americanhistory.si.edu/topics/lgbtq-history

9   https://americanhistory.si.edu/exhibitions/gay-history-beyond-stonewall

10 https://americanhistory.si.edu/blog/by-tag/LGBTQ%20History

The Library of Congress

Home to millions of books, films, photographs, manuscripts, and so much more, the Library of Congress is perhaps the number-one federal agency to reference when searching for LGBTQ+ historical resources. Whereas the Delta Collection was once a tool to sequester queer material from the public eye, it ultimately aided in preserving the LGBTQ+ historical footprint in America. Now, the Library has a wide-reaching and ever-growing collection of queer artifacts, many of which are available online due to increased digitization efforts. There are many ways to search for and to promote these items, but perhaps the most fruitful is through the Library's various research guides. A list of the most comprehensive guides can be found in Figure 2.

Research Guide Title(s)	Author(s)	Descriptions (from research guides)
Let's Talk Comics: LGBTQIA+ Titles https://blogs.loc.gov/headlinesandheroes/2021/06/lets-talk-comics-lgbtqia-titles/	Amber Paranick	Highlights "titles and anthologies within our collection that either include queer characters, were created by LGBTQIA+ talent and creators, or serve as memorable firsts in comics history."
LGBTQ+ Legal Resources: A Beginner's Guide https://guides.loc.gov/lgbtq-law	Barbara Bavis & Meg Metcalf	"This Beginner's Guide is intended to simplify this research process, and provide some helpful resources for those interested in the law surrounding gender identity and sexual orientation."
LGBTQ+ Resources in Business and the Workplace https://guides.loc.gov/lgbtq-business	Gulnar Nagashybayeva	"A guide to sources of information for those researching the issues that affect the economic circumstances of the LGBTQ+ community."
LGBTQIA+ Studies: A Resource Guide https://guides.loc.gov/lgbtq-studies/introduction	Meg Metcalf	"This research guide serves as an introduction into the excellent collection of LGBTQ+ resources available at the Library of Congress."

Figure 2   Library of Congress Research Guides

Promotional Roadblocks

Including web resources does more than simply expand a collection's historical scope, however. In recent years, the GPO has expressed an emerging interest in prioritizing digital-born material. In fact, the Depository Library Council has an entire task force dedicated to the researching and planning of a Digital Federal Depository Library Program. While this does not mean the extinction of print resources in the government info sphere, it does indicate a fundamental switch towards electronic material.

A majority of recent LGBTQ+ publications are digital-born and/or on-line-only, with many print resources dating back to the pre-2000s. Consequently, while some of these print materials offer a timely view on attitudes towards queer people throughout the decades, others are simply outdated. For example, a number of print titles are publications from the U.S. Department of Health & Human Services. One such document, *Lesbians, Gay Men, and Bisexuals*, is a 1994 annotated bibliography on research surrounding alcohol, tobacco, and drug use within the lesbian and gay communities. While the research presented in this resource might be of some value, it largely excludes other parts of the LGBTQ+ community and has since been superseded by online counterparts. Documents like this one are very much the product of a time when the public perception of queerness was limited to the LGB in LGBTQ+, ignorant to the complexities of sexuality and often exclusionary towards trans individuals altogether. Thus, while web resources have their own currency issues, they typically update in real time and have evolved to cover a broader understanding of the LGBTQ+ community as a whole.

However, while this growing amount of online material might compensate for a lack of tangible documents, issues still crop up in regard to government document promotion. Relying too heavily on web resources can create problems with visibility; namely, with a lack of print resources, there is little a patron can find when browsing library shelves. Additionally, many web resources are not cataloged by GPO to the same degree as other electronic documents, and consequently, do not have applicable bibliographic records. With a lack of discoverable records in library OPACs, then, it might seem like government document departments have little to offer their LGBTQ+ patrons. Therefore, while external censorship is still a major issue to contend with, *self*-censorship potentially becomes the bigger problem for government document collections. The question to ask, then, is how can FDLs make these invisible documents more visible?

Providing Visibility

There are a few suggested solutions. A good start is to evolve the way libraries view traditional avenues for library promotion.

Library Displays

While displays might be more difficult with limited print resources, there are still ways to shine a light on digital-born materials. One such way is to incorporate "print previews" in physical displays. This might entail printing the cover page and/or table of contents of a relevant PDF and pointing to where patrons might find the full document should they be interested. With this kind of tool, it is important to include as much detail as possible so that patrons are able to trace the abbreviated resource to its digital counterpart (see Image 1). This means including the document's SuDoc number[11] (should it have one), providing either the PURL[12] or the URL, and possibly even creating a QR code that patrons can scan directly.

In general, QR codes are another great tool to consider when looking for ways to make online-only documents more visible. Most patrons, especially those in academic libraries, will have access to a smartphone or electronic device of some kind. QR codes, then, can offer patrons more immediate access to resources on display. For example, QR codes can be used in tandem with print previews (as shown in Image 1) or even be used as supplements to other display material. For instance, the Library of Congress has a wonderful collection of LGBTQ+ documentaries, such as *Gay and Proud* by Lilli Vincenz, footage from the first Christopher Street Liberation Day Parade held in 1970. These artifacts might not be tangible but still offer a wonderful way to expand the scope of government documents, and utilizing tools like QR codes allows libraries to better promote these materials.

Another reason QR codes are such useful tools to consider is because of what they offer in terms of gathering user data. Specifically, there are two types of QR codes that a library might consider trying: static and dynamic. For libraries on a budget, static QR codes are the better option because they are mostly free to create with websites like

---

11 Government publications are arranged under the SuDoc classification system (i.e. SuDoc = call number).

12 PURLs are Persistent Uniform Resource Locators; essentially, more stable URLs.

QRCode Monkey or even *Canva*. While static codes are neither edit-
able nor trackable, they still fulfill their primary purpose. In contrast,
dynamic QR codes can be revised even after creation and can typically track a variety of other useful user data, such as how many times
the code has been scanned. For libraries hesitant to promote materials that include no way of tracking usage statistics, dynamic QR codes
offer a possible solution. Dynamic QR codes do have a couple drawbacks, however; namely, they generally require a subscription to a QR
code generator. While these costs are typically quite low, it is still an
important budgetary consideration.

Besides QR codes, there are a variety of other ways to spruce up displays lacking print resources. For example, while there are certainly
ways to promote digital documents directly, it can also be useful to
utilize these sources in creating separate supplementary material: developing informative pamphlets, brochures, and/or posters is another
way to mobilize stagnant library displays. LGBTQ+ web resources are
a necessary part of any government documents collection, but they
can sometimes be hard to streamline and promote directly. By taking
the information available from those resources and curating display
handouts with specific themes or focuses, libraries are able to both

promote online material while expanding on and creating congruency between different agencies and departments. Additionally, display handouts are another great way to track patron interaction with material. By putting out a concrete number of supplementary resources, it is easier to figure how many of those resources were taken by patrons. While this method does not account for more passive interactions with display materials, it does allow for a semi-tangible way to examine what kinds of LGBTQ+ resources are most popular.

For libraries with limited print resources, a combination of these tools can help to broaden and create a more comprehensive LGBTQ+ library display. A good example of this can be shown through the University of South Alabama's 2022 and 2023 Gov Doc Pride Month displays (see Images 2 and 3). With both displays, I employed a combination of the tools described above, and both were a success. For instance, in 2022 I created a brochure that aimed to share brief snapshots of LGBTQ+ American history. Relevant sections included a brief timeline of the Pride movement, important landmarks in queer legislation, and even a selection of LGBTQ+ historical figures. Information from each section was curated from agency websites, all of which were also listed in the brochure's references. Additionally, print previews and QR codes were included to expand the small selection of print resources that our library had available. All in all, both displays saw a good

amount of interaction for the month they were public. In 2023, over 20 of the brochures were taken and over 50 of the pride stickers were claimed. While these numbers might seem relatively small, they ultimately showcased that LGBTQ+ materials are of interest to the university's patron population.

Library Guides and Other Pathfinding Tools

Besides traditional library displays, other tools to take advantage of are things like digital library guides. The world of LGBTQ+ government documents is constantly growing and evolving, so it can be difficult to navigate what is available to find the most relevant material. Additionally, with the great migration to online-only resources, digital pathfinding tools are an especially great place to start when promoting queer material in government document collections. They can be wonderful reference tools, especially when librarians curate sources with particular criteria or questions in mind. Which U.S. agencies have relevant LGBTQ+ material? What kinds of LGBTQ+ materials are actually out there? With library guides, all these questions and concerns can be easily streamlined and addressed.

Library guides themselves can be as brief or as comprehensive as libraries make them. In regard to LGBTQ+ government documents, this could mean narrowing resources to those dealing with a specific group within the community or even curating resources that fit under a specific topic. Additionally, libraries can make these guides as general or as customized as possible. For example, sometimes the best library guides result from a really good reference question or even a successful display. Perhaps a patron visits the department looking for resources on transgender healthcare. While the specific concerns of this patron might be fully addressed during this in-person meeting, the question itself showcases a possible area of interest for this special population.

This example ultimately showcases another reason why these pathfinding tools are helpful at getting LGBTQ+ government documents to the communities that need them. Namely, depending on a patron's personal circumstances, they may either not be ready or not be able to openly check-out or discuss queer library resources. For instance, someone who still lives in a conservative home might not find it safe to openly engage with LGBTQ+-themed material. Instead, this population makes up much of what Jennifer Downey calls "stealth" library use (Downey, 2013, p. 105). Consequently, utilizing tools like online library guides would allow patrons to more discreetly browse library collections while still retaining the in-depth and comprehensive guidance that comes from actual library professionals.

There are many different ways to actually create and utilize LGBTQ+ library guides in the government documents community. For example, LibGuides have become one of the most popular ways to design and publish library guide content. Available through Springshare, this content management system is currently employed by thousands of libraries worldwide and offers an easy way to streamline, reuse, distribute, and maintain library guide content. If a library does not have access to the LibGuides platform, however, there are other options. Wix, for instance, is a website builder that can be used to create various pathfinding sites. Wix offers both free and paid subscription plans, each of which include a number of great features that can be used to construct comprehensive resource guides. While it might be more laborious to streamline content and keep-up regular maintenance, Wix still offers a way for libraries to curate library materials in a single space.

When creating library guide content, there are a few best practices to keep in mind. First, it is important to keep information clear and concise. Library guides should be easy to peruse and allow patrons a quick but comprehensive look at what library collections have to offer.

Stay away from using heavy jargon and keep descriptions short and simple to help users avoid wading through dense amounts of content.

Next, consider the best way to organize the material you are promoting. Providing an alphabetized bibliography might get the job done on some occasions, but unless a patron already has a specific title in mind, this general "list" format can potentially be confusing when dealing with large amounts of information. Instead, keep the guide's theme in mind and ponder more logical ways to organize content. Is it better to group material by agency, resource type, subject area, etc.?

Lastly, always keep up regular guide maintenance. While digital guides are particularly helpful at streamlining online content, broken links can be a pitfall. Broken links occur when a URL points to a page that no longer exists. This could mean the page/content was simply moved or sometimes even deleted entirely. While this issue rarely occurs with GPO PURLs, agency websites do not have a similar permanence. Consequently, it is important to perform routine library guide maintenance to ensure all links are up-to-date and fully accessible.

Saying all this, it is not always necessary to reinvent the wheel in terms of original LGBTQ+ pathfinding content. For example, the FDLP has an entire webpage dedicated to the collection of library guides related to the LGBTQ+ community.[13] These guides include those created by different federal depositories and even some by the Library of Congress. They focus on a variety of topics, from legal research to lists of primary sources relevant to LGBTQ+ studies. Additionally, here at the University of South Alabama, I recently developed a LibGuide titled "Gov Docs: LGBTQ+ Resources."[14] It includes a variety of health, legislative, and historical resources available from the federal government and had over 100 hits within its first month of being public. Consequently, if a library lacks the time and/or resources to create unique guides of their own, it could be just as beneficial to link or provide access to those that have already been developed.

---

13   https://libguides.fdlp.gov/LGBTQIA

14   https://libguides.southalabama.edu/lgbtq

LGBTQ+ Advocacy in the Gov Info Sphere

While taking advantage of this rise in online material allows for more fruitful government document collections, there is absolutely still a need for LGBTQ+ advocacy in the government information sphere. Primarily, this means pushing for the official cataloging of more digital resources and further supporting the documentation of queer voices in America's written history.

"Unreported Publications"

While the GPO works tirelessly to ensure that relevant material is discoverable through the Catalog of Government Publications, resources are still liable to slip through the cracks. As explained at the beginning of this chapter, an "unreported publication" is identified as any federal publication that cannot be found in CGP or was not distributed through the FDLP, and the number of unique LGBTQ+ titles currently discoverable through CGP is relatively small. This could ultimately cause visibility issues for libraries that use this catalog as a primary tool when searching for relevant material, especially since there is actually more available than what is shown.

For example, when searching for resources dealing with LGBTQ+ health, a 2021 issue brief from the Office of the Assistant Secretary for Planning and Evaluation (ASPE) was found: "Health Insurance Coverage and Access to Care for LGBTQ+ Individuals: Recent Trends and Key Challenges."[15] The document itself offers some very relevant information involving community demographics and trends in insurance coverage within LGBTQ+ populations, but it is not cataloged or discoverable within CGP itself. When libraries find and report these types of "unreported" publications, it ensures that other institutions are not ignorant to the full scope of LGBTQ+ government resources. The act of reporting is actually very easy and can be done through the *askGPO* portal.[16] Simply select the "Unreported Publications" category on their inquiry form and fill in all the necessary information, such as publication title and publishing agency.

---

15 https://aspe.hhs.gov/reports/health-insurance-coverage-lgbtq

16 https://ask.gpo.gov/

Documenting Queer Voices

Perhaps the most substantial way to advocate for the LGBTQ+ community within the gov info sphere is to further champion queer voices in America's recorded history. Until recently, queer stories have not been a priority, but change is already underway with campaigns like the National Park Service's LGBTQ Heritage Initiative. Since May 2014, the NPS has slowly been working to identify significant places and events of LGBTQ+ heritage. In doing so, noteworthy areas and figures within queer history will be better preserved and recognized. For example, the Stonewall National Monument became the first LGBTQ+ national monument on June 24, 2016. It now has its own NPS website with a multitude of educational resources and various materials to help patrons plan in-person visits.[17] Stonewall is just the start, however. Anyone can get involved and help to identify places and people deserving of preservation and recognition. For those with locations already in mind, it could be as simple as submitting a nomination form to the National Register of Historic Places.[18]

But the National Park Service is not the only federal agency working to bridge this gap between LGBTQ+ history and American history. For example, the Library of Congress's Veterans History Project is a special collection of first and secondhand accounts of U.S. military veteran experiences, starting from WWI to present day. Collection items include things such as oral histories, journal entries, photographs, and so much more. Within the project itself are additional sub-collections, including one specific to LGBTQ+ service members, titled "Serving in Silence: LGBTQ+ Veterans."[19] This particular collection is an important step in further recognizing members of the community and honoring their place in U.S. history. Anyone can participate and submit relevant material, so for those who might want to share their own stories or celebrate those who came before, the Veterans History Project is another great avenue to expand the LGBTQ+ footprint in America's chronology.[20]

---

17 https://www.nps.gov/ston/index.htm

18 https://www.nps.gov/subjects/nationalregister/how-to-list-a-property.htm

19 https://www.loc.gov/collections/veterans-history-project-collection/serving-our-voices/diverse-experiences-in-service/lgbtq-veterans/

20 https://www.loc.gov/programs/veterans-history-project/how-to-participate/

Conclusion

LGBTQ+ censorship is not a new issue for federal depositories. But while the rising importance of digital publications presents its own set of problems, there are still many ways that libraries can address a lack of queer materials in the gov info sphere. From highlighting more web-based resources through traditional library promotion to ensuring unreported publications get proper accountability in CGP, FDLs have a variety of ways to better combat issues surrounding LGBTQ+ visibility in government document collections. Perhaps the most substantial suggestion, though, is to further advocate for queer voices in the sphere of this very distinct collection. The LGBTQ+ community plays an integral part in America's widely growing melting pot, and we deserve to have our voices heard too.

No matter how libraries choose to address these issues, it is important to keep accessibility at the forefront of any efforts. Government documents can often be intimidating to library patrons but are generally some of the most pertinent resources to their everyday lives. Therefore, presenting government material in more practical, user-friendly ways helps to negate any misconceptions about what government documents actually are and who they are for. FDLs should not be afraid to shed light on the resources available to their patrons, especially when it is abundantly clear that there are special populations that would greatly benefit from their promotion.

References and Additional Resources

Adler, M. (2017). *Cruising the library: Perversities in the organization of knowledge.* Fordham University Press.

Crippen, L. (2018) [*Series*] *Finding our place: LGBTQ heritage in the United States.* National Park Service. https://www.nps.gov/articles/series. htm?id=0B81BB73-1DD8-B71B-0B676B91F1D446A7

Downey, J. (2013). Self-censorship in selection of LGBT-themed materials. *Reference & User Services Quarterly, 53*(2), 104–107. https://doi. org/10.5860/rusq.53n2.104

Federal Depository Library Program, 44 U.S.C. § 1911 (2021). https:// www.govinfo.gov/app/details/USCODE-2021-title44/ USCODE-2021-title44-chap19-sec1911

Federal Depository Library Program. Then and now experiences of the LGBTQ+ community. FDLP. https://libguides.fdlp.gov/tne-lgbtq-community/

GPO Access Act, 44 U.S.C. § 4101 (1993). https://www.govinfo.gov/content/pkg/STATUTE-107/pdf/STATUTE-107-Pg112.pdf

Halpern, N. GPO Response to Council's Letter Regarding Censorship (June 21, 2023). https://www.fdlp.gov/file-repository-item/gpo-response-councils-letter-regarding-censorship-june-21-2023

Library of Congress. *Serving in silence: LGBTQ+ veterans*. Veterans History Project. https://www.loc.gov/collections/veterans-history-project-collection/serving-our-voices/diverse-experiences-in-service/lgbtq-veterans/

Metcalf, M. (2021, June 28). *Pride night online: LGBTQ collections at the Library of Congress* [Video]. https://www.loc.gov/item/webcast-9907/?

Moody, K. *Gov docs: LGBTQ+ resources*. University of South Alabama. https://libguides.southalabama.edu/c.php?g=1315231&p=9670407

National Park Service. (2016). *LGBTQ America: A theme study of lesbian, gay, bisexual, transgender, and queer history*. Springate, M. (Ed.). https://purl.fdlp.gov/GPO/gpo135555

National Park Service. (2023.) *Stonewall: National Monument, New York*. NPS. https://www.nps.gov/ston/index.htm

Pritchard, L. Letter from DLC Chair Lisa Pritchard to GPO Director Halpern Regarding Censorship (April 23, 2023). https://fdlp.gov/file-repository-item/letter-dlc-chair-lisa-pritchard-gpo-director-halpern-regarding-censorship

Smithsonian Institution. (n.d.) *LGBTQ+ history*. National Museum of American History. https://americanhistory.si.edu/explore/topics/lgbtq-history

Task Force on a Digital FDLP. (2022). *Feasibility of a digital federal depository library program: Report of the GPO director's task force*. Government Publishing Office. https://www.fdlp.gov/file-repository-item/feasibility-digital-federal-depository-library-program-report-gpo-directors

The Closeted Collections
An Analysis of LGBTQ+ Censorship in Irish Secondary School Libraries

Phoebe Doyle

Introduction

The censorship of LGBTQ+ content in libraries is one of the biggest controversies currently facing librarians and the political landscape. There has been a significant rise in anti-LGBTQ+ rhetoric and queer-phobia in the news in the 2020s, with the library becoming a highly publicized area in this regard. This can be seen with the book burnings conducted by Paul Dorr and protests against Drag Story Hour, situations in which it has been deemed that the presence of LGBTQ+ people in the library is unacceptable (Stevens, 2020). This is a space where LGBTQ+ books are met with hostility by the surrounding population and where members of the LGBTQ+ community are discouraged from making their voices heard.

It highlights the difficult position librarians are in; they are supposed to serve their community, but LGBTQ+ patrons and material are being antagonized by others from within that same space. "Librarians find themselves in a unique position of serving both sides of the community: those who oppose LGBTQ+ materials and the LGBTQ+ community itself" (Stevens, 2020, p. 56). As repositories where all books are seen as having the equal right to be accessible, libraries containing LGBTQ+ books are being targeted with complaints and book bannings. In 2020, it was confirmed by the American Library Association (ALA) that 273 books were banned (Higgins-Dailey, 2021), and in their list of the "Top 10 Most Challenged Books of 2021," three of the most banned books focused on LGBTQ+ topics (Albanese, 2022). Despite this popular image of the role of the library within its community, it has always been a space constantly subjected to cries for censorship and inaccessibility for marginalized groups.

This idea is complicated further when addressing school libraries, a space solely intended for young people. Here, librarians must be aware of how parents and other groups may react to certain books within their collection, all while trying to serve their students. While the anti-LGBTQ+ backlash against libraries in the United States has been well documented via social media and news articles, and the legacy of Section 28[1] in the UK remains strong, little academic work has been published on this phenomenon within Irish secondary schools. Given the importance of youth literacy, representation, and acceptance during such a tumultuous period of development, it is crucial to examine how Irish secondary school libraries match those in other countries. On top of the recent protests against Swords/Cork City Council libraries, and the reclassification of certain books in Irish libraries depending on their content (Lee, 2023), it is vital that librarians in Ireland are prepared against future censorship efforts.

This chapter aims to explore how the censorship of LGBTQ+ content in Irish secondary school libraries takes place and how library workers can fight against it. The central focus will be on how censorship of books based on their LGBTQ+ content is conducted within Irish secondary schools, how it signals the rejection of LGBTQ+ youths to students, and how it acts as a testing site for future censorship among other libraries.

Defining Censorship

To understand how the censorship of LGBTQ+ books in school libraries operates, the concept must be clearly defined. Knox (2014, p. 741) defines censorship as "an amalgamation of practices, including the redaction of text in a document, cutting pages out of a book, or denying access to materials," which can range from not choosing to stock a text (passive) to removing a text from shelves. It is easy to regard complaints levied at libraries for the inclusion of certain books, or cries for the books to be inaccessible for certain groups, as forms of censorship. However, this definition can hold alternate meanings for both librarians and the public.

---

1   See "History of Libraries" section for further details.

The most popular images of censorship can be divided into several camps—internal censorship (self-censorship), external censorship (public backlash against LGBTQ+ events, book burnings), and institutional censorship (methods of cataloging, library subject headings) (Stevens, 2020). This allows for a deeper understanding of the issue, and of how censorship operates, than lumping them all under one umbrella. The act of self-censorship or evaluating how subject headings impact the ability to find books requires different solutions from combating book burnings, but these other kinds of censorship are crucial to address if LGBTQ+ youths are to feel welcome within their school library. In the context of Irish secondary school libraries, internal and external censorship are the most prevalent, and as such will be the focus of this chapter.

On self-censorship, McMenmey (2009, p. 4) states censorship is an anti-democratic practice that librarians combat through ethics policies and community support, but that may still take place through the library's omission of specific books/authors from its collections to avoid controversy. This may take the form of avoiding purchasing those books or authors, and if a librarian makes that decision based on backlash of LGBTQ+ content, this practice functions as a form of self-censorship. A 2008 *School Library Journal* survey, analyzing 653 schools in the United States, found that 47% of school librarians would avoid collecting books containing homosexual content due to fears of parental backlash (Jamison, 2018). This has as much of a negative impact on LGBTQ+ patrons as external censorship based on outside pressure, with both leading to the same result: little to no representation or support in a seemingly democratic space. Participating in self-censorship goes against one of the main tenets of the library profession—intellectual freedom. Defined by Busha (1972, p. 84) as the library user's right to access whatever content they desire without restriction, this concept is what allows otherwise maligned works to remain on library shelves, including LGBTQ+ books. As protests against LGBTQ+ books being accessible for young people within libraries have increased in recent years, this is a practice that librarians need to be aware of among their peers and themselves.

School librarians must remain conscious of how the above forms of censorship may manifest within their libraries if they are to ensure a growing collection in which LGBTQ+ students are represented. Labeling, a process in which books are marked as containing elements such as sexual content and violence, is also a form of self-censorship that signals internally that the book may be controversial for containing LGBTQ+ content (ALA, 2010, as cited by Knox, 2014). The most rudimentary form of labeling LGBTQ+ content in secondary school libraries might inspire requests from some parents to remove the books from shelves just as much as it would aid LGBTQ+ students in finding representation.

External censorship—outcries from people outside the library—constitutes the bulk of the expected image of censorship. The aforementioned advocacy for the removal of LGBTQ+ library events and books from children's sections shows that librarians have a minefield to traverse if they are to do their jobs. Thus, there is a temptation to self-censor to avoid risk, linking both forms of censorship. Knowing how would-be censors operate is another useful method of upholding values of intellectual freedom in the library and meeting the needs of LGBTQ+ students. Some of the traits shared by censors are the wish to control what people believe, the "correctness" of their values, a lack of having read the book they are objecting to, and a belief that vulnerable groups such as children need protecting from these books (Kravitz, 2002, as cited in Williams, 2020). These mindsets cleanly align with the arguments for preventing young people's access to LGBTQ+ books in school and public libraries. This can be seen in an Irish context with the case of controversy around Susan Kuklin's *Beyond Magenta: Transgender and Nonbinary Teens Speak Out*, in which a far-right activist complained that libraries in Cork were hosting an LGBTQ+ book that she claimed "normalises abuse and even paedophilia" (Kelleher, 2020). This incident illustrates both the notion that young people are to be protected from LGBTQ+ content and that those who object to this material's inclusion are in the moral right. It is this framework which frames the current debate happening within libraries. One of the libraries in this case even highlighted the lack of said content in *Beyond Magenta*, showing how books that may prove instrumental to the lives of LGBTQ+ young people are being attacked by groups who have not read these books to support their claims.

This connects to another major reason external censorship occurs within school libraries—power. Those who seek to limit young people's access to books want to exert power over what these readers consume, rather than have said young people be "negatively influenced" by said books. As Knox writes, "censorship is primarily about power and control...Censorship is generally discussed as a coherent, consistent activity, but in reality, censorship is a constellation of practices" (2017,

p. 269). Knox goes on to name several of these practices as redaction, restriction, relocation, and removal (2017, p. 269), which stresses the point that the censorship of LGBTQ+ books in libraries can take place even as the books remain on the premises. External pressure to move LGBTQ+ books out of young people's sections or obscuring the content within the text are all methods to exert power over the libraries, LGBTQ+ representation, and the ways in which LGBTQ+ young people see themselves. Much of the urge to censor books featuring marginalized groups also stems from parents/community leaders not wanting children to hold different values. "People are looking at books as dangerous knowledge. In the library field, we say we never know how any individual person will react to a book. But people who ban and challenge books collectivize everybody" (Ismail, 2022). The act of banning and censoring LGBTQ+ books implies that the people who complain about these materials represent the entire community, eliminating the voices of LGBTQ+ people and allies. This fear that books may influence children's behaviors or beliefs revolves around vague, unsupported notions of danger within these books, such as fears that young people reading these books may become normalized to abuse or have their sexuality changed. This raises a question of "whose harm do we care about?" (Patin, 2022, 39:40), and of how discussions of previously obscured topics provoke discomfort in people against the inclusion of such content (2022, 45:12). Such censorship places the concerns of a vocal minority of parents above those of the wider community, as the increasing visibility of LGBTQ+ people in public life is seen as inappropriate. The act of banning LGBTQ+ books serves to comfort a vocal minority more than young people themselves, sending a message that LGBTQ+ youths are undeserving of safety and self-definition.

History of Libraries

The phenomenon of LGBTQ+ materials being censored in libraries or removed from young people's sections is not new, but has been going on for decades. As stated at the beginning of this chapter, the history of LGBTQ+ representation within libraries has been fraught and arduous, with librarians having to fight for the ability to properly represent those within the community. One of the biggest international examples of this with school libraries is Section 28 within the United Kingdom, which from 1988 to 2003 "prohibited 'promotion' of 'the acceptability of homosexuality as a pretended family relationship' by local education authorities in the UK (except Northern Ireland)" (Nixon and Givens,

2007, p. 450). This left an entire generation of British youths without positive knowledge or representation of the LGBTQ+ community. This is notable, given that Section 28 was enacted during the 1980s, when the AIDS crisis was at its peak and popular coverage of the gay community was of a tone of contagion and fear. The denial of positive LGBTQ+ representation within the library space pushes one singular narrative, an image painted by those outside of the community, and sends the message to LGBTQ+ youths that they do not matter. The legacy of Section 28 continues to be felt today regarding the quality of LGBTQ+ collections, as these collections are stated to be severely underdeveloped despite nearly two decades of no restrictions: "despite the obvious benefits of high quality LGBTQ provision in libraries, almost unanimously in the literature it is stated that library services for the LGBTQ community remain poor" (Walker & Bates, 2016, p. 271). While Ireland never had an equivalent law to Section 28 instated, it is nonetheless valuable to see how challenges to LGBTQ+ content within secondary schools harm collection development and the well-being of students.

Irish Context

To analyze how the censorship of LGBTQ+ books operates within Irish secondary schools, it is important to recognize how Ireland's culture and approach to censorship laid the groundwork for how censorship is currently present in secondary school libraries. Ireland's relationship with the Catholic Church since gaining independence in 1921 is an inescapable fact that has shaped the moral framework of citizens. The Church became the structure on which Ireland based its moral values, its teachings, and the way of life for citizens. These religious values seeped their way into every facet of culture, including how schools operate and the values that children should learn. According to Keating (2015), the Church's insistence on preventing foreign influence into the country framed citizens as being akin to children who need parental guidance (p. 289-290). This dynamic is evident in how supporters of censorship against LGBTQ+ books believe children need to be morally shielded from such content. Many church-affiliated schools in Ireland face additional religious conflicts when trying to integrate LGBTQ+ books into the curriculum/libraries, on top of the usual parental concerns. Additionally important, in an Irish context, is the matter of how influential the Catholic Church has been in the education system since the creation of the State. From having religious teachings make up part of the school curriculum (Catechism) to many of the secondary schools being convent schools, with students being taught by clergy members, "historically, religious education has been central to the Irish school curriculum, reflecting the largely religious nature of Irish society" (Carmody, 2019, p. 251). Much of the discourse surrounding school libraries, or young people accessing LGBTQ+ texts in general, revolves around the idea that children must be protected from such content, and this wish overshadows the library's reputation for intellectual freedom. "Censorship in school libraries is an issue often subject to unbridled passion and controversy. All of the contenders, however, believe themselves to be acting in the best interests of the children" (Duthie, 2010, p. 92). The lasting moral legacy of such a system, and its continued presence in some areas, suggests that secondary school librarians must greatly consider this cultural context when shaping their LGBTQ+ collections for students.

Interview and Findings

As there is a dearth of published work on censorship in Irish secondary schools, I decided to interview a secondary school librarian to get a better understanding of the current censorship of LGBTQ+ books. For the purpose of publishing, this school will be referred to as "School A."

When asked how much of their collection was dedicated to LGBTQ+ books, it was estimated that less than 20% of the fiction section was dedicated to LGBTQ+ topics, with none falling under the non-fiction category. This indicates that amongst the readership of secondary school students, who often have very busy work-life schedules, fiction is a more appealing mode than non-fiction. For Stand Up Awareness Week every November, there is a display of LGBTQ+ books for students and visitors who come into the library. This is in addition to their traditional Pride display organized every June, which can be seen in Figure 1. During the COVID-19 pandemic, the Sora app was used so students could continue to read books during the school year. There were 252 LGBTQ+ books available on the app. The library has shown that it is remaining up to date with technological advancements in libraries and is using the growing popularity of ebooks to supply students with LGBTQ+ books.

The library has reported a significant increase in the number of LGBTQ+ books over the past decade, including Becky Albertalli's *Simon vs. the Homo Sapiens Agenda* and Alice Oseman's *Heartstopper*. Some of the reasons behind this increase include the large-scale popularity of young adult fiction in recent years, and a general increase in LGBTQ+

Figure 1 A display of various LGBTQ+ books amongst a large Pride flag, organized by School A within the library to celebrate Pride month. Author's photo, 2022.

stories being published in this genre. The librarian reported that there would be large queues of students looking for copies of *Heartstopper*. Book Two of *Heartstopper* is also accessible on the Sora app, allowing students who cannot get a physical copy to read it online. Other books include Juno Dawson's *This Book Is Gay*, Alex Gino's *George*, and Mariko Tamaki and Rosemary Valero-O'Connell's *Laura Dean Keeps Breaking Up with Me*. Many of these books are popular on BookTok (a subsection of TikTok), which has become a new method for students to discover LGBTQ+ books. Positive representation across a diverse range of media can change the attitudes of the cisgender-heterosexual population, whilst making LGBTQ+ people feel less isolated (Levina et al, 2006, p. 739). This is essential when looking at the secondary school library space, as these forms of representation have the power to carry this impact for young people across the country.

As demonstrated by the success of *Heartstopper*, both amongst students and in wider culture, graphic novels have vastly grown in popularity in recent years and should not be overlooked: "graphic novel collections in libraries are increasing in popularity, as the medium gains respectability and popularity as a form of art and literature, and as libraries seek ways to connect with teen audiences" (Greyson, 2007, p. 130). If secondary school librarians integrate graphic novels into their collections, this may inspire students more interested in those types of books/looking for a specific book to come to the library, which they may find a more accepting space than expected. According to Downey (2013, p. 105), people can engage in practices such as "under the radar browsing," where they will engage with a text without checking it out of the library itself, an action which needs to be understood in light of the possible backlash the student may face if they were to publicly read LGBTQ+ books (Downey, p. 105). While the books are being read and enjoyed, their use is untraceable by conventional means. Some solutions provided by Downey are to see whether common wear and tear is occurring on the LGBTQ+ books, indicating their use, and having a robust collection of such books (pp. 105–06). It is crucial to note when there is a call for LGBTQ+ texts to be removed, as when they are targeted, it sends a message to the wider community that this group is not worthy of representation or the same rights within the library space as the broader population (Downey, p. 106).

In the library field, matters of technology, LGBTQ+ subject matter, and bias training are constantly evolving and shaping how the library space operates, and letting LGBTQ+ young people receive up-to-date information on LGBTQ+ matters. The librarian of School A stated that the City of Dublin Education and Training Board (CDETB) and BelongTo (an LGBTQ+ youth organization) training have been utilized to train librarians/teachers. This allows libraries to remain knowledgeable on how best to incorporate LGBTQ+ books/inclusive language into the library space. There have also been several large electronic screens donated to the school, displayed within the library, which allow for the advertising of certain books during Pride. This keeps interested students informed about new books entering the library and lets them see how their school supports the inclusion of LGBTQ+ voices.

Libraries, be it for young people or the general public, function as safe spaces where people can learn about subject matter in a secure environment. The librarian of School A stated that the library is known as a safe space for LGBTQ+ students, that students are comfortable and satisfied with how the library covers LGBTQ+ topics (e.g., respecting names and pronouns), and it has been reported that students in third year have been coming out. This highlights a level of comfort both within the school and the library, as students feel secure in discussing and exploring their identities.

Fortunately, in the case of School A, there has been a lack of parental, principal, or government influence in the hosting of LGBTQ+ books within the library. The general concept of LGBTQ+ representation has been positively received. The school's lack of affiliation with the Catholic Church indicates that the Church's influence does not impact the library. Historically, there is a conflict between integrating an inclusive ethos/curriculum within Irish secondary schools and the influence of the Church: "the idea of state intervention in the internal workings and in the social, cultural and religious aims of each school would still be considered as unacceptable interference by most religious patrons" (Fischer, 2016, p. 179). Modern changes made within secondary schools, such as more LGBTQ+ inclusion with the school curriculum and the library, would be resisted by schools affiliated with the Catholic Church, with librarians operating in those schools facing greater challenges than their state school peers.

In April 2022, it was announced that Minister for Education Norma Foley would allocate €20 million for the School Library Book Grant, which will subsidize the purchase of books and other necessities for Irish schools (Department of Education, 2022). While this specific grant may not be withheld if a controversy occurred based on LGBTQ+ books present within the collection, the fear of controversy may be enough for librarians to engage in self-censorship to prevent unwanted conflicts. Applying for grants through Children's Books Ireland and Libraries Ireland is another external way for the library to gather funds.

Technology plays a significant role in how LGBTQ+ topics are spread in the library and School A. The school's Instagram page contains information on Pride/LGBTQ+ books both throughout the year and in June. Programs such as Sora and Accelerated Reader, as well as Kindle devices, allows LGBTQ+ books to be accessible to students. This helps in resolving the problem of a lacking physical collection. The quiz website Kahoot and the activity database Lookit have been used as ways to educate students on LGBTQ+ topics in an engaging way by allowing them to discover the answers themselves.

In 2018, over 60% of Irish primary school children use phones and tablets to access the internet, and that smartphone usage increases in the transition from primary to secondary education (Everri & Park, 2018, p. 4). Merging support shown in the physical library space with technology/social media-based support further reinforces to students that their school library is a safe space for LGBTQ+ identities. Libraries should lean into this increased use in technology, as well as physical books, in order to meet the needs of students. This encourages them to use the library as a digital information resource, which can prompt exploration into its physical books.

Solutions

For Irish librarians interested in improving young people's access to LGBTQ+ books and in avoiding censorship within their libraries, much of their research will be reliant on the internet for pieces that specifically address Irish libraries. There is research available for Irish librarians aiming to improve their practice around supplying materials to LGBTQ+ patrons; the most notable example is Mark Ward's "The Library as a Queer Space: Investigating Access and Provision for LGBTQ+ Patrons" (2019), which details how LGBTQ+ people in Dublin feel about their access to books in Dublin libraries, and what librarians need to implement or avoid in order to improve this experience. However, the content of this presentation is based on survey responses, and it is acknowledged within that there is little information from academic papers that focus on the censorship of LGBTQ+ text in an Irish context. If Irish librarians want to research this topic further, their sources primarily consist of news reports and social media posts.

Academics in Ireland need to evaluate the recent trends occurring in the United States and the United Kingdom, in conjunction with press and social media announcements within Ireland, to analyze the state of LGBTQ+ censorship within libraries. The recent Liveline scandal on RTÉ, where guests were permitted to make transphobic statements on air, shows how bigoted rhetoric is creeping into mainstream Irish media (Linehan, 2022). It should then be considered whether recent attacks on LGBTQ+ representation in young people's sections within libraries represent an extension of said bigotry or the first sign of its emergence. If librarians are to represent a positive change for the future, they need to identify trends within their own communities by gauging reactions to their LGBTQ+ collections, so they can plan how best to serve younger patrons.

There are numerous steps secondary school librarians in Ireland can take to reduce the censorship of LGBTQ+ books within their collections and stand by their students. There are many international examples of school librarians fighting back against the censorship of LGBTQ+ books, one being the #FReadom Fighters who fought back against the censorship of books deemed "pornographic" by parents (Montgomery, 2022). Their website contains information on how other people can fight back against censorship, including using the hashtag #FReadom on social media.[2] This highlights both how social media can be used to spread awareness of the fight against censorship within libraries, and how librarians are invested in the fight to keep intellectual freedom a top priority within young people's sections of libraries.

School librarians should consider how they can develop larger LGBTQ+ collections and resources within their libraries. This can range from weekly library-based events for students to attend or having LGBTQ+ books available to access online (e.g., having a database for the library that students can access). Making these books easier for young people to access through events which highlight their presence and databases and can greatly help LGBTQ+ students who otherwise feel isolated within their experiences. The school library then transforms into a safe space, one not impacted by usual external factors (e.g., gender/class/religion), and works to improve the overall well-being of students: "international research shows that inclusive and affirmational community services have a proven, positive effect on mitigating the statistically higher mental and physical health risks associated with LGBTQ+ youths" (Snapp et al., 2015, as cited in Hicks & Kerrigan, 2020).

Library industry journals and outsourcing to vendors are said to be the most popular methods of finding specific books (Moody, 2004, p. 5, citing Lee, 1998), but further action should be taken. Conducting research into social media posts, YouTube videos, and LGBTQ+-based blogs is another useful method of finding books that will speak to the experience of LGBTQ+ students. One recent example drawing on social media posts is displays in bookshops for titles popular on "BookTok." Downey et al. (2013, p. 105) recommend utilizing the resources of ALA's GLBT Round Table[3] (now called the "Rainbow Roundtable") and the Lamb-

---

2   https://www.txfreadomfighters.us

3   www.ala.org/glbtrt

da Literary Foundation[4] in lieu of scant LGBTQ+-focused reviews on more popular book lists. The social media pages of librarians invested in LGBTQ+ topics are another useful resource: an example would be the Pinterest board of Jenna Ingham,[5] who keeps an up-to-date list of LGBTQ+ young adult books which secondary school students may find interesting. If school libraries want to get young people engaged with the library space, they should also listen to young people's suggestions of which books to add to their collections. This solves the issue that many librarians run into of failing to meet the needs of the group they are trying to support, so becoming engaged with members of the community and students is the best way to ensure they are represented (Goodwin, 2018, p. 77). This also permits school libraries to be stocked with quality LGBTQ+ books that will meet student demand, fulfilling a need missed by many other school libraries.

Librarians need to also examine how funding works with regard to school libraries and consider how they can defend themselves should an issue of controversy arise. Knowing one's rights is key to any form of employment, and this is especially true for school librarians, who must uphold values of intellectual freedom while working with young people. Using the case of the ALA as a parallel example of funding subsidizing a library-adjacent organization, it can be seen how private foundations have helped this association remain in place today and carry out work against censorship (Asato, 2011, p. 302). School librarians in Ireland should examine where the funding they are currently receiving comes from (as—such as with School A—the source of funding differs between Catholic and non-denominational schools), whether those funding bodies will stand by a censorship controversy, and where else in the State they can receive funding from—those who will stand by them. This will alleviate fears of funding cuts, which may incentivize many school librarians to self-censor. Another bonus is that extra funds will be on hand to purchase more LGBTQ+ books, invest in technological upgrades for the library, and host after-school events. This benefits both librarians and students, while cushioning the blow that a potential censorship controversy may cause.

Librarians should use the increased presence and expectations of technology within the library (e.g., reliable Wi-Fi, access to computers, ability

---

4   www.lambdaliterary.org

5   https://www.pinterest.ie/jennakingham/lgbt%2B-spectrum-ya-books/

to print) to their advantage when attempting to build collections and services for their LGBTQ+ students. Attention must be paid to how up to date their collections are and what can be done to serve the needs of their students. While the physical presence of LGBTQ+ books may be the target of objections, online databases providing access to related books and articles can be of major benefit to students, thus maintaining intellectual freedom. These resources can allow students questioning their own identities, or curious about LGBTQ+ subject matter, to browse free from scrutiny. The extent to which young people are online today shows that having a strong online presence via social media or accessible databases is an overall benefit to school libraries, and can serve to draw attention to online resources such as ebooks and articles.

The practice of labeling has led to more LGBTQ+ books undergoing censorship by preventing access to the people who most require them. One counterpoint to consider, though, discussed in Antell et al. (2012) is that this system is useful to students new to understanding where LGBTQ+ books are stored in the library, allowing them to find what they need: "students' time is limited during school hours, and browsing must be taught as an efficient skill" (p. 91). Through this system, students learn how to efficiently navigate academic libraries and physical repositories going into adulthood.

Current Master in Library and Information Studies (MLIS) degrees cover censorship in certain modules, with the question of "how much interference should the librarian have in which texts are accessible" being posed to students. However, this question emerges more from the consideration of books within the library that may carry anti-LGBTQ+ sentiment, rather than LGBTQ+ books themselves. The issue of LGBTQ+-based censorship does emerge in class readings, but it is easy to for students who don't choose these particular classes to avoid this topic. I found the topic engaging due to being a member of the LGBTQ+ community and already being aware of emerging news of anti-LGBTQ+ backlash within the library field. But given its now-prominent presence, I would encourage that this topic be included in core modules, and that it should be one all students hear about. This would leave them equipped to tackle the topic in their future careers and in continuing their professional development.

School librarians must be knowledgeable of the relevant ethics policies to ensure they are standing by LGBTQ+ students and protecting themselves from backlash. The ALA provides several guides and policies to help librarians facing outside cries for censorship. There is the *Newsletter on Intellectual Freedom,* which highlights the issue of censorship on a deeper level (Sloan, 2012, p. 183) and the ALA offers on its website a "Sample Request for Reconsideration of Library Resources" form, a template for formal requests for the removal of books (American Library Association, 1995, as cited in Steele, 2018). The Library Association of Ireland (LAI) states that it values professionalism, impartiality, and integrity while serving library patrons (2013). The descriptions of each of these values points to supporting users' rights to access books that they need, which in turn supports the existence of LGBTQ+ books within the library space. Other bodies, such as the Australian Library and Information Association (ALIA) and International Federation of Library Associations (IFLA), all state that censorship is not acceptable within the library and that the right for users to seek a specific book must be protected (Duthie, 2010, p. 87). School librarians should make it clear that their role is to support the value of intellectual freedom, emphasizing the importance of young people having control of what they read, and to develop that interest.

School libraries need to remain well-stocked with quality LGBTQ+ books regardless of circumstance, without fears of funding being cut due to threats of censorship. LGBTQ+ young people should not continue their developmental journeys without books to help guide them through the process. Their right to representation by presence of these materials within school libraries should also not be boiled down to a debating point, or framed as something inappropriate. School libraries, in line with their roles as defenders of intellectual freedom, should stand ready to defend the rights of LGBTQ+ students, ensuring they have everything they need for accepting who they are and preparing them for the world going forward. If school libraries are to be framed as the first point of attack by those opposed to LGBTQ+ rights, librarians are needed to uphold these principles to ensure a bright future for LGBTQ+ youth.

References

Albanese, A. (2021, April 6). *ALA releases 2020 Most Challenged Books List.* Publishers Weekly. https://www.publishersweekly.com/pw/by-topic/industry-news/libraries/article/86000-ala-releases-2020-most-challenged-books-list.html.

American Library Association. (1995). *Sample Request for Reconsideration of Library Resources.*

American Library Association. (2010). *Intellectual freedom manual* (8th ed.). ALA Editions.

Antell, K., Strothmann, M., Hunt, L., & Wachsmann, M. (2012). Does labeling children's books constitute censorship? *Reference and User Services Quarterly, 52*(2), 90-92. https://doi.org/10.5860/rusq.52n2.90.

Asato, N. (2011). The origins of the Freedom to Read Foundation: Public librarians' campaign to establish a legal defense against library censorship. *Public Library Quarterly, 30*(4), 286-306. https://doi.org/10.1080/01616846.2011.625598.

Busha, C. H. (1972). *Freedom versus suppression and censorship: With a study of the attitudes of Midwestern public librarians and a bibliography of Censorship.* Libraries Unlimited.

Carmody, B. (2019). Ecclesial to public space: Religion in Irish secondary schools. *Religious Education, 114*(5), 551-564. https://doi.org/10.1080/00344087.2019.1643273.

Department of Education. (2022, April 16). *Minister Foley announces €20 million School Library Book Grant* [Press release]. https://www.gov.ie/en/press-release/2edde-minister-foley-announces-20-million-school-library-book-grant/.

Downey, J. (2013). Self-censorship in selection of LGBT-themed materials. *Reference and User Services Quarterly, 53*(2), 104-107. https://doi.org/10.5860/rusq.53n2.104.

Duthie, F. (2010). Libraries and the ethics of censorship. *The Australian Library Journal, 59*(3), 86-94. https://www.tandfonline.com/doi/abs/10.1080/00049670.2010.10735994.

Everri, M., & Park, K. (2018). *Children's online behaviours in Irish primary and secondary schools.* Zeeko, NovaUCD, University College Dublin. https://zeeko.ie/wp-content/uploads/2018/06/ZEEKO-TREND-REPORT-.pdf

Fischer, K. (2016). *Schools and the politics of religion and diversity in the Republic of Ireland: Separate but equal?.* Manchester University Press.

Goodwin, G. (2018). *A helping hand for queer and questioning youth: Provision for young LGBTIQ people in Irish public libraries.* Dublin Business School. https://esource.dbs.ie/handle/10788/3486.

Greyson, D. (2007). GLBTQ content in comics graphic novels for teens. *Collection Building, 26*(4), 130-134. https://doi.org/10.1108/01604950710831942.

Hicks, P., & Kerrigan, P. (2020). An intersectional quantitative content analysis of the LGBTQ+ catalogue in Irish public libraries. *Journal of Librarianship and Information Science, 52*(4), 1028-1041. https://doi.org/10.1177/0961000619898212.

Higgins-Dailey, J. (2021, April 5). *ALA's Top Ten Most Challenged Books of 2020*. Intellectual Freedom Blog. https://www.oif.ala.org/alas-top-ten-most-challenged-books-of-2020/.

Ismail, A. (January 31, 2022). *There's a simple reason that demands to "ban" books like* Maus *are soaring*. Slate. https://slate.com/human-interest/2022/01/maus-banned-tennessee-holocaust-graphic-novel.html.

Jamison, A. (2018, May 8). *Librarians Beware: Self-Censorship* [Blog post]. https://www.oif.ala.org/librarians-beware-self-censorship/.

Keating, A. (2015). Censorship: The cornerstone of Catholic Ireland. *A Journal of Church and State, 57*(2), 289-309. https://doi.org/10.1093/jcs/cst097.

Kelleher, P. (2020, August 10). *Libraries remove vital trans teen book after disgraceful far-right letter writing campaign linking LGBT+ lives to paedophilia*. PinkNews. https://www.pinknews.co.uk/2020/08/10/beyond-magenta-susan-kuklin-cork-city-library-ireland-far-right-homophobia-kelly/.

Knox, E. (2014). "The books will still be in the library": Narrow definitions of censorship in the discourse of challengers. *Library Trends, 62*(4), 740-749. https://doi.org/10.1353/lib.2014.0020.

Knox, E. J. M. (2017). Opposing censorship in difficult times. *The Library Quarterly, 87*(3), 268-276. https://doi.org/10.1086/692304.

Kravitz, N. (2002). *Censorship and the School Library Media Center*. Libraries Unlimited.

Lee. E. (1998). *Libraries in the age of mediocrity*. McFarland & Co.

Lee, N. (2023, July 14). *Some libraries in Ireland are restricting access to young adult LGBTQ+ books, employee says*. GCN. https://gcn.ie/ireland-libraries-restricting-access-lgbtq-young-adult-books/.

Levina, M., Waldo, C. R., & Fitzgerald, L. F. (2000). We're here, we're queer, we're on TV: The effects of visual media on heterosexuals' attitudes toward gay men and lesbians. *Journal of Applied Social Psychology, 30*(4), 738-758. https://doi.org/10.1111/j.1559-1816.2000.tb02821.x.

Library Association of Ireland. (2013). *Code of Professional Practice*. https://www.libraryassociation.ie/wp-content/uploads/2018/11/Code-of-Professional-Practice-2013_council-approved.pdf.

Linehan, A. (2022, June 14). *RTÉ Liveline criticised for enabling transphobic hate speech*. GCN. https://gcn.ie/rte-liveline-enabling-hate-speech/.

McMenemy, D. (2009). Censorship or recklessness? Obligations and legality regarding controversial materials in libraries. *Library Review 58*(2), 85–88. https://doi.org/10.1108/00242530910936899.

Moody, K. (2004). *Zero Censorship! Who Are We Kidding? An exploratory analysis of the opinions and experiences of Queensland-based public librarians with regard to the censorship of materials in public library collections*. e-Lis. http://eprints.rclis.org/6208/

Montgomery, D. (2022, Jan 18). *Librarians fight back against efforts to ban books in schools*. Education Week. https://www.edweek.org/teaching-learning/ librarians-fight-back-against-efforts-to-ban-books-in-schools/2022/01.

Nixon, D., & Givens, N. (2007). An epitaph to Section 28? Telling tales out of school about changes and challenges to discourses of sexuality. *International Journal of Qualitative Studies in Education, 20*(4), 449-471. https://doi. org/10.1080/09518390601176564.

Patin, B., et al. (Hosts). (2022, February 21). The censors are coming! The censors are coming! (No. 18) [Audio podcast episode]. In *Libraries Lead in the New Normal*. https://www.acechicagoevents.com/libraries-lead-episode-18.

Sloan, S. (2012). Regional differences in collecting freethought books in American public libraries: A case of self-censorship? *The Library Quarterly, 82*(2), 183-205. https://doi.org/10.1086/664577.

Snapp, S. D., et al. (2015) Social support networks for LGBT young adults: Low cost strategies for positive adjustment. *Family Relations* 64(3): 420–430. https://doi.org/10.1111/fare.12124.

Steele, J. E. (2018). Censorship of library collections: An analysis using gatekeeping theory. *Collection Management, 43*(4), 229-248. https://doi.org/10.1080/014 62679.2018.1512917.

Stevens, T. (2020). Suppressing communities: An analysis of LGBTQ+ censorship in libraries. *Pathfinder: A Canadian Journal for Information Science Students and Early Career Professionals, 1*(2), 51-62. https://doi.org/10.29173/ pathfinder15.

Walker, J., & Bates, J. (2016). Developments in LGBTQ provision in second-ary school library services since the abolition of Section 28. *Journal of Librarianship and Information Science, 48*(3), 269-283. https://doi. org/10.1177/0961000614566340.

Ward, M. (2019) *The library as a queer space: Investigating access and provision for LGBTQ+ patrons* [PowerPoint slides]. Library Association of Ireland. https://conference.libraryassociation.ie/portfolio/the-library-as-a-queer-space-investigating-access-and-provision-for-lgbtq-patrons-mark-ward/.

Williams, R. N. (2020). *Self-censorship in secondary school libraries*. [Doctoral dis-sertation, Cambridge College]. Cambridge College ProQuest Dissertations Publishing. https://www.proquest.com/dissertations-theses/ self-censorship-secondary-school-libraries/docview/2469515374/se-2

Disappearing Queers
A Survey of Queer Material Accessibility in Mainstream Archives

Kestrel Ward and Evangeline Giaconia

Introduction

Queer materials have a tendency to disappear into archives, whether through historical suppression of openly queer identities or current responses to censorship (Brown, 2011; Jules, 2016). Though non-queer archives, such as national and state repositories or university special collections, may not be dedicated to queer history, they nevertheless contain queer materials, as queer people have always been part of society, whether seen or unseen. In the current atmosphere of censorship of queer materials and culture, especially in the state of Florida, it is critical that we understand the lives of queer materials in these "mainstream"[1] archives, including how they are cataloged, used, or disappeared.

Queer archives have done integral work in preserving queer history on our own terms. The Canadian Lesbian and Gay Archives,[2] Lambda Archives of San Diego,[3] GLBT Historical Society,[4] and so many more, create unimaginably important spaces to document history that mainstream archives have not seen fit to include. There is extensive

---

1 For the purposes of this chapter, we use the term "mainstream" to mean any archive or collection that is not primarily focused on LGBTQ archiving.

2 Now known as The ArQuives https://arquives.ca/

3 https://www.lambdaarchives.org/

4 https://www.glbthistory.org/

literature on the invaluable contributions of these institutions (Barri-ault, 2009; Brown, 2011; Sizemore-Barber, 2017; etc.). And yet there is a large gap in the literature surrounding the fate of queer materials in mainstream archives, those collections in large national, state, and university repositories. It is critical to establish an understanding of how queer materials are being collected, cataloged, used, and made accessible in these institutions, especially as we in the state of Flor-ida face increasing government censorship of queer voices and lives.

With state bills like the so-called "Don't Say Gay" bill (CS/CS/HB 1557), attacks on academic freedom like CS/HB7[5] and SB266 (formerly HB999)[6] signed by Governor Ron DeSantis with a host of other bills in the spring of 2023, and rollbacks on LGBTQ+ rights like SB254,[7] Florida is facing a wave of oppression. Similar attacks are happening across the United States, from Texas to Indiana to Idaho. Regressive legislation and an increase in calls for the removal of queer books from libraries (primarily school and public) creates a hostile atmosphere for those who use queer archival materials and produce queer scholarship. This includes archives, where archivists have, throughout time, been culpable in burying queer mate-rials among their collections rather than describing or promoting them adequately (Brown, 2011; Freeman, 2023; Knowlton, 1987).

In this chapter, we outline the literature on the exclusion of queer ma-terials in archives, working in decreasing scale from the archive as a colonial institution to individually-enacted processes of archival cen-sorship. We demonstrate that there is a lack of scholarly attention to the fate of queer materials within "mainstream" institutions, and sug-gest that work needs to be done to address this gap. We offer our own interventions: an account of a discussion panel we led at the Society of Florida Archivists in which archival professionals shared their ex-periences and concerns around queer materials in their archives, and a nationwide survey we created to collect data on the ways in which

---

5   The "Individual Freedom Bill" makes requiring Diversity, Equity, Inclusion, and Justice (DEIJ) training for any employee or student of the state illegal, as well as revising the teaching of African American history, as well as various other amendments to the ways American history is taught in Florida public schools.

6   A higher education bill that took aim at higher education unions, preventing the teaching of certain theories about institutionalized sexism and racism, nullifying tenure at state institu-tions, removing DEIJ statements from hiring paperwork, and making it illegal to spend state funds on DEIJ programs at higher education institutions, as well as a variety of other anti-intel-lectual and anti-DEIJ measures.

7   https://www.flsenate.gov/Session/Bill/2023/254

archives utilize and make accessible—or obscure—their queer collections. Finally, we present actions that anyone, no matter your position in the archive, can take in order to promote queer materials in your collections.

Those who want to make queer archival materials more accessible must contend with a legacy of archival suppression. In combination with the current fear-based and repressive legislation in the United States, these barriers seem insurmountable. But with a community of archivists committed to fighting for their queer materials, archival professionals at every level can ameliorate this harm and work to strengthen their collections in a number of ways.

Who We Are

As two White, queer researchers at an academic library, we approach this research from a very specific positionality. We live in the Gainesville, Florida area and work at the University of Florida Libraries. As such, we recognize that the main campus of the University of Florida (UF) is located on the ancestral territory of the Potano and of the Seminole peoples.

Kestrel is a nonbinary librarian. They are a recent graduate of the Florida State University School of Information, and did their final internship in the University of Florida archives. Evangeline is a queer librarian and recent graduate of the Museum Studies program at UF, where she focused on the ethics of housing and digitizing Indigenous materials. As part of Kestrel's internship, they visited a number of archives along the East Coast, from the National Archives to state and college archives, to evaluate their queer collections. They found that the accessibility and scope of these collections varied greatly. Some archives had dedicated space and people to work with the queer materials and assist researchers, while others barely knew what they had in terms of queer collections. Kestrel's frustration with the results of their search led them to question the overall state of queer archiving, and whether difficulties and inconsistencies were systemic or simply bad luck. Evangeline's background in archival ethics provided the project with a starting point to look at the suppression of queer archival materials.

We hope to begin to fill the gap in literature around this question and work towards understanding how mainstream archives handle their queer collections. At the Society of Florida Archivists Annual Meeting in May of 2023, we led a discussion session which allowed us to begin to reveal patterns, concerns, and hopes regarding the state of queer archival materials across the country.

Archives, Neutrality, and Bias

It is often taken for granted that archives are neutral spaces. However, archives themselves are a product of imperialism and colonialism—not to mention the content within them which has historically been sourced from colonized cultures (Tuhiwai-Smith, 1999). The fundamental presumption that archives are neutral is based on the assumption that Western cultural knowledge is the "default" and therefore a neutral starting point. On the contrary: Linda Tuhiwai-Smith shows how the project of imperialism is inherently tied to processes of classification, organization, and naming, beginning with classifying who counts as human through the hierarchies of race and societies (1999). Existence in the archive implies a form of national legitimacy: "the idea that a person can find their families, or those whose lives mirrored theirs, in an acid-free box, and in doing so, find themselves, be recognized by the historical record, and claim their right to take up space in the world" (Watts, 2018, p. 104). Omission from the archive, then, is a form of historical silencing (Carter, 2006). And from the beginning, archives have worked to reinforce a specific norm that excludes marginalized peoples from the national narrative—including queer people.

It is critical not to reduce this process of exclusion to an abstraction. Adams-Campbell et al.'s concept of "settler-archival labor" is highly useful in examining how archival suppression—or exclusion, or violence—happens on an everyday, grounded level (2015). Adams-Campbell et al. show that these harmful processes do not happen without the everyday work of individuals. In their discussion of "settler archives," they describe how settler-colonialism is enacted in archives through processes including the regulation of access to archival holding, controlling the content and rhetorical strategies of archives, and denying Indigenous knowledge and records as legitimate evidence. For example, when Indigenous materials are attributed solely to the White researcher who "found" them, rather than the Indigenous person who created them, the legacy of Indigenous ownership, knowledge, and authority is obliterated (Anderson & Christen, 2019).

While these authors focus specifically on the suppression of Indigenous narratives, these strategies can be used more broadly to perpetrate the suppression of queer narratives within archives. For example, Brown (2011) writes of the families of queer individuals whose papers were contained in archives, who requested that materials be returned, hidden, or not identified as queer, and Knowlton (1987) of the reluctance of archivists to label queer materials as such. As Adams-Campbell et al. purport, in regard to Indigenous materials, these acts—the demand to cover a family history perceived shameful, the obscuring of evidence of queer lives—happen by the everyday work of individuals (2015).

Yet individual actions which perpetuate archival harm are symptomatic of bias at the institutional level. After all, "mainstream" archives themselves did not begin intentionally identifying their queer material until the 1990s as the gay rights movement began to have an effect on public opinion and archival practice, much less begin to purposefully collect it (Brown, 2011, p. 122). Queer history has been actively excluded from collections, as queerness has been variously oppressed, prohibited, and villainized throughout the history of the country. The lack of overt queerness in the archive gave rise to a process of reading "against the grain": reading between the lines to infer queer historical realities (Barriault, 2009, p. 8). This legacy of exclusion leaves us with just thirty years of queer materials even being sought after by archives.

Additionally, we must contend with the repercussions of queer materials now being shoehorned into archival systems that were not intended to house them. Bergis Jules reminds us that "who writes the software, who builds the tools, who produces the technical standards, and who provides the funding or other resources for that work" determines the bias inherent in the tools produced (2016, para. 4). Bias is baked into archival structures and tools by those who developed them, which can make them unsuitable for use by outside groups. The Library of Congress Subject Headings (LCSH), for example, were developed through the normative perspective of White, male Christians (Moyse, 2021). The LCSH focus on "uniformity and efficiency" (Moyse, 2021, p. 11), reduces the complexity of queer categories, and has led to the development of alternative vocabularies like the Homosaurus, an internationally linked data vocabulary of queer terms meant to augment systems like the LCSH. This kind of built-in bias in metadata schemas can work to ensure queer subjects are invisibilized (Rawson, 2010). After all, incorrectly or insufficiently described materials in archives may as well not exist. And this erasure is not equitably distributed. Greenblatt (2011) discusses how the LCSH conflates the terms "sex" and "gender," obscuring a distinction that is critical to queer conceptions of identity, the erasure of which obscures transgender and gender-nonconforming people from the catalog.

Censorship in the archives is another major form of harm to queer materials, one that we as archivists are most easily poised to see in our own institutions. Archival censorship can appear many different ways, whether explicit or implicit, a distinction we offer here. Explicit censorship encompasses the exclusion of queer materials due to explicit personal biases or biased policies. For example, the assumption that queer individuals do not engage with an institution, and therefore there is no reason to cater to them, creates explicitly biased ways of dealing with the public and making materials accessible. Alternatively, archivists may believe that obtaining queer materials is tantamount to promoting queer lifestyles, and direct their collections management choices to exclude acquiring those materials (Gough & Greenblatt, 2011). Implicit censorship, on the other hand, includes negligence towards materials. This negligence may go unrecognized as purposeful censorship, and can result in a lack of programming, digitization, research guides, or attention to accurate metadata, such as the ways mentioned above.

In sum, archival harm to queer materials is perpetuated through both the everyday actions of archivists and the greater, historical processes of institutions not intended to house queer collections. Harm is furthered when tools like cataloging systems are incongruous with queer identities, and materials are fit into categories which obscure their complexity. On top of these processes, modes of censorship at the level of individual decisions made by archivists can have devastating effects on the accessibility and use of queer materials. Truly, we as archivists have a number of barriers to reckon with in bringing queer materials into the light—but luckily, we are not working alone.

Interventions

SFA Discussion Session

At the 2023 Society of Florida Archivists (SFA) Annual Meeting, we moderated a discussion session in which librarians, archivists, and other Galleries, Libraries, Archives, and Museums (GLAM) professionals from the state of Florida and the Southeast shared their own experiences with their queer materials. The responses illuminated the critical importance of this work in the current oppressive political climate.

Our presentation and discussion, "Discussion of Access and Usage of LGBTQ Archival Material," covered a truncated version of the preceding literature review, offered insights from our own work to understand the current landscape of the field, and provided a foundation for a robust discussion of participants' own experiences, fears, and hopes.

A major topic of discussion was the impact of current repressive legislation in the Southeast on participants' acquisition and metadata decisions at their institutions. Responses revealed that many archivists and institutions are already feeling pressure in these areas. By and large, the largest impact has been the creation of an atmosphere of fear: fear of censorship, fear for the fate of collections, and for personal safety—especially the safety of the vulnerable members of participants' institutions. One conference attendee reported postponing a student-curated exhibit featuring LGBTQ+ and gender-related themes to evaluate the political climate and considered omitting certain curatorial information to shield the student creators from potential backlash. [See chapter 8, "Stop WOKE Gave Me Pause," by David Benjamin in this book.] Other participants discussed how news and TV coverage of a Pride event made student workers afraid to be associated with the event. We heard from university librarians that there is widespread concern that political censorship will affect collections, despite the fact that they are a state institution.

Another strong theme of our discussion session is how archivists are rethinking the language used in their exhibitions, deciding to couch collections and exhibits in less "inflammatory" language to avoid possible negative repercussions. University and public libraries alike have hurriedly pulled back from "Banned Books" events, once a common area of programming in libraries. The interactions between university and public institutions are also shifting in this time: one archivist shared that their institution is preparing itself to ingest the archival materials of a Diversity, Equity, and Inclusion (DEI) organization under threat. Around acquisitions, fears are high regarding the future of materials: as archivists, how can we assure potential donors their collections will be held safe in the public trust in these times, when we are uncertain of the fate of our own collections?

Participants also shared their barriers to using queer materials. These were largely material concerns: a lack of time and resources to describe queer oral histories, the barrier of text searchability, dealing with the mire of preexisting collection development policies, and attempting to dig out buried materials. And in Florida especially, we all deal with the legacy of the Florida Legislative Investigation Committee or more popularly known as the Johns Committee, a McCarthyist legislative investigative committee that in the 1960s terrorized the queer community and left a legacy of fear still felt today (Hof-Mahoney & Gentilhomme, n.d.).

Beginning in 1961, the Johns Committee investigated faculty and students at public colleges in Florida, particularly the University of Florida, Florida State University, and the University of South Florida, for suspected homosexuality, threatening prosecution and jail time if queer people did not out their fellows to the committee. The committee's reign of terror in Gainesville resulted in dozens of faculty being fired and students leaving UF. The student body vehemently opposed the Johns Committee actions, but Gainesville residents more or less supported it. Though the atmosphere on campus today is much more accepting than those troubled times, queer people in Gainesville and UF still face discrimination today, and the fear of such recent community persecution lingers.[8]

Finally, in our SFA session, we discussed work going forward. It is easy to get mired down in the great challenges we face, and working together to think of solutions is necessary to alleviate the fear we are all experiencing. Going forward, archivists felt that revising and updating metadata is one of the greatest priorities when it comes to making queer materials in archives more usable. With proper metadata, materials are easier to find, allowing for increased usage.

Another high priority for finding queer material in the archives is to identify historic coded language—community terms that researchers today may not recognize, such as referring to a partner as a "special friend" or the term "Boston Marriage" for two women who were living together in a committed relationship. Such terms are common in documents dating from times when queerness was criminalized. Community collaboration was also discussed as another high priority, engaging the expertise of queer community members who might be able to provide new insight into old records.

---

8   For more information, consult the Matheson Museum's online exhibition McCarthy Moment: The Johns Committee in Florida at mathesonmuseum.org/online-exhibitions and the documentaries *Behind Closed Doors* (https://www.youtube.com/watch?v=crrF1h9L708) and *The Committee* (https://www.pbs.org/video/committee-committee/).

Additionally, a priority across participants is implementing better OCR (Optimal Character Recognition) text searching.[9] Text searchability transforms the accessibility and usage potential of archival materials, decreasing the time spent searching for resources by an order of magnitude. With the number of community and standardized terms used to describe queer materials over the years, findability is paramount.

LGBTQ+ Material Survey

For ourselves, one of the steps we are taking is the creation of a survey regarding the specifics of how LGBTQ+ materials are handled and used in mainstream institutions. This survey, "The Survey of Accessibility and Usage of LGBTQ+ Archival Materials," is our first step to filling in the gap in the literature and understanding the landscape of queer archival materials.

Our survey was conducted over the course of three months, from March through May of 2023, with participation from the SFA discussion participants as well as over a hundred respondents from across the United States. Demographic information will allow us to sort our data by region and type of institution, while the bulk of the survey covers the specifics of how queer materials are collected and used. While our data is still in the process of being fully analyzed, several trends have emerged that echo the concerns shared during the discussion session, such as lack of funding and finding aids.

When the detailed results of our survey are fully published, we hope that they will inspire archival institutions to put more resources into making their LGBTQ+ collections more accessible and visible to the public. By showing overall trends for the country or by specific region, archives can allocate resources to where there is the greatest need. Archival associations such as the Society of American Archivists or regional associations like the Society of Florida Archivists can allocate funds and programming to those areas with the greatest disparity in how their LGBTQ+ collections are handled in mainstream archives.

---

9   OCR is the mechanical or electronic conversion of a scanned image to a searchable text. It uses automated machine learning to translate the image into text files.

Next Steps

Our interventions—the discussion panel and survey—are the beginning of a long road, not an end result. Recognition of problems is the first step towards correcting them, and we hope that this chapter serves as a call to action to begin correcting the disappearance of queer materials within archives. These conversations are a starting point for archivists and those in positions of power to look at the state of LGBTQ+ materials within mainstream archives. We urge all archival professionals, whatever your level of decision-making power within your institution, to work towards ameliorating archival negligence through policy-making, funding and staffing decisions, and making queer materials more accessible to researchers and the public.

Archives that strive to be representative must not only include queer materials, but should strive to make those items findable to even casual researchers—especially since queer researchers are often not formally trained in archival research. Practices such as using community terms like "gay," "lesbian," "bisexual," and "transgender" in metadata, creating full-text search functions for digital items, and creating finding aids for queer items all increase the accessibility of these items to researchers.

The Homosaurus[10] can be implemented to bolster lacking metadata. This resource is an international linked data vocabulary that can be used alongside other metadata schema such as Library of Congress Subject Headings. Full-text searching for digitized items can be achieved through the use of Optical Character Recognition (OCR). OCR technology enables handwritten documents to become keyword searchable. This is an important step that fills gaps where metadata improvements cannot. All the inclusive metadata in the world might not find older community terms that are no longer used. Text searchability will revolutionize not only outside researchers' experience, but allow you to know your own collections more deeply, possibly finding queer histories in unexpected places.

GLAM institutions with any identified queer materials should create finding aids available online. Researchers—especially amateur ones—may not know where to start with your collections. Creating a finding aid that highlights material and/or provides context for the items

---

10   https://homosaurus.org/

in your collections will facilitate researchers' work and make queer people feel more welcome in your spaces. Furthermore, queer items should be included in archives outreach, education, and display work. Visibilizing queer history makes you a safer space for queer people, and actively combats our disappearance into the archive.

Cultivating relationships with local queer community members and organizations is a great way to connect your collections to those you represent, and even recruit volunteers for projects. In the Southeast, the Invisible Histories Project assists archives in Mississippi, Alabama, Georgia, and the Florida Panhandle to connect to their local LGBTQ+ community.[11] Creating volunteer-run task forces to target specific areas of concern, such as updating metadata or creating finding aids, can not only lighten the load of archival work on staff, but connect community members with archives in a more personal way.

For those in colleges and universities, supplementing staff time with student workers can be a good option. Through the Federal Work Study program, students can be hired on a semester-by-semester basis without great cost to your department. For alternative funding sources, look to state-based queer history grants, such as the California State Library's LGBTQ+ Preservation & Accessibility grant.[12]

Updating metadata, making materials accessible through text searchability and finding aids, and involving the local queer community in your work are excellent places for any GLAM institution to begin with their queer collections. There are resources available to support this work, and people willing to help. While the current atmosphere of political suppression has created a feeling of fear, it is critical that we keep pushing forward with our efforts—as our predecessors have always done.

References

Adams-Campbell, M., Falzetti, A. G., & Rivard, C. (2015). Introduction: Indigeneity and the work of settler archives. *Settler Colonial Studies, 5*(2), 109-16.

---

11   https://invisiblehistory.org/

12   Found here: https://www.library.ca.gov/services/to-libraries/lgbtq-preservation/

Anderson, J., & Christen, K. (2019). Decolonizing attribution: Traditions of exclusion. *Journal of Radical Librarianship, 5*, 112-152.

Barriault, M. (2009). Archiving the queer and queering the archives: A case study of the Canadian Lesbian and Gay Archives (CLGA). In J. A. Bastian & B. Alexander (Eds.), *Community Archives* (pp. 97–108). Facet.

Brown, A. (2011). How queer 'pack rats' and activist archivists saved our history: An overview of lesbian, gay, bisexual, transgender, and queer (LGBTQ) archives, 1970–2008. In E. Greenblatt (Eds.), *Serving LGBTIQ library and archives users: essays on outreach, service, collections and access* (pp. 121-35). McFarland and Company, Inc.

Carter, Rodney G. S. (2006). Of things said and unsaid: Power, archival silences, and power in silence. *Archivaria 61*(September), 215–33.

CS/HB 7 2022 Bicameral 2022 Regular Sess (FL 2022) https://www.flsenate.gov/Session/Bill/2022/7/?Tab=BillText

CS/CS/HB 1557 2022 Bicameral 2022 Reg Sess (FL 2022) https://www.flsenate.gov/Session/Bill/2022/1557

Freeman, E. (2023). Defying description: Searching for queer history in institutional archives. *Archival Science 23*, 447–470.

Gough, C., & Greenblatt, E. (2011). Barriers to selecting materials about sexual and gender diversity. In E. Greenblatt (Ed.), *Serving LGBTIQ Library and Archives Users: Essays on Outreach, Service, Collections and Access* (pp. 165–173). McFarland and Company, Inc.

Greenblatt, E. (2011). The treatment of LGBTIQ concepts in the Library of Congress Subject Headings. In E. Greenblatt (Ed.), *Serving LGBTIQ Library and Archives Users: Essays on Outreach, Service, Collections and Access* (pp. 212–228). McFarland & Company, Inc., Publishers.

HB 999 2022 Bicameral 2023 Reg Sess (FL 2023) https://www.flsenate.gov/Session/Bill/2023/999

HB 254 2022 Bicameral 2023 Reg Sess (FL 2023) https://www.flsenate.gov/Session/Bill/2023/254

Hof-Mahoney, K., & Gentilhomme, S. (n.d.) *McCarthy moment: The Johns Committee in Florida.* Matheson History Museum. https://express.adobe.com/page/n2RaGQ69SDhcj/

Jules, B. (2016, November 11). Confronting our failure of care around the legacies of marginalized people in the archives. *On Archivy.* https://medium.com/on-archivy/confronting-our-failure-of-care-around-the-legacies-of-marginalized-people-in-the-archives-dc4180397280

Knowlton, E. (1987). Documenting the gay rights movement. *Provenance, 5*(1), 17–30.

Moyse, E. (2021). *Queer browsing and the Library of Congress Subject Headings: Can user-generated tags enhance subject access to LGBTQ+ material?* [Doctoral dissertation: City University London]. Humanities Commons.

Rawson, K. J. (2010). *Archiving transgender: Affects, logics, and the power of queer history* [Doctoral dissertation, Syracuse University]. Surface. https://surface.syr.edu/wp_etd/1/

SB 254 2022 Bicameral 2023 Reg Sess (FL 2023) https://www.flsenate.gov/Session/Bill/2023/254/ByCategory/?Tab=BillText

Sizemore-Barber, A. (2017). Archival movements: South Africa's Gay and Lesbian Memory in Action. *Safundi, 18*(2), 117–130. https://doi.org/10.1080/17533171.2016.1270568

Tuhiwai-Smith, L. (1999). *Decolonizing methodologies: Research and indigenous peoples.* Zed.

Watts, G. (2018). Queer lives in archives: Intelligibility and forms of memory. *disClosure: A Journal of Social Theory, 27*, 103–111. https://doi.org/10.13023/disclosure.27.15

Here, Queer, But Catalog Records Aren't Used to It
The Discoverability of LGBTQIA+ Representation in Library Collections

Amanda Melilli, Alicia G. Vaandering, and James W. Rosenzweig

Introduction

Recent years have shown a substantial increase in the number of published books that include LGBTQIA+ characters and content. While these still make up a small percentage of total published books, readers in the 2020s are significantly more likely to have access to books with LGBTQIA+ representation than were readers in the 20th century or even the early 2000s. However, finding these materials remains a challenge. Too often, readers have to rely on the knowledge of librarians who have taken a personal interest in queer materials and collections in order to find rich and diverse LGBTQIA+ representation. This can be a barrier for library users, particularly for LGBTQIA+ library patrons who have, due to privacy concerns or fear of discrimination, historically been less likely to ask for help from librarians (Seidel, 1998; Stewart & Kendrick, 2019). Independent access to library materials is an essential aspect of the library user experience, so library systems must evolve to ensure that these materials are discoverable.

More needs to be understood about the nuances of LGBTQIA+ visibility and invisibility in library catalogs to enable the development of inclusive systems that increase the discoverability of diverse materials. In our previous research, we have examined LGBTQIA+ representation in library picture book collections by asking what stories are being shared about LGBTQIA+ experiences and who is being depicted in text and illustrations (Vaandering & Rosenzweig, 2023; Vaandering et al., 2023). This study builds upon our previous research by treating recently published children's picture books as a microcosm of the North American publishing industry in order to examine how the catalog describes the representation of LGBTQIA+ identities.[1] We approach this research not as catalogers but as public service librarians at academic libraries, centering our perspectives and experiences of how library users search library catalogs to meet their information needs. In analyzing what terminology is used in WorldCat, a popular resource for library patrons, catalogers, and other librarians, we aim to increase awareness of both the visible and invisible aspects of LGBTQIA+ representation in the classification of literature in library search tools.

The Evolution of Cataloging LGBTQIA+ Content

Early in the 2000s, researchers established that the accessibility and discoverability of LGBTQIA+ content in libraries was a challenge for patrons. Books on LGBTQIA+ subjects were not always widely held, and librarians provided inconsistent levels of service in response to requests for this material (Clyde & Lobban, 2001; Curry 2005). Discoverability has posed a particular obstacle for patrons due to the limitations of the Library of Congress Subject Headings (LCSH) in addressing LGBTQIA+ topics. Some identities continue to go unmentioned in LCSH, while others remain bound to outdated language that has failed to keep pace with linguistic developments in the queer community (Edge, 2019, p. 82).

One basic challenge in cataloging systems has been the dilemma between universalization and minoritization. Universalization values the unified whole, promoting "unmarked representation" to avoid accentuating differences, which contrasts with efforts to classify and draw attention to differences through minoritization (Christensen, 2008, p. 237). For example, those drawn to universalization would likely value "homosexuality" as a subject heading because it encompasses both gay men and lesbians within the context of same-sex relations and relationships. This simplifies discovery, allowing a search for a single term to gather a lot of material. For those drawn to minoritization, separate subject headings for gay men and lesbians would likely be

---

1   We use the term "LGBTQIA+ identities" to encompass diverse gender identities and sexual orientations, as both are part of one's social identity.

preferable as a means of increasing the visibility of each group: minoritized cataloging terms simplify discovery when the searcher wants to make more subtle distinctions or to use more precise query language. As Christensen (2008) noted, the tensions between universalization and minoritization are not easily resolved and will continue to challenge catalogers.

Some researchers have suggested that the drawbacks of LCSH can be addressed by implementing gender and sexuality subject headings from the Homosaurus, a controlled vocabulary that was developed specifically for describing LGBTQIA+ identities in library materials (Fischer, 2023, pp. 8-9). Another study, however, noted that the Homosaurus still lacks coverage of some aspects addressed by LCSH terms (e.g., connections of queer identity to other aspects of identity, like "lesbian businesswomen") (Dobreski et al., 2022, p. 505). Both vocabularies also share some limitations as pre-coordinated vocabularies which, like most cataloging approaches used widely in libraries, pre-designate subject headings and therefore can be slow to adapt to areas where language and terminology are in flux (Dobreski et al., 2022, p. 505). As yet, there is no clear solution to the cataloging problem. In fact, Drabinski (2013) argued that a solution is neither possible nor desirable. She maintained that bias and inaccessibility are endemic to any system of classification and that the application of queer theory to this problem should lead us to interrogate and augment cataloging language rather than seek to fix a problem that, according to her argument, cannot be "fixed" (pp. 108-109). Some portions of Drabinski's argument have been challenged by other scholars. For instance, McAuliffe (2021) countered that Drabinski's approach may alienate patrons or subject them to experiences of othering and rejection through problematic catalog language (pp. 217-218). However, Drabinski's underlying assertion that the catalog is not perfectible seems to be widely accepted.

Toward a Nuanced Understanding of LGBTQIA+ Representation

While there has been extensive valuable research into how existing cataloging systems have evolved in their classification of LGBTQIA+ and other diverse content, some researchers have worked outside the catalog to develop additional tools that provide a deeper understanding of diverse representation, particularly in youth collections. For example, the popular Diverse BookFinder website and its collection analysis tool builds upon the research of Aronson et al. (2018) that identified narrative themes in picture books with BIPOC characters. Our initial research, conducted by Vaandering and Rosenzweig (2023), adapted this approach to develop the *Rainbow Representation Rubric* (RRR) in order to better understand LGBTQIA+ representation in picture books. We identified nine themes across picture books with queer representation (see Table 1). Our work also classified the representation of specific LGBTQIA+ identities in our book sample, applying the *Rainbow Representation Rubric Glossary for Gender Identity & Sexual Orientation* to improve consistency in LGBTQIA+ terminology used in analysis.

Theme	Description
Beautiful Life	Features LGBTQIA+ protagonists whose sexual orientation or gender identity helps drive the storyline.
Any Child	Features LGBTQIA+ protagonists whose sexual orientation or gender identity is clear but does not impact the storyline.
Community	Features cisgender, heterosexual (cishet) protagonists with LGBTQIA+ secondary/background characters whose sexual orientation or gender identity impacts the storyline.
Incidental	Features cishet protagonists with LGBTQIA+ secondary/background characters whose sexual orientation or gender identity do not impact the storyline.
Biography	Outlines the real-life experiences of a person or group of people who are part of the LGBTQIA+ community.
Coming Out	Highlights the experiences of characters who explicitly and voluntarily share their sexual orientation or gender identity.
Concepts	Defines aspects of human difference related to sexual orientation or gender identity.
Informational	Provides factual information, including depictions of members of the LGBTQIA+ community.
Resilience	Depicts resilience of characters in response to cruelty or mistreatment related to sexual orientation or gender identity.

Table 1   Rainbow Representation Rubric Narrative Themes

After adding an additional researcher to the team, we built upon that previous research to expand our sample size of picture books with queer representation (Vaandering et al., 2023). In our current study, we draw from this larger sample to analyze the visibility of queer materials in the catalog. This bears similarities to the research conducted by McClary and Howard (2007), who examined the subject headings of

40 YA and adult novels that had been identified as having "GLBT" content in an existing book list. By utilizing a larger book sample, applying more granular data of queer representation and narratives, and analyzing catalog subject headings and summaries, we hope to gain deeper insights into how well WorldCat highlights LGBTQIA+ identities and narratives.

Collecting Subject Headings and Book Summaries

We began our current study with a sample of 202 queer picture books published from 2018-2022. In our previous research, we had analyzed each of these books to determine what LGBTQIA+ identities and narrative themes were represented as well as the rate at which LGBTQIA+ terminology was used in professional reviews of these books (Vaandering & Rosenzweig, 2023; Vaandering et al., 2023). For this present study, we collected the subject headings and book summaries for these titles from WorldCat, a tool that is popular with library patrons, catalogers, and other librarians.

One complication that we experienced in analyzing subject headings from WorldCat was that these headings are not limited to Library of Congress Subject Headings (LCSH). WorldCat catalog entries also include subject headings from other controlled vocabularies, including the Homosaurus. Given that LCSH are the most ubiquitous subject headings in use, we wanted to determine whether there's a meaningful gap between searching only LCSH and searching all available WorldCat subject headings in terms of discoverability. To accomplish this, we checked each queer subject heading from our sample in authorities.loc.gov to identify which headings were Library of Congress subject headings. We then created two sets of queer subject headings to be used in our analysis: LCSH-only subject headings and all WorldCat subject headings in our sample, which included LCSH and any other vocabularies. We assigned the subject headings from these two sets to either a category that aligned with our RRR identities or a general queer content category, which encompassed subject headings not associated with a specific identity or person, for example, "Civil rights (LGBTQ)" or "Neopronouns."

After we had identified and classified the subject headings, we were able to determine how often the categories of subject headings were applied to the books in our sample. We then compared this analysis to our previous research data to determine the rate at which subject headings included specific LGBTQIA+ identities (e.g., transgender, non-binary) or general queer content (e.g., sexual minorities) and how often they lacked any reference to LGBTQIA+ characters or content.

Because searching subject headings is only one strategy used by librarians and library patrons to discover queer materials in library records, we wanted to examine other potential search elements of WorldCat records as well. In particular, we were curious to learn whether LGBTQIA+ terminology is present in catalog summaries for books, which would allow patrons an additional means to discover queer representation in the catalog by keyword searching. To that end, we applied the methodology used in our prior research which analyzed queer terminology in professional book reviews by using a list of words and phrases that describe LGBTQIA+ identities (Vaandering et al., 2023). For this present study, we implemented the same list to search each summary field to determine the rate at which LGBTQIA+ identities were mentioned in WorldCat summaries. While we acknowledge that there are limitations to this approach, given that LGBTQIA+ terminology continuously evolves, our method allows us to determine if summaries are including terminology as frequently as capsule professional book reviews.

What We Found

Identities vs. Subject Headings

A comparison of RRR identities to WorldCat/LC subject headings revealed that a large portion of our sample lacks identity-specific subject headings (see Table 2). Out of the 202 books in our sample, only 86 had an identity-specific WorldCat heading, with 82 of those including an identity-specific LCSH. We were surprised at how similar those two numbers were: our hypothesis had been that a vocabulary like the Homosaurus, designed specifically for the description of the identities we were examining, would lead to the explicit labeling of LGBTQIA+ representation in far more titles than in LCSH. The fact that so few additional books were labeled in WorldCat with identity-specific LGBTQIA+ subject headings beyond LCSH suggests that the problems with using subject headings for discoverability can't simply be addressed by adding supplemental controlled vocabularies.

	RRR Titles	% with WorldCat Subject Headings	% with LC Subject Headings
Sexual Orientations			
Gay	105	42%	42%
Lesbian	96	22%	21%
Bisexual	13	8%	8%
Asexual	5	0%	0%
Pansexual	5	0%	0%
Aromantic	2	0%	0%
Polyamorous	1	0%	0%
Gender Identities			
Mahu	1	100%	0%
Two-Spirit	4	50%	50%
Transgender	55	42%	40%
Gender Non-Conforming	70	17%	13%
Nonbinary	48	2%	2%
Gender-Queer	25	0%	0%
Gender Fluid	13	0%	0%
Intersex	11	0%	0%
Agender	8	0%	0%
General			
Queer	28	254%	93%
Questioning	Did not evaluate in this study due to lack of specific terminology (subjective analysis)		
Queer Metaphor	Did not evaluate in this study due to lack of specific terminology (subjective analysis)		

Table 2   RRR identities and WorldCat/LC Subject Headings

Our analysis revealed that LGBTQIA+ identities have been included in subject headings at varying levels. Some identities were regularly employed as subject headings (e.g., gay, lesbian, transgender), while others (e.g., agender, intersex, gender fluid) were nonexistent in our findings (see Table 2). While we initially expected that this might be due to corresponding gaps in cataloging language, that didn't appear to be the case. Of the eight identities in our book sample that were not labeled by WorldCat subject headings (including LCSH), every one of these had a subject heading in LCSH and/or the Homosaurus, which suggests that those headings are not being applied consistently.

The identity most prevalent in the subject headings was queer identity, which reflects a major distinction between our data and the approach taken by vocabularies like LCSH and the Homosaurus. We adopted a minoritized approach, preferring identity-specific labels wherever possible and only designating representation as queer when characters seemed to be claiming that particular label for themselves. LCSH and the Homosaurus, on the other hand, contain a large number of more universalized subject headings. This explains why, as shown in Table 2, WorldCat subject headings have identified many more books in our sample as queer than we did.

To some extent, the gaps in subject headings can be explained by cataloging practices. For instance, aromantic people are represented in two books in our sample, neither of which was assigned an aromantic subject heading. Both books address a wide array of identities rapidly and briefly. It may not be that surprising that a cataloger wouldn't explicitly label every identity present in books like these that provide an alphabet of LGBTQIA+ terms, like *ABC Pride* and *The GayBCs*. Another possible reason for the limited application of identity-specific subject headings is that these LGBTQIA+ labels have been created over time. For example, we observed genderqueer representation in 25 books in our sample, but none of these books have a genderqueer subject heading. One factor may be that the subject heading "genderqueer" was only recently authorized, meaning this term would not have been available at the time of publication for some of these titles. However, these cataloging practices don't easily explain why subject terms were twice as likely to identify the representation of gay men than they were to identify the representation of lesbian women. Catalog users, whether librarians or patrons, who rely on subject headings for searches are likely to miss a large proportion of LGBTQIA+

representation and to have a skewed understanding of that representation in their library collections, based on what we saw in this sample.

Our analysis was not wholly critical of subject headings, whether those offered by LCSH, the Homosaurus, or any other source. The language offered by headings can yield important insights for librarians and patrons seeking the right book. For instance, a subject heading like "Children of gay parents" in LCSH (the Homosaurus has several similar labels, including "Children of gay men" and "Children of lesbians") conveys not merely representation of identity, but also relationship. Other subject headings, like "African American transgender people," which is used in both LCSH and the Homosaurus, convey not only representation of LGBTQIA+ identity, but also intersectional depictions of other marginalized identities (in this case, race). Additionally, even when a subject heading is general and not identity-specific, that doesn't necessarily indicate that it was poorly chosen. The LCSH headings "Gay pride parades" and "Gay pride celebrations" (the Homosaurus uses the label "Gay pride week" for this material) don't specify an LGBTQIA+ identity, but they clearly communicate to catalog users about a type of content related to an important cultural activity for many LGBTQIA+ people.

The patterns we did see, though, reinforce the limited viability of relying on subject headings to discover LGBTQIA+ representation in World-Cat. In our sample, no LGBTQIA+ identity was given an identity-specific LCSH in more than 50% of the titles that depicted that identity. For all WorldCat subject headings, "Mahu" was the only outlier, as the single book in our sample representing that identity had at least one identity-specific heading. Subject headings were not missing in equal proportions: while over 40% of gay male representation was represented in subject headings, lesbian representation received queer subject headings about half as often. Transgender representation was among the most widely documented in subject headings (roughly 40% of the sample), while nonbinary representation was nearly invisible in the catalog, showing up in subject headings for only one book in our sample. These imbalances seem to indicate problematic biases in how material is described, leaving catalog users who rely on subject headings with very different search experiences depending on which LGBTQIA+ identity they're looking for in the catalog.

Based on previous research on queer representation in subject headings (Edge, 2019; Dobreski et al., 2022), it is not surprising that specific identities are being left out of WorldCat subject headings. The RRR identity data for each title was based on a close reading of the text, in which any kind of representation, however brief, was noted and classified. This level of detail isn't possible in standard cataloging environments. Our comparisons, therefore, aren't offered as a critique of cataloging practices, but rather as an attempt to spotlight how catalog users will need to adapt to overcome notable gaps in the ways the catalog identifies, or fails to identify, representation.

Identities in WorldCat Summaries vs. Professional Reviews

As mentioned earlier, we also wanted to examine whether keyword searching of catalog summaries might be an additional aid in the discovery of titles with LGBTQIA+ content. Our analysis indicated that terminology highlighting identify-specific queer content is often missing in WorldCat summaries. For sexual orientations, only gay content was found through a summary field terminology search, and this was at a very low rate of 5% of books with gay representation (see Table 3). Some gender identity categories fared better, with transgender and Two-Spirit representation having specific terminology used in 22% and 25% of the books identified in our sample; however, the only other gender identity to have specific terminology used in the World-Cat summary was non-binary at 4%. General queer terms were only found in the summary field for 19 books. Overall, the majority of books identified in our analysis did not have queer terminology used in their WorldCat summary field.

Table 3. LGBTQIA+ Terminology in WorldCat Summaries & Professional Reviews]

	RRR Titles	% with WorldCat Summaries	% with Reviews
Sexual Orientation			
Gay	105	5%	30%
Lesbian	96	0%	10%
Pansexual	5	0%	20%
Bisexual	13	0%	7.69%
Asexual	5	0%	0%
Aromantic	2	0%	0%
Polyamorous	1	0%	0%

Gender Identities			
Transgender	55	22%	60%
Two-Spirit	4	25%	50%
Nonbinary	48	4%	44%
Mahu	1	0%	100%
Intersex	11	0%	55%
Gender Fluid	13	0%	15%
Gender Non-Conforming	70	0%	1%
Gender-Queer	25	0%	0%
Agender	8	0%	0%

When comparing this data to our previous analysis of queer terminology used in professional book reviews, we found that LGBTQIA+ identities were labeled in reviews at a much higher rate than in WorldCat summaries (Vaandering et al., 2023). While the lack of queer terminology used in summaries is disappointing, the current disparity between summaries and professional reviews is understandable. Summary writers have not been subjected to the requirements many professional review journals now impose that require the identities of characters to be clearly articulated. That said, the far greater breadth of identity-specific language in professional reviews indicates that catalog summaries can do more to facilitate access to LGBTQIA+ representation in books. The reviews we examined were capsule-length, brief enough to be manageable as catalog summaries, and they were much more successful at documenting LGBTQIA+ identities.

We also observed that although queer content does exist in catalog summaries, in many cases it requires library users to draw their own conclusions about queer context rather than search for specific terminology. For example, the summary for *Jerome by Heart* reads "A young boy expresses his love for his friend Jerome." Library users might draw the conclusion that this book is about a boy with a crush on another boy, based on the name Jerome typically being associated with male identities. They might, though, simply conclude that the word "love" is being used here in a non-romantic context. Another example is *They, She, He, Easy as ABC*, which is clearly identified in the summary (and title) as a book about inclusive pronouns, yet the summary does not mention specific gender identities: "Inclusive pronouns are learned alongside the alphabet in this joyously illustrated take on the classic ABC book." Summaries like these provide contextual clues about LGBTQIA+ content, but these books may be left out of search results reliant on queer keyword searching.

Narrative Themes & WorldCat

Determining who is represented in picture books is only one aspect of representation that library users are looking for when seeking out these materials. It is also important to explore what narratives are visible in the catalog for catalog users searching by queer subject headings. Narrative themes are present in recently published picture books at varying rates with *Beautiful Life, Resilience*, and *Incidental* being the most prominent and *Coming Out, Concepts*, and *Any Child* being the least (see Figure 1) (Vaandering et al., 2023). When we examined the application of queer subject headings based on narrative, we found that *Beautiful Life* and *Resilience* had the highest number of books with LGBTQIA+ subject headings, but that the other largest category in our sample, *Incidental*, had the least. When we then analyzed our data as percentages of each narrative theme, we observed that some of the least represented themes in our sample were unexpectedly well-documented with LGBTQIA+ subject headings. *Beautiful Life* and *Resilience* books were still well represented at 72% and 71%, but *Community* and

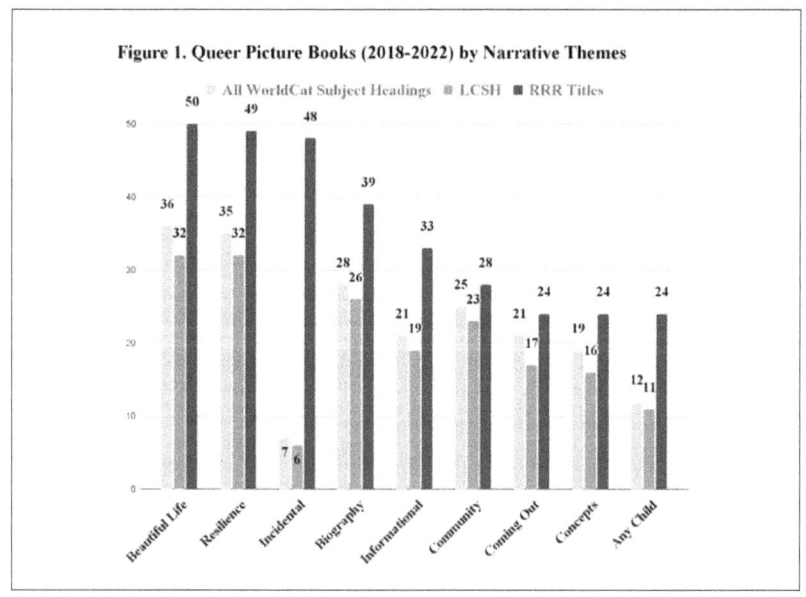

Figure 1. Queer Picture Books (2018-2022) by Narrative Themes

Figure 2. Proportion of RRR Narrative Themes Represented by Queer Subject Headings

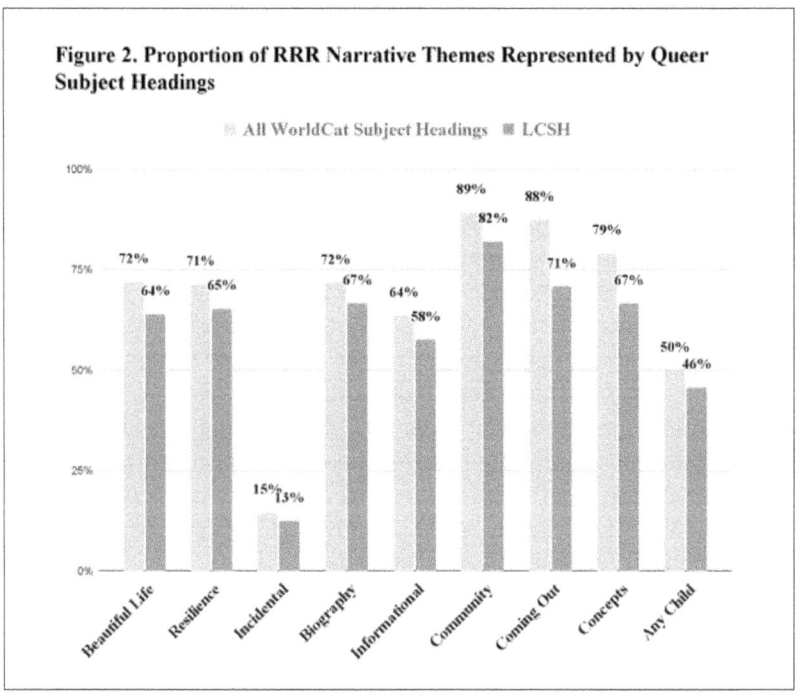

Coming Out books had the highest rate of representation in subject headings at 89% and 87% (see Figure 2). As already noted, *Incidental* made up a large portion of our sample but only 15% of these titles had an LGBTQIA+ subject heading. *Any Child* was also low, with only 50% of these books described with an LGBTQIA+ subject heading.

Because subject headings focus on the key topics of a book, it makes sense that *Incidental* and *Any Child* books had a lower rate of queer representation in subject headings, because those themes encompass stories with non-LGBTQIA+ primary characters. However, these books are still critical when it comes to LGBTQIA+ representation in library collections, given the importance of providing nuanced, diverse narratives for young readers (Melilli et al., 2023). While it is heartening to see that many *Community* books were correctly described as having queer representation in WorldCat subject headings, these books center the experiences of characters outside the LGBTQIA+ community. For this reason, libraries need to consciously develop collections of books that center queer characters, balancing ongoing singular queer stereotypes (i.e., *Resilience* and *Coming Out* narratives) with stories that celebrate queer joy by making books with *Concepts*, *Biography*, and *Beautiful Life* narratives more visible.

Recommendations for Increasing the Discoverability of Queer Materials

One important conclusion we've reached in doing this work is that providing good service to library patrons in search of LGBTQIA+ representation is difficult when relying on cataloging language alone. Library of Congress Subject Headings have strengths in labeling certain LGBTQIA+ identities and in articulating the presence of LGBTQIA+ representation in some narratives; however, gaps in the use of LCSH do continue to impair discoverability. Other library catalog elements designed to address these gaps, whether the use of vocabularies like the Homosaurus or the inclusion of more detailed written summaries, have not been successful in meaningfully resolving this issue. Given these limitations, librarians need to be aware of and employ a number of strategies in order to connect library users with queer materials. While we acknowledge that the following list of suggestions is not comprehensive, we feel they are a helpful place to start.

Understand the Importance of Visibility and Discoverability

As schools and libraries throughout the United States face an increasing number of book bans and challenges, it is essential that librarians continue to uphold the values of professional librarianship while acknowledging and understanding any restrictions in their specific communities. Some librarians have questioned the wisdom of making LGBTQIA+ representation explicit in catalog records and book lists, arguing that this makes diverse books easy targets for book bans and challenges. However, providing library patrons with access to materials is a core responsibility of libraries and librarians. Candid communication about LGBTQIA+ representation in books aids readers who want these materials, and it also informs readers who, for their own reasons, do not want them. A recent analysis by the *Washington Post* found that 60% of book challenges in the U.S. during the 2021-2022 school year were initiated by a mere 11 individuals (Natanson, 2023). As librarians, we need enforceable policies that allow us to serve all voices in our communities rather than catering to the prejudices of a select few.

Know When the Catalog Will Help and When Additional Resources Are Needed

Librarians need to be aware of their particular catalog's strengths and when additional tools are necessary for meeting the LGBTQIA+ representation needs of their library users. Resources like the Rainbow Representation Rubric,[2] Cooperative Children's Book Center (CCBC),[3] Diverse BookFinder,[4] and NoveList Plus can be used to locate less visible themes (e.g., *Incidental, Informational*) and identities (e.g., intersex, bisexual, asexual). Professional reviews, particularly *Kirkus Reviews*, are also useful for finding books if LGBTQIA+ identity is central to the storyline (Vaandering et al., 2023). Finally, established awards and book lists that highlight exceptional and authentic queer books are invaluable to librarians. For example, each year the American Library Association publishes the Rainbow Book List, an annual bibliography of quality LGBTQIA+ titles for young readers, and bestows the Stonewall Book Awards, which recognize notable LGBTQIA+ fiction and nonfiction for adults, young adults, and children.

Create Displays and Resources to Increase Discoverability of LGBTQIA+ Content

Finding other opportunities to increase the discoverability of LGBTQIA+ library materials is essential. Social media, LibGuides or other library guides, and programming can all be effective ways to call attention to LGBTQIA+ books, videos, and other resources. Representation of LGBTQIA+ people can and should also infuse a variety of displays during and outside of Pride Month. These displays could include spotlights on specific genres and formats, stories of love and romance, struggles for civil rights, coming-of-age stories, and biographies of notable athletes, scientists, artists, and inventors. The Rainbow Representation Rubric can be a useful tool for finding relevant materials, as can the other resources mentioned above.

---

2   https://research.ewu.edu/rainbowrepresentation

3   https://ccbc.education.wisc.edu/

4   https://diversebookfinder.org/

Be Proactive: Participate in Ongoing Self-Education

Librarians need to engage with their LGBTQIA+ communities and read widely with open minds in order to develop more nuanced and complex understandings of the breadth of queer experiences. This ongoing education is essential in adapting to changes in language and labels as communities find new ways to express themselves and their identities. When librarians are knowledgeable, both about LGBTQIA+ books in their collection and about LGBTQIA+ experiences, they are able to provide better service to patrons.

Conclusion

While our research has focused on LGBTQIA+ children's picture books, our findings have implications for materials published for all ages and in any format: the limitations of catalog summaries and subject headings are a shared problem for all books. Furthermore, our sample's categorization allows us to analyze not only the prevalence of LGBTQIA+ language in catalog records but also which identities and narratives are being missed by existing cataloging approaches. While library collections face external threats through censorship of LGBTQIA+ materials, the limitations of our catalogs create an internal barrier to library patrons, especially those who do not feel safe asking openly for LGBTQIA+ resources. As librarians, we should not assume that existing tools will adequately serve readers' needs in finding materials with diverse representation. Rather, we need to understand the existing limitations of our catalogs. In the short term, this knowledge equips us to use the catalog more effectively. In the long term, it enables us to work together to improve the library catalog as a resource for discovery. Developing a better understanding of barriers to discoverability is critical if we are to connect our communities to the resources they desperately need.

References

Aronson, K. M., Callahan, B. D., & O'Brien, A. S. (2018). Messages matter: Investigating the thematic content of picture books portraying under-represented racial and cultural groups. *Sociological Forum, 33*(1), 165-185. https://doi.org/10.1111/socf.12404

Christensen, B. (2008). Minoritization vs. universalization: Lesbianism and male homosexuality in LCSH and LCC. *Knowledge Organization, 35*(4), 229–238. https://doi.org/10.5771/0943-7444-2008-4-229

Clyde, L. A., & Lobban, M. (2001). A door half open: Young people's access to fiction related to homosexuality. *School Libraries Worldwide, 7*(2), 17-30.

Curry, A. (2005). If I ask, will they answer? Evaluating public library reference service to gay and lesbian youth. *Reference & User Services Quarterly, 45*(1), 65–75.

Dobreski, B., Snow, K., & Moulaison-Sandy, H. (2022). On overlap and otherness: A comparison of three vocabularies' approaches to LGBTQ+ identity. *Cataloging & Classification Quarterly, 60*(6/7), 490–513. https://doi.org/10.1080/01639374.2022.2090040

Drabinski, E. (2013). Queering the catalog: Queer theory and the politics of correction. *Library Quarterly, 83*(2), 94–111. https://doi.org/10.1086/669547

Edge, S. J. (2019). A subject "Queer"-y: A literature review on subject access to LGBTIQ materials. *The Serials Librarian, 75*(1–4), 81–90. https://doi.org/10.1080/0361526X.2018.1556190

Fischer, R. K. (2023). Using the Homosaurus in a public library consortium: A case study. *Library Resources & Technical Services, 67*(1), 4–15. https://doi.org/10.5860/lrts.67n1.4

McAuliffe, B. (2021). Queer identities, queer content and library classification: Is 'queering the catalogue' the answer? *Journal of the Australian Library and Information Association, 70*(2), 213–219. https://doi.org/10.1080/24750158.2021.1915618

McClary, C., & Howard, V. (2007). From "homosexuality" to "transvestites": An analysis of subject headings assigned to works of GLBT fiction in Canadian public libraries. *Canadian Journal of Information & Library Sciences, 31*(2), 149–162.

Melilli, A., Vaandering, A.G., & Rosenzweig, J.W. (2023, June 25). *Stories to empower our communities: Promoting diverse LGBTQIA+ narratives in picture book collections* [Conference session]. American Library Association Annual Conference 2023, Chicago, IL.

Natanson, H. (2023, September 28). She challenges one school book a week. She says she'll never stop. *Washington Post.* https://www.washingtonpost.com/education/2023/09/28/virginia-frequent-school-book-challenger-spotsylvania/

Seidel, H. (1998). The "invisibles": Lesbian women as library users. *Progressive Librarian, 14*, 34–40.

Stewart, B., & Kendrick, K.D. (2019). "Hard to find": Information barriers among LGBT college students. *Aslib Journal of Information Management, 71*(5), 601-617. https://doi.org/10.1108/AJIM-02-2019-0040

Vaandering, A.G., Melilli, A., & Rosenzweig, J.W. (2023). *Sharing pride through curriculum materials collections: The evolution of LGBTQIA+ representation in picture books.* ACRL Conference Proceedings, Pittsburgh, PA, March 15-20, 2023. http://www.ala.org/acrl/conferences/acrl2023/papers

Vaandering, A.G., & Rosenzweig, J.W. (2023). Every color of the rainbow: A framework for analyzing LGBTQIA+representation in children's picture books. *Journal of LGBT Youth.* https://doi.org/10.1080/19361653.2023.2182395

Out and Open
Promoting LGBTQ+ Resources that Defy Censorship

Stacey Ewing and Colleen Seale

Introduction

This chapter provides an annotated list of online resources that are openly available to our LGBTQ+ communities and allies both on and off campus to circumvent the increased scrutiny and potential challenges, bans, and even removal of LGBTQ+-related print collections in academic libraries. Free access to these authoritative, web-based materials can work to defy censorship which has been steadily increasing over the past two decades. To effectively support and provide inclusive representation to the LGBTQ+ community at large, it is crucial to evince and promote these resources and maintain unfettered access to them for a group that has been historically maligned, marginalized, and closeted.

To streamline this collection of resources, we focused on selections in English based in North America. For a more comprehensive list that includes international resources and additional materials, please refer to our LGBTQ+ Open Resources LibGuide.[1] Our primary consideration when choosing resources was their ease of access with a simple internet connection. While numerous library guides and online resources were freely available, some of the content was often limited to academic institutions and their affiliates, such as faculty, students, and researchers, and therefore, they are not included. Also, we

---

1 https://guides.uflib.ufl.edu/LGBTQOpenResources

encountered some resources labeled as "open access" that proved challenging to retrieve on the provider websites. These were resources that skilled librarians might navigate, but they posed difficulties for the average user and were omitted.

Furthermore, we tried our best to categorize this compilation of resources. Still, we observed an overlap among many of them as they often fell into multiple categories, such as historical, archival, or organizational. This diversity in categorization presented a unique challenge in resource organization, but the intent is to be as inclusive as possible. We want to emphasize that this is a curated list of these resources and by no means exhaustive. Additionally, the resources listed here are not ranked by perceived importance but are offered alphabetically. The lists and their respective categories are simply suggestions to help folks create new reference guides or add to existing ones they provide for their patrons.

Regarding the use of the LGBTQ+ acronym, we have chosen to align with the title of this book. However, it is essential to emphasize that our research and provided resources encompass not only LGBTQ+ but also intersex, Two Spirit, and other identities under the inclusive "+" umbrella. Additionally, references to internet websites and URLs were accurate at the time of writing.

Digital Archives

Digital archives of essential organizations in the LGBTQ+ movement are a crucial source of historical information and offer a mix of resources from images of posters, pins, and t-shirts to personal papers and organizational records. Scholar Dr. Emily Skidmore notes that "any sort of marginalized population has had a hard time finding their sources present in traditional archives" (Agarwal, 2018), and the following selected institutions not only safeguard the diverse stories and experiences of the LGBTQ+ community but also make them readily available to the public.

These archives and collections not only preserve LGBTQ+ history but also celebrate the diversity and resilience of the LGBTQ+ community. Through their digital resources and dedicated efforts, they ensure these vital stories are embraced and shared with all.

- Launched in January 2016, the Digital Transgender Archive (DTA) (https://www.digitaltransgenderarchive.net) is a testament to trans-organizational collaboration. With over sixty participating in-stitutions, including colleges, universities, nonprofit organizations, public libraries, and private collections, the DTA's mission is clear: to increase the accessibility of transgender history. They achieve this by providing a central hub for digitized historical materials, born-digital resources, and information about transgender-relat-ed archival holdings worldwide. Of particular note is their focus on materials created before 2000, emphasizing a trans-historical and trans-cultural collection.

- GLBT Historical Society Museum & Archives (https://www.glbthisto-ry.org/online-resources) offers a treasure trove of digital resources. Among these are thousands of freely accessible photographs, au-diovisual recordings, documents, and periodicals illuminating the LGBTQ+ experience. In addition to its rich digital collections, the in-stitution provides primary source sets organized by topic for educa-tors and students, as well as online exhibitions and research guides allowing for deeper exploration of its archival holdings which span the spectrum of LGBTQ+ history.

- Lesbian Herstory Archives (https://lesbianherstoryarchives.org) is a repository for preserving the history of lesbian lives and activities. Since 1979, its mission has been twofold: to gather and protect re-cords often overlooked or denied by patriarchal historians and to empower current and future generations to analyze and reevaluate the lesbian experience. Doing so brings to light the vibrant and re-silient history of lesbian individuals and communities.

- LGBTQ Video Game Archive (https://lgbtqgamearchive.com) is a cu-rated collection of information on LGBTQ and queerly read game content in more than 1,200 digital and non-digital games dating back to the 1970s. Games may be searched by decade and by category.

- ONE Archives (https://one.usc.edu) is housed within the University of Southern California and boasts a digital collection that contains interviews, images, and digitized materials. These resources serve as a valuable repository of LGBTQ+ history, enabling researchers and enthusiasts to explore a wide range of materials that shed light on the struggles and triumphs of the LGBTQ+ community.

- Queer Digital History Project (QDHP) (https://queerdigital.com/we-bresearch) is a dynamic community-led initiative focused on docu-menting and preserving pre-2010 LGBTQ+ spaces online. This vital effort includes three core collections: the *Queer Digital Community Catalog*, housing information on LGBTQ+ online communities before 2010; the *Primary Documents Archive*, featuring key documents related to LGBTQ+ life online; and *Mapping TGNet*, which plots the bulletin board systems of TGNet, an early international, transgender, digital communication network.

- Stonewall and Its Impact on the Gay Liberation Movement (https://dp.la/primary-source-sets/stonewall-and-its-impact-on-the-gay-liberation-movement#tabs) is a collection housed within the Digital Public Library of America (DPLA), that delves into the iconic Stonewall Inn Uprising. Curated by Lucy Santos Green at the University of South Carolina, it features interviews, letters, photographs, and primary resources that offer invaluable insights into the events and impact of Stonewall, a pivotal moment in LGBTQ+ history.

- Wearing Gay History (http://wearinggayhistory.com) showcases the evolution of LGBTQ+ expression through t-shirt collections. This digital archive houses images of t-shirts from LGBTQ+ archives across the United States and twenty other countries, spanning four decades. These t-shirts serve as tangible symbols of the LGBTQ+ community's rich history and culture.

Electronic Resources

The following is a selected list of openly available ebooks related to LGBTQ+ topics. There is a growing movement among publishers and authors to make these books available to a broader audience of students, researchers, and the community at large. Open-access peer-reviewed electronic journals have also emerged as crucial platforms for disseminating knowledge and promoting diverse perspectives. The following selection of books and journals contributes to LGBTQ+ studies and feminist scholarship, encourages interdisciplinary research, and fosters critical dialogues on gender, sexuality, identity, and social justice.

These open-access books and journals are essential for disseminating peer-reviewed LGBTQ+ and feminist research and scholarship, fostering inclusivity, and advancing interdisciplinary dialogues in these fields of study.

Ebooks

- Directory of Open Access Books (DOAB) (https://directory.doabooks. org/discover (search "Queer Studies" as an example)) is a discovery service for open access books. It offers a searchable index of peer-reviewed monographs and edited collections published under open access licenses, providing links to the full texts on the publisher's website or repository. DOAB aims to enhance discoverability, maximize dissemination, and improve the visibility of open access books by collecting and providing information on publishers' peer review practices and offering certification services. Librarians can integrate DOAB into their catalogs using freely available metadata feeds, and it collaborates with major library suppliers such as Ex Libris and EBSCO Discovery Service. The publications are also integrated into WorldCat and BASE for broader accessibility.

- Big Ten Open Books (https://www.fulcrum.org/bigten) is a collaboration between the university presses and libraries of the Big Ten Academic Alliance to advance equity and inclusion by connecting readers to fully accessible books from leading university presses. Their first collection is about gender and sexuality studies, and they have instituted a standard for unified open-access publishing of scholarly monographs.

- Internet Archive Open Library (https://openlibrary.org/collections/ LGBTQ) includes over a thousand LGBTQ+ titles, including everything from young adult and historical fiction to anthologies, classic pulp, and academic texts. They also have special collections such as the Stonewall Book Awards, Bisexual Book Awards, and Lambda Literary Awards, among others. Please note that many books may be borrowed with a free account.

Electronic Journals

- InterAlia: A Journal of Queer Studies (https://interalia.queerstudies.pl) is an open-access, peer-reviewed scholarly journal dedicated to queer theory. It welcomes contributions in English, Spanish, and Polish encouraging exploration of queer concepts across cultural and linguistic borders. Additionally, it embraces various aspects of the queer community, from gender and race to activism. *InterAlia* is distinctive for its inclusive approach, publishing not only traditional academic research but also literary works, art, book reviews, and more—all without publication fees, making it accessible to a broad audience.

- Lesbian, Gay, Bisexual, and Transgender Commons (https://network. bepress.com/arts-and-humanities/feminist-gender-and-sexuali- ty-studies/lesbian-gay-bisexual-and-transgender-studies) is a digi- tal resource offering free access to LGBTQ+ research with over 4,000 full-text articles from universities worldwide. It is a collaborative effort by librarians and institutions, providing a wealth of peer-re- viewed content.

- Queer Cats Journal of LGBTQ Studies (https://escholarship.org/uc/ queercatsjournal), affiliated with the Lesbian, Gay, Bisexual, Trans- gender, and Queer Studies Program at UCLA, is a peer-reviewed journal that serves as a platform for interdisciplinary LGBTQ+ re- search. In addition to its scholarly contributions, the program also hosts the annual QGrad Conference, fostering critical discourse and expanding the dialogue on LGBTQ+ issues. The journal's name com- memorates one of the earliest LGBTQ uprisings in the United States (pre-Stonewall) that began on New Year's night, 1967, when the pa- trons of the Black Cat Tavern in the Silverlake neighborhood of Los Angeles protested police brutality in the name of queer freedom.

Government Documents and Resources

The LGBTQ+ movement has seen significant progress over the years, with numerous organizations, government agencies, and institutions actively contributing to documenting and advancing LGBTQ+ rights and history. The following collection of selected government resourc- es sheds light on various aspects of LGBTQ+ history, advocacy, and statistical data. From government documents to activist records, these sources provide valuable insights into the evolution of LGBTQ+ rights and persisting challenges.

- Census Bureau LGBTQIA+ Pride Month–Key Stats (https://www.cen- sus.gov/newsroom/stories/lgbt-pride-month.html) offers vital sta- tistics related to LGBTQ+ households, couples, and demographics. These statistics help policymakers, researchers, and advocates bet- ter understand the LGBTQ+ population's diversity and needs.

- Centers for Disease Control and Prevention (CDC) Sexual Orientation Information Statistics (https://www.cdc.gov/nchs/nhis/sexual_ori- entation/statistics.htm) presents a comprehensive compilation of reports and stand-alone tables derived from the National Health Interview Survey (NHIS) sexual orientation data. This resource plays a crucial role in providing data-driven insights into the health disparities and healthcare needs of LGBTQ+ individuals.

- The Federal Bureau of Investigation (FBI) Records Vault serves as the FBI's Freedom of Information Act (FOIA) Library, which contains over 6,700 digitized records and media. Notable among these archives are two distinct records collections, the Gay Activist Alliance FBI records (https://vault.fbi.gov/gay-activist-alliance-part-01-of-02) and the Mattachine Society FBI records (https://vault.fbi.gov/mattachine-society). The Gay Activist Alliance records provide valuable historical insights into the LGBTQ+ rights movement. Established in 1969 in New York City, the Gay Activists Alliance was a non-violent organization committed to securing civil and social rights for the gay community. These records offer a unique window into the FBI's documentation of the organization's activities, shedding light on the challenges and triumphs that marked early LGBTQ+ rights advocacy. Similarly, the Mattachine Society FBI records furnish essential historical context for the nascent LGBTQ+ rights movement. These records pertain to the Mattachine Society, which was founded in 1950 as one of the pioneering organizations advocating for homosexual rights.

- The LGBT History in Government Documents UC San Diego guide (https://ucsd.libguides.com/lgbtdocs/home) serves as a valuable resource that highlights primary sources documenting the U.S. Federal Government's stance on LGBTQ+ issues with a timeline from the 1800s to the present. It illustrates the evolution of government policies toward LGBTQ+ individuals, focusing on the progress and setbacks in LGBTQ+ rights.

- LGBTQ Pride Month: Fact Sheet (https://crsreports.congress.gov/product/pdf/R/R47281/2) by the Congressional Research Service (CRS) serves as a guide designed to assist congressional offices in understanding LGBTQ+ issues on a legislative level. It offers resources such as census data, reports, and historical information to enhance policymakers' understanding of LGBTQ+ concerns.

- LGBTQIA+ Issues in Records at the National Archives (https://www.archives.gov/research/lgbt/lgbtqia) constitutes a rich documentary history of the LGBTQIA+ community, reflecting the evolution of societal attitudes and government policies towards LGBTQ+ rights, including Lesbian, Gay, Bisexual, Pansexual, Transgender, Gender-queer, Queer, Questioning, Intersex, Agender, Asexual, Ally, and other queer-identifying community records.

- The National Park Service offers several excellent LGBTQ+ resources:

  - LGBTQ Heritage (https://www.nps.gov/subjects/tellingallamericansstories/lgbtqheritage.htm) highlights the historical significance of various LGBTQ+ sites and communities, acknowledging their contributions to the broader American narrative.

  - The National Park Service Pride Guide: An Interactive Workbook for Exploring Lesbian, Gay, Bisexual, Transgender, and Queer (LGBTQ) History and Places (https://permanent.fdlp.gov/gpo135582/www.nps.gov/subjects/tellingallamericansstories/upload/prideguide_all-508-compliant.pdf) is an interactive workbook derived from the National Park Service's thematic study of LGBTQ+ history and offers a hands-on approach to exploring and understanding LGBTQ+ history and places in the United States.

  - The National Park Service LGBTQ America: A Theme Study of Lesbian, Gay, Bisexual, Transgender, and Queer History (https://permanent.fdlp.gov/gpo135555/lgbtqtheme-vol1.pdf), edited by Megan E. Springate and published by the National Park Foundation for the National Park Service, provides an in-depth exploration of LGBTQ+ history across the United States. Each chapter, written and peer-reviewed by experts in LGBTQ+ studies, contributes to a comprehensive understanding of LGBTQ+ heritage.

Health Resources

In today's diverse and inclusive world, resources and programs supporting gender-diverse individuals and their families are essential. This annotated section of selected resources highlights key organizations promoting gender inclusivity and LGBTQ+ healthcare. The following entities offer vital information, foster community, and advocate for equitable healthcare. They serve as valuable sources of guidance and support for individuals and families navigating the complexities of gender diversity.

The organizations and resources discussed here are at the forefront of promoting inclusivity, education, and advocacy for gender-diverse individuals and their families. From building supportive communities to setting global healthcare standards, they exemplify dedication to acceptance and empowerment and stand as beacons of hope, offering essential tools and information for self-discovery and acceptance, playing a pivotal role in shaping a more inclusive and compassionate society.

- Centers for Disease Control and Prevention (CDC) Lesbian, Gay, Bisexual, and Transgender Health (https://www.cdc.gov/lgbthealth/health-services.htm) provides information and resources on some of the health issues and inequities experienced by members of the LGBTQ+ community. Some of the information on their website is specifically intended for members of the general public, while other information and data have been developed for health care providers, public health professionals, and public health students.

- Children's National Gender Development Program Resources for Families (https://childrensnational.org/departments/gender-development-program/resources-for-families) provides support and information for families dealing with gender-related issues. Their website includes FAQs about their program and offers parent support groups, fostering a sense of community. They also have a support group for children, emphasizing their commitment to gender-diverse youth.

- The Fenway Health Institute (https://fenwayhealth.org/the-fenway-institute), founded in 2001 and based in Boston, advocates for and delivers innovative, equitable, accessible health care, supportive services, and transformative research and education. Their primary mission is to optimize health and well-being for sexual and gender minorities (SGM) and those affected by HIV.

- Established in 2006, Gender Spectrum (https://www.genderspectrum.org) is dedicated to creating inclusivity for children and youth, regardless of gender identity, using Stephanie Brill's "Three Dimensions of Gender" approach (i.e., each dimension [body, identity, social] is a spectrum). Their website serves as a resource hub, including extensive programs, professional development opportunities for educators, and support groups for families.

- HealthHIV (https://healthhiv.org) is a national non-profit organization with a mission to promote effective prevention, care, support, and health equity for those living with or at risk for HIV and hepatitis C, particularly within LGBTQ and underserved communities. HealthHIV works with healthcare entities to enhance HIV, HCV, STI, and LGBTQ healthcare, harm reduction, and health equity through various initiatives and programs. Healthcare partners include the HealthHCV initiative, the National Center for Health Care Capacity Building, the National Coalition for LGBTQ Health, and platforms such as PleasePrepMe.org, AgingWithHIV.org, ReduceHarmDC.org, and the HIV Prevention Certified Provider (HIVPCP) Certification Program.

- Human Rights Campaign (HRC) Resources for LGBTQ+ Patients (https://www.hrc.org/resources/patient-resources) provides helpful information for members of the LGBTQ+ community. HRC offers education on healthcare rights, protecting visitation and decision-making rights, Affordable Care Act resources, finding LGBTQ+-friendly healthcare providers, how to be open with healthcare providers, resources for autistic trans patients, and what to do when experiencing healthcare discrimination.

- LGBT National Help Center (https://www.lgbthotline.org), established in 1996, is a non-profit organization dedicated to offering peer support, community connections, and resource information for individuals dealing with issues related to sexual orientation and/or gender identity and expression. As the oldest and most comprehensive national organization of its kind in the United States, its services are available to people of all ages and geographical locations. The Help Center offers several hotlines: the LGBT National Hotline, the LGBT National Youth Talkline, the LGBT National Senior Hotline, and the LGBT National Coming Out Support Hotline. Emphasizing confidentiality, the organization ensures that conversations remain private and are not recorded or shared with external parties.

- Mental Health America: LGBTQ+ Mental Health Resource Center (https://mhanational.org/lgbtq) recognizes the mental health struggles many members of the LGBTQ+ community face due to societal stigma. The center offers resources on LGBTQ+ mental health and provides guidance on finding LGBTQ+-friendly therapy, support for questioning individuals, and resources for LGBTQ+ youth. It also covers intersecting identities, coming out guides, and mental health support for educators. Recently, they founded the Transgender Mental Health Resource Center to address specific challenges faced by the trans community. Overall, the Center aims to foster understanding, support, and affirming mental health care for the LGBTQ+ community.

- NALGAP: The Association of Lesbian, Gay, Bisexual, Transgender Addiction Professionals and Their Allies (https://nalgap.org) is a membership organization founded in 1979 and dedicated to the prevention and treatment of alcoholism, substance abuse, and other addictions in lesbian, gay, bisexual, transgender, and queer communities.

- National Domestic Violence Hotline: Abuse in LGBTQ+ Communities (https://www.thehotline.org/resources/abuse-in-lgbtq-communities) provides information specific to members of the LGBTQ+ community. Contacts to the hotline can expect free, confidential, and compassionate support 24 hours a day, seven days a week, 365 days a year, along with crisis intervention information, education, and referral services in over 200 languages.

- National LGBT Cancer Network (https://cancer-network.org) strives to improve the lives of LGBT cancer survivors and at-risk individuals through education on increased cancer risks and the importance of early detection. They also provide training for culturally competent healthcare and advocate for LGBT survivors in mainstream cancer organizations, media, and research.

- National LGBTQIA+ Health Education Center (https://www.lgbtqiahealtheducation.org) specializes in training health centers to improve access to quality healthcare for LGBTQIA+ populations. They develop curricula in collaboration with experts, focusing on LGBTQIA+ concepts, addressing unique health challenges, and promoting data collection on sexual orientation and gender identity (SOGI). They also help create welcoming environments for LGBTQIA+ patients, students, and staff.

- Paths (Re)membered Project (https://www.pathsremembered.org), under the Northwest Portland Area Indian Health Board, is dedicated to centering the Two-Spirit (2S) and LGBTQ+ community in pursuing health equity. They engage in community-based research and advocacy, aiming to create a liberated 2SLGBTQ+ future while honoring the wisdom of elders and nurturing the creativity of young people. Their approach focuses on restoring the historical significance of Two-Spirit people within their communities and contributing to their overall well-being.

- Seattle Children's Hospital Gender Clinic: Resources for Patients & Family (https://www.seattlechildrens.org/clinics/gender-clinic/patient-family-resources) provides an array of resources to support gender-diverse youth and their families. These resources cover topics such as mental health, gender-affirming social transition, and gender-affirming medical care. By offering these resources, the clinic aims to provide comprehensive support for individuals and families navigating the complexities of gender diversity and healthcare.

- World Professional Association for Transgender Health (WPATH) (https://www.wpath.org) is based in the United States and is a global authority promoting high standards of healthcare for transgender individuals. Their Standards of Care (SOC) provide clinical guidance for healthcare professionals, encompassing primary care, mental health services, hormonal and surgical treatments, and more. Their *Standards of Care* publication (freely available) also serves as a valuable resource for individuals, families, and institutions supporting transgender and gender-nonconforming individuals.

Legal and Advocacy Organizations, Websites, and Resources

The following selected organizations provide legal assistance, advocate for LGBTQ+ rights, gather information to inform policy decisions, and provide educational programs, resources, and a source of community for diverse groups.

- Advocates for Youth (https://www.advocatesforyouth.org) works in coalition with economic and social justice organizations by engaging, empowering, and mobilizing young people from marginalized communities to serve as activists and leaders in the field of sexual health. They advocate for youth rights to bodily autonomy and aim to transform policies, programs, and systems to ensure sexual health and equity for all youth. Their approach involves collaborating with both young people and their adult allies, including youth-serving institutions, to shift the prevailing cultural paradigm. Advocates recognize that factors such as poverty, homophobia, transphobia, ageism, racism, and sexism contribute to sexual health disparities and actively work to address these issues.

- Founded in 1998 by Dr. Fritz Klein, the American Institute of Bisexuality (https://www.bisexuality.org) (also known as the Bi Foundation) encourages, supports, and assists research and education about bisexuality through programs to enhance public knowledge, awareness, and understanding about bisexuality.

- Established in 2011, the Black Trans Advocacy Coalition (https://blacktrans.org) focuses on addressing the inequities faced by Black transgender individuals. Led by Black trans people, this social justice organization advocates for ending poverty, discrimination, and various human inequities rooted in systemic racism. Their efforts span areas such as health, employment, housing, and education to improve the lived experience of transgender people.

- Founded in 1985, GLAAD (https://glaad.org) is a non-profit organization dedicated to LGBTQ advocacy and cultural change. Their mission is to ensure fair, accurate, and inclusive representation of LGBTQ individuals in media and society. They also develop national and local programs aimed at advancing LGBTQ acceptance.

- GLMA: Health Professionals Advancing LGBTQ+ Equality (https://www.glma.org), a national organization, is dedicated to ensuring health equity for LGBTQ+ communities and equality for LGBTQ+ health professionals. Initially founded in 1981 as the American Association of Physicians for Human Rights and later known as the Gay & Lesbian Medical Association (GLMA), it is the world's largest and oldest association of LGBTQ+ healthcare professionals. Beyond addressing HIV, GLMA's mission encompasses a comprehensive LGBTQ+ health agenda, including issues like cancer, mental health, and access to affirming care for trans and non-binary individuals. Initially exclusive to physicians, residents, and medical students, GLMA expanded its mission in 2002 to represent tens of thousands of diverse LGBTQ+ health professionals, with approximately 1,000 member physicians, nurses, researchers, and others across various specialties and disciplines worldwide.

- GLSEN (Gay, Lesbian, and Straight Education Network) (https://www.glsen.org/school-climate-survey) conducts research and provides age-appropriate resources for K-12 education. Their flagship report, the *National School Climate Survey*, sheds light on the experiences of LGBTQ+ youth in our nation's schools. GLSEN advocates for comprehensive policies protecting LGBTQ+ and marginalized students, actively opposing discriminatory legislation in over fifteen states. With a network spanning 43 chapters in 30 states, GLSEN empowers students to create positive change in their schools and communities. Their network exceeds 1.5 million members, and over 500,000 of their resources are downloaded annually, all aimed at eliminating bullying and harassment while fostering safe, affirming school environments for LGBTQ+ students.

- Established in 1980, the Human Rights Campaign (HRC) (https://www. hrc.org) is one of the largest mainstream advocacy organizations advocating for LGBTQ+ rights. The HRC, with over 3 million members, a digital reach of over 9 million people, and 40 years of advocacy, aims to inspire and engage individuals and communities to end discrimination against LGBTQ+ people and achieve fundamental fairness and equality in every aspect of society.

- Founded in 1973, Lambda Legal (Lambda Legal Defense and Education Fund) (https://www.lambdalegal.org) is an American civil rights organization that focuses on lesbian, gay, bisexual, and transgender communities as well as people living with HIV/AIDS through impact litigation, societal education, and public policy work.

- Log Cabin Republicans (https://logcabin.org) is the nation's largest organization advocating for LGBT conservatives and allies within the Republican Party (GOP). Their mission is to make the GOP more inclusive on LGBT issues, aiming for equality through education and participation. Originating in the late 1970s, the Log Cabin Republicans emerged from defeating the anti-gay Briggs Initiative in California. They stress the importance of LGBT Americans engaging with the GOP for civil equality and striving to transform the party for a brighter, more inclusive future.

- Movement Advancement Project's (MAP) Snapshot: LGBTQ+ Equality by State (https://www.lgbtmap.org/equality-maps) tracks over fifty LGBTQ-related laws and policies for each state, the District of Columbia, and the five populated U.S. territories. The major categories of laws covered by the policy tally include "Relationship and Parental Recognition," "Nondiscrimination," "Religious Exemptions," "LGBTQ Youth," "Health Care," "Criminal Justice," and "Identity Documents."

- SAGE Advocacy & Services for LGBTQ+ Elders (https://www.sageusa. org) is the world's largest and oldest organization dedicated to improving the quality of life of LGBTQ+ older people. SAGE advocates for elders and "fosters a greater understanding of aging in all communities, and promotes positive images of LGBTQ+ life in later years" (SAGE, 2023, para. 1).

- Sylvia Rivera Law Project (https://srlp.org) was named after civil rights pioneer Sylvia Rivera. A veteran of the 1969 Stonewall Uprising, Sylvia was a tireless advocate for all those who have been marginalized. The Law Project seeks to increase the political voice and visibility of low-income people and people of color who are transgender, intersex, or gender nonconforming with legal services and public education, among other benefits.

- Williams Institute (https://williamsinstitute.law.ucla.edu), originally the Williams Project, founded in 2001, is a leading research center on sexual orientation and gender identity law and public policy. They work to ensure that facts and not stereotypes inform laws, policies, and judicial decisions that affect the LGBT community.

Lesson Plans, Teaching Resources, and Online Courses

In the evolving landscape of education, it is crucial to adapt curricula to meet the diverse needs of students. This includes integrating LGBTQ+ history and gender studies into lesson plans and teaching resources. Several organizations and educational institutions have stepped up to provide valuable materials that facilitate teaching LGBTQ+ history and gender-related topics. The following are a few resources offering educators a range of tools to incorporate LGBTQ+ history into their classrooms.

Collectively, resources such as these contribute significantly to the ongoing effort to create more inclusive and diverse educational materials, empowering educators to engage students with LGBTQ+ history and gender studies, further enriching their understanding of the past and present. By leveraging these tools, educators can create a more inclusive and equitable learning environment for all students.

- American Social History Project: Teaching and Learning LGBTQ+ History of the United States (https://ashp.cuny.edu/teaching-and-learning-lgbtq-history-united-states) resource provides primary sources, teaching activities, and classroom resources covering LGBTQ+ history in various time periods. It is celebrated for blending humanities content with innovative presentation methods, making it invaluable for educators.

- GENDER: A Four-Lesson Unit Plan for High School Psychology Teachers (https://www.apa.org/ed/precollege/topss/lessons/gender.pdf) is a resource offered by Teachers of Psychology in Secondary Schools

(TOPSS), a division of the American Psychological Association. This four-lesson unit plan that delves into the psychology of gender is a comprehensive resource for high school psychology teachers, addressing complex topics like the biopsychosocial construct of gender and pronoun usage.

- LGBTQ History Lesson Plans (https://www.onearchives.org/lgbtq-lesson-plans) were created by the ONE Archives Foundation in partnership with the UCLA History-Geography Project and provides LGBTQ+ history lesson plans. These plans align with California's FAIR Education Act, promoting fair and inclusive representations of LGBTQ+ history in K-12 classrooms.

- UC Berkeley History Social Science Project LGBTQ History Lesson Plans (https://ucbhssp.berkeley.edu/teacher-resources/lgbtq) were created in collaboration with teachers and scholars to develop LGBTQ+ history lesson plans for various grade levels and history subjects. One lesson plan, "The Lavender Scare and McCarthyism," received recognition from the Committee on LGBTQ History of the American Historical Association. UC Berkeley History Social Science Project's dedication to comprehensive LGBTQ+ history education is evident in its offerings, providing educators with robust resources to engage their students effectively.

Library Resource Guides

Library resource guides serve as valuable tools for researchers, students, and individuals interested in exploring specific topics within the vast realm of information resources. In this summary, we examine five examples of library guides that cater to the LGBTQ+ community and related fields of study. Each guide offers a unique perspective and resources for understanding LGBTQ+ history, culture, and academic research.

Library guides offer a wealth of resources and information to explore the diverse and dynamic world of LGBTQ+ studies and related subjects for scholars, students, or curious individuals seeking information curated by library professionals.

- Library of Congress LGBTQIA+ Studies: A Resource Guide (https://guides.loc.gov/lgbtq-studies) is an indispensable introduction to the Library of Congress's vast holdings highlighting LGBTQIA+ politics, history, literature, and the performing arts. Organized by subject, format, and time period, this guide is a valuable resource for anyone delving into LGBTQIA+ research.

- Society of American Archivists Diverse Sexuality and Gender Section's "Lavender Legacies" (https://www2.archivists.org/groups/diverse-sexuality-and-gender-section/lavender-legacies-guide). While this guide is no longer updated due to the proliferation of online finding aids and digital hubs, it remains an important historical resource for those interested in LGBTQIA+ archival materials.

- University of Illinois Queer Theory Guide (https://guides.library.illinois.edu/queertheory) offers an overview of queer theory and assists users in finding materials that engage with queer theory concepts within the University of Illinois Library's collections and beyond. It is an excellent resource for those exploring the intellectual underpinnings of LGBTQIA+ studies.

- University of North Texas LGBTQ Guide (https://guides.library.unt.edu/LGBTQ/welcome) supports the University of North Texas' LGBTQ Studies Program. It is a wonderful example of a guide that comprehensively explores global gender and sexual identities, communities, practices, and politics.

- University of Toronto Two Spirit and LGBTQIA Indigenous Resources Guide (https://guides.library.utoronto.ca/2spirit) explores the intersection of LGBTQIA+ identities within Indigenous communities and provides access to research reports, documents, books, films, and community resources, serving as a starting point for in-depth research in this field.

Online Reference and Referral Sources

In today's digital age, online reference and referral sources have emerged as indispensable tools for fostering inclusivity within the LGBTQ+ community and promoting a deeper understanding of sexual orientation, gender diversity, and LGBTQ+ identities. These resources encompass glossaries, style guides, directories, biographical databases, and encyclopedias, each catering to various audiences, from educators and journalists to individuals seeking comprehensive insights into these important topics.

Glossaries

- APA Psychology Teacher Network Guide to Sexual Orientation and Gender Diversity Terms (https://www.apa.org/ed/precollege/psychology-teacher-network/introductory-psychology/diversity-terms) offers definitions, distinctions, and historical context for LGBTQ+ terms, authored by the APA Psychology Teacher Network, making it a credible educational resource.

- Asexuality Archive (http://www.asexualityarchive.com/glossary) serves as a comprehensive collection of information on asexuality, featuring an essential glossary for comprehending this facet of sexual orientation. It is presented in a manner that is approachable and informative.

- *GLAAD Media Reference Guide* (https://glaad.org/reference) is a well-established resource for journalists and media creators, emphasizing fair, accurate, and inclusive respectful storytelling about LGBTQ+ topics, focusing on pronoun usage and respect for subjects' self-identification. This reference also provides several fact sheets and media guides helping journalists cover news about transgender people, LGBTQ+-related topics, legislation, and community calendar events.

- Homosaurus (https://homosaurus.org) functions as a linked data vocabulary centering on LGBTQ+ terms and is valuable for researchers and educators interested in lesbian, gay, bisexual, transgender, and queer identities.

- Human Rights Campaign Glossary of Terms (https://www.hrc.org/resources/glossary-of-terms) facilitates inclusive conversations about sexual orientation and gender identity by providing definitions for commonly used terms.

- LGBTQIA Resource Center Glossary (https://lgbtqia.ucdavis.edu/educated/glossary) acknowledges the evolving nature of LGBTQ+ terminology and encourages individuals to define themselves, offering a starting point for understanding various LGBTQ+ identities.

- PFLAG LGBTQ+ Glossary (https://pflag.org/glossary) offers definitions and explanations of terms related to sexual orientation and gender identity, making it a trusted resource for knowledge expansion.

- Pronouns.org (https://pronouns.org) focuses on the inclusive use of personal pronouns in English, providing guidance on respectful pronoun usage while addressing the complexities of gender.
- Trans Language Primer (https://translanguageprimer.com) presents an extensive collection of terms related to gender diversity and transgender experiences, documenting the complexity of gender within its historical and cultural context, offering clear definitions and example sentences for each term to aid in understanding diverse gender identities.

Style Guides

- NLGJA: The Association of LGBTQ+ Journalists Stylebook (https://www.nlgja.org/stylebook) The NLGJA, a journalist-led organization founded in 1990, promotes accurate LGBTQ+ media coverage. Their stylebook supplements existing publication guides and the *AP Stylebook*, focusing on LGBTQ+ terminology. It offers comprehensive coverage, reflecting the association's mission of inclusive reporting, and encourages journalists to use preferred terminology.
- Trans Journalists Association Style Book (https://styleguide.transjournalists.org) equips reporters and editors with tools to improve trans-related news coverage. Acknowledging the evolving language of gender and sexuality, this guide provides direction while respecting individual terminology preferences. Sections cover various aspects such as editorial best practices, gender, name and pronoun usage, and politicized or inaccurate phrases, making it a comprehensive resource for nuanced reporting.

Directories, Biographies, and Encyclopedias

- Campus Pride Index (https://www.campusprideindex.org) is a directory for evaluating LGBTQ+ inclusivity in U.S. colleges and universities. Since its launch in 2007, it has helped students, families, and educators find LGBTQ+-friendly campuses committed to improving campus life.
- GLBTQ Archives (http://www.glbtqarchive.com) is an archival encyclopedia on LGBTQ+ culture and history. Though not frequently updated, it remains a valuable resource for understanding the LGBTQ+ community's historical and cultural context. It provides a

wide range of articles, preserving the community's legacy and heritage for future generations.

• The biographical database QueerBio.com (https://queerbio.com) comprises biographies of over 17,000 LGBTQ+ figures. It covers a diverse range of LGBTQ+ identities, including notable individuals from art, sports, politics, entertainment, business, academia, and activism. It offers robust search and sorting features and is a valuable resource for research and inspiration. It is recognized for its cultural importance and archived by the Library of Congress to preserve LGBTQ+ heritage.

Oral Histories

As Roque Ramírez and Boyd (2012) wrote in their co-edited volume, *Bodies of Evidence: The Practice of Queer Oral History*:

> Queer oral histories begin with an agreement between a narrator and a researcher to record memories of queer genders, sexualities, and desires. If there is not a narrator to claim the sexual space of queer historical being and its retelling and a queer researcher to hear, record, and draw out more details, desire and meaning from it, no queer oral history is possible. (p. 1)

Although not every oral history researcher or recorder may identify as queer, all professionals are theoretically committed to recording a faithful recounting of those histories. The list of selected resources below includes links to a comprehensive directory and some of the most well-known oral history projects in the United States.

• ACT UP (AIDS Coalition to Unleash Power) Oral History Project (https://hollisarchives.lib.harvard.edu/repositories/31/resources/6341/digital_only) (2002-2015) at the Harvard University Library is a collection that chronicles the collective and individual stories of those involved in ACT UP/New York, an activist organization responding to the AIDS epidemic in the late 1980s. The interviews, organized chronologically, capture the profound influence of ACT UP on AIDS-related efforts, LGBTQ+ issues, arts, human rights, and activism in the United States.

• Among Dreams LGBTQI Military Archive (ADMA) (http://amongdreams.com) highlights the courageous stories of LGBTQ+ individuals who have served in the U.S. military despite historical and present challenges to their personal freedoms. Curated by Chelsea Rae Klein since 2011, the archive features first-person narratives from intergenerational LGBTQI active-duty members and veterans, shedding light on moments often overlooked in U.S., LGBTQI+, and military history. As an ongoing, independent production, the ADMA aims to document a diverse and largely untold history through interviews that emphasize both the struggles and resilience of these individuals in the face of discrimination and adversity.

- Archives of Lesbian Oral Testimony (https://wayback.archive-it. org/12142/20230110160617/https://alotarchives.org) collects and makes available the oral histories of people who presently or at one time identified as same-sex and same-gender attracted women. Materials in the archives include oral history audio and video recordings, radio and television programs, and associated materials.

- Lesbian Herstory Archives Audio/Visual Collections (http://herstories.prattinfoschool.nyc/omeka/collections/show/45) includes over 3,000 oral history cassettes and 950 videotapes, with approximately 385 hours, or roughly 16 days worth of content, digitized and accessible to the public on the LHA Audio/Visual Collections website as of May 2021. The earliest recorded item in this collection dates to 1971, with most of the publicly available content originating from the 1970s to the 1980s. Periodically, new files are added to the collection, typically through class projects, resulting in one to two updates per year, each consisting of about 20-30 newly digitized items.

- LGBT Religious Archives Network (https://lgbtqreligiousarchives. org/oral-histories) provides in-depth interviews with more than 70 early leaders of LGBT religious movements. Audio versions of the interviews are available, along with transcripts, biographical information, and photographs.

- Established in 2014, the Oral History Hub: LGBT History Digital Collaboratory (https://lgbtqdigitalcollaboratory.org/oral-history-hub) is the largest LGBTQ+ oral history initiative in North America, linking archives in Canada and the United States to provide a portal for researching LGBTQ+ oral histories. Through collaborations with institutions like the ArQuives, the Transgender Archives, the Digital Transgender Archives, and the Archives of Lesbian Oral Testimony, this project preserves and shares hundreds of life stories.

- Outspoken Oral History from LGBTQ Pioneers (https://www.outspo-ken-lgbtq.org) aims to preserve LGBTQ history by collecting and sharing firsthand oral accounts from the pioneering activists who shaped the modern LGBTQ movement following the 1969 Stonewall Rebellion. Their stories offer unique insights into the development of LGBTQ political activism, particularly distinct from earlier movements, making them invaluable to future historians, students, and the LGBTQ community.

- Stonewall Uprising Interviews Collection (https://openvault.wgbh.org/collections/stonewall-uprising/interviews) is comprised of forty-eight raw interviews of community leaders, activists, and authors from the *American Experience* documentary of the same name.

Podcasts and Streaming Video

Podcasts

Podcasts are generally a series or collection of digital audio files that may be downloaded or listened to online. They usually have a theme and may be hosted by an individual or group. The list below is a selection from a growing number of podcasts related to LGBTQ+ topics.

- Making Gay History (https://podcasts.apple.com/us/podcast/making-gay-history-lgbtq-oral-histories-from-the-archive/id1162447122) With 131 episodes, this collection offers intimate, personal portraits of both known and long-forgotten champions, heroes, and witnesses to history from rare archival interviews. From the episode website, a transcript, additional resources, and archival photographs are available for each episode.

- Making Queer History Public (https://ashp.cuny.edu/podcast) delves into LGBTQ+ public history, exploring archives, museums, art, and education initiatives. The series highlights how queer and trans histories are evolving in public discourse, offering insights into LGBTQ+ contributions and leading listeners to valuable queer and trans-led projects and experiences.

- Sexing History (https://www.sexinghistory.com) is a series of podcasts about how the history of sexuality shapes our present. Topics covered include "Bandstand and the Closet," "Sex over the Phone," and "Sexism Takes Flight," among others. Summaries of each pod-cast are provided, as well as suggested readings.

Streaming Video

- In 2012, the UCLA Film & Television Archive was entrusted with pre-serving and providing free online access to the 20-year collection of *In the Life* (https://www.cinema.ucla.edu/collections/inthelife/epi-sodes), television's longest-running LGBTQ news magazine. The show, a trailblazer in LGBTQ representation, covered milestones, provided a voice to LGBTQ artists, and offered political insights. The online re-source includes over 190 episodes, interviews, unseen footage, es-says, and photos, providing a comprehensive view of LGBTQ history.

- Begun in 1984 as a conference that combined technology, enter-tainment, and design, TED Talks are recorded presentations by ex-pert speakers on a vast array of topics. Viewers have the option to watch the video online or read the transcript. LGBTQ-related TED Talks (https://www.ted.com/search?q=LGBTQ) and Queer-related TED Talks (https://www.ted.com/search?q=queer) are available on the TED website.

Serial Publications

The following selected serial publications represent a tapestry of LGBTQ+ voices and experiences, showcasing the importance of LGBTQ+ newspapers as invaluable windows into the past. As we explore these archives, we honor the struggles and triumphs of LGBTQ+ individuals and their enduring contributions to society.

Magazines

The following section highlights various significant LGBTQ+ collections, publications, and resources, each offering unique insights into differ-ent aspects of LGBTQ+ history and community.

- Chris Gonzalez GLBT Archive Collection (https://ulib.iupui.edu/digi-talcollections/GonzalezGLBT) offers a unique understanding of the early GLBT community in a Midwestern city. The collection features digital versions of *The Screamer* (1966-67) and *The Works*, later re-named *The New Works News*, which was Indiana's "gay news maga-zine for gay men and women" (1982-1989).

- *The Empty Closet* (https://rbscp.lib.rochester.edu/EmptyCloset) is one of the oldest continuously published LGBTQ+ papers in the U.S. and originated at the University of Rochester by Bob Osborn and Larry Fine, founders of the Rochester Gay Liberation Front. Later transferred to the Gay Alliance of the Genesee Valley, the paper marked its 40th year in 2010. Covering local and international LGBTQ+ news, the Department of Rare Books and Special Collections archived and preserved physical copies with funding for digitization supported by the Gay Alliance.

- *The Ladder* (https://digitalassets.lib.berkeley.edu/sfbagals/The_Ladder/tl_index.html), published from 1956 to 1972, was the first nationally distributed lesbian magazine in the U.S. It served as the primary communication tool for the Daughters of Bilitis, the nation's first lesbian organization, and was supported by ONE, Inc. and the Mattachine Society.

- *OutWeek Magazine* (http://outweek.net/index.html), published from June 1989 to July 1991, was a seminal LGBTQ+ publication during the peak of the AIDS activism era. Founded by Gabriel Rotello and Kendall Morrison, it employed about thirty staff in Manhattan and redefined activist gay press by not only reporting but also frequently making news. Despite its two-year existence, *OutWeek* left a lasting legacy, transforming the landscape of gay publications and expanding the scope of gay and AIDS awareness, earning recognition as one of the most influential 20th century gay publications. All 105 issues of this magazine are accessible via the Internet Archive.

- *Two Spirit Journal (2SJ)* (https://twospiritjournal.com) is an interactive multi-platform media outlet focused on the Two Spirit community in the United States and Canada, providing news, current events, research, editorials, and community features.

- *University of Florida LGBTQIA+ Collection* (https://ufdc.ufl.edu/collections/lgbtqia) showcases digitized materials from LGBTQIA+ organizations in Florida, including bulletins, journals, magazines, newsletters, newspapers, photographs, and assorted ephemera. Resources in the collection also represent a wide range of issues and happenings, including neighborhood spaces and assistance programs, political activism, and artistic and educational events.

- *Vice Versa* (https://queermusicheritage.com/viceversa0.html) was published between June 1947 and February 1948 and was produced by Lisa Ben using carbon paper on her office typewriter. Although it had a limited print run, it likely reached numerous readers. *Vice Versa* symbolized early LGBTQ+ visibility and provided a platform for self-expression and community building during a time of marginalization.

- Village Voice Pride Collection (https://www.villagevoice.com/category/from-the-archives/vv-pride-archives) showcases historical LGBTQ+ materials from the *Village Voice*, a renowned Pulitzer Prize and National Press Foundation award-winning, alternative newsweekly magazine known for its investigative watchdog journalism, cultural coverage, and comprehensive arts and entertainment listings.

Newspapers

LGBTQ+ newspapers, often overlooked gems of historical documentation, provide invaluable insights into the struggles and triumphs of the LGBTQ+ community.

- *Alabama Forum* (https://apps.lib.ua.edu/blogs/alabamaforum), active from 1977 to 2002, served as a prominent and enduring news outlet for the LGBTQ community in Alabama. This digital collection houses 245 issues published between 1981 and 2002, comprising over 4,500 pages, offering a valuable resource for researchers exploring gay and lesbian culture in the Southeast. It not only reported local and national LGBTQ news but also served as a platform for community engagement, allowing readers to share their experiences through editorials, letters, and creative pieces while also providing a vital directory for LGBTQ-friendly organizations and businesses.

- *Bay Area Reporter* via the Internet Archive (https://archive.org/details/bayareareporter) was established in 1971 and stands as the longest-running LGBTQ weekly newspaper in the U.S., catering to the San Francisco Bay Area's LGBTQ communities with the highest circulation. The newspaper covers original news, cultural, and entertainment content for LGBTQ individuals, distributing its print edition free of charge in San Francisco and surrounding cities. The GLBT Historical Society in San Francisco is currently digitizing the newspaper's archives from 1971 to mid-2005, supported by a grant from the Bob Ross Foundation, enhancing accessibility to a significant LGBTQ historical resource.

- Founded in 1983, *Bay Windows* (https://baywindows.com) is New England's largest publication for LGBTQ+ readers and is distributed weekly throughout the greater Boston area and all of New England at 400 locations. For thirty-three years, it has brought its readers "award-winning articles and editorials on everything from the AIDS crisis to Vermont civil unions and Massachusetts marriage battles" (Bay Windows, n.d., para. 1).

- *Dallas Voice* (https://dallasvoice.com) has been continuously published since 1984 and is the primary newspaper serving the LGBTQ+ community in Dallas, Texas. With a circulation of 20,000 papers per week, it boasts a print readership of over 50,000. The University of North Texas has digitized the print archives, offering access to nearly 1,500 digital objects (https://digital.library.unt.edu/explore/collections/DALVO).

- Library of Congress Historic LGBTQIA+ Periodicals (https://guides.loc.gov/lgbtq-studies/format/serials) is a valuable resource for researchers and includes tips for searching newspaper archives using terminology from the era of publication to help maximize researchers' success when using these archives.

- *Philadelphia Gay News (PGN)* (https://epgn.com/print-edition), founded in 1976, has been integral to Philadelphia's LGBTQ+ community for decades. When mainstream media often ignored the AIDS crisis, and LGBTQ+ community members remained closeted, *PGN* provided visibility and reliable news. They continue to strive to keep the LGBTQ+ community informed about areas of concern, such as health issues and legislation, and also to celebrate community successes.

- Washington Blade (https://www.washingtonblade.com) was founded in 1969 as a one-sheet community newsletter and has evolved into an award-winning LGBTQ+ news source, marking its 40th anniversary in October 2009. Despite facing bankruptcy in November 2009, the community rallied to resurrect the publication. Today, The *Washington Blade* remains a vital source of news for the D.C. area LGBTQ community, with a rich history dating back to its emergence in the aftermath of the Stonewall Uprising in 1969.

Zines and Comics

Short for "magazines," zines are independently created and self-published by individuals or small groups. Often non-profit ventures, zines serve as platforms for artistic expression, community engagement, and amplifying underrepresented voices. They facilitate connections, foster dialogue, provide event updates, and raise awareness about various issues. Consequently, zines have found favor within communities such as feminist, punk, and LGBTQ+ circles, which tend to resist established norms and capitalist structures (LGBTQ+ Cultural Heritage, n.d.).

- Elon University's Guide to Zines/Queer History (https://elon.libguides.com/queerhistory/zines) is an excellent round-up of LGBTQ+ zines, articles about LGBTQ+ zines, and related primary resources. It also includes a second collection of AIDS/HIV activism through zines.

- In 2003, Queer Zine Archive Project (QZAP) (https://archive.qzap.org/index.php) was launched to preserve queer zines and make them available to other queers, researchers, historians, punks, and anyone else who has an interest in DIY publishing and underground queer communities. This resource provides an online, searchable database of the collection with links allowing the users to view or download electronic copies of zines. The archive strives to make the historical canon of queer zines more accessible to diverse communities and reach a wider audience.

Queer Comics Databases

The following are two examples of databases that serve freely available queer comics. These databases showcase marginalized comics and their creators.

- Queer Cartoonists Database (https://queercartoonists.com) was created in 2014 and is maintained by cartoonist MariNaomi. This database contains references for approximately 1,532 creators. Search fields include the creator's name, city, state, country, gender, ethnicity, genre, and roles.

- Queer Comics Database (http://queercomicsdatabase.com) currently holds 507 titles and aims to enhance access to comics featuring queer representation. It encompasses works from various sources, such as major publishers, independent creators, and self-published comics, spanning different age groups.

Promotion and Outreach Opportunities

The authors encourage outreach and the promotion of these "out and open" resources throughout the year, especially during key commemorative events. For example, creating library guides, flyers, and posters to celebrate Pride and LGBTQ+ alum events, library and community-related celebrations for Pride Month (June), Bisexual Awareness Week (September), LGBT History Month (October), Transgender Awareness Week (November), and Transgender Remembrance Day (November). In addition, online displays and social media posts should be a significant part of the overall promotion plan. As Wexelbaum notes, "Wikipedia, YouTube, blog feeds, Twitter, Facebook, Goodreads, LGBTQ social media apps, and other media channels currently serve as alternatives to library resources and services for LGBTQ information seekers around the world" (2017, p. 1). So, it is indeed vital to promote what libraries have to offer to the LGBTQ+ community.

Conclusion

In conclusion, this chapter underscores the critical importance of advocating for and ensuring open access to LGBTQ+ resources that are resilient against censorship, making these core online resources indispensable. These resources serve as lifelines for LGBTQ+ communities and their allies, both within and beyond the academic realm, helping to counteract historical marginalization and discrimination.

Furthermore, in anticipation of potential future threats to LGBTQ+ materials within academic libraries, maintaining vigilance and preparedness is essential. Resources like the American Library Association's *Intellectual Freedom Manual* (2021) offer valuable insights and advocacy strategies for preserving access to these materials. Additionally, libraries should consider proactively writing or updating their challenged materials policies. For example, the University of Florida recently drafted a "Policy on Withdrawing Materials on Request"[2] in preparation for any challenges to the collections.

By persistently promoting, disseminating, and safeguarding LGBTQ+ resources that resist censorship, librarians can contribute significantly to fostering a more inclusive and equitable academic environment that benefits all individuals.

---

2   https://acquisitions.uflib.ufl.edu/selector-resources/policy-on-withdrawing-materials-on-request

References

Agarwal, K. (2018). What is trans history? From activist and academic roots, a field takes shape. *Perspectives on History, 56*, 17-20. https://www.historians.org/research-and-publications/perspectives-on-history/may-2018/what-is-trans-history-from-activist-and-academic-roots-a-field-takes-shape

Bay Windows (n.d.). *About Us*. https://www.baywindows.com/pages.php?screenID=20531

LGBTQ+ Cultural Heritage. (n.d.). *Zines*. https://www.lgbtculturalheritage.com/zines

The Office for Intellectual Freedom (2021). *Intellectual Freedom Manual, 10th ed.* (M. Garnar and T. Magi, eds.). American Library Association.

Roque Ramírez, H. N., & Boyd, N. A. (2012). *Bodies of evidence: the practice of queer oral history*. Oxford University Press.

SAGE – Advocacy & Services for LGBTQ+ Elders (2023). *Resources for Older LGBTQ+ People and Those Who Care for Them*. https://www.sageusa.org/resourcehub/

Wexelbaum, R. (2017). *Global Promotion of LGBTQ Resources and Services through Social Media*. https://repository.stcloudstate.edu/cgi/viewcontent.cgi?article=1062&context=lrs_facpubs

From Research to Practice
How Studies of Drag Storytimes Can Inform an Evidence-Based Toolkit for Public Libraries

Vanessa Kitzie, Sarah Barriage, and Shannon M. Oltmann

Introduction

Drag storytimes are children's events that feature drag performers reading children's books and engaging in other storytime activities. Drag performers are diverse and include drag queens, AFAB (assigned female at birth) queens, drag kings, and non-binary and gender
non-conforming performers, among other forms of drag artistry. Drag
storytimes broadly promote reading and diversity, but their outcomes
go beyond this focus, with emerging research demonstrating how storytimes advance pedagogical and critical literacy skills (Montague &
Latham, 2019; Radis et al., 2022). Specifically, storytime attendees reported increased knowledge about gender diversity and difference
from the books, performers, and activities; opportunities to tap into
their creativity through play-based approaches; and development of
open and honest communication skills, modeled by performers during
storytime (Radis et al., 2022). Further, drag storytimes are crucial in
promoting queer visibility, allowing children to critically examine what
people take for granted as "normal," and encouraging them to recognize ways in which they and others might queer, or challenge, these
norms (Dorsey, 2020; Keenan & Lil Miss Hot Mess, 2020). An example
would be children asking a drag performer their gender or why they
have dressed a certain way, and the performer responding with questions such as "'Why does it matter if I'm a boy or a girl?'" or "'Why
shouldn't I wear sequins and feathers and lots of makeup?'" (Keenan

& Lil Miss Hot Mess, 2020, p. 452). Despite, or perhaps in response to, these benefits, there has been a growing backlash among social conservatives and fascists against these events, as various groups try to legislate and intimidate these programs out of existence (Ellis, 2022; Rojas et al., 2023). Recent examples include protestors harassing parents and children attending storytimes, hate groups like neo-Nazis making violent threats against drag storytimes, and laws passed by states attempting to bar minors from attending events with drag performers. As a result of this backlash, some library staff members engage in self-censorship by deciding not to host drag storytimes (Barriage et al., 2021; Kitzie et al., 2022; Oltmann, Kitzie, & Barriage, 2022).

In this chapter, we summarize three studies we have conducted about drag storytimes: 1) a survey of over 450 North American library staff who have hosted and not hosted drag storytimes about their perceptions and experiences with the program (Barriage et al., 2021; Oltmann, Kitzie, & Barriage, 2022); 2) interviews with 26 library staff (11 from hosting libraries, 15 from non-hosting libraries) and 11 drag performers that more deeply investigate findings from the survey (Kitzie et al., 2022); and 3) a content analysis of 103 picture books reported by research participants and in news articles and scholarly/professional literature as being read at drag storytimes (Barriage et al., under review). Findings address factors influencing decisions to host or not host these storytimes, the supports and challenges encountered when hosting them, strategies to address these challenges, and how drag storytimes may relate to existing library programs and services. Findings also discuss narratives of queerness and belonging within libraries and perceptions of connections between drag storytime, intellectual freedom, neutrality, and other core librarianship values. Finally, the findings address how picture books read during drag storytimes represent diversity.

Based on these findings, we propose a toolkit outline for libraries considering hosting drag storytimes. While guides like the Urban Librarians Unite "Drag Story Hour Planning and Safety Support Guide" (see Appendix) have taken essential steps in supporting libraries hosting drag storytimes, our outline builds on this guide in the following ways:

1. It supports public library decision-making to host these programs.

2. It expands the focus from urban libraries in progressive areas to other library types and locales based on empirical evidence from

library staff and performers who have hosted storytimes in these environments.

3. It has an advocacy component.

4. It suggests books to complement specific storytime goals and learning activities.

The authors presented the outline to a small focus group of public library staff recruited from the ALA's Rainbow Roundtable Advocacy Committee and revised it based on their feedback. Public libraries and other spaces hosting drag storytimes, such as bookstores, academic libraries, and community centers, can readily adapt this outline to promote authentic queer visibilities.

Background

The first U.S.-based drag storytime occurred in 2015 at the Eureka Valley/Harvey Milk Memorial Branch Library in the Castro district of San Francisco, California. Author Michelle Tea organized it as part of the programming for queer literary-arts organization RADAR Productions (Montague & Latham, 2019; Drag Story Hour, 2023). Originally known as "Drag Queen Story Hour," the term "Queen" has since been removed to encompass various forms of drag and drag performers. While stakeholders have established a network of self-managed and financed Drag Story Hour chapters in multiple states (e.g., Arizona, New Jersey), this network predominantly exists in progressive cities (e.g., Los Angeles, Charlotte, El Paso). As some drag storytimes are planned and implemented without the involvement of local Drag Story Hour chapters, drag storytime programming does not always follow the Drag Story Hour model.

Drag storytimes occur in public libraries, community spaces (e.g., LGBTQ+ centers), bookstores, and academic libraries, and are typically geared toward 3- to 8-year-old children and their families. However, as evidenced by drag storytimes occurring in academic libraries and in our interviews with drag performers and library workers who have hosted storytimes, sometimes LGBTQIA+ adults attend storytimes to feel seen and included (Liang & Stokalko, 2023).

Some research and practitioner literature has highlighted the benefits of drag storytimes for children and families. These include fostering an enhanced knowledge and acceptance of diverse identities and expressions and improving communication between children and their families by "modeling engaging ways to talk about topics around difference" (Montague & Latham, 2019; Radis et al., 2022, p. 346). For families with LGBTQIA+ parents and/or children (often called "rainbow families"), storytimes can make them feel seen, included, and supported. Research evidence shows that when gender-diverse youth experience a supportive family system, they experience better mental health outcomes (Westwater, Riley, & Peterson, 2019). Drag storytimes can foster such supportive family systems.

Further, storytimes cultivate critical literacies among attendees by teaching them to interrogate gender and other social structures that promote "normalcy" (Dorsey, 2020; Keenan & Lil Miss Hot Mess, 2020). For instance, Keenan and Lil Miss Hot Mess (2020) argue that drag storytimes "run deeper than morals and role models" (p. 448) by challenging attendees to engage in aesthetic self-expression that challenges or expands how they might typically present, such as by encouraging youth to make crowns, wear boas, or use glitter; highlighting how the ways we express ourselves (even the most "normal" ones) are often rooted in performance through camp and parody, such as a performer enacting the role of a schoolteacher; and instilling healthy curiosity within children by teaching them to ask questions rather than simply responding with, "because that's the way it is" or "because I told you so." These literacies foster critical thinking, enhancing skills that students can apply in classroom-based storytime interventions (Sipe, 2008). For instance, by reading *Everyone Poops* by Taro Gomi at a drag storytime, performers are implicitly asking children to question the narrative they often hear in school that defecation is private, shameful, and not to be discussed, when it is something that everyone does (Keenan & Lil Miss Hot Mess, 2020). Drag performers involved in storytimes often possess experience in early childhood education and training (Montague & Latham, 2019). For example, all performers from Drag Story Hour chapters are trained in storytime best practices. In our research, library workers who have hosted drag storytimes often reported also training performers, and some performers reported professional experience within early childhood education. Additionally, drag performers are often researchers, with drag storytime performers authoring the above-cited Dorsey (2020) and Keenan & Lil Miss Hot Mess (2020) articles.

Other literature focuses on what happens during storytimes. For instance, Dorsey (2020) and Keenan and Lil Miss Hot Mess (2020) discuss several dramaturgical and pedagogical strategies regarding how they perform in drag. Examples include unscripted interactions with children, such as the performer answering questions about their gender expression and the performer parodying popular songs or stories. Book selection is a critical storytime component, and the books read during drag storytimes often focus on diverse characters, some of whom are LGBTQIA+ (Naidoo, 2018). Library workers have expressed concerns with available LGBTQIA+ titles as only some align with the best read-aloud strategies. Read-aloud strategies represent effective instructional practices where librarians, teachers, caregivers, and drag performers, among others, read texts aloud to children. An example of an effective read-aloud strategy would be reading at an appropriate pace or stopping to let a child react or ask questions. Titles that are too wordy or do not have pictures may not foster effective read-aloud strategies among young children because they cannot engage with the text. Some available LGBTQIA+ titles have these characteristics; as one library director stated, "Some of the books about diverse gender expression can be long and we have an audience of very young children at these programs" (Naidoo, 2018, p. 19). Drag storytimes may be the only instances in which children are exposed to these critical literacy skills and books, as less than half of public library respondents to one survey reported offering LGBTQIA+ children's programming (e.g., Pride storytimes) other than drag storytimes (Naidoo, 2018).

It is disheartening that drag storytimes have faced increasing opposition despite their many benefits. Larger discursive frames that criminalize and pathologize LGBTQIA+ people (e.g., viewing an LGBTQIA+ person as a "groomer") characterize this backlash (Ellis, 2022, 2023). This backlash often occurs on social media, but also extends to the physical storytime location. In our research, we have heard from library workers that people can coordinate opposition outside of the library's service area, with people from outside the community calling the library to protest against an upcoming storytime because they heard about it on social media. Groups like Moms for Liberty and social media accounts like LibsofTikTok can also amplify negative visibility around drag storytimes by posting about upcoming events. Storytimes often face cancellations and postponements (Stone, 2019) and, when held, can draw dangerous and violent protestors, including gun-carrying neo-Nazi and white supremacist groups (Clarke, 2023; Livingston, 2023). After events, backlash can also come in the form of an unsupportive library board or administration terminating library workers involved with planning and conducting the event. For example, in Greeneville, South Carolina, a library branch manager settled a suit in which he claimed wrongful termination for refusing to cancel a drag storytime (Walters, 2020).

Legislative opposition also exists, with Tennessee recently becoming the first state to pass a bill that makes staging an "adult cabaret" in a public place or anywhere a child could see it a criminal offense (Rojas et al., 2023). However, a federal judge later ruled the law unconstitutional because it violated the First Amendment (Cochrane, 2023). Other states like Montana have been trying to pass similar legislation. Despite this backlash, LGBTQIA+ and allied communities organize and show up to these events to attend and counter-protest, displaying their solid capabilities for social and political organizing (Ellis, 2022, 2023).

Of course, opposition to drag storytimes often manifests in censorship and self-censorship within libraries. Examples include a library canceling a drag storytime as result of backlash (censorship) or library workers not considering the possibility of hosting drag storytimes because they are too "controversial" (self-censorship). However, unlike other forms of censorship, no specific titles, authors, or content is challenged. Instead, people question how the stories are read to children and by whom (Stone, 2019). Research examining intersections between drag storytimes, censorship, and intellectual freedom demonstrates that voices supporting drag storytimes connect their arguments to libraries' core ethics and values, including their obligation to be inclusive and promote equity and justice. Such discussions also critiqued concepts of library neutrality. This contested concept is not an officially recognized library value, but an ambiguous idea of being objective or not taking sides. The concept is contested for many reasons, among them the question of whether any institution or individual can truly be neutral, and the more significant critique that neutrality often serves as an implicit justification for maintaining an oppressive status quo (Gibson et al., 2017; Gibson et al., 2020). For example, library workers might decide to cancel a "drag storytime" because they regard it as political and the library is supposed to be neutral. On the other hand, arguments against drag storytimes tend to rely on personal beliefs about the library rather than supporting evidence from professional organizations like ALA Core Values (Chabot & Helkenberg, 2022).

The research we have discussed examining drag storytimes has several implications that have informed our research and the toolkit suggestions below. We now briefly discuss these implications, but will go into more depth when presenting our toolkit later in this chapter. One implication centers on a need for training and planning resources for libraries and other institutions implementing drag storytimes (Naidoo, 2018). Examples of training and planning resources could include training in de-escalation techniques and creating a plan that protects the safety of performers and storytime attendees. These institutions should also consider establishing partnerships and collaborations with LGBTQIA+ and other organizations related to performing arts, education, and literacy that have already conducted drag storytimes (Naidoo, 2018), such as Drag Story Hour. Training for performers is another opportunity and can cover topics like best storytime practices, book-sharing techniques, and critical information about childhood development (Naidoo, 2018). Libraries and other institutions can strategically plan for storytimes by catering to specific developmental ranges (e.g., for all ages, toddlers and infants, school-aged children) (Radis et al., 2022). They can also develop new policies and procedures for programming complaints, which may draw from selection and reconsideration policies for collections, and brainstorm communications with key stakeholders (e.g., local parent groups, activist groups, elected officials, government affairs offices, supporters of the library, PTAs at local schools), administration, drag performers, and the public (Davey, 2020; Urban Librarians Unite, n.d.). In addition, institutional leadership, especially in libraries, requires a vital education in intellectual freedom rights and core library values to distinguish between voices aligning with library values and those not (Chabot & Helkenberg, 2022). Specifically, there needs to be an understanding at the leadership level that ideas like neutrality are not in actuality library values and that suppressing programming like drag storytimes is an act of censorship, which is antithetical to the library value of intellectual freedom.

An example of a resource already produced to address this issue is a drag storytime planning guide created by Urban Librarians Unite (n.d.). This guide offers several invaluable worksheets, checklists, templates, and other considerations for planning drag storytimes. For example, the guide includes a community mapping worksheet and outreach tracker, safety and de-escalation guidelines, a space mapping tool, and a day-of-event checklist (Urban Librarians Unite, n.d.). The community mapping worksheet asks library workers to brainstorm at three levels—individuals, groups, and institutions—the various stakeholders that would be most beneficial to reach out to when planning a drag storytime. The outreach tracker provides a spreadsheet of contacts from this list so that workers can document who they have spoken to and take notes about their responses. The safety and de-escalation guidelines provide some tips to prepare for the event and how to engage with hostile people in ways that support keeping library workers, storytime attendees, performers, and other relevant stakeholders safe. The space mapping tool is one example of putting the guidelines into action, and it asks library workers to draw out the physical layout of the space in and outside the library where potentially threatening people may be located and then plan specific practices like where drag performers and attendees should enter the library to mitigate these threats. Finally, the day-of-event checklist provides some ideas of logistical items to consider before, during, and after the storytime, like checking in with families after the event and debriefing with staff.

Our Research

We are a team of library and information science (LIS) researchers residing in the American South with expertise in early childhood studies, youth librarianship, intellectual freedom, and LGBTQIA+ inclusion in libraries. We wanted to research (predominantly) U.S.-based drag storytimes, based on our commitment to intellectual freedom within libraries and the necessity to make information about LGBTQIA+ people, identities, and issues accessible to people of all ages. We identified several drag storytime-related areas we could research to complement and extend the work of researchers and practitioners in LIS and related fields.

The first area concerns gathering more widespread perspectives from public library workers across North America (primarily the U.S.) who have hosted ("hosts") and not hosted ("non-hosts") drag storytimes about their perceptions and experiences with the program. These latter perspectives are particularly critical as, to our knowledge, no other literature captures insights of non-hosts, including those who considered hosting but ultimately decided against it. We captured 458 responses from survey results: 341 (74%) from non-hosts and 117 (26%) from hosts. Key findings include:

- Hosts debated whether drag storytimes were one-time events or ongoing programming.

- Promotion to local LGBTQIA+ organizations, Pride events, and word-of-mouth advertising was infrequent.

- Many libraries integrated drag storytimes into established story-time and literacy practices.

- Library staff typically initiated drag storytimes (n = 89, 74%), followed by local LGBTQIA+ organizations (n = 19, 16%) and someone other than drag performers or library staff (n = 14, 12%), including library patrons, local politicians, local organizations, and library administration.

- Decision-making factors included alignment with the library's mission, community support, and values.

- While supportive of LGBTQIA+ services, spaces, and collections, some workers hesitated to host drag storytimes due to personal discomfort. Respondents evidenced this personal discomfort in their responses to a survey item asking them to indicate their comfort level with hosting a drag storytime at a library. Twenty-two percent (n = 99) of respondents selected "Uncomfortable, and would not do it." This discomfort could be due to the threat of potential backlash for hosting the event, the event going against their personal or moral beliefs, or other reasons.

- Library workers saw hosting drag storytimes as a pro-intellectual freedom stance (Barriage et al., 2021).

We wanted to know the "why" or context behind these findings, so we recruited 26 library workers (11 hosts, 15 non-hosts) for interviews to elaborate on the survey. Additionally, we interviewed 11 drag performers who have participated in storytimes, adding to the vital literature capturing performer perspectives (Dorsey, 2020; Keenan & Lil Miss Hot Mess, 2020). We wanted more information about the finding that library workers envision hosting drag storytimes as a pro-intellectual freedom stance. Below are key findings from library staff interviews and open-ended survey responses:

- Library workers generally supported the ALA's endorsement of drag storytimes, viewing opposition to these events as censorship.

- Some non-hosts expressed concerns about the polarizing nature of drag storytimes and sought alternative ways to serve LGBTQIA+ communities, such as through displays or having LGBTQIA+ titles in their collections.

- The core values of librarianship, particularly diversity, were cited in favor of hosting drag storytimes to support communities.

- In rural, conservative areas, some workers questioned the relevance of LGBTQIA+ topics for their communities.

- Library workers invoked the concept of neutrality to justify both pro- and anti-drag storytime positions (Oltmann, Kitzie, & Barriage, 2022).

When comparing library worker interviews with drag performer ones, we noticed that visibility was an essential factor not explicitly identified in the survey data, which impacted how library workers perceived and drag performers experienced storytimes. Specifically, in some instances, drag storytimes bring important visibility to LGBTQIA+ communities. Respondents, for example, noted things like, "[Drag storytime] gives visibility to a group that you don't get to see, or they're not visible in a lot of regular library programming." In other situations, an unwanted and harmful focus on these events rendered them hypervisible, leading to violent results. Finally, in some cases, various people and institutions sought to make drag storytimes invisible. An example would be a concerted social media campaign to cancel the event by threatening the library and performers that the library administration cedes to by asking workers to cancel the event. Key findings from interviews with library workers include:

- Drag storytimes foster LGBTQIA+ community connections, spark supportive counter-protests, and champion diversity and acceptance messages.

- Unwanted visibility for drag storytimes encompasses protest campaigns, event disruptions, and police presence, along with harmful stereotyping, such as questioning the age appropriateness of drag performers for young children.

- Some library workers unintentionally diminish drag storytime visibility through trivialization, assumptions about attendance, and self-censorship due to anticipated backlash (Kitzie et al., 2022).

Key findings from interviews with drag performers include:

- Drag storytimes validate diverse identities, offering visibility and support to underrepresented children.

- Counter-protests, sometimes joyous, can also draw attention to protestors, potentially leading to conflict. As one drag performer explained, "I am not going to organize a counter protest for people that are clearly unhinged. It doesn't make sense to me. And it worked for us. They stopped showing up because if you don't pay attention. They are like Tinkerbell. They just want the attention."

- Drag performers noted unwanted visibility, possibly exacerbated by how libraries or other institutions promote storytimes. For instance, one performer indicated that in training they give to libraries, they suggest that "when you can, lead with a king on your flyers or with an assigned female at birth queen, because a lot of the folks who will give the most vocal pushback, their big fear or issue is the drag queen. They don't know what drag kings are. They see 'women' as safe and they generally don't bother us once they see us as much as they bother a queen by herself."

- Some performers raised concerns about storytimes potentially diluting the subversive nature of drag in mainstream culture. For instance, one non-binary performer noted that they experienced difficulties with certain forms of drag being popularized, which could lead to gatekeeping of who can perform at storytimes, "I weirdly faced a lot of gatekeeping and a lot of difficulties being able to do my programming from, like, white, gay men."

- Performers may prefer urban, progressive venues with potentially less backlash against the event (Kitzie et al., 2022).

Finally, we wanted to respond to a troubling problem identified in the literature. While drag storytimes centered books focusing on diversity and acceptance, these books were not necessarily LGBTQIA+ due to a perceived lack of suitability for read-aloud. For example, some of these books were not considered suitable because of issues related to the format, such as too much text and insufficient images—not because they contained LGBTQIA+ characters or themes. We performed a content analysis of 103 picture books reported by research participants and in news articles and scholarly/professional literature as being read at drag storytimes. We compared results to prior research investigating diversity in picture books read during non-drag storytimes and included in early childhood classroom libraries. Key findings from this study include:

- Lead characters in the books read were primarily White, cis, hetero, and able-bodied.

- While more books featured LGBTQIA+ and disabled characters than found in prior research of other storytime and classroom contexts, LGBTQIA+ representation among lead characters remained limited.

- Nearly all books were in English.

- When we considered non-lead characters in our review, there was greater diversity in race, gender, sexuality, disabilities, and health status (Barriage et al., under review).

In conversation with relevant literature, these findings led us to identify several practice recommendations we saw as un- or under-addressed. These recommendations form the basis for a brief toolkit centering on four areas: 1) decision-making, 2) storytimes in non-urban areas, 3) advocacy, and 4) book selection.

Toolkit

Public Library Decision-making to Host Drag Storytimes

The literature shows that drag storytimes contribute to developing critical literacies by engendering creativity and intellectual curiosity among children and bringing unique pedagogical benefits, such as the ability to think subversively by identifying and questioning social norms. They promote core ALA library values, including access, diversity, the public good, intellectual freedom, and social responsibility. Further, they are one of the only forms of LGBTQIA+ programming public libraries offer. Therefore, drag storytimes are a vital programming option for public libraries to consider.

Nevertheless, a concentrated attack on LGBTQIA+ people in the U.S. has extended to libraries. A growing number of challenges and subsequent decisions to censor LGBTQIA+ titles in public and school libraries exemplify this attack (ALA, n.d. -a; Friedman & Johnson, 2022). Specifically in 2022, ALA's Office for Intellectual Freedom reported the highest number of attempted book bans in the twenty years since tracking this data. The majority of these bans are for books written by or about members of the LGBTQIA+ community and/or by and about Black people, Indigenous people, and people of color (ALA, n.d. -a). State-level departments and commissions breaking ties with national and regional library groups that indicate support for LGBTQIA+ people exemplify another area concerning the attack on LGBTQIA+ people in libraries (Garcia, 2023; Wolfe & Hager, 2023). A key recent example is the dissolution of state libraries' ALA memberships (including Montana, Missouri, and Texas) in response to the ALA President's tweets identifying herself as a "Marxist lesbian" (Riedel, 2023). An additional area of the attack relates to library workers experiencing harassment and perceiving their employment as tenuous if they support LGBTQIA+ visibility in libraries. One example is a 2020 incident in which a South Carolina library branch manager settled a wrongful termination suit for being fired after allowing a private group to organize a drag story-time and have it in the library space (Walters, 2020).

Given these conditions, what should library workers consider when deciding to host drag storytimes? One question library workers could ask if their library has not hosted a storytime is, *why?* Is it because the library engages in other programming that celebrates LGBTQIA+ people and achieves similar literacy goals? Or are there particular challenges that prevent the library from hosting this program? If challenges exist, what are they? What are some of the ways that the library might take initial steps to combat them?

A good way to think about making these initial steps comes from one of the librarians we interviewed. She spoke to us about hosting drag storytimes when she was the director at a library in a rural, conservative area. She spent over a year bringing LGBTQIA+ people, collections, services, and programming into the library to ensure her community was ready for drag storytime programming. Note that being in a rural, conservative area was not a precursor for this director to say "no" to hosting a drag storytime. Instead, she considered: How are we currently engaging with LGBTQIA+ people who are part of the community the library serves? Remember, no location is too rural or conservative for LGBTQIA+ people to exist. If no LGBTQIA+ people engage with the library, that is an indication that they do not consider it a safe space. The library director also asked: What steps can I take to bring LGBTQIA+ people into the library? Here are some recommendations and resources for addressing these questions:

1. Community Mapping and Outreach:

    a. Use Urban Librarians Unite's (n.d.) community mapping and outreach trackers to focus exclusively on identifying and reaching out to local LGBTQIA+ organizations and communities.

    b. Look for local chapters of national organizations like PFLAG, GSA, and GLSEN for a general sense of community activities and their locations.

   c.   Look up the Pride events hosted near your library, then look at the event websites for lists of local LGBTQIA+ organizations. Cross-reference with local organization websites.

2.   <u>Engagement with LGBTQIA+ Organizations:</u>

   a.   Collaborate with these organizations to understand their needs and how the library can assist.

   b.   Host a community forum between LGBTQIA+ community leaders and library workers, using the World Café method (Brown, 2005; see also Kitzie et al., 2020) as a conversation starter. This method is well-suited for community conversations, asking relevant attendees, such as LGBTQIA+ community leaders and library workers, to engage in small table conversations based on broad questions meant to elicit shared goals and ideas for actions to accomplish them.

3.   <u>Pace for Change Framework:</u>

   a.   Review Martin and Murdock's Pace for Change Framework to assess where your library stands regarding policies, programming, and practices (2007, pp. 125-135). The framework has three categories, "Red Light," "Yellow Light," and "Green Light." Each category denotes a level of LGBTQIA+ inclusivity to develop policies, programming, and practices at an appropriate pace, aiming to reach the "Green Light" level of making sustained, structural changes.

   b.   Identify initiatives to move into the next category. For example, if your programming is currently in the "Red Light" category, such as not having any LGBTQIA+ programming, your next step could be advertising drag storytime events hosted by other locations.

   c.   ALA's *Open to All Toolkit* (2018a) provides additional ideas for LGBTQIA+ inclusive policies, programming, and practices. Toolkit topics include practical tips for library services and how to address collection challenges.

4.   <u>Drag Storytime Promotion:</u>

   a.   If hosting drag storytimes, ensure you advertise them to the LGBTQIA+ organizations and communities you engage with.

5.   <u>Long-term Perspective on Drag Storytimes:</u>

a. Shift from viewing drag storytimes as one-time events to sustained programming, aligning with learning goals and drag performers' perspectives (Kitzie et al., 2022).

b. Incorporate drag performers' viewpoints into planning by reviewing resources such as storytime marketing materials and day-of-event safety plans with them and incorporating their feedback (Dorsey, 2020; Keenan & Lil Miss Hot Mess, 2020; Drag Story Hour, n.d.).

Hosting Drag Storytimes in Non-Urban Settings

Metronormativity represents the assumption that no LGBTQIA+ person wishes to reside in a non-urban setting. In reality, many LGBTQIA+ people reside in rural and conservative locales, sometimes because they do not have the means to go elsewhere, but in many cases because they enjoy living there (Gray, 2008; Movement Advancement Project, 2019). Further, these settings are home to rich, often visible displays of LGBTQIA+ people and activism from organizations such as Southerners on New Ground. Libraries in "red" states and rural areas should not assume that drag storytimes can only occur in progressive, urban locales. But there are unique considerations for libraries planning drag storytimes in these areas:

1. Alternative Locations for Drag Storytimes:

    a. If local LGBTQIA+ communities or drag performers express safety concerns with hosting storytimes at the library, consider hosting or sponsoring the event in alternative spaces like bookstores, churches, LGBTQIA+ centers, or parks. Online storytimes are also an option, but ensure patrons have the necessary resources for streaming and take necessary precautions to ensure protestors do not disrupt the event. These precautions may include asking people to RSVP and then giving them a link and password to the event, using security features like hiding people's profile pictures and suspending participant activities such as unmuting during the event, and removing participants or putting them in a waiting room if they attempt to disrupt the event.

    b. Relatedly, if your library administration will not allow you to host drag storytimes, consider volunteering or attending drag storytime events in alternative places during non-work hours.

2. Collaborate with Other Libraries and Allied Organizations:

   a. Partner with libraries within your branch/system or across branches/systems for planning and coordination. In rural areas, consider mobile venues like bookmobiles. Use the Urban Libraries Unite (n.d.) community mapping and outreach trackers, and refer to ALA's (n.d. -b) guide for libraries that have faced challenges in hosting drag storytimes.

   b. Seek support from local organizations backing libraries and LGBTQIA+ communities in your area. Examples from the authors' home states include the SC Freedom to Read Coalition, Get Ready Stay Ready, Free Mom Hugs SC, Derby City Sisters, the Fairness Campaign, and Queer Kentucky.

3. Diverse Drag Performers:

   a. Ensure a diverse selection of drag performers beyond queens, such as drag kings and non-binary performers, especially in rural areas with limited visibility. Highlight different types of performers in marketing materials to counter potential negativity given to drag queens.

   b. For example, one of the drag performers we interviewed includes drag kings on marketing materials because many people "don't know what drag kings are" and thus may be less likely to push back against the programs.

4. Evaluate Protest Areas:

   a. Assess *both* the storytime and protest spaces. Ensure that library staff arrange these spaces to maintain a safe and respectful environment for all attendees, such as keeping counter-protesters closest to the library. Adapt the Urban Librarians Unite (n.d.) space evaluation tool for outdoor areas.

2. Community-Based Policing Alternatives:

   a. Address law enforcement presence concerns by exploring community-based policing options like Sisters of Perpetual Indulgence and the Parasol Patrol. Drag Story Hour also recently created the Shields Up! Program, which is a volunteer-based safety marshal program trained in de-escalation techniques and safety contingency planning. These groups can provide visual and auditory distractions from protestors.

Advocating for Drag Storytimes

It is critical to convince relevant stakeholders—such as board of trustees, library administration, community members, and local politicians—of drag storytime's benefits. Luckily, many already-named resources include talking points and other communication strategies, including Urban Librarians Unite (n.d., p. 5) and ALA (n.d. -b). Additional resources include the Movement Advancement Project (n.d.) for talking points supporting LGBTQIA+ people more generally. Our research has shown that aligning these talking points with ALA's core library values, including diversity, access, service, the public good, social responsibility, and intellectual freedom, can be effective. Specifically, our librarian participants reported feeling empowered or supported to conduct programming like drag storytimes based on their alignment with these values. But what if you reside in a state that actively rejects ALA as an organization, such as Montana, Missouri, or Texas? These additional advocacy-based considerations are for you:

1. Align with Library Mission and Values:

    a. Clearly articulate how drag storytimes support your library's mission and values. Incorporate these key points into event communications. For example, one participant emphasized how drag storytimes enhance early literacy components in children's services. Their team unified messaging and provided talking points to the director, who shared them in an all-staff memo.

2. Incorporate into Library Norms:

    a. Establish clear policies and procedures to support drag storytimes. A framework is crucial for explaining the program's inclusion in your overall programming plan. Similar to policies for book challenges, consider consulting resources from organizations like Lambda Legal, GLAAD, AAS, and ALA's Office for Intellectual Freedom toolkit.[1]

Ideas for Activities and Books from Drag Performers

Two of our research findings inform this final toolkit area. First, drag storytimes should be sustained literacy programs rather than

---

1   See appendix.

one-shot events. Second, books read at drag storytimes could better represent LGBTQIA+ identities specifically and intersectional, diverse identities more generally in their lead characters. Therefore, we recommend some activity ideas to organize different drag storytimes and book recommendations. We prioritized the feedback of our drag performer participants in offering the following ideas and suggestions. Here are some activity ideas:

1. Voting-Themed Storytime:

    a. Conduct storytimes that emphasize the significance of voting without endorsing specific candidates. As one of our drag performer participants explained: "I'm not going to tell you who to vote for but I am going to encourage you to vote because that's your voice and your voice matters. And *Grace for President pushed my message further. So I was able to share my message and the author's message to the children that came [that] working together to make a difference you know, Grace was wanting to be the first woman president, you set a goal. People told you that you couldn't do it, well, you and your support system, your friends pushed you to do it and you were able to make that happen." Following this performer's insights, encourage children to understand that their* voices matter, as exemplified by reading books like *Grace for President* written by Kelly DiPucchio and illustrated by LeUyen Pham.

2. Balloon Diversity Lesson:

    a. Use balloons to illustrate diversity and inclusion. Different colors represent uniqueness, while all serve a common purpose in bringing joy and catching attention.

3. Interactive Performer Q&A Sessions:

    a. Include performer Q&A sessions during and after storytimes to engage children and address their questions.

4. Dress-Up Activities:

    a. Provide opportunities for children to dress up using accessories like boas, hats, and sunglasses. Performers can incorporate them into craft activities, such as making crowns or accessories with chenille stems.

5. Inclusive Crafts:

a. Create crafts with inclusive messages, like having children put handprints in different colors on a canvas to make a Pride flag, which the library can display.

6. Tailored Storytimes:

   a. Offer storytimes for specific audiences, including neurodiverse children, older children, and adults. Consider reading books in various languages and incorporating diverse cultures, like "Sparkle Havdalah," a Jewish version of Drag Storytime centered around the Havdalah ritual. Approaches to inclusivity during drag storytime programming act as natural inclusion points for diverse audiences that other storytimes may exclude. For instance, one drag performer participant explained that their motivation for creating drag storytime events was to create a safe space for their autistic child: "My older son is on the autism spectrum and we had been to some local story times where people weren't welcoming. They wanted children to sit still. They were not welcoming to a small child who needed to flap his arms or make a funny noise or speak his own language. I wanted to create an environment where every family who attended could feel really welcome and could feel safe and feel good about being there." In turn, libraries can point to drag storytime's inclusion of wider, intersectional audiences to defend this programming.

The following book recommendations all feature LGBTQIA+ lead characters, lead characters with other diverse identities, and/or LGBTQIA+ themes. Further, these recommendations represent books that have formats facilitating effective read-alouds for children:

1. *If You're a Drag Queen and You Know It* written by a founding member of Drag Story Hour, drag performer, and academic Lil Miss Hot Mess and illustrated by Olga de Dios.

2. *Neither* written and illustrated by Airlie Anderson.

3. *Red: A Crayon's Story* written and illustrated by Michael Hall.

4. *I Am Famous* written and illustrated by Tara Luebbe and Becky Cattie.

5. *From the Stars in the Sky to the Fish in the Sea* written by Kai Cheng Thom and illustrated by Kai Yun Ching and Wai-Yant Li.

6. *Harrison Dwight, Ballerina and Knight* written by Rachael Macfarlane and illustrated by Spencer Laudiero.

7. *Introducing Teddy* written by Jessica Walton and illustrated by Dougal MacPherson.

8. *Ogilvy* written by Deborah Underwood and illustrated by T. L. McBeth.

9. *A Day in the Life of Marlon Bundo* written by Jill Twiss and illustrated by E. G. Keller/Gerald Kelley.

10. *Harriett Gets Carried Away* written and illustrated by Jessie Sima.

11. *I'm Not a Girl* written by Maddox Lyons and Jessica Verdi, illustrated by Dana Simpson.

12. *I am Perfectly Designed* written by Karamo Brown and Jason "Rachel" Brown, and illustrated by Anoosha Syed.

13. *Jaime is Jaime* written by Afsaneh Moradian and illustrated by Maria Bogade.

14. *Mary Had a Little Glam* written by Tammi Sauer and illustrated by Vanessa Brantley-Newton.

15. *Bunnybear* written and illustrated by Andrea J. Loney.

Chapter Summary

This chapter overviewed current research on drag storytimes, focusing on three of our own studies on the topic. These studies explore the perspectives of library staff and drag performers. Findings address factors influencing the decision to host or not host drag storytimes, challenges faced, strategies to address them, and the representation of diversity in picture books. Based on the findings, the chapter proposes a toolkit for libraries considering hosting drag storytimes, emphasizing decision-making, inclusivity, advocacy, and book selection.

The toolkit includes recommendations for public library decision-making, hosting drag storytimes in non-urban settings, advocating for these events, and incorporating activities and book recommendations from drag performers. It aims to support libraries in navigating challenges and promoting authentic queer visibility while aligning with core library values.

Acknowledgements

Findings from this chapter were supported by an ALA Diversity Research Grant awarded to Sarah Barriage, Vanessa Kitzie, Shannon Oltmann, and Diana Floegel (co-PIs).

References

American Library Association (n.d. -a). *Top 13 Most Challenged Books of 2022.* Accessed September 13, 2023, from https://www.ala.org/advocacy/bbooks/frequentlychallengedbooks/top10

American Library Association (n.d. -b). *Libraries respond: Drag queen story hour.* https://www.ala.org/advocacy/libraries-respond-drag-queen-story-hour

Barriage, S., Betler, S., Lawler, R., Byrd-Fort, V., Myers, J., Kitzie, V., & Oltmann, S. M. (under review). A content analysis of picture books read during drag storytimes in public libraries.

Barriage, S., Kitzie, V., Floegel, D., & Oltmann, S. M. (2021). Drag queen storytimes: Public library staff perceptions and experiences. *Children and Libraries,* 19(2), 14-22.

Brown, J. (2005). *The World Café: Shaping our futures through conversations that matter.* Berrett-Koehler Publications.

Chabot, R., & Helkenberg, D. (2022, August). The discourse of drag queen story time challengers and supporters: A case study from the Okanagan Regional Library. In *Proceedings of the Annual Conference of CAIS/Actes du congrès annuel de l'ACSI.*

Clarke, F. (2023). Storytime is dragged into the guns row. *Index on Censorship: A Voice for the Persecuted,* 52(1), 50-51.

Cochrane, E. (2023, June 03). Judge finds Tennessee law aimed at restricting drag shows unconstitutional. *The New York Times.* https://www.nytimes.com/2023/06/03/us/politics/tennessee-drag-ruling.html

Davey, D. (2020). The fabulousness and the fury: Preparing for a drag queen storytime. *Partnership: The Canadian Journal of Library and Information Practice and Research,* 15(20), 1-10.

Dorsey, Z. A. (2020). When fierceness and kindness collide: The dramaturgy of a drag storytime. *Review: The Journal of Dramaturgy,* 26(1) 3-11.

Drag Story Hour (n.d.) *Homepage.* Accessed September 13, 2023, from https://www.dragstoryhour.org/

Ellis, J. R. (2022). A fairy tale gone wrong: Social media, recursive hate and the politicisation of drag queen storytime. *The Journal of Criminal Law,* 86(2), 94-108.

Ellis, J. R. (2023). *Representation, resistance and the digiqueer: Fighting for recognition in technocratic times.* Bristol University Press.

Friedman, J., & Johnson, N. F. (2022). Banned in the USA: The growing movement to censor books in schools. *PEN America.* https://pen.org/report/banned-usa-growing-movement-to-censor-books-in-schools/

Garcia, R. (2023, July). American Library Association responds to Montana State Library Commission's decision to withdraw Montana State Library's membership. *ALA News.* https://www.ala.org/news/press-releases/2023/07/american-library-association-responds-montana-state-library-commission-s

Gibson, A. N., Chancellor, R. L., Cooke, N. A., Dahlen, S. P., Lee, S. A., & Shorish, Y. L. (2017). Libraries on the frontlines: Neutrality and social justice. *Equality, Diversity and Inclusion: An International Journal, 36*(8), 751-766.

Gibson, A. N., Chancellor, R. L., Cooke, N. A., Dahlen, S. P., Patin, B., & Shorish, Y. L. (2020). Struggling to breathe: COVID-19, protest and the LIS response. *Equality, Diversity and Inclusion: An International Journal, 40*(1), 74-82.

GLAAD (2023). *Book bans: A guide for community response & action.* https://assets.glaad.org/m/53362a0a022def24/original/Book-Bans-Community-Guide.pdf

Gray, M. L. (2009). *Out in the country: Youth, media, and queer visibility in rural America.* NYU Press.

Keenan, H., & Hot Mess, L. M. (2020). Drag pedagogy: The playful practice of queer imagination in early childhood. *Curriculum Inquiry, 50*(5), 440-461.

Kitzie, V., Floegel, D., Barriage, S., & Oltmann, S. M. (2022). How visibility, hypervisibility, and invisibility shape library staff and drag performer perceptions of and experiences with drag storytimes in public libraries. *The Library Quarterly, 92*(3), 215-240.

Kitzie, V. L., Pettigrew, J., Wagner, T. L., & Vera, A. N. (2020). Using the World Café Methodology to support community-centric research and practice in library and information science. *Library & Information Science Research, 42*(4), 101050.

Lambda Legal (n.d.). *Preventing censorship of LGBT information in public school libraries.* https://legacy.lambdalegal.org/sites/default/files/publications/downloads/fs_preventing-censorship-of-lgbt-information-in-pubilc-school-libraries_1.pdf

Liang, A., & Stokalko, L. (2023). *Drag story time for adults.* Saskatchewan Library Association Conference: Saskatoon, Saskatchewan. https://hdl.handle.net/10388/14804

Livingston, D. (2023, March 11). Two arrested after protesters and supporters clashed at Wadsworth drag queen story hour. *Akron Beacon Journal.* https://www.beaconjournal.com/story/news/2023/03/11/dozens-demonstrate-at-drag-story-hour-for-children-at-wadsworth-park/69997506007/

Martin, H. J., & Murdock, J. R. (2007). *Serving lesbian, gay, bisexual, transgender, and questioning teens: A how-to-do-it manual for librarians.* ALA Neal-Schuman.

Montague, R. A., & Latham, J. (2019). Queer reflections: New views from library drag storytimes. *IFLA WLIC.* http://library.ifla.org/2585/1/191-montague-en.pdf

Movement Advancement Project (2019). *Where we call home: LGBT people in rural America.* Accessed September 13, 2023, from www.lgbtmap.org/rural-lgbt

Movement Advancement Project (n.d.). *Messaging guides.* https://www.lgbtmap.org/talking-about-lgbt-issues-series

Naidoo, J. C. (2018). A rainbow of creativity: Exploring drag queen storytimes and gender creative programming in public libraries. *Children and Libraries, 16*(4), 12-22.

Oltmann, S. M., Kitzie, V., & Barriage, S. (2022). "For me, it is an intellectual freedom issue": Drag storytimes, neutrality, and ALA core values. *Journal of Librarianship and Information Science, 55*(3), 734-743. https://doi.org/10.1177/09610006221100853

Radis, B., Wenocur, K., Jin, J., & Keeler, C. (2022). A rainbow for reading: A mixed-methods exploratory study on drag queen reading programs. *Journal of Creativity in Mental Health, 17*(3), 332-349.

Riedel, S. (2023). 8 states are pushing to leave a national library group because its president is a Marxist lesbian. Them. https://www.them.us/story/marxist-lesbian-librarian-american-library-association

Rojas, R., Cochrane, E., Sasani, A., & Paulson, M. (2023, March 05). Tennessee law limiting 'cabaret' shows raises uncertainty about drag events. *The New York Times.* https://www.nytimes.com/2023/03/05/us/tennessee-law-drag-shows.html

Sipe, L. (2008). *Storytime: Young children's literary understanding in the classroom.* New York: Teachers College Press.

Stone, D. R. (2019). News: Drag queen storytimes. *Journal of Intellectual Freedom & Privacy, 4*(1), 67-70.

Urban Libraries Unite (n.d.) *Drag story hour: Planning & safety support guide.* Accessed September 13, 2023, from https://urbanlibrariansunite.org/drag-story-hour-support/

Walters, H. (2020, August 11). Greenville County settles lawsuit with ex-librarian in relation to Drag Queen Story Hour. *Greenville News.* https://www.greenvilleonline.com/story/news/2020/08/11/drag-queen-story-hour-greenville-county-settles-librarian-lawsuit-sc/3333813001/

Westwater, J. J., Riley, E. A., & Peterson, G. M. (2019) What about the family in youth gender diversity? A literature review. *International Journal of Transgenderism, 20*(4), 351-370. https://doi.org/10.1080/15532739.2019.1652130

Wolfe, J., & Hager, M. (2023, September 08). EXCLUSIVE: State librarian president resigns after state superintendent cuts ties with organization. *Carolina News & Reporter.* https://carolinanewsandreporter.cic.sc.edu/exclusive-state-librarian-president-resigns-after-state-superintendent-cuts-ties-with-organization/

Appendix

Web-Based Resources

<u>Drag Story Hour</u>

- Drag Story Hour. https://www.dragstoryhour.org/
- Urban Libraries Unite. *Drag Story Hour Planning and Safety Support Guide.* https://urbanlibrariansunite.org/drag-story-hour-planning-and-safety-support-guide/

<u>American Library Association Resources</u>

- Rainbow Round Table. https://www.ala.org/rt/rrt
- *Core Values of Librarianship.* https://www.ala.org/advocacy/advocacy/intfreedom/corevalues
- *Libraries Respond: Drag Queen Story Hour.* https://www.ala.org/advocacy/libraries-respond-drag-queen-story-hour
- *Open to All* toolkit. https://alair.ala.org/bitstream/handle/11213/14839/160309-glbtrt-open-to-all-toolkit-online.pdf?sequence=1
- Selection & Reconsideration Policy Toolkit for Public, School, & Academic Libraries: Selection Criteria. https://www.ala.org/tools/challengesupport/selectionpolicytoolkit/criteria
- *Selection & Reconsideration Policy Toolkit for Public, School, & Academic Libraries:* Support for Intellectual Freedom. https://www.ala.org/tools/challengesupport/selectionpolicytoolkit/intellectualfreedom
- American Association of School Librarians (AASL). Defending intellectual freedom: LGBTQ materials in school libraries. https://www.ala.org/sites/default/files/aasl/content/aaslissues/toolkits/LGBTQ%2BResource%20Guide_FINAL-180709.pdf

<u>Southern LGBTQIA+ Organizations</u>

- Derby City Sisters. https://derbycitysisters.org/
- The Fairness Campaign. https://www.fairness.org/

- Free Mom Hugs SC. https://freemomhugs.org/index.cfm?nodeID=41

- Get Ready, Stay Ready. https://www.getreadystayready.info/

- Queer Kentucky. https://queerkentucky.com/

- South Carolina Freedom to Read Coalition. https://my.lwv.org/south-carolina-state/freedom-read-sc-coalition

- Southerners on New Ground. https://southernersonnew-ground.org/

National LGBTQIA+ Organizations

- GLAAD. https://glaad.org/

- Lambda Legal. https://lambdalegal.org/

- Movement Advancement Project. https://www.lgbtmap.org/

- Parasol Patrol. https://parasolpatrol.org/

- The Sisters of Perpetual Indulgence. https://www.thesisters.org/

Part 4
Gird Your Loins:
Where (and How)
We Go from Here

At What Cost?
The Personal Stakes of Intellectual Freedom

Jason D. Phillips and Jordan Ruud

Introduction

Being an advocate can hurt you. There's no getting around this, and we've seen it time and time again in our own professional experiences and in those others have faced. Moral injury, tokenism, and emotional labor ("queer battle fatigue") are not concepts we learned in library school. In response to the Black Lives Matter movement, the pandemic, and bans on books by or about people of color (POC) or the LGBTQ+ community, it seems we, as a profession, are finally grappling with these concepts, in articles, in conference presentations, in online discussions, and other forums.

Given our work in what is inherently a public service profession, advocacy seems second nature to many librarians. We want to serve our community—all of its members. But the acts of selecting books, making programming decisions, and/or carrying out services to the traditionally underserved POC and/or LGBTQ+ communities, face challenges—within the library from internal censorship, and public pressure from groups such as Moms for Liberty, library boards, and/or elected officials. Advocating for these communities comes with the potential for negative consequences, such as microaggressions, targeting (disciplinary action for unrelated and potentially trivial offenses), harassment from members of the public, or even potential termination. There's also the mental cost—the potential for advocates to experience stress, anxiety, and/or depression. It is not a good place to be when you feel like you're under a microscope, with a target on your back.

This chapter is a cautionary tale. It calls for its readers to carefully consider the costs and toll that advocacy may take on their lives. Professionally. Mentally. We do not want to discourage would-be advocates from taking up the cause so much as it is important for you to be informed.

Defining Our Terms

As we set about writing this chapter, we searched for a term to best describe the condition LGBTQ+ people experience when they constantly, persistently are put into positions where they have to advocate for or speak on behalf of themselves or their community. Tokenism, emotional labor, moral injury, and moral fatigue are all components or results of this form of advocacy, yet none seem to speak holistically to this concept. A colleague, Dr. Nicki Stancil, suggested considering William A. Smith's framework of "racial battle fatigue," leading us to find the conceptual framework of queer battle fatigue in the work of Boni Wozolek, Ross Varndell, and Taylor Speer (2015). Intersectionally drawing on Smith's work, Wozolek et al. conceptualize queer battle fatigue as the exhaustion of LGBTQ students and allies in a situation of "simply being themselves in schools and universities, regardless of whether they are out or closeted for their own protection" (2015, p. 3). For the purposes of this framework, and placing the concept within a different social framework than do Wozolek et al. (who primarily center their discussion around schools), queer battle fatigue speaks to the experience of LGBTQ+ people in the workplace while incorporating elements of tokenism, emotional labor, moral injury, and moral fatigue.

These LGBTQ+ individuals, voluntarily or involuntarily, are placed into formal or informal situations where they serve as advocates for or educators about the LGBTQ+ community to a largely White, cisgender, heterosexual audience and power dynamic. This is a constant, persistent situation, whether it means being approached by someone seeking information about pronouns and why we share them or explaining to an official why one should use "sexual orientation" in place of "sexual preference." Or having to explain other parts of the LGBTQ+ spectrum you may not be as familiar or well-versed with, such as explaining the difference between bisexual and pansexual. In other scenarios, openly LGBTQ+ (or out) individuals may be selected to serve on committees for the sake of token LGBTQ+ representation. The persistence of this situation and the emotional labor involved can result in a sense of moral fatigue of always having to serve in this role, particularly the heavy lifting involved with proffering a perspective counter to the heteronormative viewpoint.

Advocacy does not have to be on behalf of the community, but for oneself. Living openly as an LGBTQ+ person in a predominantly heterosexual and cisgender society is in itself a form of emotional labor: visibility in itself can arguably be a form of advocacy. For many LGBTQ+ people, the process of "coming out" is one they experience for most of their lives in situations where they need to introduce their pronouns, their sexuality, whether they're transitioning, or other facets of their LGBTQ+ identity. This does feel like a form of labor, particularly when you need to gently correct someone's assumptions. In professional environments, we sometimes face microaggressions or more blatant forms of phobia (homo-, bi-, trans-, etc.), which are not always treated with the seriousness they deserve or they are brushed off entirely. "You're just wearing your heart on your sleeve." "You should remember where you live." "Oh, they're not homophobic—they have a gay cousin they're fond of." It wears on you when your identity is under attack and those in power dismiss it because they cannot imagine themselves in your situation, experiencing it as you do.

This advocacy, either for oneself and/or the community, likely may fly in the face of accepted mores, creating the potential for friction. Those in the dominant cisheteronormative community may experience a spectrum of reactions: acceptance, surprise, disbelief, embarrassment, defensiveness, and/or a bigoted response to the shared information, placing the LGBTQ+ person in a vulnerable situation of having to potentially explain or defend the information. This is a situation where one's personhood and sense of self becomes inextricably tied with the information delivered, or in other words, a potential situation where the messenger is endangered. There is an accretive, potentially corrosive effect that occurs from each encounter, both for the LGBTQ+ individual and the person(s) encountered. Advocating for a gender-neutral restroom policy can lead to one being branded as a "troublemaker," for what should seem to be an innocuous matter (but sadly isn't). Requests for both equality and equity on behalf of the LGBTQ+ community challenge the heteronormative power dynamic, thus presenting the requester as someone to be watched, or worse: the enemy.

In the library context, to give an example, queer battle fatigue (and moral injury) can be experienced by LGBTQ+ library staff in a situation where books, programs, or services are challenged. Library administrators or other forms of authority may force libraries to remove books or cancel programming or services, effectively succumbing to public pressure. In many situations, this feels like a slow-moving bullet, potentially creating a stressful, tense situation that may pit a LGBTQ+ librarian against other librarians, staff, and/or administrators, ending with an outcome that violates principles of our profession, such as intellectual freedom or representation for underserved communities. In the context of queer battle fatigue, this is especially injurious for librarians and library staff who themselves are LGBTQ+, because not only are our identities under attack, but the decision ultimately erases or denigrates our status and dignity.

Queer battle fatigue speaks not only to the emotional labor and tokenism involved with advocating or educating on behalf of yourself and/or the LGBTQ+ community, but also to the cumulative effects (moral fatigue, moral injury) this has on the advocate.

Fee Fie Fo Fum: A Drag Storytime Event Gone Awry

An anecdote that is frankly upsetting to share because of the emotional labor and toll this incident took on us begins with our experiences with helping to coordinate a drag storytime in our academic library in December of 2018. The planning for the event led to many fruitful partnerships across campus and with the local community, but the local response led to a high cost to the organizers of the event.

This event arose as an idea for stress relief at finals. The LGBTQ+ student organization, PRIDE at UAFS sponsored the event (full disclosure: one of the librarians involved was the sponsor of the organization at the time). The library coordinated with other campus offices (such as Student Housing and the Student Activities Office) to promote the event. While the Fort Smith Public Library declined to serve as a co-sponsor, two of their librarians, on their personal time, did come to help by selecting books to be read aloud, bringing props for the participants, and facilitating the story hour element of the event. The library, working in cooperation with the local LGBTQ+ non-profit organization, River Valley Equality Center (RVEC), secured the participation of a drag queen, Chloe Jacobs, the then-reigning Miss Gay Arkansas America (2018). Chloe generously agreed to perform for free; RVEC provided an honorarium to cover travel and lodging expenses. And we can report that the university's administration was supportive of the event during the planning stages.

Prior to the event, two state senators got wind of it and one immediately launched a loud social media campaign to bring the event to the public's attention, stating that representatives of our employer would be called on to "explain themselves" before a legislative committee (which, to the best of our knowledge, never happened). Another state senator stated of the event, in effect, that it was intended to undermine traditional values.

The first state senator's post drew immediate attention within the state and then nationally. (The senator followed up with a quote from Ronald Reagan: "we can't expect [God] to protect America in a crisis if we just leave Him over on the shelf in our day-to-day living.") We were amused to note that in the comments section of the post, gay men from near each other within the state were becoming acquainted with one another. But despite the pushback many members of the public directed at the senators' posts, the posts, in addition to privately communicated complaints from alumni and other local leaders, *did* get the attention of our employer's administrators, who were reasonably concerned about the public response and state senators' vague threats of legislative sanction.

The public criticism for the event focused on three issues: hosting the event on campus (state-owned property); the use of public funds (taxpayer dollars) for the event; and perceived university sponsorship (read: endorsement of drag culture). In response to the first issue, the Student Activities Office maintained the firm stance that registered student organizations can bring speakers or host events on campus if they go through the approval process, which PRIDE at UAFS did. The second issue was a bit murkier since technically the library fronted the funds for refreshments and would be reimbursed by the student organization via budget transfer, but, ultimately, student fees and not public funds were used.

The third issue, perceived sponsorship, is where we did make a crucial error. When we, as the library, began promoting the event on-site and online, our poster design included the library's logo, a variation of the university logo, indicating official sponsorship (though the logo's inclusion was intended more as a simple statement of the hosting venue for the event). The university's administration asked us to recreate the event's promotional materials without any indication of the university's sanction (removing the library's logo) and to clarify that the event was happening without any funding from the university.

Despite the criticism and firestorm that erupted, the university gave its approval for the event to go ahead as scheduled (with protection from campus police). Somewhere in the range of 30-40 members of the university community and public, including a camera crew from a local television station, showed up to safely enjoy the drag storytime.

LGBTQ+ Advocates Under Siege

The period leading up to this event was a fraught one, with semi-panicky texts flying back and forth. Though the event itself went off without a hitch, the impact remained: since this event, we have become more guarded about programming, and an event like this is unlikely to be repeated here in the near future. This was 2018, and in the intervening five years between then and the time of writing, the attitude of certain sectors of the public toward events like this has only grown more openly hostile. What has changed, or simply become more apparent, in the meantime? A combination of factors, in our view, informs the tenuous situation many librarians face when it comes to programming and collection decisions under attack.

Moral panic, as discussed elsewhere in this collection, is at a point of white heat: while clearly the voices screaming about the horrors of LGBTQ materials and programming in libraries are a minority bent on enforcing their own norms, they are a *loud* minority and capable of leading to action from others. As Justin R. Ellis writes, citing Lauren Berlant's work:

> Outrage against DQS reflects the episodic invocation of a 'sexual emergency.' Such 'emergencies' might include prejudice-based government policies and '...defensiveness, rage, and nostalgia among ordinary citizens who liked it better when their sexuality could be assumed to be general for the population as a whole.' This protest reflects the tension between sexual citizenship as a method of achieving broader rights bearing inclusion for LGBTQ communities and the enhanced capacity to generate partisan outrage through digital media technologies. (Ellis, 2022, p. 99)

This is precisely the dynamic we saw at work in our own event.

Libraries and the people who staff them are good at many things, but outreach and self-justification are not inherently among those things.

A library carrying out an event that may be of a politically charged nature (even politically charged within the niche parameters under discussion here, such as adversity from a handful of ostensibly concerned parents, clergy, or politicians) without justifying that event—or pushing back against those attacking it—is a library that is not in a position to defend itself. There may also be a drastic asymmetry between the resources that a library can marshal in its own defense and the resources militating against a controversial programming or collections decision. A politician attacking a library for a drag storytime—or for that matter a Proud Boys chapter showing up to protest such an event, or a Moms for Liberty chapter attacking a library for housing a copy of *Gender Queer: A Memoir*—could easily draw a greater, louder audience, an audience more willing to go on the offensive, than the library and its allies can muster.

Attacking libraries has become a favored tactic of political opportunism in some quarters. In the current political sphere, one running for office, for example, stands to gain a lot of exposure in the news media and support from their conservative flank by attacking low-hanging fruit, and libraries may be seen as an easy target. As public institutions, libraries dangle perilously over the precipice, as we again see an asymmetry between the library's own resources and the political resources that may be marshaled against programming/collections decisions.

This period of public attack on libraries and librarians coincides with the erosion of tenure and/or contract protections for library employees. Without job security or the assurance of defense from above, librarians are left twisting in the wind in the face of voices attacking their work in this area.

Paying the Piper: The Toll Advocacy Takes

The simple truth is that not everyone needs to be a martyr or put themselves at even the risk of risk, as it were. Not every library is equipped to handle the pushback that may result from controversial decisions. If we had our drag event to do over again, given the current climate toward intellectual freedom and LGBTQ programming/materials in libraries (as compared to the situation in 2018 when we carried out our event), it's very likely that we'd decide against going ahead with it. The librarians involved felt distinctly uncomfortable and nervous from the intense scrutiny leading up to the event. Drop-ins from senior administrators sharing updates and concerns, news coverage, social media posts, and vague threats from state legislators all took their toll on the organizers. In conversations between the organizers, they refer to that time as "dark days" and what should have been a feat to be celebrated became a focal point of stress and anxiety. This was traumatic—a situation in which the event organizers sincerely perceived themselves to be at risk—and emblematic of the previously discussed queer battle fatigue. Other libraries are still unapologetically carrying out events of this nature, with drag storytime events or other forms of LGBTQ+ programming, and we wholeheartedly celebrate that as their prerogative. We trust their judgment in knowing their communities, calculating the possibility of pushback and the rewards of such an event, and going ahead with their events.

There is a personal and professional toll to these kinds of programming and collections decisions, and, more generally, to being an advocate. We're confident that everyone in this collection who carried out an LGBTQ-oriented event, or made an LGBTQ-centric collections decision, did so with selfless ends in mind. That is simply the nature of public-facing library work: we do what we do with the intention of helping others, whether it be the entertainment of a drag event or the intense empathy of finding oneself reflected in a book. Xochitl Gonzalez, reflecting on the personal plight of librarians at this challenging moment, notes: "Librarians who showcase books about underrepresented groups, including LGBTQ people, surely believe that these stories are valuable. But the librarians I spoke with insisted that they're making these choices because an assessment determined that there was a patron need for these books, not to push some personal social agenda" (2023, para. 17).

But as we've seen throughout this collection, this all comes at a cost. Bringing one's identity—either as an LGBTQ person or as a proactive ally—to the workplace is itself a form of emotional labor and queer battle fatigue. When one's work in programming or collection development is attacked, even granting that this work is with the goal of fulfilling the public's needs, rather than pushing personal agendas, one's own identity is implicitly under attack as well. Even with backup from administrators and colleagues, it can still hurt to have one's work attacked this way. The toll is that much greater when work like this puts one's job at risk. Fobazi Ettarh (2018, para. 16) discusses the burnout-inducing emotional toll of the "expectation of 'whole-self' librarianship," a toll clearly also present in cases where one's identification of oneself in one's library work leads to personal attacks.

As an example, one author has moved on to a new job at a new university. Years of LGBTQ+ advocacy within the library, on campus, and in the community as a volunteer in an LGBTQ+ non-profit led to intense feelings of queer battle fatigue. The trauma from the drag storytime event (and resulting fallout), microaggressions, and targeting necessitated a fresh start and hard reset. He has been able to step back from his advocacy role and pursue other professional and personal interests. But an advocate was lost in this process, a voice was silenced because the load became too much to bear.

Once More Unto the Breach: How to Gird One's Self

How can librarians minimize their exposure in multiple ways, not only in terms of protecting their jobs, but also protecting their emotional (and even physical) well-being in the face of retrogressive forces working in opposition to events and collection decisions like these? One strategy is to figure out where the buck stops. If you conceive of a particular programming idea that may be controversial, even if you've previously more or less had carte blanche when it comes to programming decisions, now is the time to ensure that administration explicitly approves of this idea. Get that person's (or that body's) investment, and if it turns out that you'll be standing on your own, left in a potentially vulnerable position, now is the time to rethink whether this event is really something you want to do. This may even rise to the point of preemptively consulting with counsel, if that's an option available to you, to get a read on whether they'll truly have your back. You need to be able to anticipate as clearly as possible how things will play out for your institution, and more importantly for you.

"Our tax dollars are paying for this!" is one common motif of outrage directed at LGBTQ+ programming and materials. In the case of programming, if your institution is public, be especially careful with how the event is paid for. Of course, it may be possible to make a compelling, effective argument for LGBTQ programming as rightly subsidized by public funds. The benefits of drag storytimes and LGBTQ+-centered displays have repeatedly been discussed, with their detractors unable to demonstrate any dire consequences of these events. But we've seen that there can be scrutiny directed at use of public funds for funding controversial events. Student fee money (as in the resources of a registered student Pride organization) and nonprofit support (as in local LGBTQ-serving nonprofits) may be the way to go. If you're interested in hosting such an event, and a local organization along these lines has the resources, you may be pleasantly surprised to learn with what enthusiasm they step up to subsidize your event, and even to coordinate from a logistical perspective.

We'll note in passing that it is *always* useful for librarians with an interest in LGBTQ causes or allyship to have a clear read on community resources for these populations. Do you know whether you have a local LGBTQ group? Are you familiar with community health resources for these populations, for example, trans healthcare resources? Having this information at hand, and having some connections built up with such resources and organizations, not only helps when it comes to finding logical outreach partners for programming, but also could help with ongoing public service (as in the case of someone needing a referral for services). In our case, it was prior connections with and participation in our local equality center that led to the opportunity for external funding for our event. We're very aware that this is likely preaching to the choir, but a librarian with their thumb on the pulse of the local LGBTQ community is one better equipped to carry out their work in areas including public service and acquisitions.

Having a close connection with organizations and resources like these additionally offers an easy channel for finding advocates in the event of adversity. One case of advocates proactively stepping up on behalf of their assailed library is representative. A footnote in the chapter titled "Building and Defending LGBTQ+ Collections" points to the situation of a public library under attack for its LGBTQ+ inclusive materials. The director left under a severance agreement, but public advocacy on behalf of the materials in question—and, by extension, on behalf of the personnel who made the decision to collect those materials—continued. On one level, advocates carried out the work of drawing attention to the library's situation: "In response, a group of advocates began speaking out against the new policies in library board meetings. Sarah Ramirez makes TikTok videos poking fun at...board members, some of which have millions of views," one story reported of the situation in Crawford County, Arkansas (Lenora, 2023, para. 11). Challenges in an effort to get the materials reinstated to their original locations, and even a lawsuit challenging materials relocations, were another outcome of public advocacy (Dale, 2023).

Assessment of the value of programming and collections is always a crucial consideration in libraries, and that goes for situations like those under discussion as well. If you have specifics to bring to the table—circulation and attendance figures for materials and programming in these areas—you can make your case that much more effectively.

It's also critical to thoughtfully circumscribe the limits—or lack of limits—under which a library is operating in terms of playing host to different types of programming. Consider the example of evangelist Kirk Cameron's recent tour on behalf of the publishing line Brave Books. Many have argued that this book tour, ostensibly intended to carry out storytimes at public libraries, was in fact intended to make a point about libraries. Kelly Jensen argues, discussing these nationally coordinated "See You at the Library" events, that "[t]hese are coordinated efforts to prove a point; in the sake of Cameron and Brave Books, it's to find a 'gotcha' with censorship. If you don't give them what they want, they can cry censorship, even if they themselves are the perpetrators who purposefully subvert the rules and policies" (2023, para. 28). Ultimately, we can ascribe whatever motives we want to Cameron and those carrying out these events: we can assume good faith (or as Cameron put it, lofty faith that "good is going to triumph over evil"), or we can view these events in the light of an organization intending to hurt libraries by disingenuously putting the appearance of a double standard in place (Washington Examiner, 2023, para. 4). Either way, consistent policy toward such events can actually be a fail-safe for LGBTQ+-centric programming. Put simply, a library permitting evangelical storytimes should not be able, with any philosophical consistency, to deny drag storytimes as well.

A phrase one commonly hears in the context of social opprobrium against controversial collections and programming is "community standards." For example, one draft of an Arkansas law widely viewed as targeting drag performances forbade minors from attending events that "[depict] sexual behavior in a way that is patently offensive under community standards as applied to a minor" (Mizelle, 2023, para. 6). A similar piece of legislation (also from Arkansas) appealed to "the average adult applying contemporary state standards with respect to what is suitable for minors" (Arkansas State Legislature, 2023). In this case, "average adult," without further explanation, could easily be viewed as any member of the public with a majority identity—not an LGBTQ person. "Community standards" are a moving target that nebulously defines the viewpoints and perspectives of diverse people—minorities and the materials and programming that represent them—out of the running for consideration, and deliberately others these people, treating them as not part of the "community."

As we've previously discussed in "Building and Defending LGBTQ+ Collections," a library with allies and advocates is a stronger library when it comes to potentially contentious materials and programming. The notion of "community standards" implies that minorities and their interests stand on their own. How better to put the lie to that than by drawing on the help of others in the community? Community partnerships, established as a pre-existing groundwork prior to a possibly controversial program, for example, can serve as the face of an event and can serve to indicate that the event has real community support.

Our Revels Now Are Ended: Parting Thoughts

Ultimately, the story we've seen recapitulated over and over—from many of our authors, from our friends in the profession, from other practitioners who've put themselves at risk by carrying out events like drag storytimes and making LGBTQ+ focused collections decisions—is a story of bravery. Sometimes one will have the strongest and most welcome institutional support in carrying out such things, but other times there's real adversity and the potential for real risk. In these circumstances, going ahead with these events, or unapologetically buying these materials, is to be commended. However, it's no less praiseworthy to evaluate the risks and make a well-informed decision against these things. The effects of queer battle fatigue are real and cumulative. They can lead to feelings of burnout, targeting, and/or take a toll on one's mental health resulting in stress, depression, anxiety, or unhealthy behaviors. If you choose to proceed, be cognizant of the potential toll your advocate role may take—and gird yourself accordingly. Have healthy coping mechanisms in place. And seek out a support network. It's important work that we're all doing, and we shouldn't ever feel the need to go it alone.

References

Arkansas State Legislature. Senate Bill 81 (draft). Reg. Sess.
2023 (2023). https://www.arkleg.state.ar.us/Home/
FTPDocument?path=%2FBills%2F2023R%2FPublic%2FSB81%
2FSB81011920231600.pdf

Dale, T. A. (2023). *Crawford County Library Board again delays action to hire new
director*. Talk Business & Politics. https://talkbusiness.net/2023/12/
crawford-county-library-board-again-delays-action-to-hire-new-director/

Ellis, J. R. (2022). A fairy tale gone wrong: Social media, recursive hate and the
politicisation of Drag Queen Storytime. *The Journal of Criminal Law, 86*(2),
94–108. https://doi.org/10.1177/00220183221086455

Ettarh, F. (2018, January 10). *Vocational awe and librarianship: The lies we tell
ourselves*. In the Library with the Lead Pipe. https://www.inthelibrary-
withtheleadpipe.org/2018/vocational-awe/

Gonzalez, X. (2023, May 15). *The librarians are not okay*. The Atlantic.
https://www.theatlantic.com/ideas/archive/2023/03/
book-bans-censorship-librarian-challenges/673398/

Jensen, K. (2023, June 5). *Brave Books, Kirk Cameron plan public library events
August 5; Public libraries need to prepare*. Book Riot. https://bookriot.
com/kirk-cameron-public-library-events-august-5/

Lenora, J. (2023, June 15). *Crawford County officials, residents debate LGBTQ
books in library children's section*. Little Rock Public Radio. https://www.
ualrpublicradio.org/local-regional-news/2023-06-15/crawford-county-of-
ficials-residents-debate-lgbtq-books-in-library-childrens-section

Mizelle, S. (2023, February 5). *Republicans across the country push legislation to
restrict drag show performances*. CNN. https://www.cnn.com/2023/02/05/
politics/drag-show-legislation/index.html

Washington Examiner (2023, August 2). *Kirk Cameron gears up for 'See You at
the Library' despite ALA opposition: 'Confident good is going to triumph.'*
https://www.washingtonexaminer.com/news/2583683/kirk-cameron-
gears-up-for-see-you-at-the-library-despite-ala-opposition-confident-
good-is-going-to-triumph/

Wozolek, B., Varndell, R., & Speer, T. (2015.) Are we not fatigued?: Queer battle fatigue at the intersection of heteronormative culture. *International Journal
of Curriculum & Social Justice, 1*(1), 1-35.

Queering the Undisturbed
Reflections on the Construction of Queer Space Through LGBTQIA+ Materials and Programs at the Quezon City Public Library (QCPL)

Ernani A. Agulto

As a queer, Filipino teacher-librarian, I have always imagined a library as a place where everyone is welcome. I envisioned it being a safe space where people from different walks of life can study, gather, and have meaningful conversations, evoking a sense of comfort and belonging. Back in college, I vividly remember frequenting the university library and was interested in pursuing a certificate in women's studies (which did not materialize, sadly). I used to spend my free time, even Saturdays, wandering through the dim aisles of the library and running my fingers over dusty books' spines, trying to memorize specific call numbers and locations of Simone de Beauvoir's *Second Sex* and Elie Wiesel's *Night*. Even though I felt the pleasure of being in a space filled with books, there was a certain feeling of disconnect. Looking back, I realize that this feeling of detachment stemmed from the academic library's lack of visibility of queer resources, services, and programs intended for queer students like me. To be candid about it, I never saw myself in Filipiniana books, nor in the library activities and programs that talked about Filipino queerness, which I was still trying to explore back then. There was an unrecognizable inexistence of space for materials and programs dedicated to LGBTQIA+. I did not question it. At the time, it was an absence I thought was acceptable, legitimized by the library's inability to provide materials and programs dedicated to the queer community. I acknowledge the impact it had on me as a queer-identifying individual.

Contemplating this particular experience allowed me to feel and see the absence of materials and programs that reflected my identity. It affected how I identify and connect with my true self and the community I have been seeking. The enlightenment this personal struggle brought led me to look for a possible, valid space where queer people like me would be allowed to feel visible, included, and accepted.

This personal pursuit has taken on a new form as I have become a librarian, ushering in a critical reflection on the practice and notion of library space, particularly *queer space*—a concept of space discussed by Edson Cabalfin in his article "Mala-baklang Espasyo Arkitekturang Filipino: Estetika, Morpolohiya, Konteksto [Queer Space in Filipino Architecture: Aesthetics, Morphology, Context]" (2000). Cabalfin defines *queer space* as an appropriation of meaning and a concept wherein queer identity is used as a foundation in understanding the concept of space (2000). Moreover, Cabalfin asserts that "giving meaning" and "making sense" of *queer space* as a category is a way for queer people to seize power from the politics of heterosexual dominance. For Cabalfin, writing his paper was a means of empowering these kinds of spaces—spaces that already exist but have been marginalized—including those who create and use these spaces. Therefore, this chapter is a brave attempt to critically engage the concepts of public librarianship and *queer space* as I relate how I, as a queer, Filipino teacher-librarian and LGBTQIA+ advocate, was able to "give meaning" and "make sense" of the reachable spaces (physical, virtual, and hybrid) by implementing queer-oriented library programming during the 2021 Pride Month Celebration at the Quezon City Public Library (QCPL).

I also use this opportunity to forward and amplify narratives of queer, Filipino librarians in possible, vital spaces (for instance, in publication) that have not yet been explored, to encourage other queer, colored voices that otherwise remain unheard. Hence, this chapter aims to empower queer librarians by constructing a personal queer narrative and by doing so, to forge the reclamation of queer spaces for and by queer people.

Queer Context

This chapter represents my experience as a queer, Filipino teacher-librarian and LGBTQIA+ advocate currently living and working in a highly urbanized Metro Manila, Philippines. On a professional level, my work as a librarian is bound by prescriptions set by the professional governing bodies in the field of librarianship in the Philippines and the bureaucracy of the local government. As a licensed librarian, I am obliged to comply with the prescribed ethical practice set by Republic Act No. 9246, also known as "The Philippine Librarianship Act of 2003," and the Philippine Librarians Association, Inc. (PLAI). Meanwhile, as a librarian working for a public library, I have to comply with professional standards set in the "Code of Conduct and Ethical Standards for Public Officials and Employees" implemented by the Civil Service Commission (CSC) and with the agenda set by the local government of Quezon City.

By using the words LGBTQIA+, queer, and gay, I do not claim that such labels sufficiently embody the specific social and linguistic meanings of other widely used local terms. For instance, the Tagalog label *bakla* has been a slippery term encompassing "homosexuality, hermaphro-ditism, cross-dressing, and efficacy" (Manalansan, 2003, p. 221). Can-nell (1999) and Johnson (1997) noted that *bakla* is associated with the process of transformation and shifting selves that refuse any fixed category. *Bakla* is also appropriated as an alternative term for tran-sexual due to the inadequacy of the Tagalog vocabulary.

Hence, I deliberately use the terms LGBTQIA+, queer, and gay through-out the paper to fill in the moments when these specific, local terms cease to yield collective and political meanings.[1] Through this, I can discuss my personal experience as a *bakla* in relation to other Fili-pino LGBTQIA+ members of my community and vice versa, in a more intentional and inclusive manner. Given this intention, however, I do recognize the Western terms' universalist connotation (Garcia, 2008, p. 537) and their irreconcilable contradiction vis-à-vis the local terms and their particular sociopolitical dynamics with the concepts of sex-uality and gender. It is not my intention to epistemologically recon-cile these terms, but simply to utilize these foreign terms as linguistic support in conveying my personal narrative, and to allow this to enrich existing intersectional discourses on public libraries and queer space.

Queer Politics in the Philippines

In a study conducted by the Pew Research Center in 2013 and 2019, the Philippines scored high as one of the countries that believes

---

1 Existing studies on gender and sexuality have asserted the collective and political meanings of LGBTQIA+ (Ceatha et al., 2019), queer (Kornak, 2015), and gay (Mathews, 1987).

homosexuality should be accepted. Although this may project a positive impression, this contradicts what is actually happening on the ground.

For more than a decade, the Philippines have struggled in passing a SOGIE (Sexual Orientation and Gender Identity or Expression) Bill, intended to protect the lives and rights of LGBTQIA+ individuals. To address this, various cities and municipalities in the country passed SOGIE-oriented ordinances to provide proper protection against any form of violence and discrimination on the basis of gender and sexuality. Quezon City is one of the first cities that passed and implemented a comprehensive ordinance, known as the Quezon City Gender-Fair Ordinance (No. SP-2357 2014). This local ordinance complemented the Quezon City Gender and Development Code (QC GAD Code) and at the same time, supported the establishment and mandates of the Quezon City Pride Council (QCPC) and the Quezon City Gender and Development Council Office.

While there were efforts at promoting LGBTQIA+ rights in the local government, instances of homophobia and transphobia still persist. On August 13, 2019, a transwoman named Gretchen Custodio Diez was prevented from using a woman's restroom in a mall in Cubao, Quezon City by a janitress who insisted that she use the men's restroom instead because she still had a penis (Talabong, 2019). Diez recorded the incident live via Facebook and was arrested for filming live while inside a female restroom. As a response, Quezon City Mayor Joy Belmonte condemned the discrimination that had transpired, insisting that the mall had clearly violated the Gender-Fair Ordinance, which requires all public, private, and commercial establishments to provide all-gender restrooms.

In Philippine politics, participation of the LGBTQIA+ at the national level has always been repressed, if not dismissed as insignificant. Ang Ladlad, an LGBTQIA+ political organization, applied for registration with the Commission on Elections (COMELEC) in 2006. The group was disqualified by the COMELEC, citing that the organization did not have enough members. In 2009, Ang Ladlad filed an application a second time, but was again dismissed on moral and religious grounds. Based on the published case, the COMELEC cited that group "tolerates immorality" which offends Christian and Muslim beliefs and supports LGBTQIA+ issues that violated civil code statutes such as "public morals" and "moral norms." The court's decision maintained that Ang Ladlad must be recognized by the COMELEC as a legitimate political party in the Philippines. In 2015, the group was one of the 38 party-list groups delisted by the COMELEC for failing to gain at least two percent (2%) of the votes cast for party-list during 2010 and 2013 elections (Gran-ali, 2015). Although this appeared as discouraging, hope for LGBTQIA+ representation in the Congress sparked anew when Geraldine Roman secured a seat, making her the first elected transgender woman leg-islator (Chen, 2016). Months before this victory, boxer and politician Manny Pacquiao made homophobic remarks that allowing homosexu-al relationships will make men "worse than animals." Pacquiao's state-ment started intense discussion online and was slammed by queer Fil-ipino celebrities and Ang Ladlad. In an Instagram post, Pacquiao later expressed his apology but was firm that he is against same-sex mar-riage and held his anti-gay belief on the basis of the Bible. Ironically, Geraldine Roman attracted opposing comments online over her state-ment against a recent drag performance by Pura Luka Vega. Roman re-ceived support from her fellow politicians and the LGBTQIA+ commu-nity. However, the Congresswoman drew flak from other members of the queer community, criticizing her contradicting views on the issue as a Catholic devotee while as a legislator, she favored the death pen-alty and kept mum on misogynistic remarks during the administration of then-President Rodrigo Duterte.

Library Space as a Queer Space

Library space is historically viewed as an absolute space, like cathe-drals, temples, and other culturally symbolic spaces, having a defi-nite sociocultural function (Elmborg, 2011). Particular to this ideologi-cal tradition is the perception of library space as a "service place" and a "learning space" (Bennet, 2003). Bennet defines a library as a service place where information is held, organized, and managed, while the li-brary as a learning space is a place where "learning is the primary activ-ity and where the focus is on facilitating social exchanges through which information is transformed into the knowledge of some person or group of persons" (2003, p. 4). These ideas conventionalize the functions of li-brary spaces based on what is deemed as the needs of library users.

Another popular view that shapes library space is the concept of "third place." Third place is defined as a place that is outside work or home (Oldenburg, 1999) and where library users can meet and create a sense of community (Montgomery & Miller, 2011). Third place em-phasizes adopting commercial practices of space and how these ideas can be applied to libraries in order to attract and accommodate the demand for social interactions and collaborations. James K. Elmborg (2011) discusses library space as a "third space." Echoing Henri Lefebvre (1991), Elmborg defines third space as an indeterminate and flexible space that is open for appropriation by its users for their own benefit. Contrasting with previous concepts of space, Elmborg argued that applying third space as a concept will give libraries room "to aim to be socially meaningful institutions with a higher role and calling" (2011). However, he maintained that following the idea of third place, having a stress on the commercial practices of space, would transform the library from an absolute space to an abstract space, devoid of any real meaning or purpose (Elmborg, 2011).

Although these perspectives offer interesting yet opposing ideas, I would like to push the discussion of library space a little further by welcoming Cabalfin's notion of "queer space." In his devised theoretical scheme, Cabalfin (2000) mentioned that the discourses of queer (*bakla*) are employed as a metaphor to create the category of space (*espasyo*). Thus, the concept of queer space (*mala-baklang espasyo*) can be interpreted as an appropriation of meanings and concepts attached to the word *bakla*. Here, the concept of space can be seen as an operation of identification, where the dynamics of queer identity are utilized as a foundation. Initially, Cabalfin expounds on Aaron Betsky's idea of queer space, which Betsky views as a space of queers whose primary purpose is to serve as a site for *jouissance* (or, as Betsky phrases it, orgasm: "leav[ing] you vulnerable and happy in that vulnerability, because you are at the center of your experiences" (Betsky, 1997, p. 17)). Betsky adds that queer space pertains to space created and utilized essentially by queers. Cabalfin's own writing expounds on Betsky's (1997) idea that "Queer space does not confidently establish a clear, ordered space for itself.... It is altogether more ambivalent, open, leaky, self-critical or ironic, and ephemeral. Queer space often doesn't look like an order you can recognize, and when it does, it seems like an ironic or rhetorical twist on such an order" (p. 18).

Meanwhile, contrary to Betsky's concept, George Chauncey as quoted in Cabalfin (2000) asserts that there is no queer space, but:

> ...only queer spaces used by queers or put to queer use. Space has no natural character, no inherent meaning, no intrinsic status as public or private. As Michel de Certeau has argued, it is always invested with meaning by its users as well as its creators, and when its

creators have the power to define its official and dominant meaning, its users are usually able to develop tactics that allow them to use the space in alternative, even in oppositional ways that confound the designs of is creators. (2000, p. 7)

Cabalfin opposes Chauncey's claim. Using de Certeau's argument, Cabalfin agrees that people dictate the meaning of space and adds that the transformation and categorization by those who utilize space hold power in producing its meaning. Therefore, Cabalfin continues, similar to queer space, the interpretation and meaning of queer as a category of space, is a way to seize power from the dominant. In this case, the dominant is the heterosexual. For Cabalfin, writing his paper is a way of empowering these kinds of spaces that already exist but have been marginalized, including those who create and use these spaces.

Cabalfin (2000) also highlights overpasses and basketball courts/plazas as vital examples, while exploring multifunctionality and paradox (*kabalintunaan*) as observable qualities of queer space. Overpasses and basketball courts/plazas are common structures in urbanized cities in the Philippines, serving as multifunctional spaces where individuals from different backgrounds and with different communal activities in mind converge. Multifunctionality is referred to as a combination of activities on the user's part that may be a form of deviation from the intended function of a space. Furthermore, Cabalfin makes a distinction that the paradox in the utility of an overpass may occur simultaneously (for example, utilizing space to sell street food instead of using it solely to cross a street) while in a basketball court/plaza, this paradox happens with respect to the time and needs of the community (for example, utilizing space for Christmas party or Lenten activities instead of using it only for basketball games). Note that the author emphasizes the appropriation of space as a clear manifestation of multifunctionality and paradox. He also underlines the multisensory experience of users in these specific spaces and how it influences their behavior in a specific way. For Cabalfin, these structural examples are important because they possess qualities of queer space and therefore, a piece of evidence that queer space exists in Philippine architecture.

The theoretical idea offered by Cabalfin instigated my awareness of the potential of the library as a queer space. This informed my plans and the execution of library programming for the 2021 Pride Month Celebration.

QCPL 2021 Pride Month Celebration

Situated at the heart of Quezon City, the QCPL has been an active agent in shaping the mind of its community. The conception of the QCPL came from the joint initiative of the National Library of the Philippines (NLP) and the Local Government of Quezon City. Inaugurated on August 16, 1948, under the administration of late Mayor Ponciano A. Bernardo, the library was established at a time when Quezon City had undergone various socio-economic developments. For several years, the local government of Quezon City was under male leadership, until 1976 when Adelina Santos Rodriguez assumed the position and served for ten years later as city mayor.

Fast forward to 2017. The newly constructed QCPL was opened, now boasting thousands of print and non-print library materials, and has 27 branch libraries located across the city. According to QCPL's annual report 2019-2020, there were 244,685 library users in attendance. Forty-five percent (45%) or 110,849 were male, while fifty-one percent (51%) or 133,836 were female. Furthermore, there was an apparent absence of activities, programs, or any available data on LGBTQIA+ users until 2021.

The QCPL had its first Pride Month celebration since the establishment of the library in June 2021. The programming crafted for Pride Month was intentional, inclusive, diverse, and…queer. The aim was to come up with library activities that would honor and celebrate the LGBTQIA+ as a community, whether in virtual or physical modalities and establish it as one of QCPL's important celebrations. Hence, the theme *Tunay na Inkulsibo. Mapagpalayang Espasyo* [Genuinely Inclusive. Liberating Space]. As a proponent of this project, LGBTQIA+ advocate, and queer individual, this meant a great deal, because I felt it was not just a mere project, but rather part of something bigger than myself.

The activities were a series of social media posts (virtual), forum (hybrid), and LGBTQIA+-sensitive initiatives (physical). A couple of months prior to the celebration, I conceptualized library activities and partnered with librarians from the Readers' Services Division (RSD). Librarians and library staff of the RSD were assigned to implement activities with the approval of the RSD head and in coordination with other QCPL divisions. The preparation and execution of the activities happened at the height of the pandemic. While there were efforts from the healthcare, government, and non-government sectors, there was an overwhelming sense of fear of going to work and health was still a top priority. Hence, most of the activities were done virtually, while other

Figure 1 QCPL 2021 Pride Month
Official Poster

activities were physical and hybrid, which strictly followed health protocol guidelines.

Pre- and post-activity collaterals, or media materials used to support a program or service, such as an official poster, recorded storytelling videos, and other images, were created using Canva, a free online design and visual communication platform, and channeled through QCPL's official Facebook page and digital signboards. For the record, online posts posted on the official Facebook of the library gained a total of 913 reactions, 723 shares, 34 comments, and 8,552 views.

Utilizing QCPL's official Facebook account helped in marketing and accomplishing the pre- and post-activities. Based on the data, the account has 43,000+ followers (74.8% are women, while 25.2% are men) residing mainly in Quezon City. Most of its followers are 25-34 years old, followed by 35-44 years old and 18-24 years old, while the least is 65+ years old.

Kicking off the QCPL Pride Month activities was a 56-second introductory video[2] and an official poster (figure 1). The materials served as a sneak peek for the upcoming celebration. We registered and dedicated a basic account to carry out all pre- and post-activity collaterals. As a background, I used mainly the colorful LGBTQIA+ flag. Meanwhile, the foreground was composed of the QCPL logo and text (theme and official hashtags).

---

2   QCPL Pride 2021 introductory video: https://www.facebook.com/quezoncitypubliclibrary/videos/193537999312998

Figures 2, 3, and 4

QCPL 2021 Pride Month
video screenshots

For the introductory video, we edited each slide using a template to present lined-up activities. At a glance, the video was predominantly in pink and used varied colors, emulating the LGBTQIA+ flag. The chosen images and graphics (see figures 2-4) were free and taken from the online design editing platform. The use of color and images, both in the video and official poster, was deliberately done to directly convey the intended message of the celebration. The text was backed up by the chosen color and images associated with the queer community.

Following the video and poster was a series of social media posts. Each post was scheduled from the first week up to the fourth week of June 2021. The schedule was made to ensure that Pride Month celebration was promoted on the official Facebook account of QCPL through continuous posting of online activities.

The first in the series of posts was recorded storytelling sessions of select queer-themed Filipino children's picture books (see figure 5). We selected four Filipino children's picture books with queer themes:

Dalawa Ang Daddy ni Billy (Billy Has Two Daddies) written by Michael P. de Guzma and illustrated by Daniel Palma Tayona,[3] *Uncle Sam* written by Segundo D. Matias and illustrated by Jason Moss,[4] *Ang Bonggang Bonggang Batang Beki (The Fierce and Fabulous Boy in Pink!)* written by Rhandee Garlitos and illustrated by Tokwa Salazar Peñaflorida,[5] and *Ikaklit sa Aming Hardin (Ikaklit in Our Garden)* written by Bernadette Villanueva and illustrated by CJ de Silva.[6] To carry out the storytelling session, staff from the RSD were assigned books and asked to record their readings; recorded storytelling sessions were posted on the official Facebook page of QCPL. One staff member recorded her storytelling session at the QCPL's Children's Section, with a green screen as her background. Other library staff opted to record their storytelling at home due to the ongoing health protocol guidelines implemented throughout Metro Manila. All of the staff used mobile phones to record and accompanied the recorded sessions with images taken from selected children's picture books.

One of the social media posts highlighted titles of LGBTQIA+ print Filipiniana books (see fig. 6). Because of the scarce titles of queer-centered books in the local publication, there were only a few titles included. Some of these titles were: *Ladlad: An Anthology of Philippine Gay Writing* edited by Neil C. Garcia and Danton Remoto,[7] *Brusko Pink, King Kong Barbies, and Other Queer Files* by Louie Cano,[8] *Gaydar* by Danton Remoto,[9] *Global Divas: Filipino Gay Men in the Diaspora* by Martin F. Manalansan IV,[10] and *Rampa: mga Sanaysay* by Danton Remoto.[11]

Another social media post highlighted five LGBTQIA+ organizations that championed queer rights and activism in the Philippines, namely:

---

3   *Dalawa Ang Daddy ni Billy (Billy Has Two Daddies)*: https://www.worldcat.org/title/1086610044; https://www.worldcat.org/title/1129083140

4   *Uncle Sam*: https://www.worldcat.org/title/1111788369

5   *Ang Bonggang Bonggang Batang Beki (The Fierce and Fabulous Boy in Pink!)*: https://www.worldcat.org/title/875477419

6   *Ang Ikaklit sa aming Hardin (Ikaklit in Our Garden)*: https://www.worldcat.org/title/957965488; https://www.worldcat.org/title/1391155742

7   *Ladlad: An Anthology of Philippine Gay Writing*: https://www.worldcat.org/title/906798707

8   *Brusko Pink, King Kong Barbies, and Other Queer Files*: https://www.worldcat.org/title/70635118

9   *Gaydar*: https://www.worldcat.org/title/53307932

10 *Global Divas: Filipino Gay Men in the Diaspora*: https://www.worldcat.org/title/779896741

11 *Rampa: mga Sanaysay*: https://www.worldcat.org/title/300289344

Figure 5 Selected children's picture books

UP Babaylan (UP Diliman),[12] Metro Manila Pride,[13] Rainbow Rights,[14] Galang,[15] and Ladlad.[16] These LGBTQIA+ organizations were selected because of their indispensable contributions in forwarding queer struggles and fighting for LGBTQIA+ rights, as well as in asserting queer representation in politics, as well as in other equally important spaces that demand a queer presence and voice.

---

12 UP Babaylan: https://upbabaylan.org/about-us/

13 Metro Manila Pride: https://mmpride.org

14 Rainbow Rights (Facebook): https://www.facebook.com/rrightsphl/

15 Galang: http://www.galangphilippines.org

16 Ladlad (Facebook): https://www.facebook.com/LadladPartyListOfficial/

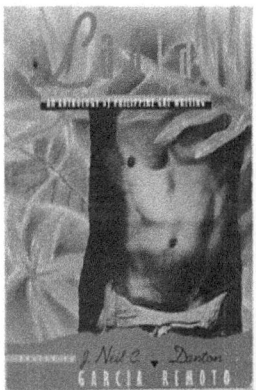

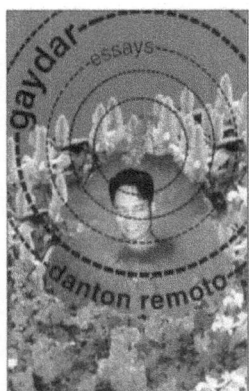

Figure 6 Selected Filipiniana books

Closing the month-long celebration was an online forum on Sexual Orientation, Gender Identity, and Expression (SOGIE), virtually attended by QCPL employees and open to the public via Facebook Live. I facilitated the online forum and was assisted by attorney Clara Rita Padilla, executive director of EnGendeRights, Inc.[17] The forum was formulated to educate the employees about the vital concepts of SOGIE and to consciously apply them in their daily work. For some attendees, it was their first-time hearing about SOGIE. Others were curious enough to ask follow-up questions. Attendees were enlightened with answers coming from the resource person. The forum engaged with issues concerning SOGIE, and proved that public libraries can provide a needed

---

17   EnGendeRights, Inc.: https://engenderights.wordpress.com/about/

Figure 7 Facebook post on LGBTQIA+ organizations

space—a critical space—for a very needed discourse involving an underrepresented sector. Indeed, echoing the words of Brooks Rainwater (2023), communities should see library space as one of the most valuable resources a public library has to offer.

One monumental activity was the inauguration of the all-gender restroom on June 8, 2021. The launch was attended by the City Librarian and other QCPL administrators. The all-gender restroom was located at the ground floor of the QCPL, adjacent to male and female restrooms. Due to insufficient space and funding, we were compelled to assign the PWD (persons with disabilities) restroom as an all-gender facility. The establishment of the all-gender restroom was compliant to SP-1309, S-2003, also known as the Gender Fair Local Ordinance. Under Section 5, the ordinance requires "government agencies, private offices, and commercial and industrial establishments to designate all-gender toilet rooms." But beyond compliance, we wanted to establish an all-gender restroom to ensure everyone could conduct their personal business in the most private manner possible. Through this, we hope we can help eliminate any form of violence or intimidation toward queer individuals.

QCPL Registration Form
Please write in print

Name:
Last First Middle Initial

Date of Birth: Citizenship:

Assigned sex at birth:
- ☐ Male
- ☐ Female
- ☐ Intersex
- ☐ Prefer not to say

Category: (Choose one)
- ☐ Preschool
- ☐ Elementary
- ☐ Junior High School
- ☐ Senior High School
- ☐ College
- ☐ Post-graduate
- ☐ Professional
- ☐ Senior Citizen
- ☐ PWD
- ☐ Out-of-School Youth
- ☐ Labor Force/ Skilled Manpower

Do you identify as part of LGBTQIA+?
☐ Yes ☐ No ☐ Prefer not to say

Address:

Contact No.: _____ Email Address:

For minors (17 years old & below)

Guardian's Name:

Relationship to the Applicant:

Address:

Contact No.:

Waiver of Confidentiality

By accomplishing this form, I agree that my personal data will be used to process my application for identification purposes in case of emergency and for demographics presentation.

Signature of Applicant

Please present a valid ID upon submitting this form

To be filled by QCPL staff

Date of Application:

Library Pass/Card No.: Processed by:

Figure 8 QCPL Registration Form

Another inclusive move was the inclusion of "Intersex" and "Prefer not to say" as sex options, and LGBTQIA+ identification as an option in the QCPL registration form. I personally observed that not all establishments, especially in public libraries here in the Philippines, were gender-sensitive in their forms. Usual registration forms would only have "male" and "female" only as gender options, or sometimes would use the terms "gender" and "sex" interchangeably as though they have the same meanings. I saw this as a long-time problem needing to be addressed. Before pursuing this initiative, I consulted my immediate supervisors and the upper management of the QCPL, before coordinating with the National Library of the Philippines (NLP). The reason for coordinating with the latter was that the NLP was the end receiver of the data taken from different public libraries, including QCPL, and proposing a form revision would have a direct effect on data to be gathered. This initiative was monumental for a public library and for LGBTQIA+-identifying library clients. Public forms were never neutral, and were part of a long-held belief system that had remained unquestioned. Being a part of this initiative felt fulfilling and liberating.

Further Ideas to Consider

Re-Imagine Library Spaces

Through my chapter, I have shown how we were able to reimagine library space during the pandemic—a time when physical and resource restrictions were magnified, creating a new reality. As a queer, Filipino teacher-librarian and LGBTQIA+ advocate, reflecting on the concept of queer space helped in redefining and reconstructing new meanings of library space grounded in the practical implementation of library programming. The potential of the library space could only be unlocked by breaking away from its rigid conception of being a one-dimensional space created for a specific function. Meanwhile, library programming should always be reconciled with the use of space and vice versa, dedicated to empowering the marginalized members of the community especially.

For instance, the establishment of the all-gender restroom at the QCPL was a clear manifestation of how the library reconciled space with library programming. At the onset, we recognized the limited library space and the obligation to provide a safe space for everyone. By dedicating a space as an all-gender restroom, we provided an inclusive space where queer people, as well as people with disabilities, were able to do their personal business without any fear of being judged and hopefully, were able to feel included. Via this library programming, we not only sought a practical, immediate outcome by providing inclusive library spaces, but also hoped to contribute to the ever-changing perspectives toward library roles and spaces—humane and grounded in the actual needs of library users.

Conceptualization, Planning, and Implementation of Library Programming

In order for successful library programming to materialize, it's crucial to have a well-thought-out concept and plan. Conceptualization and planning are critical stages that serve as the very basis for all library programs. Creating a program committee will be a great help in overseeing the program. This is something that we neglected during the 2021 Pride Month celebration, but worked out in 2022. We realized that an organized committee consisting of other people with different sets of perspectives would help in generating unique ideas, and at the same time, would offer alternative ways to look at every detail involved in the library programming. Having members of the committee come from or identify with the group or community that the library programming is intended for will make the experience more enriching and purposeful. In addition to this, one thing to note is to plan ahead of time. This may seem basic, but will be a great help to execute the program properly according to a timeline.

Highlighted previously as one of QCPL's initiatives was the revision of the library registration form, where inclusion of "Intersex" and "Prefer not to say" as an added option under "Sex" and "LGBTQIA+" under "Gender"—an initiative which came from the common experience among us queer individuals. Our lived experiences as queer individuals not only guided us to think of an initiative that aimed to create an inclusive library environment simply by recognizing queer identities but also made us sensitive to library programs or initiatives that truly matter. Moreover, advance planning and coordination worked in our favor and gave us more room to accomplish other tasks.

Budget

For most public libraries, budget considerations may not be easy. However, that should not hinder the execution of purposeful library programs. With a limited budget, one is given an opportunity to harness creativity and resourcefulness.

Library resources and free, open-source platforms or applications are an excellent starting point for finding materials that are in line with library programming and do not require any funding to develop marketing collateral. In one of QCPL 2021 Pride Month activities, we included highlighting queer-centered, Filipiniana materials about and authored by queer people. We also took advantage of Canva, a free-to-use online design and visual communication tool, to produce social media collateral, which were posted via QCPL's official Facebook page and digital signboards.

Tap into possible sponsorships and/or partnerships with the members of the community, the local government, and/or private organizations who may have the same goals to aid in accomplishing desired library programs. The support they offer, including financial and other forms of assistance, can play a significant role in making library programs a reality.

References

Bennett, S. (2003). *Libraries designed for learning.* Council on Library and Information Resources. https://www.clir.org/wp-content/uploads/sites/6/pub122web.pdf

Betsky, A. (1997.) *Queer space: Architecture and same-sex desire.* William Morrow and Company.

Cabalfin, E. R. G. (2000). "Mala-Baklang Espasyo" sa Arkitekturang Filipino: Estetika, Morpolohiya, Konteksto (Panimulang Pagtuklas at Paggalugad. *MUHON: A Journal of Architecture, Landscape Architecture, and the Designed Environment, 1*(1), 1-24. https://journals.upd.edu.ph/index.php/muhon/article/view/6329

Ceatha, N., Mayock, P., Campbell, J., Noone, C., & Browne, K. (2019). The power of recognition: A qualitative study of social connectedness and wellbeing through LGBT sporting, creative and social groups in Ireland. *International Journal of Environmental Research and Public Health, 16*(19). https://doi.org/10.3390/ijerph16193636

Chen, H. (2016, May 10). *Geraldine Roman: First transgender politician elected in the Philippines.* BBC. https://www.bbc.com/news/world-asia-36253666

Elmborg, J. K. (2011). Libraries as the spaces between us: recognizing and valuing the third space. *Reference & User Services Quarterly, 50*(4), 338–350. https://doi.org/10.5860/rusq.50n4.338

Granali, R. (2015, February 16). What to do? Ang Ladlad party list in quandary. *Philippine Daily Inquirer.* https://newsinfo.inquirer.net/673147/what-to-do-ang-ladlad-party-list-in-Quandary

Garcia, J. N. C. (2008). *Philippine gay culture.* University of the Philippines Press.

Manalansan, M. F. (2003). *Global divas: Filipino gay men in the diaspora.* Ateneo de Manila University Press.

Mathews, P. W. (1987). Some preliminary observations of male prostitution in Manila. *Philippine Sociological Review, 35*(3-4), 55-74.

Montgomery, S. E., & Miller, J. (2011). The third place: The library as collaborative and community space in a time of fiscal restraint. *College & Undergraduate Libraries, 18*(2-3), 228-238. https://doi.org/10.1080/10691316.2011.577683

Kornak, J. (2015). *Queer as a political concept* [Doctoral dissertation, University of Helsinki]. University of Helsinki Open Repository. https://helda.helsinki.fi/items/7048ef66-0c5c-4d9b-82d6-e2255ddce950

Oldenburg, Ray (1999). *The great good place.* Marlowe & Company.

Rainwater, B. (2023). *Public libraries as critical spaces for convening.* Urban Libraries Council. https://www.urbanlibraries.org/blog/public-libraries-as-critical-spaces-for-convening

Talabong, R. (2019, August 13). *Trans woman arrested after being blocked from using women's restroom in Cubao.* Rappler. https://www.rappler.com/nation/237698-transgender-woman-arrested-after-blocked-using-women-restroom-cubao/

The Library Classroom as a Safe Space
Academic Libraries, Information Literacy, and Trans Allyship

Matthew Rohweder

Introduction

Growing up as a gay kid, I often found solace and safety in my neighborhood library. A few blocks away from my house, right on the corner of a busy intersection in a very large city, my tiny neighborhood branch was a place where I could find relief from bullies or the ever-present sense of difference that clouded my brain daily. Lost amongst the tiny stacks, I found new worlds to explore and lives to live. And, as I got older and started to recognize what that sense of difference was, the library became a place to explore, intellectually, who I might be. And naturally, the librarians who oversaw this tiny branch, and who all knew me by name, were instrumental in that. They happily got *certain* books in from the city's main branch, let me check them out so I could read them quietly, and never so much as said a word when I returned them before heading home.

This is, of course, a rather clichéd and highly romanticized anecdote about growing up gay and the incredible power and safety I found in libraries. However, I believe it to be an honest one. Libraries, as Stephen Krueger notes, are reliable places where many members of the LGBTQ+ community could feel comfortable and safe (2019, p. xiii). But despite this sense that libraries can be seen as a safe space for queer kids, it is essential to explore the various spaces within a library to determine whether they are all equally safe for *all* members of the LGBTQ+ community.

Libraries, as Krueger goes on to explain, are well-placed to function as allies for trans, nonbinary, or gender nonconformist individuals. Although not necessarily tied to information literacy, he provides an example of his own experience while transitioning and having his deadname associated with his student ID. While librarians and library workers at his university's library understood his discomfort, working to provide him with a new ID with his proper name, he recognized that the library's policies held an inadvert cisnormativity. "This unintentional ignorance," Krueger notes, "meant that the library's policies made some patrons extremely uncomfortable" (2019, p. 119). The necessary takeaway is that not all members of the LGBTQ community experience the same level of acceptance, safety, and comfort within the library; however, as the librarians at Krueger's university demonstrated, we can work within or around our policies to support that community. With this in mind, I look towards the classroom and posit that, as librarians, we must strive to find ways to establish ourselves as allies.

I would argue that the classroom is one of the primary places where librarians connect the most with learners. And by striving to achieve good allyship, we can ensure that libraries are safe spaces for trans, nonbinary, or gender nonconformist individuals. This chapter is specifically concerned with information literacy (IL), how it is taught in classroom spaces, and how we can work to create safe spaces within those classrooms.

First, we will look at some theoretical understandings of allyship before turning to explore some practical ways that librarians and library instructors can engage students to establish a safe and welcoming space. Further, the work of allies is also to assist members of the LGBTQ+ community in the discovery of their identity by giving them tools and the space to explore and question; thus, some of the practical tips included in this chapter will also touch on this aim.

Allyship & Safe Spaces

Fundamentally, allyship is considered as an "active, consistent, and arduous practice of unlearning and reevaluating in which a person of privilege seeks to operate in solidarity with a marginalized group" (The Anti-Oppression Network, "Allyship," para. 1). Allyship is therefore an active state, and it is not meant as a passive identity. Calling oneself an ally is not sufficient in demonstrating an individual's solidarity to equity-deserving groups.

To further this definition of allyship, I want to consider the issue of trust within the relationship between equity-deserving groups and allies. One of the fundamental elements behind allyship is a measure of accountability and consistency, which means an ongoing process of building relationships and seeking recognition that the work of allies is benefiting equity-deserving groups (Anti-Oppression Network). This, in turn, requires trust. It is important to consider whether individuals of equity-deserving groups can trust that we will continue to show support to them, that we will use our spaces of privilege to help their advancement or to end systematic levels of oppression.

When we enter spaces of privilege (such as the classroom), we are assuming positions of power; thus, as allies, we need to be accountable in providing support for members of those communities. They are entrusting us to create spaces where their identities are not being undermined or oppressed, and we need to step up to that challenge.

Allyship in the IL Classroom

The IL classroom, despite its function to equip students with the tools and knowledge of finding and using information, is generally a neutral space. As Angela Pashia explains in her exploration of critical information literacy, "we can teach students to evaluate information sources according to a simple checklist, usually including the authority (often focused on formal credentials) of the author, publication date, and purpose of the piece, without having to examine the power structures that enabled that author to become an authority or the ideological biases represented in the piece" (2019, p. 101). The tendency to avoid such conversations pushes the IL classroom away from functioning as an allied space. Teaching IL concepts without examining the power structures behind the information students are exploring means that we, as practitioners, maintain a status quo and can reinforce notions of traditional forms of knowledge. I will discuss more on this point later in the chapter.

As I have discussed, true allyship requires demonstrating solidarity with equity-deserving groups. In an IL context, it is important to consider exactly what highlighting one form of knowledge does and whether we should be considering how that practice impacts our students, specifically those within the LGBTQ+ community.

Reexamining IL practices to build a more welcoming space should not be a seismic shift; rather, there are practical and subtle ways to change

IL practices to demonstrate strong allyship that do not require immense work or massive expense on your part. For instance, the above example about reconsidering what constitutes as scholarly authority may require some training for IL practitioners but can be easily implemented as part of a general IL session lesson plan.

What are these practical and pedagogical changes that can happen in the IL classroom to help establish a stronger sense of allyship towards the LGBTQ+ community?

Allyship Techniques in the IL Classroom

Allyship in the classroom is something that educators must continuously work at, while at the same time constantly be in a state of learning themselves. Several of the techniques that I discuss might strike you as commonsensical, but for many who want to actively engage in allyship for the first time, these are things they may have never thought about before. But even if you have been engaging in allyship or integrating pedagogical techniques that are inclusive, there is always more to learn, try, and do within a classroom.

You might regard the techniques that I discuss in this chapter as only the start of establishing your classroom as a safe space for the trans community. Or perhaps you have been actively working to create a safe space and are looking for something new to try, in which case, I hope these techniques and ideas inspire you.

One essential element to keep in mind with any of these techniques is to engage in discussion and gather feedback. You might want to anonymously solicit feedback from students about how the session went for them. Did they feel comfortable with the conversations that were happening in the classroom, or how could you have made the space more welcoming? How, for example, did they feel about pronoun sharing? Engaging with community members is one of the best ways to continuously learn and shape our allyship work. We need to act alongside and in collaboration with the community to empower them and make spaces where they feel comfortable and accepted for themselves.

Pronoun Go-Rounds

A note: While I view this strategy as an essential part of creating safe spaces within the classroom, it is important that you should not require your students to participate in pronoun introductions. There are many reasons why an individual might be uncomfortable participating in this activity; however, advocating for pronouns in a classroom can help individuals realize you are a safe person to speak to.

In an age in which including one's pronouns within your email signature or as part of your Zoom screen name is commonplace, it can be easy to forget the importance of declaring one's pronouns. Within the IL classroom, pronouns can easily be overlooked or be seen as unnecessary, especially if you are confined by the limitations of a one-shot session. However, demonstrating strong allyship is all about looking for ways to reshape IL sessions to become more inclusive. As Karen Nicholson and Maura Seale point out, "Small changes to library teaching practices offer an opportunity to resist the pedagogies of the practical that dominate library instruction but do not require substantially more labor from library workers" (2022, p. 774). The simple act of announcing your pronouns in class is one such small change.

Initially, I thought this was nothing more than low-hanging fruit, but something as simple as starting off my IL sessions with, "Hello, my name is Matt, and my pronouns are he/him" ended up being revolutionary. When I did this for the first time in 2021, a student, who also introduced themselves with their pronouns, stayed behind at the end to thank me. They told me that not many professors or instructors do this, so they often felt unsure whether those classrooms were welcoming spaces. Giving students space to share their pronouns and making sure to memorize them, as well as sharing my own, has become one of the foundational cornerstones of my pedagogical philosophies around allyship.

These activities are often called "pronoun go-rounds" and, as Davey Shlasko explains in *The Trans Ally Workbook*, "This practice works much better if supported by some explanation of why it is happening, and communicating an expectation that people call others the requested pronouns" (Shlasko, 2017, p. 58). It is important to note that while you might have the best of intentions in advocating for the sharing of pronouns, not everyone will feel comfortable doing so. Remember that nobody of any gender identity should feel obligated to share their pronouns, so you should not be surprised if some students refuse to do so. If you are creating a safe space, you won't even acknowledge this and simply move onto the next student. Thus, be sure to make clear that sharing is optional and that you are striving to create an inclusive space. Also emphasize that there are no repercussions if individuals decide not to share their pronouns. The key point here is inclusivity and positivity.

There are other techniques that can help you build upon verbal go-rounds. For instance, during online classes make sure your screen name includes your pronouns and ask if anyone wants help changing their name to include pronouns—it might surprise you how often someone will take you up on that offer. And for in-person sessions, you can use temporary name cards, which include pronouns. Again, you want to start the session by writing your own name on the board, with your pronouns, then hand out the name cards and ask everyone to copy what you've done—if they are comfortable doing so.

Techniques such as these will also ensure that you do not misgender anyone in your classroom. As Krueger points out, "To a large extent, it is up to individuals to avoid misgendering others; it is your responsibility to try to use people's pronouns correctly and to improve when you make mistakes" (2019, p. 18). The techniques discussed here are one way to help you become comfortable in using pronouns and encourage you to create gender-inclusive spaces for everyone. Further, developing strong and consistent practices around pronoun use offers instances of learning for those new to working with members of the trans community and are working towards proper pronoun usage (Shlasko, 2017, p. 58).

Finally, if you are unsure whether your practices are impacting your classroom and students in the manner you want, never be afraid to ask how you can change them to be more effective. Pronoun use is just one element of allyship and establishing safe spaces, but it is always a learning process.

Code of Conduct

Establishing a code of conduct can often be one of the easiest techniques in creating a safe space within your classroom. It can require very little work, as you can usually point to your library or institution's classroom code of conduct. You can remind students, either verbally or in a presentation, of those policies and make sure they understand you won't tolerate offensive language or inappropriate behavior. By familiarizing yourself with the larger institution's code of conduct, you can establish your own and emphasize the importance that all students respect each other.

The code you develop or draw upon does not have to be specific to the trans community, but it must include language about anti-discrimination policies. For example, Oregon State University Library's code of conduct policy states that library users must "[m]aintain the safety and security of others, free from discrimination, intimidation, and harassment" (Oregon State University, n.d., para. 3). However, it elaborates that library users must treat other users and staff with dignity and respect, as well as not engage "in discrimination, microaggressions, intimidation, or harassment of any kind, including unwanted or inappropriate advances, sexual activities, or indecent exposure" (n.d., para. 3).

A classroom code of conduct that draws on such language does not need to go into further specifics but can be easily enforced and help assure members of the LGBTQ+ community that their interests are protected.

A code of conduct might be seen as a simplistic technique in creating safe spaces, but its importance cannot be overemphasized. Again, I look to Krueger to emphasize how important these kinds of policies are within the classroom: "Given all of the difficulties trans and gender variant students face, it is extremely important that the campus library respect them and provide an environment where they can feel safe. Failure to do so is a failure to adequately support the students" (2019, p. 116). Being conscious of how you establish your classroom and what you expect from your students and yourself can go a long way to ensure that trans students and trans library users feel comfortable in that space and continue to engage with you as an educator.

Incorporating Diverse Examples

Creating a safe and welcoming space within the library classroom goes beyond just developing a code of conduct or ensuring that pronouns become part of your regular pedagogical practices. You also need to be aware that the content of your sessions—what you are teaching—can greatly impact your students. As librarians who regularly teach IL, we all have a rotating set of examples or databases or tools that we use to illustrate the skills we want students to learn. Perhaps these are tools that we've developed over time that work best for the group of students we're teaching. For instance, as a business librarian, I commonly use searches related to specific types of marketing or HR-related issues around pay equity; however, these examples may not effectively create the inclusive space we need to foster in our classrooms.

Are your examples representative of the diverse communities in your classroom? Are you drawing on ideas that can spark conversations about those communities and demonstrate to members that you are a safe individual to speak to about these issues? Consider that by using a diverse range of examples in your classes, you are actively creating a space for dialogue and showing that you are someone who can be approached to discuss further research on these and other diverse topics. For instance, in IL classes for marketing students, I often use examples about the spending power of the LGBTQ+ community, "pink money," and how different corporations market to that community. This then signals to students that I can be approached to talk to about other issues or topics relating to the LGBTQ+ community. If we begin to incorporate examples, including anti-trans laws, drag bans in libraries, book censorship, gender affirming medical care, and so on, we can not only help students see they can come to the library for information on these issues, but demonstrate that you, as a librarian, can be trusted to have these kinds of conversations.

Again, Krueger makes the point that "[v]aried examples demonstrate the range of people who make up the trans and gender variant community. Including trans subject matter in this way helps normalize the existence of trans and gender variant people, who are often erased simply through lack of representation" (2019, p. 122). If we are to create safe spaces for members of these communities and show we are true allies of those communities, then we need to look at the content of our classrooms and start to use inclusive examples and discussions. But to do that, we may need to look beyond even just the kinds of examples we're using and instead focus on what kind of information we're highlighting.

The Hard Conversations: Looking Beyond Peer Review

Teaching information literacy, as academic librarians, often involves highlighting the importance of peer-reviewed articles above all other information resources. While this is a well-established and often necessary practice, it has the potential to highlight privileged voices. And often these voices are white, cisgendered, and straight. With this understanding in place, I wonder, where are the diverse voices? And how likely is it that lived experiences will be highlighted in such a practice?

My point in critiquing this practice is not to shut down the teaching of searching for and using peer-reviewed articles, rather it is to consider how we can incorporate lived experiences into the IL classroom.

Moving beyond the system of peer review means moving beyond established notions of *accepted* information, versus *unaccepted* information. As Ian Beilin points out, "the existing information system mirrors the larger social and political order, which is characterized by a radically asymmetrical distribution of power, and is shot through, systematically and structurally, by racism, sexism, homophobia, militarism, and class oppression" (2015, para. 22). As allies, we need to consider whether the diverse voices and lived experiences that we are trying to uplift in our classrooms are getting lost when we continue to uplift those systems that have the potential to cause harm. Instead, I advocate for a more balanced or nuanced way of teaching. We can critique which voices we highlight in our lessons by blending both the authoritative peer review with the lived experience.

For academic librarians, teaching information literacy is one of the cornerstones of our practice, often relying on The Association for College & Research Libraries (ACRL) Framework[1] to give structure and definition to what and how we teach. IL is positioned as "the set of integrated abilities encompassing the reflective discovery of information, the understanding of how information is produced and valued, and the use of information in creating new knowledge and participating ethically in communities of learning" (ACRL, 2015, para. 6). As pointed out above, the forms and systems of information highlighted are what come out of the peer-reviewed system over any other.

Yet I want to consider how to best act as allies within our classrooms and whether we should be thinking about who is getting published, whose voices are being highlighted, and whose voices are being left out. Thus, as allies, it is our job to decentralize privilege and disrupt accepted or heteronormative attitudes. Naturally, this is part of a larger conversation that involves faculty, curriculum design specialists, or teaching and learning departments within our institutions where it is important to remember that you are not necessarily advocating to entirely de-emphasize peer review, but rather looking at ways to augment those voices. For instance, you might want to co-teach a session with a faculty member where you engage in discussions with students about scholarly conversations or scholarly authority and ask the question "Who is being published?" Or you may want to help faculty develop a class that includes resources highlighting lived experiences

---

1   http://www.ala.org/acrl/standards/ilframework

alongside peer-reviewed articles. In such a case, your IL session could show how to find credible examples of such resources. You could even work with your teaching and learning department to develop an IL session for faculty on finding resources that emphasize lived experiences for their classes.

There are myriad ways to raise questions of authority in information resources within the classroom, but the most important piece is the act of emphasizing lived experiences as a form of authority. This has the potential to create a safe space within your classroom and might empower students from trans, nonbinary, or gender nonconformist communities to engage with you openly about their own lived experiences. They might start to see their experiences as equally as important as a peer-reviewed article.

I utilize various resources or tools to talk about lived experiences. For instance, I have highlighted podcasts, zines, online blogs or magazines, and social media posts. In a class where students had to write essays debunking a myth or stereotypes, I showed them how to find peer-reviewed articles on that subject, but I placed those articles in conversations with the *Trans Voices Podcast* and the *Gender Stories* podcast, as well as showed them multiple zines published online that augment or help them better understand the perspective of community members. It can take time to source good, reliable material. I rely on the advice of other librarians, peers in my community, articles highlighting diverse voices, and conversations with faculty to select what I use and show students. It also helps to be open with faculty about your intentions and make sure they understand you are still going to talk about peer review, but that you want to place those resources in context or conversation with other voices. I have been consistently surprised about how receptive faculty and others are to shifts in my IL practice. I am finding more often that faculty and students respond well to my emphasizing that these resources can add a rich and unique element to an IL classroom.

We need to ensure that our IL practice includes encouraging students to critically engage with information, especially concerning questions of authority. Having conversations about scholarly and critical authority demonstrates to students from equity deserving groups that their voices can and should be highlighted. By actively taking lived experiences into account, and de-emphasizing the role peer review always plays, we are already starting to shift our IL classrooms into safe, welcoming, and questioning spaces. Providing the space for trans, nonbinary, or gender nonconformist students to consider the value of their voices is another tool in your arsenal to both demonstrate your allyship, but also working to create a safe space.

Conclusion

We do not often think of the IL classroom as a transformative space, where students or even instructors can begin to unpack questions about their identity or confront issues directly pertaining to their community. By incorporating respectful ideas and attitudes, current examples, and current language of trans- and gender-variance into your classrooms, not only are you ensuring a safe space in your classroom but are identifying yourself as someone who can be approached to discuss and research other trans- and gender-variant topics. You are essentially showing your allyship.

Always keep in mind that allyship is something you do. It is, as Shlasko points out in the *Trans Allyship Workbook*, an "informed, accountable action that contributes to other people's ability to survive and thrive in a context of inequality" (2017, p. 5). You can never be passive as an ally; you need to always be working at strengthening your toolkit and rethinking how to best create empowering spaces for trans people and other members of the LGBTQ+ community.

Right now, more than ever, the trans community needs us as keepers of information and educators to step up and demonstrate that we are willing to do the work of recognizing them by giving their voice credence and ensuring their safety in our libraries and classrooms.

References

Anti-Oppression Network. (n.d.). *Allyship.* https://theantioppressionnetwork.com/allyship/

Association of College and Research Libraries (ACRL). (2015). *Framework for information literacy for higher education.* http://www.ala.org/acrl/standards/ilframework

Beilin, I. (2015). *Beyond the threshold: Conformity, resistance, and the ACRL Information Literacy Framework for Higher Education.* In the Library with the Lead Pipe. https://www.inthelibrarywiththeleadpipe.org/2015/beyond-the-threshold-conformity-resistance-and-the-aclr-information-literacy-framework-for-higher-education

Krueger, S. G. (2019). *Supporting trans people in libraries.* Libraries Unlimited.

Leung, S. (2022). The futility of information literacy & EDI: Toward what? *College & Research Libraries, 83*(5), 751-764. https://doi.org/10.5860/crl.83.5.751

Nicholson, K. P., & Seale, M. (2022). Information literacy, diversity, and one-shot "pedagogies of the practical." *College & Research Libraries, 83*(5), 765-779. https://doi.org/10.5860/crl.83.5.765

Oregon State University (n.d.). *Library code of conduct.* https://library.oregonstate.edu/code-conduct

Pashia, A. (2019). Black Lives Matter in information literacy. *Radical Teacher, 113,* 100–102. https://doi.org/10.5195/rt.2019.611

Shlasko, D. (2017). *Trans allyship workbook : building skills to support trans people in our lives* (Updated and expanded edition.). Think Again Training.

How an Education Liaison Librarian Uses Library Information Sessions and Other Outreach Methods to Instruct Pre-Service Teachers on Using LGBTQ Children's Literature in Their Lesson Planning Efforts

Allyson Wind

Introduction

As the education department liaison librarian for East Stroudsburg University's Kemp Library, Professor Allyson Wind will discuss how she introduces pre-service teachers (PSTs) to LGBTQ children's literature during library information sessions. A PST is a college or university student who is pursuing a career in the education field. PSTs are being taught how to be educators through guided field experiences, observing, and finally, student teaching. At East Stroudsburg University, many of the PSTs are brought to the library by their professors for a Library Information Session (LIS) on how to choose the appropriate books for lesson planning purposes.

Professor Wind demonstrates how to use curricular materials for a specific subject area like social studies, language arts, or science, or for special days and holiday celebrations. Within the context of these curricular areas, she also introduces students to LGBTQ books that they can incorporate into their lessons.

A Short History of ESU and Library Services for Pre-Service Teachers

East Stroudsburg University (ESU) has a long history of educating educators. In 1893, East Stroudsburg Normal School opened. In 1983, the school was officially named East Stroudsburg University (n.d.-a). As of the 2023 Fall Semester, ESU's College of Education offers multiple graduate and undergraduate programs for education majors including Early Childhood, Middle Grades, Secondary Education, Special Education and Rehabilitation, Health and Physical Education, Reading Education, and Educational Leadership (n.d.-b). According to a timeline established by our university archivist, the first instance of a library on campus was in 1893. In 1980, Kemp Library opened in its current location on Smith and Normal Streets (n.d.-c). In 1987, the Curriculum Materials Center (CMC) was established on the ground floor at Kemp Library. The purpose of the CMC was to provide a space for collaborating with the Education Department to ensure that the pre-service teachers were supplied with the best possible books and curriculum materials to assist with lesson planning.

I serve as the liaison librarian for ESU's Education Department. My bachelor's degree is in elementary education and I am thrilled to work closely with both the faculty and PSTs in this department. At the beginning of each semester, I send out a letter to the chairs of the Education Department informing them of the services I provide, including teaching Library Instruction Sessions (LIS) on topics such as searching the education related databases for peer-reviewed articles to using specific curriculum materials to design lessons. I am also in charge of the collection development and promotion of the CMC and children's/YA Collections. I also feel that it is my obligation to prepare PSTs to be knowledgeable of LGBTQ literature and to be strong advocates for why these books belong in their future classrooms.

ESU's PSTs will be entering the teaching profession in a volatile political and social climate. Nearly every day in the news we see stories about books being challenged, classroom libraries scrutinized by parents, censorship attempts by lobbyist groups and school boards, books being removed from curriculum use, and school libraries being repurposed for "discipline centers." PSTs need to ensure that their future classrooms are welcoming spaces for all students; and one way to do that is to make available books that reflect their students' real-life experiences, which often include LGBTQ themes.

In addition to just having these books in their classroom libraries, a PST should also be knowledgeable about how to deal with any challenges that may arise regarding why the books are included in their collections or used in their curriculum. PSTs should know that their school library and librarian/library staff are essential for the success of their students academically, socially, and emotionally. I hope that through my efforts of extensive collection development, direct instruction, hosting special events such as book tastings, and creating engaging book displays, our PSTs will become confident in their knowledge and use of LGBTQ books when they graduate and start teaching.

Assess Your Current Collection and Weed

One of the first things I did with the CMC and children's collection was to assess the current collection for weeding and collection development purposes. I wanted to ensure the collection was adequate for my goals of introducing PSTs to LGBTQ literature. I strongly believe that in order to let the good things shine through in your library's collections you must regularly assess and weed. At the time of the initial assessment of the collection, I was not given any extra funds for retrospective collection development. I knew it would take me a significant amount of time to evaluate which items needed weeding and which could remain in the collection.

A quick visual assessment of the collection showed that there were multiple issues that needed to be addressed. I am not sure that these collections had ever been weeded, as I found books on the shelves that dated back to the 1920s and 1930s. Many of the books were in poor physical condition, with broken spines and missing pages or poorly repaired. Books on the top shelves were covered in layers of dust, while others were damp, and others were coated in mold and mildew. These books had to be removed immediately because mold and mildew could easily spread to and ruin any newer books placed on the shelf adjacent to them. After just a short time weeding the collection, one of my colleagues and I contracted respiratory infections, while other individuals assisting with the weeding project experienced skin and eye irritation. I would highly recommend that any individual involved in weeding a collection in the same physical condition and age as mine wear a N95 mask or respirator, long-sleeved shirt and pants, closed-toe shoes, and gloves to reduce the risk of getting ill from the contaminated items.

I utilized the CREW method for weeding the children's and YA collections. This method is outlined in *CREW: A Weeding Manual for Modern Libraries from the Texas State Library and Archives Committee* (Texas State Library and Archives Commission, 2012). I learned about this method while working as a reference librarian at a public library. The method worked well for me to weed the adult nonfiction and reference collections. Within the *CREW Manual* is a set of criteria called MUSTIE that gives a concise guide on how to weed any library collection. MUSTIE is short for Misleading, Ugly, Superseded, Trivial, Irrelevant, or obtainable Elsewhere (Texas State Library and Archives Commission, 2012, pp. 52-53). According to the CREW method, you must "aggressively weed" children's books, as they are used much more roughly than books in the regular circulating collection. They are spilled on, chewed on, or otherwise damaged while being read by children. I weeded more than 12,000 books from these collections using this method. Most of the books met the "U" (or Ugly) criteria. Other books met other criteria such as "M" (for Misleading) and "S" (Superseded by a better title on the topic).

Although the majority of the books in the collection were pedagogically sound, I was shocked to find books on the shelves that were no longer relevant to our current student body. Some books contained racist, sexist, or otherwise outdated information. I found books on topics like divorce, working mothers, sex education, drug and alcohol abuse, and disabilities that were decades out of date in terms of the information contained in the books. I found very few picture books on LGBTQ topics besides "classics" like Leslea Newman and Laura Cornell's *Heather Has Two Mommies* or Michael Willhoite's *Daddy's Roommate*.

In terms of the YA collection, I weeded it extensively in October 2023 and found that the collection did not contain many LGBTQ items at all. Most of the YA books in general were dated from the 1970s through the early 2000s and their themes definitely did not reflect LGBTQ viewpoints or have LGBTQ characters. There were some titles that were Stonewall Award winners or honor books in the YA collection. This finding accurately reflects the publication history of LGBTQ themed YA books during this time period. The first YA novel to specifically address homosexuality in the life of young adults was John Donovan's 1969 title *I'll Get There: It Better Be Worth the Trip*. From this point through the late 1990s, very few books were published with gay/lesbian issues or identities, although the visibility of gay men and lesbians had shifted dramatically (Jenkins, 1998).

If outdated LGBTQ titles are located during the weeding process, I believe they should first be assessed for physical condition. If in poor physical condition or with outdated covers, illustrations, or photographs, weed immediately according to the "U" in the MUSTIE criteria. If their physical condition is decent, I would then assess the titles for historical or research purposes. I have placed some non-LGBTQ outdated titles with historical or research purposes in our library's Rare Book Room. They are discoverable in our library catalog but are not able to be checked out unless I specifically authorize it. If the titles contain egregiously incorrect, outdated, or hurtful information about the LGBTQ community, I would weed it immediately based on the "M" criterion. There are so many modern books published with compassionate and realistic depictions of LBGTQ characters that could be ordered to replace any outdated titles.

Below are two examples of LGBTQ books I found in the children's non-fiction section of my library while weeding just recently. I am currently evaluating what I would like to do with them; I may weed them based on the "U" and "S" MUSTIE criteria, but they might have historical or research value when compared to more contemporary titles on the topic.

Zach's Story: Growing Up with Same-Sex Parents—This book, published in 1996, tells the story of Zach, an 11-year-old boy living with his two moms. He discusses how his life compares to children with a mom and a dad. Although the book does a good job of introducing this topic in an age-appropriate way, it contains outdated photographs and language, as the publication date is nearly 30 years old.

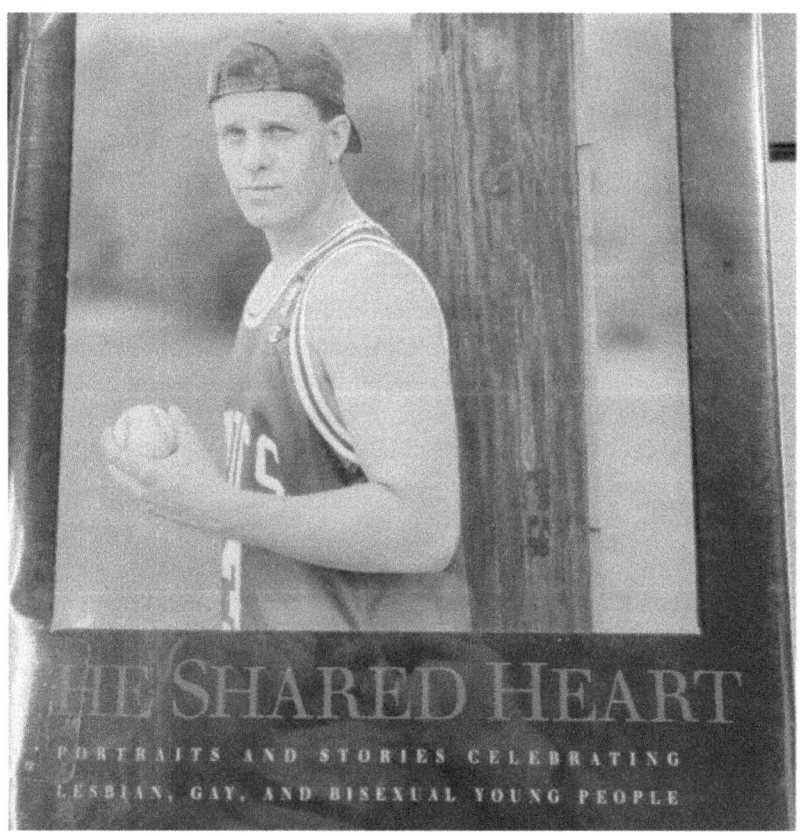

The Shared Heart: Portraits and Stories Celebrating Lesbian, Gay, and Bisexual Young People—This title was published in 1997. The portraits and primary narratives of LGBTQ young adults are compelling. The photographer, Adam Mastoon, is still actively working. The black-and-white photographs and outdated clothing and accessories of the 90s (*Details* Magazine, rollerblades, Starter jackets) may deter our students from picking it off the shelf.

Below are two examples of picture books that I weeded also based on the "U" and "S" criteria and suggestions for replacements:

Sonya's Mommy Works

In 1982 when this book was published, it was less common for mothers to be working outside of the home. Currently, there are many combinations of working adults in families, and we needed books to reflect this.

 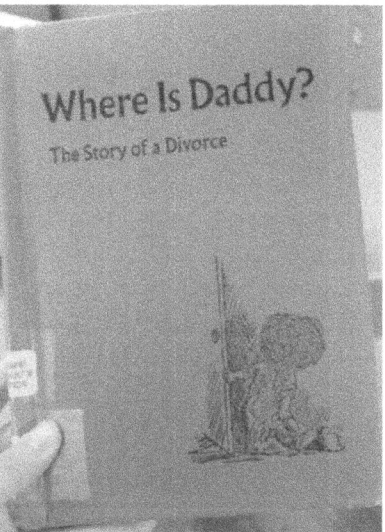

A suggestion for replacement is Arpan V. Shah's *Daddy Goes to Work*. This story is about a father going to work and the child's grandmother caring for her while he is away.

Where is Daddy? The Story of a Divorce

This book was published in 1969, when divorce was still quite uncommon. Starting in the 1970s, no-fault divorces were allowed, and divorce became a more common occurrence. Although divorce rates are falling, "traditional" nuclear families where a mother and father divorce is not necessarily the norm.

- A suggestion for replacement is Jessica Wexler and Jeric Tan's *Two Moms, Two Houses*, an age-appropriate book about divorce between two moms.

Collection Development

After the initial assessment and weeding of the CMC and children's/YA collections, I focused on the collection development step in the process. It took another five years after the initial assessment and weeding of the collections to obtain funding from the library director for purchasing new books. Our current library director allocated each of the librarians $3,000 per academic year for our collection develop-ment efforts starting in 2022. I use the funds to purchase books to re-place missing topics, including modern LGBTQ and diverse literature.

My library director remains very supportive of me ordering LGBTQ books for the collections, but this will not be the case at every library. There may be backlash to ordering these books, and it can come from any individual, internally or externally. Some possibilities include books purposefully not being ordered, or they could be hidden, stolen, or otherwise censored after their arrival at the library. I was prepared with a direct answer if I ever got any questions about why I was order-ing these books: students and faculty from the Education Department were requesting them for lesson-planning purposes.

I use several resources to locate LGBTQ books to add to the children's and YA collections. Some are more traditional tools that most librari-ans are aware of, but others are more non-traditional.

American Library Association (ALA)

The ALA is an obvious place for most librarians to start when they are looking to add LGBTQ books to their children's and YA collections. There are many lists of books that include LGBTQ topics.

- I personally started with the ALA Banned Book List (American Li-brary Association, 2023a) as many of the titles have been banned for discussing LGBTQ topics that some may deem as "age-inappropriate" for their intended audience.

- Stonewall Award Booklist: My goal for the children's and YA collec-tions is to add a new award-winning book section to the shelves to highlight the Stonewall Award titles (Rainbow Round Table, 2024a). I hope that adding this collection will let students know that one of our goals at Kemp Library is to recognize and honor LGBTQ au-thors and literature at the same level as other literary awards like the Caldecott and Newbery Award winners/honor books. Pre-Ser-vice teachers are often encouraged to use Caldecott and Newbery books in their lesson planning purposes or have them in their class-room libraries, but to my knowledge, I don't know that LGBTQ liter-ature is encouraged in the same way. I do know that when I was a PST in the early 2000s, I was not made aware of the Stonewall Award, even though it has been around since the 1970s. I discovered the

Stonewall Award list when I was searching for other medals on the ALA website.

- Rainbow Book List: I was introduced to this list while editing this chapter. The Rainbow Book List is created by the Rainbow Book List Committee of the Rainbow Round Table of the ALA. This annual book list presents an "an array of diverse stories and identities representing the LGBTQIA+ youth experience" (Rainbow Round Table, 2023, para. 1).

Social Media

Because I'm a librarian, I follow many social media pages that focus on books in general. I often see books highlighted to me while I browse social media that are diversity and inclusion or LGBTQ related. Some of my favorites to use for collection development in these topic areas are:

- Read Brightly: a blog with sections of book suggestions for babies through teens, including lists for diversity and inclusion topics (Read Brightly, n.d.).

- Library for the Kind: a Facebook group created by a children's librarian who created the group "to celebrate children's books that celebrate diversity, inclusion, gender equality, LGBT+ and kindness as a whole" (Library for the Kind, n.d.).

- We Need Diverse Books: "Founded by marginalized authors, We Need Diverse Books strives to diversify the publishing industry and make bookshelves more equitable—all to promote literacy, build empathy, and reduce bias" (We Need Diverse Books, n.d.).

- Mai Storybook Library: "The goal of MaiStoryBook is to spotlight children's illustrated books, as well as provide resources for parents, families, and teachers to inspire in children a love for books and a curiosity for the world of reading—all through a series of MaiStoryBook collections" (MaiStoryBook, n.d.).

- Ezra Jack Keats Foundation's resources for educators: "Get support for engaging lessons using the best in diverse children's literature published over the last three decades, including last year! These virtual & in-person toolkits make subjects like Bullying, Community and Equity understandable and relatable for any age group" (Ezra Jack Keats Foundation, n.d.).

Suggestions from the LGBTQ Community

As with many topics on diversity and inclusion, I like to get suggestions for books directly from the source. If you feel comfortable asking people you know in the LGBTQ community, I am sure they can give you suggestions for books that would fit in your collection. If you are working on a college campus with a Gender and Sexuality Center, you could ask the leadership there for help with book suggestions. I would be careful, though, to make sure you are not tokenizing any one person in the community, as their experiences do not reflect the entire LGBTQ community.

Label Your Books for Easier Browsing

Clearly labeling books in the collection as LGBTQ is a great way to make it easy for PSTs to locate these titles in your collection as they browse. Sometimes the students need a book for a lesson plan that is LGBTQ-related, but are unsure of which one they want. Their professors will often reach out to me in advance and let me know their students will be coming to the library to look for LGBTQ children's or YA books to use in a lesson plan or for a research assignment. In this case, I am ready to assist any students who arrive at the library for these assignments. I walk them to the collections and make suggestions based on their requirements. For example, a student came in recently and told me her professor wanted her to find a "contemporary" LGDTQ book for a 3rd grade lesson plan. I showed the student how our LGBTQ books were labeled with the LGBTQ label, but then I guided the student in choosing a book that would meet the criteria set forth by their professor. The student ended up choosing Marcus Ewert and Rex Ray's *10,000 Dresses*, about a boy who dreams of wearing beautiful, sparkly ball gowns and challenges gender stereotypes.

Other times, PSTs will come to the library to simply browse the collections for books they need. I wanted a way for PSTs to easily locate LGBTQ books when browsing, like in the evenings and weekends when there are no librarians available to assist them. I want the books to be labeled in a similar way to our labeling of books as "Disability" and "Multicultural," as these were being required for specific assignments in the past for other education classes. With the increase in need for LGBTQ books for PST assignments, these titles needed to be clearly labeled for browsing purposes. There are various companies that produce attractive spine labels for LGBTQ books. We usually order from either Demco or Brodart, the most commonly used library supply companies. In addition to labeling LGBTQ books, I started re-labeling the "Disability" and "Multicultural" books to "Diversity," which I think better reflects what my goal for the collection is; to highlight the diversity of our campus community. In the past, these books were labeled by the CMC library assistant, using labels she created herself. Although at the time, they served their purpose, I think the Demco diversity labels are easier to see and better reflect my goal for the collection.

Make Engaging LGBTQ Displays

A fun and simple way to teach PSTs about the LGBTQ books in your collection is to incorporate LGBTQ books into engaging displays. I create seasonal displays in the children's/YA area for traditionally celebrated holidays like Halloween and Christmas. I also maintain a permanent diversity and inclusion display on the main floor of the library. I add in a variety of books with LGBTQ themes to my seasonal displays all year round. I explicitly show PSTs these displays during each one of the LIS I teach. I suggest to PSTs that they should consider using books with diverse themes in their future classrooms because not every student they will have comes from a traditional family background. It's also important to me to make PSTs aware that they should consider incorporating books on LGBTQ themes during holidays and special awareness days/months throughout the academic year.

During the month of February when PSTs usually look for books on Valentine's Day, I like putting Daniel Haack's *Prince and Knight* on display during this holiday. This book tells a tale as old as time of a prince looking for a partner to rule his future kingdom with him. In his case, none of the princesses brought to the castle by his parents suit his fancy. But then the prince meets a brave knight on a white horse and falls in love, and they get married. I would instruct PSTs to consider using stories like this in their future classrooms because the plot and theme are familiar to its intended audience of young children. It would be a great catalyst to start an age-appropriate discussion about the normalization of same-sex marriage.

There are also various important awareness days or significant times throughout the calendar year for members of the LGBTQ community that can be used to make displays for PSTs. I generally reference the GLAAD website for this information (GLAAD, n.d.). The full week after Valentine's Day is Aromantic Spectrum Awareness Week. This theme

Example of a Permanent LGBTQ Display

Example of Valentines Day/Aromantic Spectrum Awareness Week Book Display

may be more appropriate for PSTs who are planning on working with middle or high school age students. Items I would put on display for Aromantic Awareness Week would include graphic novels like *Loveless* by Alice Oseman (author of the popular *Heartstopper* series) or *Gender Queer: A Memoir* by Maia Kobabe.

Book Tastings

Other ways I make sure that students are aware of LGBTQ children's literature are through programs with the university's Education Department such as a book tasting. A book tasting is an event where participants such as PSTs can get a sample of books on certain topics or genres. I have seen this event set up like you were dining at a fancy restaurant, complete with red checkered tablecloths, dinnerware, and vases of flowers for decoration. Sometimes there is actual food involved, like if the books are cooking-themed, but the main idea of a book tasting is to let pre-service teachers "sample" a number of book titles for sparking ideas for lesson-planning purposes.

For each table, a different genre of book is presented in a pleasing way for participants to "taste" and become familiar with. For the book tasting event I participated in during the spring 2022 semester with the ESU Education Department, I decided to highlight LGBTQ books from our library's collection. PSTs who attended this event received several free resources that I printed out from the Human Rights Campaign (HRC). These resources corresponded with the books from our collection. On the Human Rights Campaign website, I discovered they have a program called Welcoming Schools:

> HRC Foundation's Welcoming Schools is the most comprehensive bias-based bullying prevention program in the nation to provide LGBTQ+ and gender inclusive professional development training, lesson plans, booklists and resources specifically designed for educators and youth-serving professionals. Our program uses an intersectional, anti-racist lens dedicated to actionable policies and practices. We uplift school communities with critical tools to embrace family diversity, create LGBTQ+ and gender inclusive schools, prevent bias-based bullying, and support transgender and non-binary students (Welcoming Schools, n.d.).

Welcoming Schools has book lists, lesson plans, and many other free resources that can help PSTs learn to incorporate LBGTQ topics into their everyday lesson-planning duties. I also discovered that library companies like Brodart have websites for youth services resources. The Brodart website contains lots of great information for PSTs to use for incorporating LGBTQ literature into their lesson plans, from creating inclusive storytimes to starting a graphic novel book club. These are just two resources that I used to help our PSTs sample the LGBTQ books in our library's collection, but there are so many more. I hope to put these resources on our Education Department LibGuide so that our PSTs can come back and review them whenever they wish.

Upon conclusion of this chapter, I realize that I have a lot more work to do in order to make sure that ESU's PSTs are adequately prepared to utilize LGBTQ children's and YA literature in their classrooms. The weeding and collection development of my current collection, paired with teaching library information sessions, and hosting other special events like book tastings is really just a start for me. I also need to develop ways to more explicitly teach PSTs about the complexities of censorship and free speech as it relates to all types of children's and YA literature, including LGBTQ literature. My hope is that this chapter will serve as a guide for any librarians who may be in the same position as me, working to teach our future educators to appreciate, utilize, and defend their use of LGBTQ literature in the classroom.

Censorship of books is an issue that is not one that is going to go away anytime soon unless we all fight against it. The ALA's Office of Intellectual Freedom (OIF) continues to report that book challenges are being recorded at an alarming rate in 2023. Between January 1 and August 31, 2023, OIF reported 695 attempts to censor library materials and services and documented challenges to 1,915 unique titles— 20% increase from the same reporting period in 2022. A report authored by Phil Morehart from *The I Love Libraries Blog*, an initiative by the American Library Association, lists five actionable steps to take now if you are worried about the increasing book banning attempts happening in the United States (2023).

References

American Library Association. (2023a). *Banned & challenged books.* https://www.ala.org/bbooks

American Library Association. (2023b). *Book ban data.* https://www.ala.org/bbooks/book-ban-data

East Stroudsburg University. (n.d.-a) *About ESU: Past presidents.* https://www.esu.edu/about/history_beliefs/past_presidents.cfm

East Stroudsburg University. (n.d.-b) *College of Education.* https://www.esu.edu/college_education/index.cfm

East Stroudsburg University. (n.d.-c) *Kemp Library: About the Library.* https://www.esu.edu/library/about/index.cfm

Ezra Jack Keats Foundation. (n.d.). *For educators.* https://www.ejkf.org/for-educators/

GLAAD. (n.d.). *LGBTQ community calendar.* https://glaad.org/reference/calendar/

Jenkins, C. (1998). From queer to gay and back again: Young adult novels with gay/lesbian/queer content, 1969-1997. *The Library Quarterly: Information, Community, Policy, 68*(3), 298–334. https://www.jstor.org/stable/4309229

Library for the Kind. (n.d.). *About.* https://www.facebook.com/groups/3031859860429502

MaiStoryBook. (n.d.). *About MaiStoryBook.* https://maistorybook.com/about/

Morehart, P. (2023, December 9). *U.S. book challenges update: December 8 edition.* I Love Libraries. https://ilovelibraries.org/article/u-s-book-challenges-update-december-8-edition/

Rainbow Round Table, American Library Association. (2023). *The 2023 Rainbow Book List.* https://glbtrt.ala.org/rainbowbooks/archives/1444

Rainbow Round Table, American Library Association. (2024a). *Stonewall Book Awards list*. https://www.ala.org/rrt/award/stonewall/honored

Read Brightly (n.d.). *Diverse books*. https://www.readbrightly.com/ages-stages/pre-k/diversity/

Texas State Library and Archives Commission. (2012). *CREW: A weeding manual for modern libraries*. https://www.tsl.texas.gov/sites/default/files/public/tslac/ld/ld/pubs/crew/crewmethod12.pdf

We Need Diverse Books. (n.d.). *We Need Diverse Books*. https://diversebooks.org/

Welcoming Schools. (n.d). *Creating safe and welcoming schools*. https://welcomingschools.org/

Does This Camouflage Come in Rainbow?
Visibility of Frontline Library Workers During the Culture Wars

Patrick Connors and Debra Trogdon-Livingston

Authors' Note

We would like to acknowledge that the terminology used to describe the LGBTQ2SIA+ community is nuanced. We intentionally alternated between queer and LGBTQ2SIA+ to honor the experiences of all queer people.

Introduction

Queer visibility in public libraries is a complicated issue with high stakes. When queer workers are visible, it can be positive for patrons and the community as a whole. Being too visible, however, can be risky for library workers themselves. Current accusations of LGBTQ2SIA+ people as "groomers" or "pedophiles" have pushed many library workers to police how they perform their gender and sexual identities at work or risk negative consequences (Udesky, 2022).

Existing in a queer body in libraries can put workers at risk, but there are some considerations to improve queer library worker experiences. Kelly et al. found three commonalities which made workplaces more queer-friendly: "policies and practices which included anti-discrimination, ... disclosure, visibility and recognition, ...and protection from discrimination based on sexuality, gender, and other intersecting marginalized identities (2021, p. 1083). These three factors combine to allow people to share more of their identities in a safer emotional environment backed by solid protective policy.

Queer library workers find themselves in a position where they must decide how to perform their gender and sexuality at work in a way that is authentic to them, but inoffensive to potential critics. Not properly performing one's "worksona"[1] could mean being viewed by coworkers, patrons, and administrators as unprofessional, unserious, or worse—a sexual deviant (Retta, 2022). Speaking with a "gay voice" or dressing in a gender-nonconforming style could violate the worksona, exposing the worker to bigotry. In some states, librarians can face criminal charges for even distributing LGBTQ2SIA+ materials[2] (Sye, 2022). Sharing materials about your own community and lived experiences can cost a career—not to mention emotional devastation. Hearing patrons object to library materials—where you and your family are represented—as "obscene" is demoralizing to say the least.

Legislation sweeping across the country has made it increasingly unsafe to exist in a queer body. The clothing LGBTQ2SIA+ library workers wear can make their existence illegal. If a transgender (trans) person presents as trans during story time, does that count as "drag storytime"? Such homophobic and transphobic legislation[3] forces queer library workers to critically consider their worksona performance because a slip-up (not self-censoring one's gender expression) could result in fines, a felony, or jail time (Sye, 2022). These stakes are heightened when considering the intersectional identities of library workers. Intersectionality refers to the way layered identities "'intersect' to create unique dynamics and effects" (Center for Intersectional Justice, n.d., para 1). Examples of intersectionality can include but are

---

1   Portmanteau of "work" and "persona" coined by Twitter user @lexaprose (Little Lady Gams, 2020).

2   Indiana and Iowa introduced bills which would remove legal protections for library workers and libraries. In 2021, criminal charges were filed in Wyoming after community members accused Campbell County library workers of "disseminating obscene material to minors" a.k.a. LGBTQ2SIA+ materials (Sye, 2022).

3   In our state of South Carolina, the General Assembly is considering the "Defense of Children's Innocence" bill. This bill would prohibit any minors from viewing a drag show and would penalize state agencies (like public libraries) for exposing minors to performances or materials deemed inappropriate or perverse. The Defense of Children's Innocence bill defines drag as exhibiting "a gender identity that is different than the performer's gender assigned at birth" which could easily land transgender or gender non-conforming library workers with a felony. Additionally, Section 3 of the bill aims to penalize "the offense of disseminating harmful material to minors" which could curb book recommendations to young readers (H. 3616, South Carolina General Assembly).

not limited to a queer Black person who is also Muslim or a Two Spirit person who is also disabled. Intersectionality is a framework to comprehend the way layered marginalized identities result in individuals facing layers of discrimination and bigotry. We will explore how libraries can leverage design, allyship praxis, and establish communities of practice to create safer experiences for LGBTQ2SIA+ community members and staff.

Furthermore, how we staff libraries impacts the experiences of queer library workers and patrons. Through our lived experiences, we've seen the benefits of being "out and proud" at work: LGBTQ2SIA+ youth see that there is a future where they thrive and confirmation that their identity is not a phase or perversion. "In 2021, almost half of LGBQ+ [sic] students seriously considered attempting suicide" (Centers for Disease Control and Prevention, 2023, para. 10). Queer library workers often serve as mentors to youth wherein they see a potential future for themselves that's often not modeled elsewhere. Yet proposed legislation could deter queer people from working in libraries or could force workers to essentially go back into the closet to protect themselves.

It is also important to have the LGBTQ2SIA+ community working at all levels of librarianship because queer library workers deserve representation equal to that of our cisgender/heterosexual (cis/het) peers. Our voices deserve to be heard and supported all the time, but *especially* now when our identities are under attack at our places of work. Library workers deserve to go to work without fear of "wrong" gender performance landing the worker with a felony for simply doing their job. Cis/het patrons can benefit from LGBTQ2SIA+ library workers because they can feel freer to express their own gender identities. The public library is a space for all people and we need to keep it that way.

We will provide tips for library staff on how to alleviate the stressors experienced by queer staff due to current events like legislation targeting LGBTQ2SIA+ library materials[4] (H. 3284, 2023), hate campaigns against library workers who advocate for inclusive collections[5]

---

4   South Carolina amendment H. 3284 would mandate all public school library collections be "age appropriate." "Prohibited" items (such as *Gender Queer* by Maia Kobabe) may only be checked out after guardians submit written permission to the principal and the guardian is present to check out and return "prohibited" material (H. 3284, 2023).

5   Librarians across the country have been accused of grooming and pedophilia because they include LGBTQ2SIA+ books in their libraries. The resulting hate campaigns have "cyberbullied, threatened and doxxed" library workers in a censorship attempt (Udesky, 2022, para. 5).

(Udesky, 2022), and the distancing of state institutions from library organizations due to intellectual freedom. Our recommendations will include universal design, inclusive management practices, and allyship praxis in the library. Staff are in a unique position to create inclusive spaces for all members of the community. For example, the language we use and how we treat each library user models acceptable and equitable treatment for all library users and workers. Simple modifications in library desk interactions like using gender-neutral language and avoiding "sir" or "ma'am," multiple gender options on library card registrations, opportunities for nicknames on records instead of legal names, making it easy to change genders/names on records, and calling people by their correct pronouns can have ripple effects impacting how the public views the library and creates an environment in which people with marginalized identities feel welcome.

Visibility and Professionalism

For LGBTQ2SIA+ staff, being able to wear pronoun pins or rainbows can create a feeling of welcome. This work-acceptable visibility in the form of queer signaling can be significant to patrons but can also make queer library staff hypervisible and vulnerable to hateful conduct like "negative bias in policies, access, or direct interactions" (American Library Association, 2018, para. 4). Unless libraries are prepared, making diverse staff hypervisible can pose a risk and have consequences like hate crime victimization, which rose in libraries after Trump's 2016 election (Peet, 2018). Kitzie et al. define hypervisibility as "those scrutinized because they are not perceived as 'normal'" (2022, p. 218). Inadequate knowledge of ALA resources like the Library Bill of Rights, the Intellectual Freedom Manual, and Libraries Transforming Communities (American Library Association, 2022), or lack of clear policies to defend equity and inclusion, can lead libraries to take down LGBTQ2SIA+ displays or prohibit rainbow gear and pronoun pins (Peet, 2018; American Library Association, 2018). Censoring staff in these smaller ways signals a lack of administrative support for expression of gender identity or sexual orientation. It would be easier for the administration if we went back in the closet, but what is right is never easy.

Moreover, the entire concept of professionalism is predicated upon systems of oppression (Cheshire & Stout, 2020, p.223). Professionalism often conflicts with administrators who encourage workers to bring their "whole selves" to work without grasping how daunting it is when

little lady gams
@lexaprose

writing a cover letter is just like: here is my worksona she has no mental illnesses and hates breaks! i would like to larp her for 40 hours a week with full pay and benefits

10:29 PM · Dec 4, 2020

your whole self—especially if that self is not a cis/het white man—is inherently a "discursive performance" of gender[6] (Wallace, 2002, p. 53). Professionalism tends to reinforce the norm as seen "through the eyes of white men" (Cheshire & Stout, 2020, p. 223). The more queer people are safe and encouraged to be more true to themselves at work, the more all library workers will be able to break free from restrictive gender roles in the workplace. Library work has the opportunity to have a more expansive view of professionalism.

To exist as a queer person in a cis/heteronormative world is to be vulnerable. It seems like library administrators want queer workers to be visible, but still professional in the traditional sense. In other words, they would like queer visibility to begin and end at the rainbow pin. Administration often pays lip service by encouraging LGBTQ-2SIA+ workers to be themselves, but still requiring workers to fill a corporate mold not created with their existence in mind. Something not often seen in the library literature is the performative element of being queer in library spaces. All workers must don a worksona in the professional sphere, but that performance is heightened when compounded by the performance of gender and sexuality by queer

---

6   Queer theory purports that all gender is performance, but a discursive performance aims to "reconstruct cultural narratives" (Wallace, 2002, p. 53). Queer people have the ability to re-invent their worksona by bringing queerness into the workplace, thus challenging the pervasive "normalness" of professional mores.

workers. LGBTQ2SIA+ library workers must perform their worksona in such a way as to be inoffensive and "professional," but still serve as a token minority to benefit the institution and patrons while balancing professionalism with self-expression (Little Lady Gams, 2020; Kitzie et al., 2022). If queer workers do not perform their worksona correctly (i.e. acting "too gay" or "too trans") patrons might accuse workers of being pedophiles or perverting children's gender (as in the current right-wing argument surrounding queerness in libraries).

In her article "The Librarians Are Not Okay," Xochitl Gonzalez narrates the harassment a Texas library worker faced for wearing Pride socks while leading storytime (2023). Simply wearing rainbow socks resulted in this worker receiving a complaint filed to the city about them "grooming children" (Gonzalez, 2023, para. 9). There is no dearth of horror stories about library workers—gay or straight—receiving in-person or online harassment for being associated with LGBTQ2SIA+ staff and/or materials. Still, playing a cis-heternormative worksona could mean colluding in one's own oppression by self-censoring the performance of gender to conform for safety (Wallace, 2002, p. 55).

One example of discursive performance of gender is queer signaling. Queer signaling is the means through which people in the LGBTQ2SIA+ community discreetly signal their identity to other community members; this usually takes the form of style (wearing pins that telegraph their gender and sexual identity or wearing a thumb ring) or grooming (femmes leaving two nails on the dominant hand short or sporting an undercut). One could argue that queer signaling means more now than ever because it reminds the queer community that we're still here standing strong against organized hate campaigns. Queer library workers must consciously be "exposing heteronormativity as heterosexism, moving beyond invisibility, and the trap of double consciousness that too often leads some who identify as…LGBT [sic] to collude in their own oppression" (Wallace, 2002, p. 55). Queer library workers must grapple daily with the double standards thrust upon them by the professional world which compete with their own hard-won sense of self.

In their research, Kitzie et al. explain that LGBTQ2SIA+ library workers and patrons can be invisible or hypervisible depending on the circumstances and the needs of the institution (2022). Queer staff can be invisible when it comes to designing spaces, curating collections, or offering benefits, but become hypervisible when tokenized or over-surveilled (Kitzie et al., 2022). Both forms of in/visibility disadvantage queer employees in the library compared to cis/het peers. On one hand, queer library workers could leverage visibility to advocate for the LGBTQ2SIA+ community, but advocacy might come at the cost of their professional reputation, or at the risk of their being pigeonholed. For example, they might only have professional opportunities in the realm of diversity, equity, and inclusion (DEI) committees and such (which is its own form of emotional labor) rather than anything pertaining to their other professional interests.

Library as Theater of the Political

Who is in political power impacts LGBTQ2SIA+ library experiences for better or for worse (Wagner & Crowley, 2020). Wagner and Crowley note that in trying to combat exclusion of the LGBTQ2SIA+ community after the election of the 45th president, academic libraries leaned too hard into bathroom policies resulting in performative gestures, rather than real and systematic change like insurance covering gender-affirming care, LGBTQ2SIA+-equitable hiring policies, or having a human resources plan for employees who transition (2020). While having access to safe restrooms is vital to health and wellness, many libraries stopped there.

One of the reasons it's so difficult to change library policy is that libraries are likened to hallowed ground for book lovers and scholars. The library's elevation from a community forum to a sacred temple of learning results in vocational awe which negatively affects workers by prioritizing the institution over the people who work there (Ettarh & Vidas, 2022; Cheshire & Stout, 2020). The elevation of the library as an institution means it's somehow beyond reproach or change. Placing the library on a pedestal results in the perception that the library is "neutral" in its stances, which is simply untrue. For example, libraries continually celebrating a certain wizarding school despite the author's transphobic rants rather than thinking about how we're platforming such beliefs. Choosing, in the interest of being "neutral," to promote a book series whose author has proved to be a hateful bigot actively harms queer people on staff and in the community. Libraries make showing your pride in being a Pufflehuff more important than caring about the person on the desk next to you. Society's reverence for the library enables the public and workers to pay no attention to the ways staff are oppressed within library systems, especially those who belong to marginalized communities. More and more LIS discourse has become critical of the library's stance of "neutrality," but progress is slow moving (Booth, 2022; Cooke et al., 2022). Queer workers do not fit into the idealized picture of The Library, which is maybe why queerness in the library is perceived as a perversion of a utopia.

Library workers are frequently on the frontlines of the culture wars and face workplace conditions that include hate crimes like homophobic graffiti and vandalism of LGBTQSIA+ books (Peet, 2018). Often, working at the library means seeing a microcosm of whatever is going on politically and having to face the ramifications of that political action. Yorio noted a growing anti-LGBTQ2SIA+ sentiment (2019) which has led to book burnings and suppression of queer materials and programs. Living and working in a climate which actively seeks to destroy your stories and ignore your existence has a profoundly negative impact of queer library workers. Cisgender, queer library workers are safer in being visible at work. Gender non-conforming people may not feel safe in being visible, or safe at all, due to the transphobic rhetoric popular with conservatives currently. So much of library worker safety is dependent upon prevailing narratives which are politically motivated.

Staffing

Intentional staffing to ensure workers from the queer community are installed at all levels of librarianship, and paying them a fair market wage in comparison to their cis/het counterparts, betters the experiences of queer library workers and patrons. It reinforces equitable hiring policies instead of tokenizing and devaluing queer labor. Additionally, hiring queer administrators benefits both lower-level and higher-level staff because those administrators can provide valuable insight into queer experiences and needs for policy creation and broadens the horizons of executive leadership. Such policy changes could shift the institution away from cisheteronormativity to create inclusion beyond virtue-signaling, like advocacy only during Pride Month. Meaningful change happens only when diverse staff members are represented at all levels of the organization and are paid appropriately.

Permanent full-time employment may be especially important to library workers who may need access to health benefits to cover gender affirming healthcare (Owens et al., 2022, p. 9). Full-time work can be important for queer library workers because they may fear losing part-time shifts if people find out about their gender identity or sexual orientation (Owens et al., 2022, p. 9). Stability is an important facet of working for all people, but especially so for queer workers. The narrative needs to be shifted away from workplaces being LGBTQ-friendly to focusing on income and job security (Owens et al., 2022, p. 10). Wearing pronoun pins only takes a workplace so far, but providing inclusive benefits and comprehensive policies to protect employees will demonstrate to queer library workers that the institution's allyship is not just performative. Rainbow pins and pronouns in email signatures are great first steps to significant progress for gender and sexuality inclusivity, but better working conditions for marginalized staff will have a greater impact on the health and contentment of staff.

Seeing queer employees reassures all patrons that libraries are welcoming to all. Many patrons across my [Debra] career have approached me to say how meaningful it was to see me leading storytime. They recognized my queerness, and it made their families feel safe in programming and encouraged them to be visible themselves in the library. There have been several patrons who aren't part of the queer community who were excited for their children to be around a diverse library staff.

I [Patrick] mostly work with teenagers and so many of them feel comfortable asking me for books with queer representation because I am visibly genderqueer. The teenage years are a time of great upheaval in one's sense of self and are frequently the time people discover their gender and sexuality. They trust me with these reader's advisory interviews even when we have to be discreet because the patron is not out to their caregivers yet. Teens also feel that they can tell me that their name and/or pronouns are different from what their parents use, because they know I will believe them. Being a glimpse into queer adulthood for these teens makes the struggles of being out at work *almost* worth it.

Library Environments

Many libraries want to achieve a level of queer friendliness, but don't have human resources or collection development policies backing their intentions. When creating these policies, the importance of involving queer voices at every stage of planning and creation cannot be overstated. Strengthening allyship in administration will help with consistent follow-through of policies put in place to protect library workers who have marginalized identities.

It is common in LIS discourse to acknowledge that libraries—especially public libraries—uphold traditional hegemonic power structures like white supremacy, cis/heteronormativity, ableism, et cetera, meaning the library excludes "queer people in many aspects, including policies, cataloging, and creative spaces like makerspace" (Kitzie et al., 2022, p. 216). For example, cataloging of queer materials often means segregating them from the rest of the collection. Some libraries even place special stickers on the spines in a well-meaning attempt to make the queer books stand out, but this actually serves to "other" these books from the rest of the collection. A traditionalist librarian might defend this decision by arguing that they're marking the genre of the book, as is common practice with diverse materials. Libraries should begin to move away from thinking of diversity as a genre or a fad and begin to see diversity as a requirement for all areas of the library, since the library has an ethical obligation to serve all people. This exclusion becomes magnified when it comes to frontline workers who are meant to engage with these systems (like cataloging) and spaces (like bathrooms) daily. How do staff retain self-expression and agency while interfacing with systems that omit their existence?

Creating, implementing, and following through with inclusive and clear policies about equity for LGBTQ2SIA+ library workers offers an area of opportunity for libraries. Every policy should be inclusive of the needs of the LGBTQ2SIA+ community, including definitions of families, medical coverage, and dress codes, as a start. As Kelly et al. state, transitioning from "tolerance to full acceptance at work, queer and trans workers must be supported by policies, practices, and ideologies that resist cisnormativity, heteronormativity, and homonormativity" (2021, p. 1083). Examples of this include making sure to write inclusive language into policies (e.g., that every library will have a chestfeeding (instead of breastfeeding) pod) and including nuance in policies for example, making pronoun pins optional instead of mandating either way (this protects workers who feel unsafe disclosing their pronoun, but encourages pronoun use for those who feel safe to do so). Ultimately, an expansive view of who policies include or exclude can behoove administration seeking to increase its DEI focus and protect queer staff and patrons.

While all of these principles are good in theory, it is important to recognize that there are multiple, often conflicting, considerations to being visible at work. Topics around visibility often affect trans folks and their safety more profoundly. This population faces higher rates of violent crime. The Human Rights Campaign noted that 2021 brought a "record number of violent fatal incidents against transgender and non-conforming people" (HRC Foundation, n.d., para. 2). Whether or not to disclose sexuality or gender identities or to consider transitioning at work are multi-faceted considerations that involve personal choice and safety. To be a healthy workplace, the needs of, and direct input from, queer staff need to be included and valued.

Recommendations

While there is no one perfect solution for the unique stressors queer workers endure in libraries in the current political climate, we would like to end this section with some suggestions on how to ameliorate negative mental health effects of being a queer library worker in a time when queerness is under attack. Currently, LGBTQ2SIA+ issues in library and information science are "lamentably underdeveloped," as queer librarianship requires more scholarship and analysis, but we've compiled these recommendations for alleviating stressors experienced by queer staff due to current events (Poole, 2020, p. 350).

We'd like to pause here to say that while we as workers can take steps to protect ourselves, this does not absolve administration and institutions from any responsibility for workers' well-being. Queer library workers need to protect themselves while also continuing to push for institutional change—a tall order, but a necessary one.

Leadership

Due to the threat of hatred, queer folks are censoring their self-expression on a national scale. Kingkade details how Emily Drabinski, president of the American Library Association, is facing targeted personal attacks and professional attacks against the American Library Association after releasing one tweet (which has since been deleted by the user) identifying as a "Marxist lesbian" (2023, para. 4). This example clearly shows how unsafe it can be to share your gender identity or sexual orientation in the current political climate.

One way to fight back is by leveraging equity-driven business trends and following the lead of top organizations. The American Library Association recently released a statement of "its support for LGBTQIA+ library workers and reaffirms its commitment to equity and inclusivity" (2023b, p. 1). In this statement specific actions like creating task forces and inclusive communication plans were created to build a strategy and action (American Library Association, 2023b, p. 1). The Art Libraries Society of North America created a "statement in support of LGBTQ+

people in libraries" which unequivocally advocates for equity and access for all people (2023, para. 1). However, it would be more impactful to see state-based library associations take similar stances in a grassroots effort—especially in states where queerness in libraries is under attack (Gonzalez, 2023). As mentioned earlier, inclusive policies and procedures create safer spaces for queer library workers.

Increased Allyship!

Allyship does not begin and end at the conference or the webinar. Allies, such as administration, colleagues, and volunteers, should make an effort to be in tune with the political climate facing the LGBTQ2SIA+ community and how those hostile politics play out at the reference desk. We encourage allies to leverage their privilege to advocate for better work conditions and elevate and amplify the voices of queer colleagues and patrons.

Believe queer people! If someone tells you their pronouns, respect that those are their pronouns and use them. If someone changes their pronouns, honor that. We learn new words and information every day. Allow people room to grow and change.

Check in with them on how to best support queer library workers. The best allies (in my experience) [Patrick] have been the ones who come to me in private to say, "This is my read on this situation or here's a pattern I think I've seen played out. This is what I did about it. Is that okay with you or would you like me to do something differently?" Direct communication like this can be awkward, but it's an attestation of commitment to the well-being of queer coworkers. It's also a way for allies to show coworkers that they care and there is a place for them in libraries. Additionally, if managers hear their staff being misgendered while that worker is not around, correct them. It is important to note that explaining and educating people about the needs of the LGBTQ2SIA+ community does cause an additional burden on LGBTQ2SIA+ individuals. It is important for allies and advocates to take on their own education and awareness as much as possible to minimize that emotional burden.

How can management be allies? This could be a whole 'nother chapter, but the people in power have the capacity to do the most to advocate for staff needs without them having to ask. If you know a staff member uses pronouns not acknowledged in your library system, try to get other options added. People in management need to actively seek out instances of injustice against queer library workers. Sitting and wait-ing to be told puts an undue burden on queer library workers. Micro-aggressions often happen in plain sight. That isn't "just how a per-son is." Sticking up for your staff sets a standard of acceptability that others pick up on. Managers can use their authority to create positive work environments for everyone.

Managers can include equity in workplace professionalism expecta-tions. The American Library Association provides ideas to create more supportive environments for trans library workers from hiring practic-es to policy inclusion (2020). Ideas presented range from quick chang-es like using pronouns and avoiding adding a choice of "other" on hiring forms to planning decisions, like avoiding providing DEI train-ing only after a negative event occurs (American Library Association, 2020). Taking time to learn about the needs of trans library workers and being intentional about implementing change is an important part of equity-driven, inclusive management.

Universal Design

Administration should use universal design, the concept of "designing spaces, products, services, and more in a way that makes them as func-tional as possible for people of all ages, abilities, and backgrounds" to create better spaces for queer folks and have intersectional impact (Spina, 2017, para. 2). Bathrooms designed for families also help queer folks who may feel unsafe in gendered bathrooms. Being clear about bathrooms being open to all, and single stalls accommodating anyone uncomfortable with that, signals safety and creates options.

Duluth Public Library is one of the libraries who uses social stories, "usu-ally surrounding an idea, expectations of others, and strategies to try while engaging in everyday life events" to respectfully introduce their patrons to spaces and expectations[7] (n.d., para. 1). If libraries intentional-ly promoted the use of social stories with people of all abilities and ages, it could set expectations and help queer folks navigate space, find exits, and feel secure. With the increased threat of violence, being able to plan exits may open up library services to people who otherwise wouldn't feel safe to visit the library (American Library Association, 2023a).

---

7   The Duluth Public Library website provides virtual copies of these social stories to maximize accessibility. These social stories are simple "visual and written explanations" of library design and what a patron might encounter when they visit (n.d., para. 5).

Multi-stall restrooms are located on each floor. Single-stall restrooms, including a family restroom, are located off of the Main Street Lobby.

The CMA welcomes gender diversity. All visitors are welcome to use the restroom that best fits their identity. We ask that no one be stared at, questioned, or asked to leave. Thank you for making the museum safe, inclusive, and accessible for everyone.

Image courtesy of the Columbia Museum of Art

Placement of materials and displays matters. Interfiling books with queer themes/characters normalizes this representation, rather than ghettoizing that demographic by putting them in their own section with a rainbow sticker. Ensuring all book lists or displays have some form of diversity (in ability, gender, sexuality, race, etc.) means there is a place for queer authors and characters all year round—not just during Pride Month. Plus, all libraries should conduct diversity audits.[8] Prioritizing visibility of underrepresented authors and communities signals welcome to all people.

---

8   A diversity audit is the process of evaluating library collections and resources to ensure that a diversity of experiences and perspectives, especially "non-dominant voices," are represented in collections (Matthews & Kyrillidou, 2023, p. 18).

Worker Solidarity

Another recommendation would be to find communities of practice[9] either through existing collectives like library employee resource groups or local library association LGBTQ2SIA+ committees. There is a rich history of queer library workers building communities of practice in order to advance LGBTQ2SIA+ rights in librarianship. The ALA Task Force on Gay Liberation (later renamed the Rainbow Roundtable) was founded in 1971 and pushed the profession forward through theatrical means (like an iconic "Hug a Homosexual" booth at ALA Annual) and corrective means (changing subject headings to be more inclusive of queer topics) (Poole, 2020, p. 535). Solidarity amongst workers, even outside of a union, can be impactful. When workers collectively advocate for themselves, they can flex their power to better the library for everyone.

References

American Library Association. (2023a, March 27). *American Library Association condemns ongoing threats against libraries.* https://www.ala.org/news/press-releases/2023/03/american-library-association-condemns-ongoing-threats-against-libraries

American Library Association. (2023b, August 8). *American Library Association upholds its support for LGBTQIA+ library workers and reaffirms its commitment to equity and inclusivity.* https://www.ala.org/news/press-releases/2023/08/ala-upholds-its-support-lgbtqia-library-workers-and-reaffirms-its-commitment

American Library Association. (2022, July 14). *Challenge support.* https://www.ala.org/tools/challengesupport

American Library Association (2018, December 7). *Hateful conduct in libraries: Supporting library workers and patrons.* http://www.ala.org/advocacy/hatefulconduct

American Library Association. (2020, July 17). *Libraries respond: Protecting and supporting transgender staff and patrons.* Advocacy, Legislation & Issues. https://www.ala.org/advocacy/diversity/librariesrespond/transgender-staff-patrons

---

9   Communities of practice can be defined as a group of people who "coalesce around a common, sustained interest" (Poole, 2020, p. 533). In other words, communities of practice are often the intersection between the emotional and the actionable (ERLC, 2016).

Art Libraries Society of North America. (2023). *Statement in support of LGBTQ+ people in libraries.* https://www.arlisna.org/news/statement-in-support-of-lgbtq-people-in-libraries

Booth, H. (2022, February 23). *Newsmaker: Ibram X. Kendi.* American Libraries Magazine. https://americanlibrariesmagazine.org/2022/03/01/newsmaker-ibram-x-kendi/

Centers for Disease Control and Prevention. (2023, March 9). *CDC report shows concerning increases in sadness and exposure to violence among teen girls and LGBQ+ youth.* https://www.cdc.gov/nchhstp/newsroom/fact-sheets/healthy-youth/sadness-and-violence-among-teen-girls-and-LG-BQ-youth-factsheet.html

Center for Intersectional Justice. (n.d.) *What is intersectionality?* https://www.intersectionaljustice.org/what-is-intersectionality

Cheshire, K., & Stout, J. (2020). The moral arc of the library: What are our duties and limitations after 45?. *Reference Services Review 48*(2). 219-225. https://doi.org/10.1108/RSR-10-2019-0074.

Cooke, N. A., Chancellor, R., Shorish, Y. S., Dahlen, S. P., & Gibson, A. (2022, June 10). *Once more for those in the back: Libraries are not neutral.* PublishersWeekly.com. https://www.publishersweekly.com/pw/by-topic/industry-news/libraries/article/89576-once-more-for-those-in-the-back-libraries-are-not-neutral.html

Duluth Public Library. (n.d.). *Social Stories.* https://duluthlibrary.org/services/social-stories/

Edmonton Regional Learning Consortium (ERLC). (2016). *What is a Community of Practice?* Creating Communities of Practice. https://www.communityof-practice.ca/background/what-is-a-community-of-practice

Ettarh, F., & Vidas, C. (2022). The future of libraries: Vocational awe in a "post-COVID" world. *The Serials Librarian 82*(1-4). 17-22. https://doi.org/10.1080/0361526X.2022.2028501.

Gonzalez, X. (2023, March 15). The librarians are not okay. *The Atlantic.* https://www.theatlantic.com/ideas/archive/2023/03/book-bans-censorship-librarian-challenges/673398/

H. 3284, 2023–2024 South Carolina General Assembly, 125th Session. (SC, 2023). https://www.scstatehouse.gov/sess125_2023-2024/bills/3284.htm

H. 3616, 2023–2024 South Carolina General Assembly, 125th Session. (SC, 2023). https://www.scstatehouse.gov/sess125_2023-2024/bills/3616.htm

HRC Foundation. (n.d.). *Fatal violence against the transgender and gender non-conforming community in 2022.* Human Rights Campaign. https://www.hrc.org/resources/fatal-violence-against-the-transgender-and-gen-der-non-conforming-community-in-2022

Kelly, M., Carathers, J., & Kade, T. (2021). Beyond tolerance: Policies, practices, and ideologies of queer-friendly workplaces. *Sexuality Research & Social Policy, 18*(4), 1078-1093. https://doi.org/10.1007/s13178-020-00512-3

Kingkade, T. (2023, August 7). Top librarian calls 'Marxist lesbian'tweet backlash 'regrettable:' GOP lawmakers in several states have called for defunding the American Library Association because of Emily Drabinski's identity and political beliefs. *NBC News*. https://www.nbcnews.com/news/us-news/american-library-association-president-marxist-lesbian-rcna98254

Kitzie, V., Floegel, D., Barrage, S., et al. (2022). How visibility, hypervisibility, and invisibility shape library staff and drag performer perceptions of and experiences with drag storytimes in public libraries. *Library Quarterly 92*(3). 215-240. https://doi.org/10.1086/719915

Little Lady Gams [@lexaprose]. (2020, December 4). *Writing a cover letter is just like: here is my worksona she has no mental illnesses and hates breaks!* [Tweet]. Twitter. https://twitter.com/lexaprose/status/1335078890612649987

Matthews, J., & Kyrillidou, M. (2023, Sep). A quick test for a collection assessment using a DEI lens. *Public Libraries*, 62, 18-21. https://www.proquest.com/magazines/quick-test-collection-assessment-using-dei-lens/docview/2885844647/se-2

Owens, B., Mills, S., Lewis, N., & Guta, A. (2022). Work-related stressors and mental health among LGBTQ workers: Results from a cross-sectional survey. *PloS One, 17*(10), e0275771-e0275771. https://doi.org/10.1371/journal.pone.0275771

Peet, L. (2018). Dispute over LGBTQ display, buttons in Utah. *Library Journal, 143*(15), 10. https://www.proquest.com/trade-journals/news-dispute-over-lgbtq-display-buttons-utah/docview/2102908201/se-2

Poole, A. (2020). "Tearing the shroud of invisibility": Communities of protest information practices and the fight for LGBTQ rights in US librarianship. *The Library Quarterly 90*(4). 530-562. https://doi.org/10.1086/710255

Retta, M. (2022, December 19). *American Library Association President: Librarians are facing harassment*. Teen Vogue. https://www.teenvogue.com/story/american-library-association-president-book-bans-censorship.

Spina, C. (2017, May 5). *How universal design will make your library more inclusive*. School Library Journal. https://www.slj.com/story/how-universal-design-will-make-your-library-more-inclusive

Sye, D. (2022, March 8). *Beyond book banning: Efforts to criminally charge librarians*. Intellectual Freedom Blog: The Office for Intellectual Freedom of the American Library Association. https://www.oif.ala.org/beyond-book-banning-efforts-to-criminally-charge-librarians/

Udesky, L. (2022, March 26). *Librarians' mental health threatened by book bans, abuse and harassment*. MindSite News. https://mindsitenews.org/2022/03/26/librarians-mental-health-threatened-by-book-bans-threats-and-harassment

Wagner, T. L., & Crowley, A. (2020). Why are bathrooms inclusive if the stacks exclude?: Systemic exclusion of trans and gender nonconforming persons in post-Trump academic librarianship. *Reference Services Review, 48*(1), 159-181. https://doi.org/10.1108/RSR-10-2019-0072

Wallace, D. (2002). Out in the academy: Heterosexism, invisibility, and double consciousness. *College English(65)*1, Special Issue: Lesbian and Gay Studies/
Queer Pedagogies. pp. 53-66. https://doi.org/10.2307/3250730

Yorio, K. (2019). Libraries see anti-LGBTQIA+ trend: "State of America's libraries 2019" reveals "extreme tactics" by organized groups. *School
Library Journal, 65*(4), 10. https://www.proquest.com/trade-journals/
libraries-see-anti-lgbtqia-trend/docview/2216954556/se-2

Trans Accessible Libraries Initiative

Julie Leuzinger and Coby Condrey

Introduction

The University of North Texas (UNT) serves approximately 45,000 students and is situated in the large metroplex of Dallas/Fort Worth (University of North Texas, 2023). The UNT Libraries have become a known repository for studies related to lesbian, gay, bisexual, transgender, queer or questioning, and other sexual identities (LGBTQ+) through their Lesbian, Gay, Bisexual, Transgender, and Queer Archive[1] of many historical collections, their collaborations with campus LGBTQ+ student organizations and faculty to monitor the information needs of the LGBTQ+ campus community, and their trained personnel, including a librarian who is responsible for requesting LGBTQ+ materials for the Libraries' general collection. In addition to striving to be the LGBTQ+ history archive of the South, the Libraries are well positioned to provide effective informational resources transgender people seek. Yet recent national surveys indicate that transgender people do not typically turn to libraries for their information.

Current research, discussed below, highlights many of the barriers to information that transgender individuals face. While they are frequently simply lumped in with the rest of the lesbian, gay, bisexual, and queer community, their needs are significantly different, and the acronym LGBTQ+ likely perpetuates some of the confusion in a primarily cisgender-heterosexual world (cisgender or cis is a term that describes a person whose gender identity aligns with the sex they were assigned at birth).

---

1   https://library.unt.edu/special-collections/archives-manuscripts/lgbtq-archive/

As allies of the transgender community, we observed with dismay that by the mid-2010s, anti-transgender rhetoric in Texas and elsewhere surfaced with increasing severity and frequency. We saw proposed legislation and other measures that were actively discriminatory against transgender people. Many anti-transgender policy initiatives during this period were aimed at erasing the basic civil rights of these individuals. We were concerned that these developments endangered the physical and mental well-being of the transgender community. We wanted to do something that showed we supported this group and that we would continue to support them despite potential criticism from opponents. In addition, we wanted to ensure that the campus community had library resources to help them research these issues as well as the many others that might be of interest to a transgender audience.

Given that this population is hidden unless self-identified, we used findings documented in recent studies addressing information seeking behaviors of transgender persons and their perceptions of the library to provide more equitable access to our services and collections (Drake & Bielefield, 2017; Lyttan & Laloo, 2017). We did a pre- and post-assessment of collection usage and LibGuides to determine the success of the initiative. We also applied for, and received, $3,000 in intramural funding to address gaps in our collection and provide outreach materials. We carried out the work of the grant in late 2020 and throughout 2021. Our hope was to achieve a nationally prominent position among university libraries for serving transgender patrons, to elevate UNT's standing on internationally distributed rankings of colleges for its LGBTQ+ friendliness, and to disseminate resulting best practices to share this model with other libraries.

Needs Assessment

The needs assessment for the Trans Accessible Libraries Initiative (TALI) began in 2016 through the Texas Gender Project. One of the authors, along with two other librarians at the University of North Texas, applied for and received intramural funding through the UNT Libraries' for focus groups and travel expenses. In this study, we asked transgender Texans about their impressions of library services, then we asked Texas librarians, from all types of libraries, about their knowledge of transgender issues. The recommendations based on those findings, which mirrored those of the 2015 *U.S. Transgender Survey* conducted by the National Center for Transgender Equality, were shared with the *Texas Library Journal* (Keralis et al., 2017).

Recent national surveys, such as the one mentioned above, indicate that transgender people do not typically turn to libraries for their information. "Nearly one-quarter...of people who were out or perceived as transgender...were verbally, physically, or sexually harassed" (National Center for Transgender Equality, 2015, p. 9). Additionally, "[o]ne in five...did not use at least one type of public accommodation in the past year because they feared they would be mistreated as a transgender person..." (National Center for Transgender Equality, 2015, p.14). Libraries would be included here as a "public accommodation."

In 2017, a research survey addressed what accommodations libraries needed to make for transgender individuals to feel safe, what areas had the greatest unmet information needs, and why transgender people didn't use libraries as an information resource at all. Some of the accommodations included current transgender literature, gender identity and expression as part of their institutions' non-discrimination policy, and gender-neutral restrooms. Unmet information needs included transgender health, legal, and political advocacy information. Some reasons for the overall low level of library satisfaction were either not enough applicable resources or discomfort at interacting with library staff (Lyttan & Laloo, 2017).

Finally, the book *Supporting Trans People in Libraries* (Krueger, 2019) provided valuable insights in helping libraries become more affirming places. The author provides guidelines on issues applicable to everyone, such as pronouns, handling personal information, restrooms, job postings and interviews, patron complaints, and employee objections. The book also takes a deeper dive into issues surrounding collection development and access services. Additional resources, such as the American Library Association's "Libraries Respond: Protecting and Supporting Library Staff and Patrons" (2020), were consulted and can be found on the "For Librarians" page of the Trans Accessible Libraries Initiative LibGuide[2] (University of North Texas Libraries, 2020), but the above were some of the most impactful.

In addition to reviewing the literature, we noticed a significant amount of peer-to-peer consulting in an "Ask a Transgender Person" online

---

2   https://guides.library.unt.edu/trans

forum (open to both transgender and cisgender individuals) asking for resources based on lived experiences. Some topics were relatively innocuous, like how to find transgender-friendly service providers. Others were far more appropriate for a doctor or therapist, such as how to get hormones (without a doctor). Asking your peers is a legitimate form of research; as librarians, we also know it is important to look at multiple sources.

We wanted to make sure that our collections were current and meeting our students' needs. In addition, we wanted to advertise the collection as another way to get good information. We didn't want students not to ask their peers, as their community is a great place to start their research. Instead, we wanted students to remember to include information they can find in the library, from health practitioners and other experts. We were also subtly encouraging them to develop and use information literacy skills to determine what is right for their situation.

It was also important to us not to make students out themselves just to provide feedback, since this population is hidden unless self-identified, and we wanted to respect their privacy. We knew from our background research the general information-seeking behaviors of transgender individuals and their perceptions of the library. That, coupled with an excellent relationship with our campus gender and sexuality resource center, provided a foundation for learning the needs of our local community to make our collections, services, and resources more accessible, useful, and visible.

Collection Development

As part of the TALI project to update our collection, we used two strategies to identify materials about the transgender experience. We needed this information to evaluate the materials in our current collection and then to find materials to add to our collection. The first approach for finding transgender-related content was to search our database of available books and the Library of Congress online classification outline[3] to determine LC classification number ranges (Library of Congress, Acquisitions and Bibliographic Access Directorate, n.d.). These classification number ranges appear in Appendix 1.

---

3   https://www.loc.gov/catdir/cpso/lcco/

Then we identified current and past subject terms related to transgender topics, using books on the market and in our online catalog that were in the classification ranges from the prior step. We checked the subject terms in the online Library of Congress subject headings[4] (Library of Congress, Linked Data Service, n.d.). These entries appear in Appendix 2. Note that the terminology in the Library of Congress Classification System and the Library of Congress Subject Headings can employ words or phrases that are not appropriate for describing the transgender experience as we understand it now. We do not condone any misrepresentation conveyed by outdated meanings of words like *transvestism* or negative phrases like *Gender identity disorders. Transsexualism.*

We provided the classification ranges and subject headings to our assessment librarian, who evaluated our library's existing transgender collection. To understand usage of the collection, the assessment librarian compiled two measures for the titles in the classification ranges and subjects for transgender topics: circulation statistics and interlibrary loan requests. Circulation statistics provide evidence for how often a patron found a book valuable enough to read it in depth. Interlibrary loan requests indicate that a topic was lacking resources in the existing collection but had high enough need that a patron made an extra effort to get more information and was willing to wait for the library to provide the resource. The collection evaluation used these measures to describe the state of our collection and then to point us toward content that would be most useful to our patrons. The measures revealed that the collection size was approximately 700 monographic titles, of which only 24% were available in electronic format. The collection's holdings were concentrated in sociology (46%) and medicine, psychiatry, and psychology (25%). The dominant call numbers for these two groups were HQ77 (*Transvestism, Transexualism, and Transgenderism*), HQ1075 (*Sex roles*), BF692.2 (*Psychology of sex. Sex roles*), and RC556 (*Psychiatric aspects of personality and behavior conditions. Sexual and psychosexual conditions*). These two groups accounted for 71% of the entire collection, but only about 35% of these titles were published after the year 2000. The assessment confirmed our impression that the existing collection was relatively small, growing old, and available mostly in print. The analysis also indicated a decline in usage of the holdings, likely due to the obsolescence of the

---

4   https://id.loc.gov/authorities/subjects.html

collection and the lack of online access. Overall, the report stated that the strongest areas of the collection were in sociology despite topics in this subject area having quite weak ebook holdings and usage. It is not surprising that so much content related to transgender topics falls within the classification of sociology, as research programs on gender and sexuality studies generally find homes in social sciences departments. However, our project wanted to provide content outside of the traditional classification areas as well, so that transgender people could find well-researched academic information that does not treat them as objects of sociological study.

One very useful feature that the collection assessment provided was a qualitative matrix of subjects (Harker, 2020), where the call number ranges displayed in a color-coded way that would provide guidance for developing the collection (see Figure 1). For example, the lower right quadrant, where usage is high and ILL requests are low, should receive less attention for finding new titles to add than the upper left quadrant where there is low usage of the collection and high ILL rates.

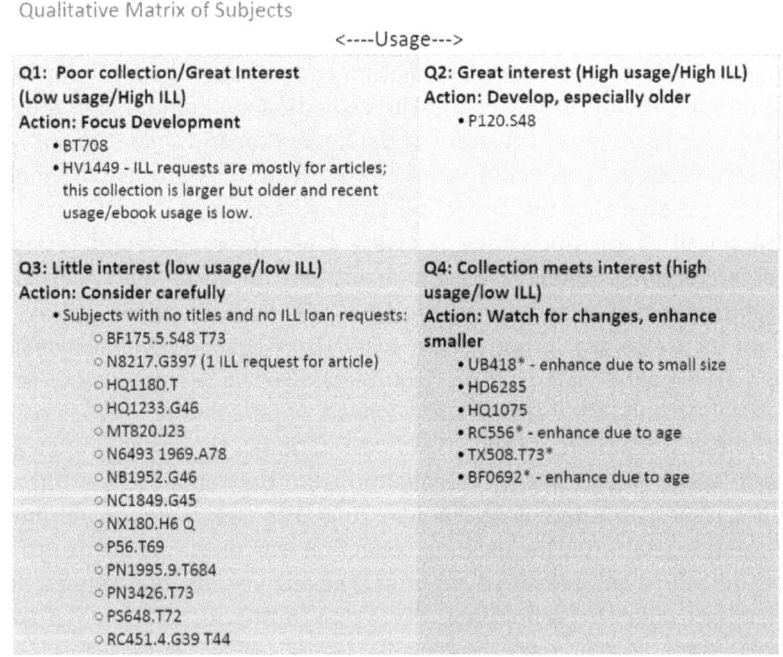

Qualitative Matrix of Subjects

<----Usage--->

Q1: Poor collection/Great Interest (Low usage/High ILL) Action: Focus Development • BT708 • HV1449 - ILL requests are mostly for articles; this collection is larger but older and recent usage/ebook usage is low.	Q2: Great interest (High usage/High ILL) Action: Develop, especially older • P120.S48
Q3: Little interest (low usage/low ILL) Action: Consider carefully • Subjects with no titles and no ILL loan requests: ○ BF175.5.S48 T73 ○ N8217.G397 (1 ILL request for article) ○ HQ1180.T ○ HQ1233.G46 ○ MT820.J23 ○ N6493 1969.A78 ○ NB1952.G46 ○ NC1849.G45 ○ NX180.H6 Q ○ P56.T69 ○ PN1995.9.T684 ○ PN3426.T73 ○ PS648.T72 ○ RC451.4.G39 T44	Q4: Collection meets interest (high usage/low ILL) Action: Watch for changes, enhance smaller • UB418* - enhance due to small size • HD6285 • HQ1075 • RC556* - enhance due to age • TX508.T73* • BF0692* - enhance due to age

Figure 1   Qualitative Matrix of Transgender Subjects in UNT Libraries Collections (Prior to Enhancement)

We now had evidence that our collection on transgender topics could use some better resources, and we also knew the classification ranges that had the highest potential to meet patron needs.

We then used the classification numbers and the subject headings to find current titles in our book identification tool for consideration to acquire. We set some basic parameters for filtering the first round of titles:

- Ebooks only, to ensure anonymous user access;

- Titles published within last 10 years, to ensure the content was "fresh";

- Titles focused on the U.S., to match the geographic location of our audience;

- Titles in English, the primary language of the university;

- Titles oriented to a young adult audience, as we wished to engage college students; and,

- No titles that focused too broadly on LGBTQ+ because much of this content had little information about transgender issues.

The filtered list of titles included 118 ebooks, the total cost for which exceeded our grant budget. At this point we deemed it critical to get input from the target audience, so we partnered with the UNT Pride Alliance, our campus gender and sexuality resource center, to help us with sending survey links to appropriate students and faculty. We asked our audience—specifically, transgender faculty and students— to answer brief, anonymous feedback questionnaires about their interest in the books we were considering for purchase. The surveys grouped books into categories by the content being primarily related to medicine, humanities, or social sciences and asked the respondents to indicate for each title "Yes, I'm interested" or "No, I'm not," with an optional textbox for additional feedback. After gathering the results, we applied the user preferences to make our final selections. The preferences that we found most noteworthy were that, overall, the respondents expressed no desire for reading memoirs but were highly interested in books that addressed medical aspects of transitioning to confirm and express their internal sense of gender.

We looked at several ways to get the most content to the users and eventually settled on 39 titles purchased outright for almost exactly the budget of $3,000. These titles generally rated the highest in the user surveys. We also decided to provide access to 71 titles by adding them to our demand-driven acquisitions (DDA) pool, as making them available this way would have no immediate cost but had the potential for permanent addition to the collection if usage over time triggered a purchase of them at some point in the future. Ultimately the grant project made 110 new titles of high interest available to patrons.

Promotion and Outreach

We needed a means of communicating with the public about the new initiative. Thus, we created a LibGuide[5] (University of North Texas Libraries, 2020) as the primary means of promoting the newly acquired items and reaching out to the community. We used the needs assessment to determine what to highlight in the guide. For example, the library services page highlights services and facilities that might concern a transgender individual. It focuses on maintaining patron privacy, from how to ensure we are using their chosen name, to using the self-checkout machine. It also covers restrooms and getting research help online. We also wanted the guide to be useful to other librarians, so we created a "For Librarians" page[6] that includes a brief description of the work of the initiative, recommendations for best practices, and additional resources to consult.

Part of the initiative was to encourage students to investigate and analyze a broader range of resources that would extend through and beyond the library, so the guide has an information literacy page that helps readers understand how to find reliable information on any topic; however, the entire guide supports the ideals of information literacy.

Given that the needs assessment revealed that many transgender individuals believe the library does not offer anything for them, we broke the guide down by topic, including everything we purchased in mental health, religion, employment, literature, medical books, etc., each on a separate page (Figure 2). We included a recommended topical database as well as web resources to encourage them to look at different types of sources. We also included film, graphic novels, government information, journals, primary sources, and datasets with a note on why you might use those formats in your research.

---

5   https://guides.library.unt.edu/trans

6   https://guides.library.unt.edu/trans/librarians

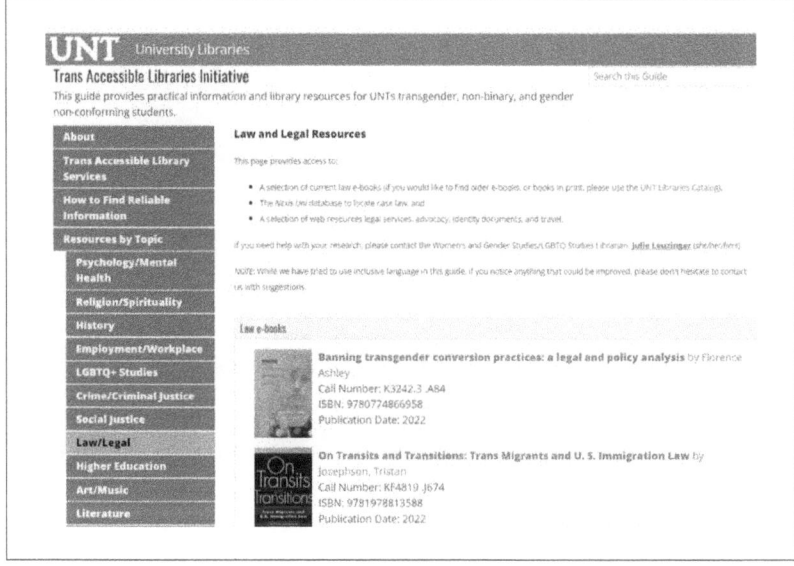

Figure 2 Topical Resources on Trans Accessible Libraries Initiative LibGuide

We had planned to have two book displays, but the COVID pandemic forced us to turn them into topic blog posts that were cross-promoted to the LibGuide and social media. One was called "Transgender Individuals in Public Policy: from 'Bathroom Bills' to Employee Protection,"[7] which highlighted items in our digital libraries government documents collection. That went out in November 2020, on Transgender Day of Remembrance. The other 2021 one, "Transgender Authors in Creative Writing,"[8] went out in March on the Transgender Day of Visibility, which we thought was a great way to celebrate some of the accomplishments of transgender individuals as well as raise awareness. Both were shared with the Pride Alliance and LGBTQ Studies-affiliated faculty. The Transgender Day of Visibility post saw more usage, likely because Transgender Day of Remembrance is so close to Fall Break.

Finally, we ordered business-card-sized promotion cards (Figure 3) through our Marketing and Communication Department, who designed a book graphic with the transgender flag colors on the front and the back, including the link to the guide, a brief description of

---

7   https://blogs.library.unt.edu/sycamore-stacks/2020/11/13/transgender-individuals-and-public-policy-from-bathroom-bills-to-employee-protection-2016-2020/

8   https://guides.library.unt.edu/trans/authors

Figure 3   (Upper Graphic of Three Book Spines in Light Blue, Cream, and Pink, the Transgender Flag Colors)

the initiative, and the library's contact information. These cards went out to our service desks in the library and to the offices of our campus gender and sexuality resource center and LGBTQ Studies Program for display there. These campus partners also shared the initiative via their social media and on their websites. We would have liked to share with our campus's LGBTQ related affinity groups, but since most people were remote due to COVID, this had to wait until 2022.

Following the initial phase of the project, we promoted awareness of it among librarians by presenting it at regional, statewide, and national conferences. Examples of two of these presentations are available from the UNT Digital Library (Leuzinger & Condrey, 2021; Leuzinger & Condrey, 2023). The overall response from the library community has been quite positive, with requests for consultations and presentations, and the "For Librarians" page of the guide (mentioned above) is now the second most-accessed page of the entire guide.

Assessment

We assessed the impact of TALI with multiple measures. We requested a follow-up collection evaluation after a year of the titles being added to our holdings; this information would include circulation statistics. We counted hits on the LibGuide, and we added a survey widget on the LibGuide asking, "Was this guide helpful?" We monitored likes or shares of the guide from social media and we tracked anecdotal user feedback.

We measured LibGuide usage for slightly more than a year; it had about 1,400 total views. To put this into context, our library published 568 LibGuides during that time frame, and only 34 guides had more usage, an excellent rate considering that the comparison includes guides on topics with much broader appeal (such as the library's makerspace and the citations & style guide.) Some three years later, the guide in 2023 has had over 7,500 views and is one of our most used topical guides. We observe that the guide's page for librarians has a significant number of uses, the second highest number among this guide's pages, due to our promotion of the project at professional conferences and due to the increased interest throughout U.S. society in transgender awareness and transgender inclusivity. Based on the usage of the TALI LibGuide, topics that were of most interest to users were graphic novels/comics (by a wide margin), film, and subject pages (specifically, medical topics and psychology/mental health).

The follow-up collection evaluation looked at circulation results from the period of September 2020 to August 2021. The assessment reported that 52% of the titles added had been used at least once, two titles in the DDA pool had received sufficient usage to trigger their purchase for permanent ownership, and the new additions were used significantly more than the legacy titles in the collection (Harker, 2021).

While we did not request survey feedback from any users after the main objectives were complete, we did state on the LibGuide that users were welcome to provide feedback directly to the guide owner via email. A handful of messages arrived, which, considering that most library users wouldn't usually write to a librarian about their perceptions of a guide or of library resources, we felt these messages indicated a strong resonance within the community. Two of the messages stated, in essence, that the readers were happy to see themselves in the books they found in the collection. Another message expressed gratitude for the work we were doing to raise awareness of and within the transgender community. Another message stated that they selected the University of North Texas for their graduate program at least in part because of the initiative.

Best Practices

A year after the launch of this initiative, we took some time to highlight our lessons learned and created a list of recommended best practices for anyone considering taking on a project of this nature. We suggest:

- Conducting a needs assessment of the targeted user group. Understanding the community's needs is the key element needed to ensure that the project meets its intended purpose.

- Developing relationships with members of the transgender community and allies. These relationships can be crucial to the success of a project of this nature, where the targeted user group is difficult to identify. Collaborators will be highly valuable in reaching the transgender community (or any community you hope to reach).

- Communicating with the community at the start to promote the initiative so that they know that the purpose of the project is to bring about improvements in services and resources (see above in the "Collection Development" section of this chapter).

- Following up with the community to demonstrate how the project team used the community's input to select materials and develop or modify services (see above in the "Promotion and Outreach" section of this chapter).

- Soliciting feedback and maintaining objectivity when the feedback indicates the library has not been meeting the information needs of the targeted group.

- Determining at the outset how to assess the initiative's success.

- Making sure that you have a policy related to challenges of content and programming offered by the library, in case there is community push-back.

Conclusion

Our hope is that others can adapt the model we describe here to serve their local transgender community or modify the initiative to serve other historically marginalized populations in their area. Even if your library cannot provide the funding for a collection enhancement, work with the time and resources you do have and update things as you are able. This could include creating service desk handouts with search tips, providing a local resource list, or attending local events to promote what you do have and to ask people what they need. We did this ourselves when we customized one of our previous presentations to make the transgender content more visible in a government documents collection (Leuzinger & Condrey, 2023).

Thank Yous

We would like to extend our thanks to the following individuals:

- Karen Harker (she/her), Head of Collection Assessment at the UNT Libraries, for the collection assessments

- Kathleen Hobson (they/them), Director of the UNT Pride Alliance, our gender and sexuality resource center, as staff advisor to the initiative

- Clark Pomerleau (he/him), UNT Associate Professor of History, faculty advisor for the initiative

- All the anonymous UNT students who provided feedback

References

American Library Association. (2020). *Libraries respond: Protecting and supporting transgender staff and patrons.* https://www.ala.org/advocacy/diversity/librariesrespond/transgender-staff-patrons

Drake, A., & Bielefield, A. (2017). Equitable access: Information seeking behavior, information needs, and necessary library accommodations for transgender patrons. *Library & Information Science Research, 39*(3), 160-168. https://doi.org/10.1016/j.lisr.2017.06.002

Harker, K. (2020). *Transgender Collection Evaluation 2020* [Unpublished report]. University of North Texas Libraries, University of North Texas, Denton, Texas.

Harker, K. (2021). *Report on the Assessment of Resources Provided by the Trans Accessible Library Initiative* [Unpublished memorandum]. University of North Texas Libraries, University of North Texas, Denton, Texas.

Keralis, S. D. C., Leuzinger, J., & Rowe, J. (2017). Providing inclusive services to transgender customers. *Texas Library Journal, 93*(3), 82-83. https://digital.library.unt.edu/ark:/67531/metadc1040567/

Krueger, S. (2019). *Supporting Trans People in Libraries.* Libraries Unlimited.

Leuzinger, J., & Condrey, C. (2021) *Trans Accessible Libraries Initiative, presentation [for Cross Timbers Library Collaborative Conference], July 23, 2021.* University of North Texas Libraries, UNT Digital Library. https://digital.library.unt.edu/ark:/67531/metadc1913256.

Leuzinger, J., & Condrey, C. (2023). *Trans Accessible Libraries Initiative, presentation [for Federal Depository Library Programs], March 22, 2023.* University of North Texas Libraries, UNT Digital Library. https://digital.library.unt.edu/ark:/67531/metadc2148976/

Library of Congress, Acquisitions and Bibliographic Access Directorate. (n.d.) *Library of Congress Classification Outline.* https://www.loc.gov/catdir/cpso/lcco/

Library of Congress, Linked Data Service. (n.d.) *Library of Congress Subject Headings.* https://id.loc.gov/authorities/subjects.html

Lyttan, B., & Laloo, B. (2020). Equitable access to information in libraries: a predicament for transgender people. *Journal of Access Services, 17*(1), 46–64. https://doi.org/10.1080/15367967.2019.1671850

National Center for Transgender Equality. (2015). *U.S. Transgender Survey.* National Center for Transgender Equality. https://transequality.org/sites/default/files/docs/usts/USTS-Executive-Summary-Dec17.pdf

University of North Texas. (2023). *UNT Fact Book 2022-2023.* University of North Texas Institutional Research. https://institutionalresearch.unt.edu/sites/default/files/factbook_dair_2022-2023.pdf

University of North Texas Libraries. (2020). *Trans Accessible Libraries Initiative LibGuide.* University of North Texas LibGuides. https://guides.library.unt.edu/trans

Appendix 1

Library of Congress Classification Numbers Related to Transgender People

Number	Descriptor
BF175.5.S48 T73	PSYCHOLOGY—Psychoanalysis—Special topics, A-Z—Sex differences
BF692.2	PSYCHOLOGY—Psychology of sex. Sexual behavior—Sex role. Sex differences—General works
BF720.S48	PSYCHOLOGY—Developmental psychology—Infant psychology. Newborn infant psychology—Special topics, A-Z—Sex. Sex role
BF723.S4+	PSYCHOLOGY—Developmental psychology—Child psychology—Special topics, A-Z—Sex
BF723.S42	PSYCHOLOGY—Developmental psychology—Child psychology—Special topics, A-Z—Sex role
BF724.3.S4	PSYCHOLOGY—Developmental psychology—Adolescence. Youth—Special topics, A-Z—Sex. Sex role. Sex difference
BM729.T65	JUDAISM—Practical Judaism—Other special topics, A-Z—Transgenderism
BR115.T76	CHRISTIANITY—Christianity in relation to special subjects, A-Z—Transgender people. Transvestism. Transsexualism
BT708	DOCTRINAL THEOLOGY—Creation—Man. Doctrinal anthropology—Sex—General works
GV708.8	RECREATION. LEISURE—Sports—Sports for special classes of persons—Gay men. Lesbians. Transgender people
HD6285	INDUSTRIES. LAND USE. LABOR—Labor. Work. Working class—Classes of labor—Sexual minorities—General works
HF5549.5.S47	COMMERCE—Business—Personnel management. Employment management—By topic—Sexual orientation
HQ18.55	THE FAMILY. MARRIAGE. WOMEN—Human sexuality. Sex—Gender identity—General works
HQ77	THE FAMILY. MARRIAGE. WOMEN—Human sexuality. Sex—Cross-dressing. Transvestism—General works
HQ777.83	THE FAMILY. MARRIAGE. WOMEN—The family. Marriage. Home—Children. Child development—Child rearing—Rearing of special categories of children—Children of transsexual parents
HQ1075	THE FAMILY. MARRIAGE. WOMEN—Sex role—General works
HQ1180.T	THE FAMILY. MARRIAGE. WOMEN—Women. Feminism—Women's studies. Study and teaching. Research—By region or country, A-Z

Number	Descriptor
HQ1233.G46	THE FAMILY. MARRIAGE. WOMEN—Women. Feminism—General special (Special aspects of the subject as a whole)
HV1449	SOCIAL PATHOLOGY. SOCIAL AND PUBLIC WELFARE. CRIMINOLOGY—Protection, assistance and relief—Special classes—Gay men. Lesbians
HV8024	SOCIAL PATHOLOGY. SOCIAL AND PUBLIC WELFARE. CRIMINOLOGY—Criminal justice administration—Police. Detectives. Constabulary—Administration and organization—Municipal police. Town constables—Organization—Officials. Personnel—Gay, lesbian, and transgender police officers
K3242.3	LAW IN GENERAL. COMPARATIVE AND UNIFORM LAW. JURISPRUDENCE—Comparative law. International uniform law—Constitutional law—Individual and state—Human rights. Civil and political rights—Sexual minorities
KD4103	LAW OF ENGLAND AND WALES—Constitutional law—Individual and state—Civil and political rights and liberties—Sex discrimination
KF505 .T73	UNITED STATES [LAW] (GENERAL)—Persons—Domestic relations. Family law—Domestic relations courts
KF4754.5	UNITED STATES [LAW] (GENERAL)—Constitutional law—Individual and state—Civil and political rights and liberties—Particular groups—Sexual minorities
LC2574.6	SPECIAL ASPECTS OF EDUCATION—Education of special classes of persons—Sexual minorities—Higher education
MT820 .J23	[MUSIC] INSTRUCTION AND STUDY—Singing and vocal technique—Physiology and care of the voice
N6493 1969 .A78	VISUAL ARTS—History—Modern art—By century—19th and 20th centuries—20th century—Special, by year or brief span of years
N8217.G397	VISUAL ARTS—Special subjects of art—Other special subjects (alphabetically)—A-Industry—Gender identity
NB1952.G46	SCULPTURE—Special subjects—Other subjects or themes in sculpture, A-Z—Gender identity
NC1849.G45	DRAWING. DESIGN. ILLUSTRATION—Posters—Special topics, A-Z—Gender identity
NX180.H6 Q	ARTS IN GENERAL—The arts in relation to other subjects, A-Z—Homosexuality
NX650.G44	ARTS IN GENERAL—Special subjects or topics, A-Z—Gender identity
P120.S48	PHILOLOGY. LINGUISTICS—Language. Linguistic theory. Comparative grammar—Philosophy, origin, etc. of language—Other aspects, A-Z—Sex. Sex differences. Sexism. Nonsexist language
PN56.T69	LITERATURE (GENERAL)—Theory. Philosophy. Esthetics—Relation to and treatment of special elements, problems, and subjects—Other special—Topics, A-Z—Transvestism. Cross-dressing

Number	Descriptor
PN1969.D73	DRAMA—Special types—Vaudeville. Varieties—Special topics, A-Z—Drag shows. Drag performance
PN1995.9.T684	DRAMA—Motion pictures—Other special topics, A-Z—Transgender people
PN3426.T73	PROSE—Prose. Prose fiction—Special topics—Special races, classes, types, etc., in fiction—Other, A-Z—Transvestites. Cross-dressers
PR428.G43	ENGLISH LITERATURE—History of English literature—By period—Modern—Elizabethan era (1550-1640)—Other special topics, A-Z—Gender identity
PS508.T73	AMERICAN LITERATURE—Collections of American literature—Special classes of authors, A-Z—Transsexuals
PS648.T72	AMERICAN LITERATURE—Collections of American literature—Prose (General)—Special forms and topics, A-Z—Transgender people
RA564.9.T73	PUBLIC ASPECTS OF MEDICINE—Public health. Hygiene. Preventive medicine—By age group, class, etc.—Other, A-Z—Transsexuals
RC451.4.G39 T44	INTERNAL MEDICINE—Neurosciences. Biological psychiatry. Neuropsychiatry—Psychiatry—By age group, profession, etc.—Gay men and lesbians
RC556	INTERNAL MEDICINE—Neurosciences. Biological psychiatry. Neuropsychiatry—Psychiatry—Psychiatric aspects of personality and behavior conditions—Sexual and psychosexual conditions—General works
RC560.C4	INTERNAL MEDICINE—Neurosciences. Biological psychiatry. Neuropsychiatry—Psychiatry—Psychiatric aspects of personality and behavior conditions—Sexual and psychosexual conditions—Other special problems, A-Z—Change of sex. Transsexualism
RC560.G45	INTERNAL MEDICINE—Neurosciences. Biological psychiatry. Neuropsychiatry—Psychiatry—Psychiatric aspects of personality and behavior conditions—Sexual and psychosexual conditions—Other special problems, A-Z—Gender identity disorders. Transsexualism
RF511.T73	OTORHINOLARYNGOLOGY—Laryngology. Diseases of the throat—Diseases of the larynx, vocal cords, epiglottis, and trachea—By age group, class, etc., A-Z—Transsexuals
RJ506.G35	PEDIATRICS—Diseases of children—Mental disorders of children and adolescents. Child psychiatry. Child mental health services—Specific disorders, A-Z—Gender identity disorders
TR681.T68	PHOTOGRAPHY—Applied photography—Artistic photography—Portraits—Special classes of persons, A-Z—Transgender people
UB418.T72	MILITARY ADMINISTRATION—Minorities, women, etc., in armed forces—By region or country—United States—Individual groups, A-Z—Transgender people

Appendix 2

Library of Congress Subject Headings Related to Transgender People

- Transgender people
- Transgender women
- Transgender men
- Transgender children
- Transgender parents
- Children of transgender parents
- Parents of transgender children
- Transgender artists
- Transgender college students
- Transgender college teachers
- Transgender journalists
- Transgender legislators
- Transgender librarians
- Transgender military personnel
- Transgender musicians
- Transgender police officers
- Transgender prisoners
- Transgender singers
- Transgender students
- Transgender teachers
- Transgender veterans
- Transgender youth
- African American transgender people
- Minority transgender women
- Older transgender people
- Transgender people in art
- Transgender people in literature
- Transgender superheroes
- Transgender people in mass media
- Transgender people in motion pictures
- Transgender people in popular culture
- Transgender people's writing
- Transgender people's writings, American
- Transgender people's writing, Canadian
- Transgender people—Employment
- Transgender people—Employment—Law and legislation
- Transgender people—Identity
- Transgender people—Legal status, laws, etc.
- Transgender people—Medical care
- Transgender people—Psychology
- Transgender people—United States
- Transgender people—Violence against
- Christian transgender people
- Jewish transgender people
- Bible—Transgender interpretations
- Libraries and transgender people
- Libraries—Special collections—Transgender people
- Church work with transgender people
- Legal assistance to transgender people
- Social work with transgender people
- Social work with transgender youth
- Gender noncomformity
- Gender noncomformity on television
- Stonewall Book Awards
- Transgender Day of Remembrance
- Transphobia
- Trans-exclusionary radical feminism

Contributors

Ernani A. Agulto is a licensed Filipino librarian-teacher, proud queer, and an interdisciplinary creative. He has been active in the field of librarianship for more than ten years and is working as a librarian under the Library and Extension Division (LED) and as the Gender and Development (GAD) Focal Person of the Quezon City Public Library (QCPL), Quezon City. In addition, he has been invited to various speaking engagements as a resource person in the Philippines. Mr. Agulto received a Bachelor of Library and Information Science from the Philippine Normal University, Manila. He took online courses on Media and Information Literacy and Intercultural Dialogue (2015) from Athabasca University and UNESCO and Visualizing Japan (1850s-1930s): Westernization, Protest, Modernity (2018) from Harvard University—Online Learning, Massachusetts Institute of Technology (MIT), and edX, under a financial assistance grant. He was a full scholarship recipient and earned a two-year Fashion Design and Marketing course from SoFA Design Institute. At present, he is pursuing a graduate degree in art studies with a specialization in art theory and criticism at the University of the Philippines, Diliman. In his spare time, he engages in creative pursuits and perceives that the intersectionality of queer issues presents an opportunity to advance queer discourses.

Maria Atilano (she/her) is the Student Engagement Librarian at the University of North Florida's Thomas G. Carpenter Library in Jacksonville, Florida. She began working in academic libraries in 2002 as a student employee while studying at the University of North Carolina at Greensboro. Before becoming a librarian, Maria held staff positions as Library Services Specialist in Public Services and Sr. Library Services Associate in Special Collections at UNF. She graduated with her MLIS from Florida State University in 2012. Maria's research interests include social media, library marketing, student engagement, and instruction.

Maureen Babb is a Science Liaison Librarian in the Jim Peebles Science and Technology Library at the University of Manitoba. Maureen obtained an MLIS from the University of Alberta, has published in the *Canadian Journal of Academic Librarianship*, the *Journal of the Canadian Health Libraries Association*, the *Journal of the Medical Libraries Association* and elsewhere, and has been Chair of the Canadian Association of Professional Academic Librarians (CAPAL)'s Research and Scholarship Committee.

Sarah Barriage, Ph.D., is an Assistant Professor in the School of Information Science at the University of Kentucky. Her research interests include the information practices of children and youth, social justice in information institutions, and the development and use of child-centered research methods. Her work has been published in scholarly journals such as *The Library Quarterly*, *Library & Information Science Research*, *International Journal of Qualitative Methods*, and *Journal of Childhood Studies*.

David Benjamin is the Head of the University of Central Florida Libraries Special Collections & University Archives department. Before working at UCF, David was the Assistant Director of the Volkerding Study Center at the University of Arizona's Center for Creative Photography and the Visual Materials Archivist at the Wisconsin Historical Society. He started his career in archives in the University of Kansas' Kansas Collection. David has a Master of Library Science from the University of Wisconsin-Madison and a Master of Architecture in American Architecture and Landscape History from the University of Kansas. An archivist for 30-plus years, David is involved with several regional, national, and international organizations, including the Society of American Archivists, Association of Moving Image Archivists, Association of College and Research Libraries Rare Books and Manuscript Section, and the Society of Florida Archivists.

Coby Condrey (he/him/his) earned his master's in library and information science from the University of Texas at Austin in 1993. He has worked in a wide range of specializations in his career in librarianship, including government documents, electronic resources, open access resources, collection development, research, and instructional services. From 1993 to 2011 he held a series of positions at the Texas State Library and Archives Commission where he participated in the collection, discovery, and preservation of print and electronic state publications. In 2012 he moved to the University of North Texas

(UNT), where he initially held positions related to acquisitions. As of 2022 he serves as a subject librarian for psychology and technical communication. Coby participates frequently in campus LGBTQ+ initiatives, including service as the chair of the Committee on the Status of the LGBTQ+ Faculty and as the assistant director of the LGBTQ+ Faculty Network. He was elected to the UNT Faculty Senate in 2022 and to the office of Faculty Senate secretary in 2023. He is active in the Texas Library Association where he routinely serves in officer and program planning roles. His research frequently focuses on government information services and resources and LGBTQ+ topics, among many other interests.

Patrick Connors (they/them) is a disabled, nonbinary Teen Services Librarian based in South Carolina. They earned their MLIS from the University of South Carolina and have 5+ years of experience in public librarianship. Their professional interests include youth services, makerspace programming, equity work, and queer librarianship. When not in the library, Connors enjoys reading, traveling, fiber arts, and hanging out with their wife and pets. *Censorship Is a Drag* is their first publication.

Phoebe Doyle is an aspiring writer from Dublin, born and raised in The Liberties, Dublin's oldest quarter. She holds an undergraduate degree in English and film studies and a Master in Library and Information Studies, both from University College Dublin. A poet at heart, Phoebe takes a similar approach to academic writing—the pairing of engaging, moving prose with facts being, as she believes, to be one of the keys to change. She continually finds inspiration through lesbian writers of the past, the beauty of her city, and the wondrous people in her life. Her other works lie haphazardly in dog-eared notebooks and will hopefully one day grace the shelves of other curious writers. Her contribution to this book marks her first professionally published piece. You can follow her on Twitter at @PhoebeEllaDoyle.

Emily Drabinski is Associate Professor at the Queens (N.Y.) College Graduate School of Library and Information Studies. She edits *Gender and Sexuality in Information Studies*, a book series from Library Juice Press/Litwin Books. Drabinski served as 2023-24 President of the American Library Association.

Stacey Ewing is the Chair of the Humanities and Social Sciences Library West branch of the University of Florida (UF) George A. Smathers

Libraries. Her scholarship and grant work is focused primarily on technologies that enhance and support the learning, teaching, and research needs of students and faculty, as well as accessibility services, resources, and technology that help boost student success. Secondary scholarship is centered around digital humanities, with the most recent project involving text mining of the *UF Independent Florida Alligator* newspaper to construct a historical timeline of transgender awareness and related community involvement on a university campus.

Evangeline Giaconia is a recent graduate of the museum studies MA program at the University of Florida. Her research focuses on the ethical treatment of Indigenous archival materials and, more recently, queer archiving. Her work can be found at ethicalarchives.worldpress.com. When not working as the Access Services Manager at the Architecture & Fine Arts Library at UF, she can be found writing and printmaking.

Lisa N. Johnston is Director of Library Services at Eckerd College. Lisa has had a lengthy career as a liberal arts college librarian specializing in public services, arts, and humanities. She is currently co-director of ACRL's College Library Director Mentoring Program (CLDMP). Lisa has been an active member of the American Library Association's Rainbow Round Table since 2000. She has served on the Stonewall Book Award jury four times. When she left Sweet Briar College after over two decades of service as associate director of the library to join Eckerd College as their director in 2015, she was honored with the appointment professor emerita of Sweet Briar College. In the summer of 2013, Lisa served as assistant librarian for Semester at Sea, which only increased her passion for travel. When she's not at the library, she can be found reading about queer history, watching British detective shows, and planning her next adventure. Lisa lives in the rainbow bubble of St. Petersburg (the Austin of Florida) with her wife and their two cats.

Vanessa Kitzie, PhD, is an associate professor in the School of Information Science at the University of South Carolina. Her recent publications have appeared in *The Library Quarterly*, *Journal of the Association for Information Science*, and *Journal of Documentation*, and she is a co-author of the book *LGBTQIA+ Inclusive Children's Librarianship: Policies, Programs, and Practices*.

Donna Langille (she/her/they/them) lives and works as an uninvited settler on the unceded traditional territory of the Syilx Okanagan peoples. She is the Community Engagement and Open Education Librarian, as well as the subject liaison librarian for film studies, theatre, media studies, and the digital humanities at the University of British Columbia Okanagan (UBCO). Their work includes connecting the wider community with UBCO Library resources, providing support to students, staff, and faculty working on open educational resources (OER), and building advocacy and awareness of OER at her institution. They are also a PhD student in Interdisciplinary Studies at UBCO, working under the supervision of Fiona P. McDonald (Anthropology) and Emily Christian Murphy (Digital Humanities). In 2019, she obtained her Master of Information Studies from McGill University. Prior to this degree, she earned her Honours B. A. in English and Gender, Sexuality, and Women's Studies from Simon Fraser University. They also hold a diploma in Film Production from Capilano University. As a queer scholar, they are interested in reframing the way we observe and acknowledge queer histories in relation to and with feminist technologies.

Julie Leuzinger (she/her/hers) received her Master in Library Science from the Texas Woman's University and has been working at the University of North Texas (UNT) Libraries since 2005. She has over 25 years of management experience that started with owning a mixed martial arts school with her brother in the Dallas area. She is currently the Women's and Gender Studies and LGBTQ Studies Subject Librarian as well as the library liaison to the campus gender and sexuality resource center. Julie is passionate about providing services and resources for queer and trans students and coordinates a library-wide collaboration along with campus partners each spring for Campus Pride Week that provides programming for queers and allies alike, highlighting what the library has to offer to this community. She is at present Vice Chair of the Women & Gender Equity Network at UNT. Julie is active in the Texas Library Association, serving on the Legislative Committee, and previously served as Chair of the College and University Library Division. Her research interests include library management-related topics and library services for the transgender community. She is currently working on a study about workplace belonging for transgender and gender-nonconforming library employees.

Amanda Melilli, Head of the Teacher Development & Resources Library at the University of Nevada, Las Vegas (UNLV), supports the teacher education programs within the UNLV College of Education and specializes in youth library collections with a focus on the discovery and evaluation of diverse children's/young adult literature. Melilli's research interests include promoting the use of often underutilized youth materials, specifically the importance of incorporating graphic novels into elementary/secondary classrooms and supporting LGBTQIA+ youth through inclusive school library collections and curriculum.

Kaitlyn Moody is a Library Technical Assistant for the Government Documents/Serials Department at the University of South Alabama's Marx Library. She has a BS in Secondary Education and English, and recently received her MLIS from the University of Southern Mississippi. She has grown a real interest in working with government documents during her time at South Alabama and wishes to more actively ensure that the LGBTQ+ community is accounted for in America's written history.

Bryn Nelson, PhD, is an award-winning science, medical, and environmental writer and the author of *Flush: The Remarkable Science of an Unlikely Treasure* (Grand Central Publishing). He is a former microbiologist trained in bacterial biochemistry at the University of Washington and a longtime fan of public and academic libraries. While a science writer at *Newsday*, Nelson wrote frequently about genetics, biomedicine, global warming, evolution, and epidemiology. He was a principal writer for "Long Island: Our Natural World," a 13-part ecology series about the natural world on Long Island, which became the basis for a book, *Newsday's Guide to Long Island's Natural World* (Globe Pequot Press / Falcon Guides). As a freelance writer, he helped cover the COVID-19 pandemic for *The Daily Beast* and *The British Medical Journal*. He has also written for a wide variety of other publications including the *New York Times*, *Scientific American*, *Nature*, *Wired*, *CNN*, *New Scientist*, *The Guardian*, and *TIME*. For other book projects, Nelson edited two chapters on microbiology and food safety for the bestselling six-volume *Modernist Cuisine: The Art and Science of Cooking* (The Cooking Lab) and contributed a chapter to *The Science Writers' Handbook* (Da Capo). He lives in Seattle.

Shannon M. Oltmann is an Associate Professor in the School of Information Science at the University of Kentucky. She obtained her PhD from Indiana University. Her research interests include information ethics, censorship, intellectual freedom, public libraries, privacy, and qualitative research methods. Oltmann is the past editor of the

Journal of Intellectual Freedom and Privacy and Associate Editor of *Library Quarterly*. She wrote the book *Practicing Intellectual Freedom in Libraries* and edited *The Fight Against Book Bans: Perspectives from the Field*. Oltmann's work has been funded by the American Library Association and the Institute of Museum and Library Services. She has presented her research at numerous academic and professional conferences and published widely.

Jason D. Phillips (he/him/his) is a Social Science Librarian holding the faculty rank of Associate Librarian at the University of Central Florida. His research interests are LGBTQ collections and services and librarian burnout, and he recently received certifications in evidence synthesis reviews. Jason is active with library and university committees and previously served on the Stonewall Book Award Committee and the River Valley Equality Center's Board of Directors for several years. For the past seventeen years he has worked at academic libraries in the Southeast. Jason holds a BA in History and Political Science, an MLIS, and an MA in History—all from The University of Alabama. Outside of work, he prefers to spend time at the beach or mountains, and is an avid RPG gamer, binger of TV series, lapsed college football fan, amateur cook, and food enthusiast.

Matt Rohweder is a Liaison Librarian at Wilfrid Laurier University in Waterloo, Ontario, Canada, is the recipient of the 2021-2022 Ontario Council of University Faculty Association's Award of Distinction in Academic Librarianship. He has worked in academic libraries since 2014 and is an advocate, activist, and ally for all equity-deserving groups. He is co-author of *Librarian's Guide to Games and Gamers: From Collection Development to Advisory Services* (Libraries Unlimited). His research interests include DEI initiatives in libraries, LGBTQ+ community libraries and education programs, and allyship in libraries. Outside of work, he is an avid reader, gamer, and vinyl collector. He and his husband live in Kitchener, Ontario, with their dog, Scarlett.

James W. Rosenzweig is a Professor and the Education and Children's Studies Librarian at Eastern Washington University. James's research interests include citation analysis and source evaluation for K-12 students and college undergraduates, diverse representation in children's and young adult literature, and Wikipedia in the classroom. He holds a Master in Teaching from Western Washington University and a Master of Library and Information Science from the University of Washington.

Jordan Ruud is the director of library services at the University of Arkansas-Fort Smith, where he serves as liaison to the humanities disciplines. His interests include user experience and intellectual freedom; he recently served as a panelist on "Intellectual Freedom: Arkansas Perspectives" at the Arkansas Library Association's annual conference. He received his MSLIS degree in 2012 from the University of Illinois Urbana-Champaign. In his spare time, he's a movie buff (keep an ear out for *The Midnight Symposium*, a forthcoming podcast about horror movies that he's been recording with colleagues).

Colleen Seale is an emeritus faculty member at the University of Florida (UF) George A. Smathers Libraries. She formerly served as Associate Chair of the Humanities and Social Sciences Library West branch of the Smathers Libraries. She was the Women's, Gender, and LGBTQI Studies Librarian and the Library West Reference Collection Manager. Her most recent scholarship includes a digital humanities project that text-mined the *UF Independent Florida Alligator* newspaper to develop a historical timeline of transgender awareness and related community involvement on a university campus.

Debra Trogdon-Livingston (she/they) serves as the User Experience and Education Strategist for Region 2 of the Network of the National Library of Medicine (NNLM) headquartered at the Medical University of South Carolina (MUSC) in Charleston, South Carolina. They provide resources, education, user experience guidance, and program evaluation services to members and communities in Region 2. Debra leads the Regional Medical Library's education strategy and advocates for equitable user experiences in and beyond Region 2. They are an instructor for both the Medical University of South Carolina and the Network of the National Library of Medicine. Debra enjoys finding ways to integrate equity practices into their instruction. Debra brings more than nineteen years of library experience and more than twelve years of health and wellness programming in multiple libraries throughout North and South Carolina with a strong emphasis on public libraries. They have presented at local, regional, and national conferences. Debra has a strong focus on mentorship, community partnerships, diversity, equity, inclusion, and accessibility, LGBTQIA2S+ equity, and health literacy. Debra actively researches LGBTQIA2S+ library worker equity and health equity.

Pat Tully grew up in Cincinnati, Ohio and was educated at Cape Cod Community College and Williams College, receiving a Master in

Library Studies from the University of Michigan in 1988. Since then, Pat has worked in technical services and library administration in public and academic libraries in Indiana, the U. S. Virgin Islands, Pennsylvania, Massachusetts, Connecticut, and Alaska. In addition to her work in libraries, Pat is active in local organizations. She has been a Rotarian for 12 years, joining the Middletown (Connecticut) Rotary Club in 2010, and has held a variety of offices in that Club and in the First City Rotary Club in Ketchikan, Alaska. Pat has long had an interest in preserving and celebrating local history, serving as a volunteer and Board members at Historic Beverly (Massachusetts), the Middlesex County (Connecticut) Historical Society, and Historic Ketchikan. In January 2017 she moved to Ketchikan, Alaska to become Director of the Ketchikan Public Library.

Alicia G. Vaandering is an Assistant Professor and the Student Success Librarian at the University of Rhode Island where she supports the learning and research of students, with an emphasis on undergraduate first-year, international, first generation, and transfer students. Her research interests include diversity in children's books collections, information literacy instruction, and alternative grading methods. Alicia completed her MLIS and MA in History at the University of Rhode Island.

Kestrel Ward is a white, disabled, neurodivergent, queer, nonbinary librarian and independent researcher. They are just starting their career in libraries and archives, having received their MLIS from the Florida State University in 2022. They have worked for the University of Florida libraries for four years, where they are active in outreach and LGBTQ+ archiving. They are also active members of ALA and SAA, and are pursuing a Digital Archives Specialist certificate currently. Their research interests are women in ancient history, digital violence prevention, LGBTQ+ archives, and digital LGBTQ+ communities. They live in central Florida with their son, German shepherd dog, and two kittens.

Allyson Wind (she/her) is the Electronic Resources Librarian at Kemp Library, on the campus of East Stroudsburg University (ESU), a Pennsylvania State System of Higher Education (PASSHE) Institution. Mrs. Wind is a tenured assistant professor and liaison librarian for the Education, Biological Sciences, Biochemistry, Chemistry and Physics Departments. Her collection development areas include the above liaison areas plus the Children's and Young Adult Collections and the Curriculum Materials Center (CMC). Mrs. Wind obtained a Diversity, Equity, and Inclusion Certificate from ESU; her research for the certificate involved investigating whether academic libraries were truly inclusive places for people with disabilities. Mrs. Wind serves as the chair of ESU's Association of Pennsylvania State College and University Faculties (APSCUF) Gender and Social Justice (GISJ) committee. Mrs. Wind attended Tunkhannock Area High School, graduated from the University of Scranton in 2006 with a Bachelor in Elementary Education, and substitute taught in several school districts in Northeastern Pennsylvania until attending graduate school. Mrs. Wind completed her Master in Library and Information Science from Drexel University's iSchool in 2012. She worked in two public libraries in New York's Hudson Valley and was the Web Services Librarian at the Geisinger Commonwealth School of Medicine (GCSOM) before accepting her current position at ESU. Mrs. Wind currently lives just outside of Scranton, Pennsylvania with her husband Kyle and their four rescue cats.

Index